CHICKEN

CHICKEN

A cook's collection of 500
fabulous chicken, turkey and
game dishes

Edited by
Valerie Ferguson

LORENZ BOOKS

First published in 2000 by Lorenz Books

© 2000 Anness Publishing Limited

Lorenz Books is an imprint of Anness Publishing Inc.
27 West 20th Street, New York, NY 10011

ISBN 0 7548 0459 3

Publisher: Joanna Lorenz
Consultant Editor: Valerie Ferguson
Designer: Carole Perks
Editorial Reader: Richard McGinlay
Production Controller: Wendy Lawson

Recipes contributed by:
Catherine Atkinson, Alex Barker, Angela Boggiano, Kathy Brown, Carla Capalbo, Lesley Chamberlain, Kit Chan, Maxine Clarke, Frances Cleary, Carole Clements, Trisha Davies, Roz Denny, Michelle Derrie-Johnson, Patrizia Diemling, Matthew Drennan, Sarah Edmonds, Joanna Farrow, Rafi Fernandez, Christine France, Silvano Franco, Sarah Gates, Shirley Gill, Rosamund Grant, Carole Handslip, Rebekah Hassan, Deh-Ta Hsuing, Shehzad Husain, Christine Ingram, Judy Jackson, Sheila Kimberley, Masaki Ko, Ruby Le Bois, Lesley Mackley, Norma MacMillan, Sue Maggs, Kathy Man, Maggie Mayhew, Norma Miller, Sallie Morris, Elizabeth Lambert Ortiz, Maggie Pannell, Katherine Richmond, Anne Sheasby, Jenny Stacey, Liz Trigg, Hilaire Walden, Laura Washburn, Steven Wheeler, Judy Williams, Polly Wreford, Jeni Wright, Elizabeth Wolf-Cohen
Photography:
Karl Adamson, Edward Allwright, David Armstrong, Steve Baxter, James Duncan, John Freeman, Ian Garlick, Michelle Garrett, John Heseltine, Amanda Heywood, Ferguson Hill, Janine Hosegood, David Jordan, Don Last, William Lingwood, Patrick McLeavey, Thomas Odulate, Juliet Piddington, Peter Reilly

Printed and bound in France

1 3 5 7 9 10 8 6 4 2

Contents

Introduction

Chicken is an extremely popular food. It is versatile and economical, and can be cooked with a wide variety of ingredients and flavorings. It is low in fat and quick to cook, with very little wastage.

Chicken can be bought in many forms: whole, quartered or divided into thighs, drumsticks, breasts and wings, with or without bones and skin,

which makes preparation very easy. Ground chicken can be found at some large supermarkets, but the skinned flesh can be ground quickly at home in a food processor. Although it is convenient to buy portions individually packaged, it can be expensive. It is much cheaper to buy a whole chicken and prepare it yourself, and cheaper still to buy a frozen chicken and defrost it thoroughly before using. The added bonus of a frozen bird are the giblets (neck, heart, liver and gizzard) found inside the cavity, which can be used for making stock. To get the best results from a frozen chicken, let it thaw slowly in a cool place overnight or until completely defrosted.

Many types of chicken are available, such as free-range and corn-fed (with yellow skin), and all are full of flavor. Some have added herbs and flavorings, and others are self-basting

with either butter or olive oil injected into the flesh. This helps keep the flesh succulent. Chicken is available all year round, although some of the more expensive types are raised only in limited numbers. Baby chickens are called poussins and can be bought to serve whole or halved, depending on their size and your appetite. In fact, chicken can be bought at any weight ranging from 1 pound to 6 pounds.

When buying, look for a firm, plump bird with no signs of damage to the limbs, flesh or skin. Unwrap the bird, immediately store it in the refrigerator and use as soon as possible, as all poultry deteriorates very rapidly.

This book offers chicken, turkey and game recipes from all corners of the world and for every occasion, from simple snacks, appetizers and light dishes, through substantial family casseroles, to luxurious presentations for celebrations and entertaining. Soups, salads and pâtés; roasts, casseroles and pies; stir-fries and sautés; hot and spicy dishes in profusion; and low-fat recipes for people who are watching their cholesterol levels or weight—there is truly something here for every taste and occasion. You need never again be at a loss for an inspiring chicken recipe.

Choosing a Chicken

When choosing a fresh chicken for cooking, it should have a plump breast, and the skin should be creamy in color. The tip of the breastbone should be pliable when pressed. A bird's dressed weight is taken after plucking and drawing, and may include the giblets (neck, gizzard, heart and liver). A frozen chicken must be thawed slowly in the refrigerator or a cool room before cooking. Never try to thaw it in hot water, as this will toughen the flesh.

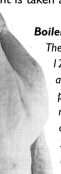

Boilers
These are about 12 months and over, and weigh 4½–6½ pounds. They require long, slow cooking, around 2–3 hours, to make them tender.

Corn-fed Chickens
These are free-range birds and are generally more expensive. They usually weigh 2½–3½ pounds.

Roasters
These birds are about 6–12 months old and weigh 3½–4½ pounds. They will feed a family.

Spring Chickens
These birds are about 3 months old and weigh 2–2½ pounds. They will serve three to four people.

Double Poussins
These are 8–10 weeks old and weigh 1¾–2 pounds They will serve two people. Poussins are best roasted, broiled or pot-roasted.

Poussins
These are 4–6 weeks old and weigh 1–1¼ pounds. They are sufficient for one person.

Cuts of Chicken

Chicken pieces today are available pre-packaged in a variety of different ways. If you do not want to buy a whole bird, you can choose from the many selected cuts on the market. Most cooking methods are suitable for all cuts, but some are especially suited to specific cuts of meat. These are ideal for frying, broiling and grilling.

Skinless Boneless Thigh
This makes tasks such as stuffing and rolling much quicker, as it is already skinned and jointed.

Ground Chicken
This is not as strongly flavored as, say, ground beef, but may be used as a substitute in some recipes.

Liver
This makes a wonderful addition to pâtés or to salads.

Leg
The leg comprises the thigh and drumstick. Large pieces with bones, such as this, are suitable for slow-cooking, such as braising or poaching.

Wing
The wing does not supply much meat. It is often grilled or fried.

Drumstick
The drumstick is a favorite for grilling or frying, either in batter or rolled in bread crumbs.

Breast
This comprises tender white meat and can be simply cooked in butter, as well as stuffed.

Thigh
The thigh is suitable for braising and other slow-cooking methods.

Techniques

Jointing a Chicken

For recipes that call for chicken joints, it is often cheaper to buy a whole chicken and joint it yourself, particularly if you are cooking for a large number of people. It is important to have a portion of bone with the wing and breast joints, otherwise the flesh shrinks during cooking.

I Hold the leg firmly with one hand. Using a sharp knife, cut the skin between the leg and breast.

2 Then, press the leg down to expose the ball-and-socket joint, cut or break the joint apart and cut down toward the parson's nose.

3 Turn the chicken over and loosen the "oyster" from the underside (this lies embedded alongside the backbone). Repeat with the other leg.

4 Now, with your finger, feel for the end of the breastbone, and, using a sharp knife, cut diagonally through the flesh to the rib cage.

5 Using strong kitchen scissors, cut through the rib cage and wishbone, separating the two wing joints.

6 Twist the wing tip and tuck it under the breast meat so that the joint is held flat. This will ensure that it has a good shape for cooking.

7 Using strong kitchen scissors, cut the breast meat from the carcass in one piece. (All that remains of the carcass is half of the rib cage and the backbone.)

8 The legs can be cut in half through the joint to give a thigh joint and a drumstick. The breast can also be cut into two pieces through the breastbone.

Spatchcocking a Chicken

This is a good way to prepare chickens for broiling or grilling, especially the smaller sizes such as poussins. By removing their backbones, poussins can be opened out and flattened, ready for even and fast cooking.

I Using a very sharp pair of kitchen scissors, cut the poussin on either side of its backbone.

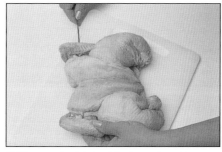

2 Flatten the bird with the palm of your hand or a rolling pin. Turn it over and cut out the fine rib cage, leaving the rest of the carcass intact to hold its shape. Thread thin skewers though the wings.

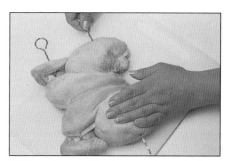

3 Then thread thin skewers through the legs and wings to hold them in position and keep the bird flat. Brush liberally with melted butter. It will take 10–15 minutes on each side, depending on the heat.

Stuffing a Chicken

Stuffing helps keep chickens moist during cooking, which is important because they have very little fat. The stuffing also helps make the meal go further. There are many different flavors of stuffing that may be used to enhance the taste of chicken, without detracting from its own delicate flavor. Bread, rice or potatoes can be used as a base to which other ingredients may be added. Fat is important in stuffing because it prevents it from becoming dry and crumbly.

1 Only stuff the small neck-end of the chicken and not the large cavity inside the carcass, as the heat from the oven will not penetrate all the way through the chicken. Any leftover stuffing should be made into small balls and fried separately or put into a shallow, buttered ovenproof dish, baked with the chicken and cut into squares for serving with the chicken.

2 Never pack the stuffing too tightly, as bread crumbs will expand during cooking and this may cause the skin to burst open. The flap of neck skin should then be tucked under the chicken and secured with the wing tips or sewn into place with a needle and fine trussing thread. Remember to weigh the chicken after it has been stuffed to calculate the cooking time accurately.

Casseroling

This slow-cooking method is good for large chicken joints with bones, or more mature meat.

1 Heat some olive oil in a flameproof casserole and fry the chicken joints until they are browned on all sides.

2 Add stock, wine or a mixture of both to a depth of 1 inch. Add seasonings and herbs, cover and cook on the stove or in the oven for 1½ hours or until the chicken is tender.

3 Add a selection of lightly fried vegetables such as pearl onions, mushrooms, carrots and small new potatoes about halfway through the cooking time.

Braising

This method can be used for whole chickens or pieces and is ideal for strongly flavored meat.

1 Heat some olive oil in a flameproof casserole and lightly fry a whole bird or chicken joints until golden on all sides.

2 Remove the chicken from the casserole and fry 1 pound diced vegetables, such as carrots, onions, celery and turnips, until soft.

3 Replace the chicken, cover with a tight lid and cook very slowly on the stove or in the oven, preheated to 325°F, until tender.

Carving a Chicken

It is best to let the chicken stand (or "rest") for 10–15 minutes before carving (while the gravy is being made). This lets the meat relax, so the flesh will not tear while carving. Use a sharp carving knife and work on a plate that will catch any juices that can be added to the gravy. The leg can be cut in half for a thigh and a drumstick.

1 Hold the chicken firmly with a carving fork, between the breast and one of the legs, down to the backbone. Cut the skin around the opposite leg, press gently outward to expose the ball-and-socket joint and cut through. Slip the knife under the back to remove the "oyster" with the leg.

2 With the knife at the top end of the breastbone, cut down parallel to one side of the wishbone to take a good slice of breast meat with the wing joint.

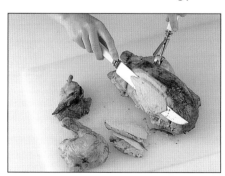

3 With the knife at the end of the breastbone, cut down the front of the carcass, removing the wishbone. Carve the remaining breast into slices.

Chicken Stock

A good chicken stock is called for in many dishes, so make a large quantity and freeze it in small batches.

1 onion
4 cloves
1 carrot
2 leeks
2 celery stalks
1 chicken carcass, cooked or raw
1 bouquet garni
8 black peppercorns
½ teaspoon salt

1 Peel the onion, cut into quarters and spike each quarter with a clove. Scrub and roughly chop the other vegetables.

How to Make Gravy

After roasting, transfer the chicken to a serving dish and remove any trussing string. Cover loosely with aluminum foil and let rest in a warm place before carving. Meanwhile, spoon the fat from the juices left in the roasting pan. Stirring constantly, blend 1 tablespoon all-purpose flour into the juices and cook gently on the stove until golden brown. Add 1¼ cups chicken stock or vegetable cooking water and bring to a boil, to thicken. Season to taste. Strain into a pitcher or gravy boat to serve.

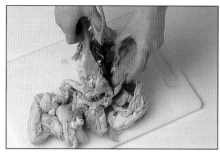

2 Break up the chicken carcass into several pieces and place in a large saucepan with the remaining ingredients.

3 Cover with 7½ cups water. Bring to a boil, skim and simmer, partially covered, for 2 hours. Strain the stock and let cool. When cold, remove the hardened fat before using.

Roasting Times for Poultry

Note: Birds should be weighed after stuffing.

Poussin	1–1½ pounds	1–1¼ hours at 350°F
Chicken	2½–3 pounds	1–1¼ hours at 375°F
	3½–4 pounds	1¼–1¾ hours at 375°F
	4½–5 pounds	1½–2 hours at 375°F
	5–6 pounds	1¾–2½ hours at 375°F
Duck	3–5 pounds	1¾–2¼ hours at 400°F
Goose	8–10 pounds	2½–3 hours at 350°F
	10–12 pounds	3–3½ hours at 350°F
Turkey (whole bird)	6–8 pounds	3–3½ hours at 325°F
	8–12 pounds	3–4 hours at 325°F
	12–16 pounds	4–5 hours at 325°F
Turkey (whole breast)	4–6 pounds	1½–2¼ hours at 325°F
	6–8 pounds	2¼–3¼ hours at 325°F

Mexican Chicken Soup

For a hearty version of this simple soup, add some cooked chickpeas or rice.

Serves 6
6¼ cups Chicken Stock
2 cooked chicken breast fillets,
 skinned and cut into large strips
1 canned chipotle chile
 or jalapeño chile,
 drained and rinsed
1 avocado
salt and freshly ground
 black pepper

1 Heat the stock in a large saucepan, and add the chicken and chile. Simmer over very low heat for 5 minutes to heat the chicken and release the flavor from the chile.

2 Cut the avocado in half, remove the pit and peel off the skin. Slice the avocado flesh neatly.

3 Remove the chile from the stock, using a slotted spoon, and then discard it. Taste the soup for seasoning, and add salt and pepper as necessary.

4 Pour the soup into warmed serving bowls, distributing the chicken evenly among them. Carefully add a few avocado slices to each bowl and serve immediately.

> **Cook's Tip**
> When using canned chiles, it is important to rinse them very thoroughly before adding them to the pan in order to remove the flavor of any pickling liquid.

Chicken Stellette Soup

The pasta shapes are the stars of this gently flavored soup in two senses, since despite their small size, they attract the eye and capture the interest.

Serves 4–6
3¾ cups Chicken Stock
1 bay leaf
4 scallions
3 cups button mushrooms, sliced
4 ounces cooked
 chicken breast fillet
½ cup stellette (tiny soup pasta)
⅔ cup dry white wine
1 tablespoon chopped
 fresh parsley
salt and freshly ground
 black pepper

1 Put the stock and bay leaf in a large saucepan and bring to a boil over medium heat.

2 Thinly slice the scallions and add to the pan of stock. Add the mushrooms.

3 Remove the skin from the chicken and discard. Slice the chicken thinly. Transfer to a plate and set aside.

4 Add the pasta to the pan, cover and simmer for 7–8 minutes. Just before serving, add the chicken, wine and parsley, season to taste and heat through for 2–3 minutes. Serve in warmed bowls.

Chicken Soup Lebanese-style

A substantial soup with a hint of cinnamon and cumin.

Serves 6
¾ cup chickpeas,
 soaked in water overnight
9 cups Chicken Stock
½ cup long-grain rice
1 onion, chopped
2 garlic cloves, crushed
2 tablespoons olive oil
½ teaspoon ground cumin
1 teaspoon ground cinnamon
2½ cups cooked chicken, diced
salt and freshly ground
 black pepper

1 Simmer the drained chickpeas in the stock for about 1 hour, until tender but not mushy. Add the rice and cook for 15 minutes, until the rice is just tender.

2 Meanwhile, gently sauté the onion and garlic in the oil for 10 minutes until soft but not browned. Stir in the spices and cook gently for 5 more minutes.

3 Add the onion mixture and the cooked chicken to the soup at the end of its cooking time, and simmer long enough to heat the chicken thoroughly. Season to taste and serve.

Chicken & Asparagus Soup

A very delicate and delicious soup. When fresh asparagus is not in season, canned white asparagus is an acceptable substitute.

Serves 4
5 ounces chicken breast fillet
1 teaspoon egg white
1 teaspoon cornstarch
4 ounces asparagus
3 cups Chicken Stock
salt and freshly ground
 black pepper
cilantro leaves, to garnish

1 Cut the chicken meat into thin slices, each about the size of a postage stamp. Season with a pinch of salt and stir in the egg white. Mix the cornstarch into a thin paste with a little water and add to the chicken.

2 Trim and discard the tough stems of the asparagus. Diagonally cut the tender spears into short lengths.

3 In a wok or saucepan, bring the stock to a rolling boil. Add the asparagus, return to a boil and cook for 2 minutes. (This is not necessary if using canned asparagus.)

4 Add the chicken, stir to separate and bring back to a boil once more. Taste the soup and adjust the seasoning as necessary. Serve hot, garnished with cilantro leaves.

> **Cook's Tip**
> When buying asparagus, look for tight buds and firm, unwrinkled stems that are evenly colored.

Pasta Soup with Chicken Livers

A soup that can be served as either a first or main course. The fried chicken livers are so delicious that even if you do not normally like them, you will love them in this soup.

Serves 4–6
1 tablespoon olive oil
pat of butter
4 garlic cloves, crushed
3 sprigs each fresh parsley,
 marjoram and sage, chopped
leaves from 1 fresh thyme
 sprig, chopped
5–6 fresh basil leaves, chopped
⅔ cup chicken livers, thawed if
 frozen, cut into small pieces
1–2 tablespoons dry white wine
2 11-ounce cans condensed
 chicken consommé
2 cups frozen peas
½ cup small pasta shapes,
 e.g. farfalle
2–3 scallions,
 diagonally sliced
salt and freshly ground
 black pepper
toasted slices of French bread,
 to serve

1 Heat the oil and butter in a frying pan, add the garlic and herbs, with salt and pepper to taste, and sauté gently for a few minutes.

2 Add the livers, increase the heat to high and stir-fry for a few minutes, until they change color and become dry. Pour the wine onto the livers, cook until the wine evaporates, then remove the pan from heat. Season to taste.

3 Pour both cans of condensed chicken consommé into a large saucepan and add water as directed on the labels. Add an extra can of water, season to taste and bring to a boil.

4 Add the peas to the pan and simmer for about 5 minutes, then add the pasta and bring the soup back to a boil, stirring. Simmer, stirring frequently, until the pasta is just *al dente*: about 5 minutes or according to the instructions on the package.

5 Add the fried chicken livers and the scallions, and heat through for 2–3 minutes. Taste and adjust the seasoning as necessary. Serve hot in warm bowls, accompanied by toasted slices of French bread.

Chinese Chicken Soup

Corn, scallions, carrots and egg noodles combine with chicken to create this tasty Eastern-style soup.

Serves 4–6
1 tablespoon sesame oil
4 scallions, roughly chopped
8 ounces chicken breast fillet, skinned and cut into small cubes
5 cups Chicken Stock
1 tablespoon soy sauce
1 cup frozen corn kernels
4 ounces medium thread egg noodles
1 carrot
salt and freshly ground black pepper
shrimp crackers, to serve (optional)

1 Heat the oil in a large, heavy saucepan, add the scallions and chicken and cook, stirring constantly, until the meat has browned all over.

2 Pour in the stock and soy sauce, and bring to a boil. Stir in the corn.

3 Add the noodles, breaking them up roughly, and simmer for a few minutes. Season to taste with salt and pepper.

4 Thinly slice the carrot lengthwise. Use small cutters to stamp out shapes from the slices of carrot. Add them to the soup and simmer for 5 minutes.

5 Pour the soup into warmed bowls and serve, accompanied by shrimp crackers if desired.

Chicken & Buckwheat Noodle Soup

This satisfying soup is given body with buckwheat or soba noodles, which are widely enjoyed in Japan.

Serves 4
8 ounces chicken breast fillet, skinned
1/2 cup soy sauce
1 tablespoon sake
4 cups Chicken Stock
2 pieces young leek, cut into 1-inch pieces
6 ounces spinach leaves
11 ounces buckwheat or soba noodles
sesame seeds, toasted, to garnish

1 Slice the chicken diagonally into bite-size pieces. Combine the soy sauce and sake in a saucepan and bring to a simmer. Add the chicken and cook gently for about 3 minutes, until it is tender. Keep hot.

2 Bring the stock to a boil in another saucepan. Add the leek and simmer for 3 minutes, then add the spinach. Remove from heat but keep warm.

3 Cook the noodles in a large saucepan of boiling water until just tender, following the instructions on the package.

4 Drain the noodles and divide among warmed individual serving bowls. Ladle the hot soup into the bowls, then add a portion of chicken to each. Serve immediately, sprinkled with sesame seeds.

Cook's Tip
Sake is a Japanese rice wine widely available at supermarkets and specialty stores. Do not confuse it with rice vinegar.

Chicken Soup with Garlic Croutons

A thick, chunky chicken and vegetable soup served with crisp fried croutons: a meal in itself.

Serves 4

4 chicken thighs, boned
  and skinned
1 tablespoon butter
2 small leeks, thinly sliced
1 tablespoon long-grain rice
3¾ cups Chicken Stock

1 tablespoon mixed chopped
  fresh parsley and mint
salt and freshly ground
  black pepper
crusty bread, to serve (optional)

For the garlic croutons

2 tablespoons olive oil
1 garlic clove, crushed
4 slices bread, cut into cubes

1 Cut the chicken into ½-inch cubes. Melt the butter in a saucepan, add the leeks and cook them until they are tender. Add the rice and chicken, and cook for another 2 minutes.

2 Pour in the stock, then cover and simmer for 15–20 minutes or until the rice is cooked and the chicken is tender.

3 To make the garlic croutons, heat the oil in a large frying pan. Add the crushed garlic clove and bread cubes, and cook until golden brown, stirring constantly to prevent burning. Drain on paper towels and sprinkle with a pinch of salt.

4 Add the parsley and mint to the soup and adjust the seasoning to taste. Serve hot in warmed bowls and pass the garlic croutons separately for sprinkling on the soup. Accompany with crusty bread, if desired.

Cock-a-Leekie

This traditional soup recipe—it is known from as long ago as 1598—originally included beef as well as chicken. In the past it would have been made from an old roaster, hence the name.

Serves 4–6

5 cups Chicken Stock
2 chicken portions,
  about 10 ounces each
1 bouquet garni
4 leeks
8–12 prunes, soaked overnight
  in water
salt and freshly ground
  black pepper
buttered soft rolls, to serve

1 Bring the stock to a boil in a large saucepan. Add the chicken and bouquet garni, and simmer gently for 40 minutes.

2 Cut the white part of the leeks into 1-inch slices and thinly slice a little of the green part. Drain the prunes.

3 Add the white parts of the leeks and the prunes to the saucepan and cook gently for 20 minutes, then add the green part of the leeks and cook for another 10–15 minutes.

4 Discard the bouquet garni. Remove the chicken from the pan, discard the skin and bones, and chop the flesh. Return the chicken to the pan and season the soup to taste. Heat the soup through, then serve hot with buttered soft rolls.

Cook's Tip

Bouquet garni traditionally consists of fresh herbs—usually a bay leaf, thyme sprigs and parsley stalks. Ready-made dried bouquets garnis are also available.

Chicken Vermicelli Soup

This soup is very quick and easy—you can add all sorts of extra ingredients to vary the taste, using up leftovers.

Serves 4–6
3 large eggs
2 tablespoons chopped cilantro
    or parsley
6¼ cups Chicken Stock or
    canned consommé
1 cup dried vermicelli or angel
    hair pasta
4 ounces cooked chicken
    breast fillet, sliced
salt and freshly ground
    black pepper

1 First, make the egg shreds. Whisk the eggs together in a small bowl and stir in the cilantro or parsley.

2 Heat a small, nonstick frying pan and pour in 2–3 tablespoons egg, swirling to cover the bottom evenly. Cook until set. Repeat until all the mixture is used up.

3 Roll up each egg crêpe and slice thinly into shreds using a sharp knife. Set aside until serving.

4 Bring the stock or consommé to a boil in a large saucepan and add the pasta, breaking it up into short lengths. Cook for 3–5 minutes, until the pasta is almost tender, then add the chicken, salt and pepper.

5 Heat through for 2–3 minutes, then stir in the egg shreds. Serve immediately in warmed bowls.

Variation
To make a Thai variation of this soup, use Chinese rice noodles instead of pasta. Stir ½ teaspoon dried lemongrass, two small whole fresh chiles and ¼ cup coconut milk into the chicken stock or consommé. Add four sliced scallions and chopped cilantro.

Chicken Broth with Cheese Toasts

A really filling, hearty soup that makes excellent use of a chicken carcass and vegetables left over from the weekend roast.

Serves 4
1 roasted chicken carcass
1 onion, quartered
2 celery stalks, finely chopped
1 garlic clove, crushed
a few fresh parsley sprigs
2 bay leaves
8-ounce can chopped tomatoes
7-ounce can chickpeas
2–3 tablespoons leftover
    vegetables, chopped, or
    1 large carrot, finely chopped
1 tablespoon chopped
    fresh parsley
2 slices toast
¼ cup grated cheese
salt and freshly ground
    black pepper

1 Pick off any little bits of flesh from the chicken carcass, especially from the underside where there is often some very tasty dark meat. Set aside.

2 Break the carcass in half and place in a large saucepan with the onion, half the celery, the garlic, parsley sprigs, bay leaves and sufficient water to cover. Cover the pan, bring to a boil and simmer for about 30 minutes or until you are left with about 1¼ cups of liquid.

3 Strain the stock and return to the pan. Add the chicken flesh, the remaining celery, the tomatoes, chickpeas (and their liquid), leftover vegetables or carrot and chopped parsley. Season to taste and simmer for another 7–10 minutes.

4 Meanwhile, sprinkle the toast with the cheese and broil until bubbling, then cut into fingers or triangles. Serve the soup hot in warmed bowls with the cheese toasts floating on top or passed separately.

Corn & Chicken Soup

This popular classic Chinese soup is delicious and very easy to make.

Serves 4–6

4 ounces chicken breast fillet, skinned and cubed
2 teaspoons light soy sauce
1 tablespoon Chinese rice wine
1 teaspoon cornstarch
1/4 cup cold water
1 teaspoon sesame oil
2 tablespoons peanut oil
1 teaspoon grated fresh ginger root
4 cups Chicken Stock
15-ounce can creamed corn
8-ounce can corn kernels
2 eggs, beaten
2–3 scallions, green parts only, cut into tiny rounds
salt and freshly ground black pepper

1 Grind the chicken in a food processor, taking care not to over-process. Transfer the chicken to a bowl and stir in the soy sauce, rice wine, cornstarch, water, sesame oil and seasoning. Cover and let sit for about 15 minutes to absorb the flavors.

2 Heat a wok over medium heat. Add the peanut oil and swirl it around. Add the ginger and stir-fry for a few seconds. Add the stock, creamed corn and corn kernels. Bring to just below the boiling point.

3 Spoon about 6 tablespoons of the hot liquid into the chicken mixture until it forms a smooth paste, and stir. Return to the wok. Slowly bring to a boil, stirring constantly, then simmer for 2–3 minutes, until cooked.

4 Pour the beaten eggs into the soup in a slow, steady stream, using a fork or chopsticks to stir the top of the soup in a figure-eight pattern. The eggs should set in lacy shreds. Serve immediately in warmed individual soup bowls with the scallions sprinkled on top.

Pumpkin, Rice & Chicken Soup

A warm, comforting soup which, despite the spice and basmati rice, is quintessentially English. For an even more substantial meal, add a little extra rice and make sure you use all the chicken from the stock.

Serves 4

1 pumpkin wedge, about 1 pound
1 tablespoon sunflower oil
2 tablespoons butter
6 green cardamom pods
2 leeks, chopped
1/2 cup basmati rice, soaked in water
1 1/2 cups milk
salt and freshly ground black pepper
generous strips of pared orange zest, to garnish
whole-wheat bread, to serve

For the chicken stock

2 chicken quarters
1 onion, quartered
2 carrots, chopped
1 celery stalk, chopped
6–8 peppercorns
3 3/4 cups water

1 First, to make the chicken stock, place the chicken quarters, onion, carrots, celery and peppercorns in a large saucepan. Pour in the water and bring to a boil over medium heat. Skim the surface if necessary, then lower the heat, cover and simmer gently for 1 hour.

2 Strain the chicken stock into a clean, large bowl, discarding the vegetables. Skin and bone one or both chicken pieces and cut the flesh into strips. (If not using both chicken pieces for the soup, reserve the other piece for another recipe.)

3 Peel the pumpkin, and remove and discard all the seeds and pith, so that you have about 12 ounces flesh. Cut the flesh into 1-inch cubes.

4 Heat the oil and butter in a saucepan and fry the cardamom pods for 2–3 minutes, until slightly swollen. Add the leeks and pumpkin. Cook, stirring, for 3–4 minutes over medium heat, then lower the heat, cover and sweat for 5 more minutes or until the pumpkin is quite tender, stirring once or twice.

5 Measure 2 1/2 cups of the stock and add to the pumpkin mixture. Bring to a boil, lower the heat, cover and simmer for 10–15 minutes, until the pumpkin is soft.

6 Pour the remaining stock into a measuring cup and add water to make 1 1/4 cups. Drain the rice and put it into a saucepan. Pour in the stock, bring to a boil, then simmer for about 10 minutes, until the rice is tender. Add seasoning to taste.

7 Remove the cardamom pods, then process the soup in a blender or food processor until smooth. Pour back into a clean saucepan and stir in the milk, chicken and rice (with any stock that has not been absorbed). Heat until simmering. Pour into warmed bowls and garnish with the strips of pared orange zest and freshly ground black pepper. Serve with whole-wheat bread.

Chicken Soup with Lockshen

To achieve the best results with this traditional Jewish dish, follow two rules: make it the day before and try to find a boiling fowl, which has much more flavor than a roasting bird.

Serves 6–8
6½-pound boiling chicken,
    including the giblets, but not
    the liver
4 cups cold water
2 onions, halved
2 carrots
5 celery stalks
handful of fine vermicelli
    (lockshen), about 4 ounces
salt and freshly ground
    black pepper
fresh bread, to serve (optional)

1 Put the chicken into a very large saucepan, together with the giblets. Add the water and bring to a boil over high heat. Skim off the white froth that comes to the top and then add the halved onions, the carrots and celery. Season to taste with ground black pepper only.

2 Bring the liquid to a boil again, then turn the heat to low, cover and simmer for at least 2 hours. Keep an eye on the water level and add a little more as needed so that the chicken is always covered.

3 When the chicken is tender, remove from the pan and take the meat off the bones, reserving it for another use. Put the bones back in the soup and continue cooking for another 1 hour. There should be at least 4 cups of soup.

4 Strain the soup into a large bowl and chill overnight. When it is quite cold, it may form a jelly and a pale layer of fat will have settled on the top. Remove the fat with a spoon and discard.

5 Bring the soup to a boil again, season to taste and add the vermicelli. Boil for about 8 minutes and serve in warmed large bowls, with fresh bread, if using.

Chicken Soup with Matzo Kleis Balls

Another classic Jewish recipe, in which herbed dumplings are cooked in delicious homemade soup.

Serves 4
2 matzo (sheets of
    unleavened bread)
2 tablespoons oil
1 onion, chopped
handful of parsley
2 eggs
pinch of ground ginger
1–2 tablespoons medium ground
    matzo meal
4 cups Chicken Soup
salt and freshly ground
    black pepper

1 Soak the matzo in cold water for about 5 minutes, then drain and squeeze them dry.

2 Heat the oil in a frying pan and sauté the onion until golden. Chop the parsley, reserving a few sprigs for the garnish. Whisk the eggs slightly.

3 Combine the soaked matzo, sautéed onion, parsley and eggs. Season with salt, pepper and ginger, and add about 1 tablespoon matzo meal. Chill for at least 1 hour.

4 Bring the soup to a boil in a large saucepan. Roll the dumpling mixture into small balls, drop them into the fast-boiling soup and cook for about 20 minutes. Serve the soup in warmed bowls, garnished with the reserved parsley.

Cook's Tip
You can make the dumplings well in advance, but they should be kept chilled. They also freeze well, so it is a good idea to make a double batch, and cook half and freeze half. To use frozen dumplings, let them defrost for about 1 hour before cooking in the soup.

Chicken Soup with Vermicelli

This traditional Moroccan soup is injected with an extra burst of flavor in the form of lemon, parsley, cilantro and saffron just before serving.

Serves 4–6

2 tablespoons sunflower oil
1 tablespoon butter
1 onion, chopped
2 chicken legs or breasts, halved
    or quartered
seasoned flour, for dusting
2 carrots, cut into 1¹/₂-inch pieces
1 parsnip, cut into 1¹/₂-inch pieces
6¹/₄ cups Chicken Stock
1 cinnamon stick
good pinch of paprika
pinch of saffron
2 egg yolks
juice of ¹/₂ lemon
2 tablespoons chopped
    cilantro
2 tablespoons chopped
    fresh parsley
5 ounces vermicelli
salt and freshly ground
    black pepper
Moroccan bread, to serve

1 Heat the oil and butter in a saucepan or flameproof casserole and sauté the onion for 3–4 minutes, until softened. Dust the chicken pieces in seasoned flour, add to the pan or casserole and cook gently until evenly browned.

2 Transfer the chicken to a plate and add the carrots and parsnip to the pan. Cook over low heat for 3–4 minutes, stirring frequently, then return the chicken to the pan. Add the chicken stock, cinnamon stick and paprika, and season to taste with salt and pepper.

3 Bring the soup to a boil, cover and simmer for 1 hour or until the vegetables are very tender.

4 While the soup is cooking, blend the saffron in 2 tablespoons boiling water. Beat the egg yolks with the lemon juice in a separate bowl and add the chopped cilantro and parsley. When the saffron water has cooled, stir into the egg and lemon mixture until thoroughly blended.

5 When the vegetables are tender, transfer the chicken to a plate. Spoon any excess fat from the soup, then increase the heat a little and stir in the vermicelli. Cook for 5–6 minutes, until the noodles are tender.

6 Meanwhile, remove the skin from the chicken and, if desired, bone and chop the meat into bite-size pieces. If you prefer, simply skin the chicken and leave the pieces whole.

7 When the vermicelli is cooked, reduce the heat and stir in the chicken pieces and the egg, lemon and saffron mixture. Cook over very low heat for 1–2 minutes, stirring constantly. Adjust the seasoning and serve with Moroccan bread.

Rich Minestrone

A special minestrone made with chicken. Served with crusty Italian bread, it makes a hearty meal.

Serves 4–6

1 tablespoon olive oil
2 chicken thighs
3 strips bacon, chopped
1 onion, finely chopped
a few fresh basil leaves, shredded
a few fresh rosemary leaves,
    finely chopped
1 tablespoon chopped fresh
    flat-leaf parsley
2 potatoes, cut into ¹/₂-inch cubes
1 large carrot, cut into
    ¹/₂-inch cubes
2 small zucchini, cut into
    ¹/₂-inch cubes
1–2 celery stalks, cut into
    ¹/₂-inch cubes
4 cups
    Chicken Stock
1³/₄ cups frozen peas
1 cup stellette or other
    tiny soup pasta
salt and freshly ground
    black pepper
coarsely shaved Parmesan cheese,
    and fresh basil leaves,
    to garnish

1 Heat the oil in a large saucepan and fry the chicken for about 5 minutes on each side. Remove and set aside. Lower the heat, add the bacon, onion, shredded basil, rosemary and parsley to the pan and stir well. Cook gently, stirring constantly, for about 5 minutes. Add all the vegetables except the frozen peas and cook for 5–7 more minutes, stirring frequently.

2 Return the chicken thighs to the pan, add the stock and bring to a boil. Cover and cook over low heat for 35–40 minutes, stirring the soup occasionally.

3 Remove the chicken thighs using a slotted spoon. Stir the peas and pasta into the soup, and bring back to a boil. Simmer, stirring frequently, until the pasta is al dente: 7–8 minutes or according to the instructions on the package.

4 Meanwhile, skin the chicken and cut the meat into ¹/₂-inch pieces. Return it to the soup and heat through. Adjust the seasoning and serve, sprinkled with Parmesan and basil leaves.

Chicken, Tomato & Chayote Soup

An unusual soup from Africa that includes smoked haddock and chayote, a squash available at gourmet grocery stores.

Serves 4

8 ounces chicken breast
  fillet, skinned
1 garlic clove, crushed
pinch of freshly grated nutmeg
2 tablespoons butter
  or margarine
1/2 onion, finely chopped
1 tablespoon tomato paste
14-ounce can tomatoes, puréed
5 cups Chicken Stock
1 fresh chile, seeded and chopped
1 chayote, peeled and diced,
  about 12 ounces
1 teaspoon dried oregano
1/2 teaspoon dried thyme
2 ounces smoked haddock fillet,
  skinned and diced
salt and freshly ground
  black pepper
fresh snipped chives, to garnish

1 Dice the chicken, place in a bowl and season with salt, pepper, garlic and nutmeg. Mix well to flavor the chicken and then set aside for about 30 minutes.

2 Melt the butter or margarine in a large saucepan, add the chicken and sauté over medium heat for 5–6 minutes. Stir in the onion and sauté gently for another 5 minutes, until the onion is slightly softened.

3 Add the tomato paste, puréed tomatoes, stock, chile, chayote and herbs. Bring to a boil, cover and simmer gently for 35 minutes, until the chayote is tender.

4 Add the smoked fish and simmer for another 5 minutes or until the fish is cooked through. Taste the soup and adjust the seasoning as necessary. Pour into warmed soup bowls, garnish with snipped chives and serve.

Tortilla Soup

You can make this Mexican-style soup as mild or as fiery as you want.

Serves 4–6

vegetable oil, for frying
1 onion, finely chopped
1 large garlic clove, crushed
2 medium tomatoes, peeled,
  seeded and chopped
1/2 teaspoon salt
7 1/2 cups Chicken Stock
1 carrot, diced
1 small zucchini, diced
1 chicken breast fillet, skinned,
  cooked and shredded
1–2 ounces canned green chiles,
  chopped

For the garnish

4 corn tortillas
1 small ripe avocado
2 scallions, chopped
chopped cilantro
grated Cheddar cheese (optional)

1 Heat 1 tablespoon oil in a large saucepan. Add the onion and garlic, and cook over medium heat for 5–8 minutes, until just softened. Add the tomatoes and salt, and cook for 5 more minutes. Stir in the stock. Bring to a boil, then lower the heat and simmer, covered, for about 15 minutes.

2 Meanwhile, to make the garnish, trim the tortillas into squares, then cut them into strips. Pour 1/2 inch of oil into a frying pan and heat until hot but not smoking. Add the tortilla strips, in batches, and fry until just beginning to brown, turning occasionally. Remove with a slotted spoon and drain on paper towels.

3 Add the carrot to the soup. Cook, covered, for 10 minutes. Add the zucchini, shredded chicken and green chiles, and continue cooking, uncovered, for about 5 minutes, until the vegetables are just tender.

4 Meanwhile, peel and pit the avocado. Cut the flesh into fine dice. Divide the tortilla strips among warmed soup bowls. Sprinkle with the avocado. Ladle in the soup, then sprinkle the scallions and cilantro on top. Serve immediately, with grated Cheddar, if desired.

Spicy Chicken & Mushroom Soup

A creamy chicken soup that makes a hearty meal for a winter's night. Serve it piping hot with lots of fresh garlic bread.

Serves 4

8 ounces chicken, skinned and boned
6 tablespoons unsalted butter
½ teaspoon crushed garlic
I teaspoon garam masala
I teaspoon crushed black peppercorns
I teaspoon salt
¼ teaspoon grated nutmeg
I medium leek, sliced
generous I cup mushrooms, sliced
⅓ cup corn kernels
I¼ cups water
I cup light cream
I tablespoon chopped cilantro
I teaspoon crushed dried red chiles (optional)

I Cut the chicken pieces into very fine, even-size strips.

2 Melt the butter in a medium saucepan. Lower the heat slightly and add the garlic and garam masala. Lower the heat even more and add the black peppercorns, salt and nutmeg. Finally, add the chicken pieces, leek, mushrooms and corn, and cook for 5–7 minutes or until the chicken is cooked through, stirring constantly.

3 Remove from heat and let cool slightly. Transfer three quarters of the mixture into a food processor or blender. Add the water and process for about I minute.

4 Pour the resulting purée back into the saucepan with the rest of the mixture and bring to a boil over medium heat. Lower the heat and stir in the cream.

5 Add the cilantro. Taste the soup and adjust the seasoning as necessary. Serve hot, garnished with the crushed red chiles, if desired.

Chicken & Almond Soup

This rich and creamy soup makes an excellent appetizer for an Indian meal or, served with naan, a satisfying lunch or supper dish.

Serves 4

6 tablespoons unsalted butter
I medium leek, chopped
½ teaspoon grated fresh ginger root
I cup ground almonds
I teaspoon salt
½ teaspoon crushed black peppercorns
I fresh green chile, chopped
I medium carrot, sliced
½ cup frozen peas
4 ounces chicken, skinned, boned and cubed
I tablespoon chopped cilantro
scant 2 cups water
I cup light cream
4 cilantro sprigs, to garnish

I Melt the butter in a large karahi or deep, round frying pan and sauté the leek with the ginger until soft.

2 Lower the heat and add the ground almonds, salt, peppercorns, chile, carrot, peas and chicken. Cook for about 10 minutes or until the chicken is completely cooked, stirring constantly. Add the chopped cilantro.

3 Remove from heat and let cool slightly. Transfer the mixture to a food processor or blender and process for about I½ minutes. Pour in the water and process for another 30 seconds.

4 Pour the soup back into the saucepan and bring to a boil, stirring occasionally. Once it has boiled, lower the heat and gradually stir in the cream. Cook gently for another 2 minutes, stirring occasionally.

5 Serve the soup immediately in warmed bowls, garnished with the cilantro sprigs.

Chicken Wonton Soup with Shrimp

This Indonesian version of wonton soup is more luxurious than the more widely known basic recipe and is almost a meal in itself.

Serves 4

11 ounces chicken breast
    fillet, skinned
7 ounces shrimp tails, raw
    or cooked
1 teaspoon finely chopped
    fresh ginger root
2 scallions, finely chopped
1 egg
2 teaspoons oyster sauce
    (optional)
1 tablespoon cornstarch
1 package wonton skins
3¾ cups Chicken Stock
¼ cucumber, peeled and diced
salt and freshly ground
    black pepper

For the garnish

1 scallion, roughly shredded
4 sprigs cilantro leaves
1 tomato, peeled, seeded
    and diced

1 Place the chicken breast, 5 ounces of the shrimp tails, the ginger and scallions in a food processor and process for 2–3 minutes. Add the egg, oyster sauce (if using) and seasoning and process briefly. Set aside.

2 Mix the cornstarch with a little water to form a thin paste. Place eight wonton skins at a time on a work surface, moisten the edges with the cornstarch paste and place ½ teaspoon of the filling in the center of each. Fold in half and pinch to seal.

3 Bring the chicken stock to a boil, add the remaining shrimp tails and the cucumber, and simmer for 3–4 minutes. Add the wontons and simmer to warm through.

4 Ladle the soup into warmed bowls and garnish with shredded scallion, cilantro leaves and diced tomato. Serve immediately in warmed bowls.

Chicken Mulligatawny

Using the original pepper water—mulla-ga-tani— this famous dish was created by the non-vegetarian chefs during the British Raj and imported to the United Kingdom.

Serves 4–6

2-pound chicken, boned, skinned
    and cubed
2½ cups water
6 green cardamom pods
2-inch piece cinnamon stick
4–6 curry leaves
1 tablespoon ground coriander
1 teaspoon ground cumin
½ teaspoon ground turmeric
3 garlic cloves, crushed
12 peppercorns
4 cloves
1 onion, finely chopped
4 ounces coconut milk
juice of 2 lemons
salt

deep-fried onions and chopped
    cilantro, to garnish

1 Place the chicken in a large saucepan with the water and cook until tender. Skim the surface, then strain, reserving the stock. Keep the chicken warm.

2 Return the stock to the pan and reheat. Add the cardamom, cinnamon, curry leaves, ground coriander, cumin and turmeric, garlic, peppercorns, cloves and onion. Add the coconut milk, the lemon juice and salt to taste. Simmer for 10–15 minutes.

3 Strain the soup again and return the chicken to the pan. Simmer for a few minutes to reheat thoroughly.

4 Taste the soup and adjust the seasoning as necessary. Divide among warmed bowls, garnish with deep-fried onions and chopped cilantro, and serve.

Thai-style Chicken Soup

A fragrant blend of coconut milk, lemongrass, ginger and lime makes a delicious soup, with just a hint of chile.

Serves 4

1 teaspoon oil
1–2 fresh red chiles, seeded and chopped
2 garlic cloves, crushed
1 large leek, thinly sliced
2½ cups Chicken Stock
1⅔ cups coconut milk
1 pound boneless, skinless chicken thighs, cut into bite-size pieces
2 tablespoons fish sauce
1 lemongrass stalk, split
1-inch piece fresh ginger root, peeled and finely chopped
1 teaspoon sugar
4 kaffir lime leaves (optional)
¾ cup frozen peas, thawed
3 tablespoons chopped cilantro

1 Heat the oil in a large saucepan, and cook the chiles and garlic for about 2 minutes. Add the leek and cook for another 2 minutes.

2 Stir in the stock and coconut milk, and bring to a boil.

3 Add the chicken, with the fish sauce, lemongrass, ginger, sugar and lime leaves, if using. Simmer, covered, for 15 minutes or until the chicken is tender, stirring occasionally.

4 Add the peas and cook for another 3 minutes. Remove the lemongrass and stir in the cilantro just before serving.

> **Cook's Tip**
> *Kaffir lime leaves are aromatic and used frequently in Southeast Asian cooking. They are available at specialty stores.*

Spiced Vegetable Soup with Chicken & Shrimp

Eggplant, green beans, red bell pepper, cabbage, succulent chicken and shrimp are given excellent flavor with a fabulous mixture of spices.

Serves 6–8

1 onion
2 garlic cloves, crushed
1 fresh red or green chile, seeded and sliced
½-inch cube terasi
3 macadamia nuts or 6 almonds
½-inch piece galangal, peeled and sliced
1 teaspoon sugar
oil, for frying
8 ounces chicken breast fillet, skinned and cut into ½-inch cubes
1¼ cups coconut milk
5 cups Chicken Stock
1 eggplant, diced
8 ounces green beans, chopped
small wedge of white cabbage, shredded
1 red bell pepper, seeded and finely sliced
4 ounces cooked peeled shrimp
salt and freshly ground black pepper

1 Halve the onion; slice one half and set aside; cut the other half in half and place both halves in a mortar. Add the garlic, chile, terasi, nuts, galangal and sugar, and grind into a paste using a pestle. Alternatively, grind in a food processor.

2 Heat a wok, add the oil and fry the paste, without browning, until it releases a rich aroma. Add the reserved onion and chicken, and cook for 3–4 minutes. Stir in the coconut milk and stock. Bring to a boil and simmer for a few minutes.

3 Add the diced eggplant to the soup, with the beans, and cook for only a few minutes, until the beans are almost cooked.

4 A few minutes before serving, stir in the cabbage, red pepper and shrimp. The vegetables should be cooked so that they are still crunchy and the shrimp merely heated through. Taste the soup and adjust the seasoning as necessary. Serve in warmed bowls.

Chiang Mai Noodle Soup

A signature dish of the Thai city of Chiang Mai, this delicious noodle soup, in fact, has Burmese origins.

I pound fresh egg noodles, blanched briefly in boiling water
salt and freshly ground black pepper

Serves 4–6
2½ cups coconut milk
2 tablespoons red curry paste
I teaspoon ground turmeric
I pound chicken thighs, boned and cut into bite-size chunks
2½ cups Chicken Stock
¼ cup fish sauce
I tablespoon dark soy sauce
juice of ½–I lime

For the garnish
3 scallions, chopped
4 fresh red chiles, chopped
4 shallots, chopped
¼ cup sliced pickled mustard leaves, rinsed
2 tablespoons fried sliced garlic
cilantro leaves
4 fried noodle nests (optional)

I Pour about one third of the coconut milk into a large saucepan and bring to a boil, stirring often with a wooden spoon, until it separates.

2 Add the curry paste and ground turmeric, stir to mix completely and cook gently until fragrant.

3 Add the chicken and stir-fry for about 2 minutes, ensuring that all the chunks are coated with the paste.

4 Add the remaining coconut milk, the chicken stock, fish sauce and soy sauce. Season with salt and pepper to taste. Simmer over low heat for 7–10 minutes. Remove from heat and stir in the lime juice.

5 Reheat the noodles in boiling water, drain and divide among warmed individual bowls. Divide the chicken between the bowls and ladle in the hot soup. Top each bowl with a few of each of the garnishes and serve.

Ginger, Chicken & Coconut Soup

The ginger flavor in this aromatic soup is provided by galangal, which belongs to the same family as the more familiar ginger.

Serves 4–6
3 cups coconut milk
2 cups Chicken Stock
4 lemongrass stalks, bruised and chopped
I-inch piece galangal, thinly sliced
10 black peppercorns, crushed

10 kaffir lime leaves, torn
11 ounces boneless chicken, cut into thin strips
1½ cups button mushrooms
½ cup baby corn
¼ cup lime juice
3 tablespoons fish sauce

For the garnish
2 fresh red chiles, chopped
a few scallions, chopped
cilantro leaves

I Bring the coconut milk and chicken stock to a boil in a medium saucepan. Add the lemongrass, galangal, peppercorns and half the kaffir lime leaves, reduce the heat and simmer gently for 10 minutes.

2 Strain the stock into a clean pan. Return to the heat, then add the chicken, button mushrooms and baby corn. Simmer for 5–7 minutes or until the chicken is cooked.

3 Stir in the lime juice, fish sauce to taste and the rest of the kaffir lime leaves.

4 Serve the soup hot in warmed bowls, garnished with chopped red chiles, scallions and cilantro.

Turkey & Lentil Soup

A fairly substantial soup, ideal for a cold day, and a great way of using up leftover cooked turkey, or other poultry, at the end of the festive season.

Serves 4

2 tablespoons butter
  or margarine
1 large carrot, chopped
1 onion, chopped
1 leek, white part only, chopped
1 celery stalk, chopped
1½ cups mushrooms, chopped
3 tablespoons dry white wine
4 cups Chicken Stock
2 teaspoons dried thyme
1 bay leaf
½ cup brown or green lentils
8 ounces cooked turkey, diced
salt and freshly ground
  black pepper

1 Melt the butter or margarine in a large saucepan. Add the carrot, onion, leek, celery and mushrooms. Cook for 3–5 minutes, until the vegetables are softened.

2 Stir in the wine and chicken stock. Bring to a boil and skim off any foam that rises to the surface. Add the thyme and bay leaf. Reduce the heat, cover and simmer for 30 minutes.

3 Add the lentils and continue cooking, covered, for 30–40 more minutes until they are just tender. Stir the soup occasionally.

4 Stir in the diced turkey and season to taste with salt and pepper. Cook until the turkey is just heated through. Ladle the soup into warmed bowls and serve hot.

Cook's Tip
Lentils are one of the few pulses that do not need to be soaked before cooking. Puy lentils have the best flavor and retain their shape well.

Asian Duck Consommé

Though a little time-consuming to make, this wonderful soup, light and rich at the same time, is well worth the effort.

Serves 4

1 duck carcass (raw or cooked),
  plus 2 legs or any giblets,
  trimmed of as much fat
  as possible
1 large onion, unpeeled, with root
  end trimmed
2 carrots, cut into 2-inch pieces
1 parsnip, cut into 2-inch pieces
1 leek, cut into 2-inch pieces
2–4 garlic cloves, crushed
1-inch piece fresh ginger root,
  peeled and sliced
1 tablespoon black peppercorns
4–6 fresh thyme sprigs
1 small bunch cilantro
  (6–8 sprigs), leaves and
  stems separated

For the garnish
1 small carrot
1 small leek, halved lengthwise
4–6 shiitake mushrooms,
  thinly sliced
soy sauce
2 scallions, thinly sliced
shredded Chinese greens
freshly ground black pepper

1 Put the duck carcass, the legs or giblets, the vegetables, spices, thyme and cilantro stems in a large saucepan, cover with cold water and bring to a boil over medium-high heat, skimming any foam that rises to the surface.

2 Reduce the heat and simmer gently for 1½–2 hours, then strain through a muslin-lined sieve into a bowl.

3 Let the stock cool, then chill for several hours or overnight. Skim off any congealed fat and blot the surface with paper towels to remove any traces of fat.

4 To make the garnish, cut the carrot and leek into julienne strips. Place in a large saucepan with the mushrooms. Pour in the stock, add a few dashes of soy sauce and some pepper. Bring to a boil, skimming off any foam. Stir in the scallions and Chinese greens. Ladle into warmed bowls, sprinkle with cilantro leaves and serve.

Chicken Liver Pâté

This is a really quick and simple pâté to make, yet it has a delicious, rich flavor. It is sealed with clarified butter, which helps maintain its freshness.

Serves 6

2 ounces butter
1 onion, finely chopped
12 ounces chicken
    livers, trimmed
¼ cup medium sherry
1 ounce cream cheese
1–2 tablespoons lemon juice
2 hard-boiled eggs, shelled
    and chopped
4–6 tablespoons Clarified Butter
salt and freshly ground
    black pepper
bay leaves, to garnish
toast or savory crackers, to serve

1 Melt the butter in a frying pan. Add the onion and livers, and cook until the onion is soft and the livers are lightly browned and no longer pink in the center.

2 Add the sherry and boil until reduced by half. Cool slightly.

3 Transfer the mixture to a food processor or blender and add the cream cheese and 1 tablespoon lemon juice. Process until thoroughly blended and smooth.

4 Add the hard-boiled eggs and blend briefly. Season with salt and pepper. Taste and add more lemon juice, if desired.

5 Pack the liver pâté into a mold or into individual ramekins. Smooth the surface.

6 Spoon a layer of clarified butter onto the surface of the pâté. Chill until firm and garnish with bay leaves. Serve at room temperature, with hot toast or savory crackers.

Clarified Butter

This is butter from which the milk solids have been removed.

Makes about 6 ounces
8 ounces butter

1 Put the butter in a heavy saucepan over low heat. Melt gently. Skim off all the froth from the surface. You will then see a clear yellow layer on top of a milky layer: carefully pour the clear fat into a bowl or pitcher, leaving the milky residue in the pan.
2 Discard the milky residue, or add it to soups.

3 The clarified butter may be stored in the refrigerator for several weeks and for longer in the freezer.

Chicken Liver Pâté with Marsala

A more sophisticated version of chicken liver pâté that contains Marsala, a soft and pungent fortified wine from Sicily, and a generous amount of garlic.

Serves 4–6

1 cup butter, softened
12 ounces chicken
    livers, trimmed
2 garlic cloves, crushed
1 tablespoon Marsala
1 teaspoon chopped fresh sage
salt and freshly ground
    black pepper
8 sage leaves, to garnish
Melba toast, to serve

1 Melt 2 tablespoons of the butter in a frying pan, add the chicken livers and garlic, and fry over medium heat for about 5 minutes or until the livers are lightly browned but still pink in the middle.

2 Transfer the livers to a blender or food processor, using a slotted spoon, and add the Marsala and chopped sage.

3 Melt 10 tablespoons of the remaining butter in the frying pan, stirring to loosen any sediment, then pour into the blender or processor and process until smooth. Season well.

4 Spoon the pâté into individual pots and smooth the surface. Melt the rest of the butter in a separate pan and pour onto the pâtés. Garnish with sage leaves and chill until set. Serve with triangles of Melba toast.

Cook's Tip
Sage has a special affinity with liver. However, it is very powerfully flavored and should be used sparingly.

Chicken Liver Mousse

This mousse makes an elegant yet easy first course. The onion marmalade makes a delicious accompaniment, along with a salad of bitter greens.

Serves 6–8
3/4 cup butter, diced
1 small onion, finely chopped
1 garlic clove, finely chopped
1 pound chicken livers, trimmed
1/2 teaspoon dried thyme

2–3 tablespoons brandy
salt and freshly ground
 black pepper

For the onion marmalade
2 tablespoons butter
1 pound red onions, thinly sliced
1 garlic clove, finely chopped
1/2 teaspoon dried thyme
2–3 tablespoons raspberry or
 red wine vinegar
1–2 tablespoons honey
1/4 cup golden raisins

1 In a heavy frying pan, melt 2 tablespoons of the butter over medium heat. Add the onion and cook for 5–7 minutes, until soft and golden, then add the chopped garlic and cook for 1 more minute.

2 Increase the heat to medium-high and add the chicken livers, thyme, salt and pepper. Cook for 3–5 minutes, until the livers are colored, stirring frequently; the livers should remain pink inside. Add the brandy and cook for another minute.

3 Using a slotted spoon, transfer the livers to a food processor with a metal blade. Pour in the cooking juices and process for 1 minute or until smooth, scraping down the sides once. With the machine running, add the remaining butter, a few pieces at a time, until it is incorporated.

4 Press the mousse mixture through a fine sieve with a wooden spoon or rubber spatula.

5 Line a 2-cup loaf pan with plastic wrap, smoothing out as many wrinkles as possible. Pour the mousse mixture into the lined pan. Cool, then cover and chill until firm.

6 To make the onion marmalade, heat the butter in a heavy frying pan over medium-low heat, add the onions, and cook for 20 minutes, until softened and just colored, stirring frequently. Stir in the garlic, thyme, vinegar, honey and golden raisins and cook, covered, for 10–15 minutes, until the onions are completely soft and jam-like, stirring occasionally. Spoon into a bowl and cool to room temperature.

7 To serve, dip the loaf pan into hot water for 5 seconds, wipe dry and invert onto a board. Lift off the pan, peel off the plastic wrap and smooth the surface with a knife. Serve sliced with a little of the onion marmalade.

> **Cook's Tip**
> *The mousse will keep for 3–4 days. If made ahead, cover and chill until ready to use. The onion marmalade can be made up to 2 days ahead and gently reheated over low heat or in the microwave until just warm.*

Chicken & Pistachio Pâté

This version of a classic of French charcuterie can be made using a whole boned bird or chicken pieces.

Serves 10–12
2 pounds boneless chicken meat
1 chicken breast fillet, about
 6 ounces, skinned
1/2 cup fresh white bread crumbs
1/2 cup whipping cream
1 egg white
4 scallions, finely chopped
1 garlic clove, finely chopped

1/2 cup cooked ham, cut into
 1/2-inch cubes
1/2 cup shelled pistachios
3 tablespoons chopped
 fresh tarragon
pinch of grated nutmeg
3/4 teaspoon salt
1 1/2 teaspoons freshly ground
 black pepper
oil, for greasing
green salad, to serve

1 Trim the chicken meat and cut into 2-inch cubes. Put in a food processor and pulse to chop the meat to a smooth purée, in two or three batches. Alternatively, pass the meat through the medium or fine blade of a grinder.

2 Preheat the oven to 350°F. Cut the chicken breast fillet into 1/2-inch cubes.

3 In a large mixing bowl, soak the bread crumbs in the whipping cream. Add the puréed chicken, egg white, scallions, garlic, ham, pistachios, tarragon, nutmeg, salt and pepper. Using a wooden spoon or your fingers, stir the mixture until very well combined.

4 Lay out a piece of aluminum foil about 18 inches long on a work surface and lightly brush oil on a 12-inch square in the center. Spoon the chicken mixture onto the foil to form a log shape about 12 inches long and about 3 1/2 inches thick. Bring together the long sides of the foil and fold over securely. Twist the ends and tie with string.

5 Transfer to a baking sheet and bake for 1 1/2 hours. Let cool, then chill overnight. Serve sliced with green salad.

Chicken & Mushroom Terrine

Ideal as an appetizer or light lunch, this delicious dish proves that low-fat cooking need not sacrifice flavor.

Serves 4
2 shallots, chopped
generous 2 cups mushrooms, chopped
3 tablespoons Chicken Stock
2 chicken breast fillets, skinned and chopped
1 egg white
2 tablespoons whole-wheat bread crumbs
2 tablespoons chopped fresh parsley
2 tablespoons chopped fresh sage
oil, for greasing
salt and freshly ground black pepper
fresh sage sprigs, to garnish
tomatoes, to serve

1 Preheat the oven to 350°F. Place the shallots, mushrooms and stock in a saucepan, and cook over low heat, stirring occasionally, until the vegetables have softened and the mixture is dry.

2 Transfer to a food processor and add the chicken, egg white, bread crumbs and seasoning, and chop coarsely. Add the chopped herbs and process briefly.

3 Spoon into a greased 3¾-cup ovenproof terrine dish and smooth the surface. Cover with aluminum foil and bake for 35–40 minutes, until the juices are no longer pink.

4 Remove from the oven and place a weight on top. Let cool, then chill. Serve sliced, garnished with sage and accompanied by tomatoes.

Potted Chicken

A simple-to-make appetizer using cooked chicken, this looks good served in attractive individual pots.

Serves 4–6
12 ounces skinless boneless cooked chicken
½ cup Clarified Butter
1½ tablespoons dry sherry
ground cinnamon
ground mace
salt and freshly ground black pepper

1 Put the cooked chicken through the fine blade of a grinder or chop finely in a food processor.

2 Heat the butter and blend half with the chicken. Add the sherry with cinnamon, mace, salt and pepper to taste.

3 Pack into individual containers and seal the tops with the remaining butter.

Chicken, Bacon & Walnut Terrine

A luxurious dish, richly textured and lightly spiced, this would make a perfect appetizer for a special occasion dinner or buffet.

Serves 8–10
2 chicken breast fillets
1 large garlic clove, crushed
½ slice bread
1 egg
12 ounces bacon (the fattier the better), ground or finely chopped
8 ounces chicken livers, trimmed and finely chopped
¼ cup chopped walnuts, toasted
2 tablespoons sweet sherry or Madeira
½ teaspoon ground allspice
½ teaspoon cayenne pepper
pinch each grated nutmeg and ground cloves
8 strips bacon, stretched
oil, for greasing
salt and freshly ground black pepper
endive leaves, chives and chopped walnuts, to garnish

1 Cut the chicken into thin strips and season lightly. Mash the garlic, bread and egg together. Work in the chopped bacon (using your hands is really the best way) and then the finely chopped livers. Stir in the chopped walnuts, sherry or Madeira, spices and seasoning to taste.

2 Preheat the oven to 400°F. Line a 1½-pound loaf pan with the bacon strips and pack in half the meat mixture. Lay the chicken strips on the top and spread on the rest of the mixture. Cover the loaf pan with lightly greased aluminum foil, seal well and press down firmly.

3 Place the terrine in a roasting pan half full of hot water and bake for 1–1½ hours or until firm to the touch. Remove from the oven, place a weight on top and let cool, draining off any excess fat or liquid while the terrine is still warm. Chill.

4 To serve, turn out the terrine and cut into thick slices. Garnish with a few endive leaves and chives, and a sprinkling of chopped walnuts.

Turkey, Juniper & Green Peppercorn Terrine

This is an ideal dish for entertaining, as it can be made several days in advance and looks beautiful.

Serves 10–12

8 ounces chicken livers, trimmed
1 pound ground turkey
1 pound ground pork
8 ounces cubetti pancetta
½ cup shelled pistachios, roughly chopped
1 teaspoon salt
½ teaspoon ground mace
2 garlic cloves, crushed
1 teaspoon green peppercorns in brine, drained
1 teaspoon juniper berries
½ cup dry white wine
2 tablespoons gin
finely grated zest of 1 orange
8 large vacuum-packed grape leaves in brine
oil, for greasing
pickles or chutney, to serve

1 Chop the chicken livers finely. Put them in a bowl and add the turkey, pork, pancetta, pistachios, salt, mace and garlic. Mix well. Lightly crush the peppercorns and juniper berries, and add them to the mixture. Stir in the wine, gin and orange zest. Cover and chill overnight.

2 Preheat the oven to 325°F. Rinse the grape leaves under cold running water. Drain them thoroughly. Lightly oil a 5-cup ovenproof terrine dish or loaf pan. Line the terrine or pan with the leaves, letting the ends hang over the sides. Pack the meat mixture into the terrine or pan and fold the leaves over to enclose. Brush lightly with oil.

3 Cover the terrine. Place it in a roasting pan and pour in boiling water to come halfway up the sides of the terrine. Bake for 1¾ hours, checking the level of the water occasionally.

4 Let the terrine cool, then pour off the surface juices. Cover with plastic wrap, then aluminum foil, and place a weight on top. Chill overnight.

5 Serve in slices, at room temperature, with pickles or chutney.

Chicken & Pork Terrine

A delicate-flavored, smooth pâté with a contrasting strip of coarser-textured meat in the center.

Serves 6–8

8 ounces bacon
13 ounces chicken breast fillet, skinned
1 tablespoon lemon juice
8 ounces lean ground pork
½ small onion, finely chopped
2 eggs, beaten
2 tablespoons chopped fresh parsley
1 teaspoon salt
1 teaspoon green peppercorns, crushed
oil, for greasing
green salad, radishes and lemon wedges, to serve

1 Preheat the oven to 325°F. Put the bacon on a board and stretch it using the back of a heavy knife so that it can be arranged in overlapping slices over the bottom and sides of a 2-pound loaf pan.

2 Cut 4 ounces of the chicken into strips about 4 inches long. Sprinkle with lemon juice. Put the rest of the chicken in a food processor or blender with the ground pork and the onion. Process until fairly smooth.

3 Add the eggs, parsley, salt and peppercorns to the meat mixture, and process again briefly. Spoon half the mixture into the loaf pan and then level the surface.

4 Arrange the chicken strips on top, then spoon in the remaining meat mixture and smooth the top. Give the pan a couple of sharp taps to knock out any pockets of air.

5 Cover with a piece of oiled aluminum foil and put in a roasting pan. Pour in enough hot water to come halfway up the sides of the loaf pan. Bake for 45–50 minutes, until firm.

6 Let the terrine cool in the pan before turning out and chilling. Serve sliced, with a green salad, radishes and wedges of lemon to squeeze on top.

Country Terrine

The terrine must have a lid, to seal in all the flavors during the cooking time.

Serves 8
8 ounces bacon
8 ounces chicken liver, ground
1 pound ground pork
1 small onion, finely chopped
2 garlic cloves, crushed
2 teaspoons dried mixed herbs

8 ounces game (e.g. hare, rabbit, pheasant or pigeon)
1/4 cup port or sherry
1 bay leaf
1/4 cup all-purpose flour
1 1/4 cups aspic jelly, made per package instructions
salt and freshly ground black pepper
fresh parsley and thyme sprigs, to garnish

1 Stretch each strip of bacon with the back of a heavy knife. Use to line a 4-cup ovenproof terrine dish.

2 In a bowl, combine the liver and pork with the onion, garlic and dried herbs. Season with salt and pepper. Cut the game into thin strips and put it in another bowl with the port or sherry. Season with salt and pepper.

3 Put one-third of the liver and pork mixture into the terrine. Cover with half the game and repeat the layers, ending with a liver and pork layer. Level and lay the bay leaf on top.

4 Preheat the oven to 325°F. Put the flour in a bowl and mix into a dough with 2 tablespoons cold water. Cover the terrine with a lid and seal it with the flour paste.

5 Place the terrine in a roasting pan and pour around enough hot water to come halfway up the sides of the dish. Cook in the oven for 2 hours.

6 Remove the lid and place a weight on top of the terrine. Let cool. Remove any fat, then cover with warmed aspic jelly. Cool, then chill. To serve, turn out, cut into slices and garnish with parsley and thyme.

Duck & Calvados Terrine

This classic dish from Normandy uses the regional apple brandy.

Serves 4
oil, for greasing
1 1/4 pounds boneless duck meat, coarsely chopped
8 ounces pork belly, ground
2 shallots, chopped

grated zest and juice of 1 orange
2 tablespoons calvados
10 strips bacon
2 eggs, beaten
2 tablespoons chopped fresh parsley
salt and freshly ground black pepper
mixed salad and hot toast, to serve

1 Grease and line the bottom of a 2-pound loaf pan or ovenproof terrine dish. Place the chopped duck meat in a bowl with the ground pork, shallots, orange zest and juice, calvados and seasoning. Mix well, cover and chill for 1–2 hours.

2 Preheat the oven to 350°F. Stretch the bacon strips with the back of a heavy knife and use them to line the loaf pan or dish, leaving any excess hanging over the edge.

3 Stir the eggs and parsley into the meat mixture, then spoon it into the prepared pan or dish. Smooth the surface, fold the bacon over, then cover with aluminum foil.

4 Stand the terrine in a roasting pan and pour in boiling water to come about two thirds of the way up the sides.

5 Bake for 1 1/4 hours, then remove the terrine from the water bath, lift off the foil and let cool. Cover with clean aluminum foil and a weight, and chill for 3–4 hours, until firm.

6 Turn out the terrine and cut it into slices. Serve with a mixed salad and hot toast.

Cook's Tip
Marinating the meat for a few hours will develop the flavors.

Chicken Livers in Sherry

This dish, which could hardly be quicker to prepare, makes an excellent simple appetizer. Serve with crusty bread.

Serves 4

8 ounces chicken livers
1 small onion
2 small garlic cloves
1 tablespoon olive oil
1 teaspoon fresh thyme leaves
2 tablespoons sweet sherry
2 tablespoons sour or
   heavy cream
salt and freshly ground
   black pepper
fresh thyme sprigs, to garnish

1 Trim any green spots and sinew from the chicken livers. Finely chop the onion and garlic.

2 Heat the oil in a frying pan and cook the onion, garlic, chicken livers and thyme leaves for 3 minutes or until the livers are colored on the outside but still slightly pink in the middle.

3 Stir in the sherry and cook gently for 1 minute. Add the sour or heavy cream and cook over low heat for 1–2 more minutes.

4 Stir in salt and pepper to taste, and serve immediately, garnished with thyme sprigs.

Fresh Tomato Sauce

Adding a little tomato paste gives extra strength of flavor to this sauce.

Makes 1¼ cups

1 onion, chopped
1 garlic clove, crushed
1 tablespoon olive oil
1 pound tomatoes, peeled
   and chopped
2 teaspoons tomato paste
1 teaspoon sugar (optional)
salt and freshly ground
   black pepper

1 Cook the onion and garlic in the oil for about 5 minutes until softened but not brown. Add the tomatoes, tomato paste, sugar (if using imported tomatoes, out of season) and seasoning.

2 Cover and simmer for 15–20 minutes, stirring occasionally. If the sauce seems a little thin, remove the lid and simmer for a few more minutes to reduce slightly.

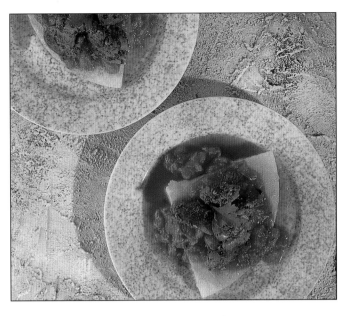

Polenta with Chicken Livers

The richness of the livers is perfectly balanced here by the mild-flavored polenta and fresh tomato sauce.

Serves 4

3 cups Chicken Stock or water
generous 1 cup polenta
about ¼ cup butter
2 tablespoons olive oil
1 pound chicken livers, trimmed
   and cut in half
1–2 garlic cloves, finely chopped
¼ cup chopped fresh parsley,
   preferably flat-leaf
1 teaspoon chopped fresh
   oregano or ½ teaspoon
   dried oregano
squeeze of lemon juice
salt and freshly ground
   black pepper
1½ cups Fresh Tomato Sauce,
   heated

1 Bring the stock or water to a boil in a large saucepan. If using water, add a little salt. Gradually stir in the polenta and cook over low heat until very thick, stirring constantly. Pour the polenta into a buttered 8-inch round pan. Set aside for at least 30 minutes to firm.

2 Invert the block of polenta onto a board. Cut it into four wedges. Fry in 1½ ounces of the butter until golden brown on both sides, turning once.

3 Heat the remaining butter and the oil in a frying pan over medium-high heat. Add the livers and fry for 2–3 minutes or until they are starting to brown, turning once. Add the garlic, herbs, lemon juice and seasoning. Continue cooking for another 1–2 minutes or until the livers are lightly browned on the outside but still pink in the center.

4 Place a wedge of polenta on each warmed plate. Spoon on the tomato sauce and put the chicken livers on top.

Variation
Use 6 cups sliced mushrooms sautéed in 1½ ounces butter instead of the chicken livers.

Thai-style Chicken Livers

This dish is full of the flavors of Thailand.

Serves 4–6
3 tablespoons vegetable oil
1 pound chicken livers, trimmed
4 shallots, chopped
2 garlic cloves, chopped
1 tablespoon roasted ground rice
3 tablespoons fish sauce
3 tablespoons lime juice
1 teaspoon sugar
2 lemongrass stalks, bruised and
   finely chopped
2 tablespoons chopped cilantro
10–12 fresh mint leaves and
   2 fresh red chiles, chopped,
   to garnish

1 Heat the oil in a wok or large frying pan. Add the livers and fry over medium-high heat for about 4 minutes, until the livers are golden brown and cooked, but still slightly pink inside.

2 Move the livers to one side of the pan, and add the shallots and garlic. Sauté for about 1–2 minutes.

3 Add the ground rice, fish sauce, lime juice, sugar, lemongrass and cilantro. Stir and remove from heat, and discard the lemongrass. Serve garnished with mint leaves and chiles.

Chicken Livers with Chinese Chives

This popular Thai dish is simplicity itself.

Serves 4
1 pound chicken livers, trimmed
3 garlic cloves, finely chopped
3 tablespoons peanut oil
1 pound Chinese chives, cut into
   ½-inch lengths
2–3 tablespoons fish sauce
2 tablespoons oyster sauce
1 tablespoon sugar

1 Cut the livers into thin strips using a sharp knife.

2 Stir-fry the garlic in the oil for 1–2 minutes, until golden. Add the livers and stir-fry over high heat for 3–4 minutes. Add the Chinese chives, fish and oyster sauces and sugar, and cook for 1 more minute.

Spiced Chicken Livers

Chicken livers combine perfectly with ground coriander, cumin, cardamom, paprika and nutmeg to make this tasty first course or light meal.

Serves 4
12 ounces chicken
   livers, trimmed
1 cup all-purpose flour
½ teaspoon ground coriander
½ teaspoon ground cumin
½ teaspoon ground
   cardamom seeds
¼ teaspoon ground paprika
¼ teaspoon grated nutmeg
6 tablespoons olive oil
salt and freshly ground
   black pepper
salad and garlic bread, to serve

1 Dry the chicken livers on paper towels. Cut any large livers in half and leave the smaller ones whole.

2 Mix the flour with the coriander, cumin, cardamom, paprika, nutmeg, salt and pepper.

3 Coat a small batch of livers with spiced flour, separating each piece. Heat the oil in a large frying pan and fry the livers in batches. (This helps keep the oil temperature high and prevents the flour from becoming soggy.)

4 Fry quickly, stirring frequently, until crispy. Keep warm and repeat with the remaining livers. Serve immediately with salad and warm garlic bread.

Cook's Tip
Although always milder than chile or cayenne pepper, paprika varies in strength from mild, (sometimes called sweet), to hot.

Tandoori Chicken Sticks

This aromatic chicken dish is traditionally baked in a clay oven called a tandoor.

Makes about 25
1 pound chicken breast
   fillets, skinned

For the cilantro yogurt
1 cup plain yogurt
2 tablespoons whipping cream
½ cucumber, peeled, seeded and
   finely chopped
1–2 tablespoons fresh chopped
   cilantro or mint
salt and freshly ground
   black pepper

For the marinade
¾ cup plain yogurt
1 teaspoon garam masala or
   curry powder
¼ teaspoon ground cumin
¼ teaspoon ground coriander
¼ teaspoon cayenne pepper
   (or to taste)
1 teaspoon tomato paste
1–2 garlic cloves, finely chopped
½-inch piece fresh ginger root,
   peeled and finely chopped
grated zest and juice of
   ½ lemon
1–2 tablespoons fresh chopped
   cilantro or mint

1 First, make the cilantro yogurt. Mix all the ingredients and season with salt and pepper. Cover and chill.

2 To make the marinade, place all the ingredients in a food processor and process until smooth. Pour into a shallow dish.

3 Freeze the chicken fillets for 5 minutes to firm them, then slice in half horizontally. Cut the slices into ¾-inch strips and add to the marinade. Toss to coat well. Cover and chill for 6–8 hours or overnight.

4 Preheat the broiler and line a baking sheet with aluminum foil. Using a slotted spoon, remove the chicken from the marinade and arrange the pieces in a single layer on the baking sheet. Scrunch up the chicken slightly so it makes wavy shapes. Broil for 4–5 minutes, until brown and just cooked, turning once.

5 Thread 1–2 pieces of cooked chicken onto toothpicks or short skewers and serve immediately with the bowl of cilantro yogurt as a dip.

Sesame Seed Chicken Bites

Best served warm, these crispy coated bites are delicious accompanied by a glass of chilled dry white wine.

Makes 20
6 ounces chicken breast fillet
2 garlic cloves, crushed
1-inch piece fresh ginger root,
   peeled and grated
1 small egg white
1 teaspoon cornstarch
¼ cup shelled pistachios,
   roughly chopped

¼ cup sesame seeds
2 tablespoons grapeseed oil
salt and freshly ground
   black pepper

For the dipping sauce
3 tablespoons hoisin sauce
1 tablespoon sweet chili sauce

For the garnish
finely shredded fresh ginger root
roughly chopped pistachios
fresh dill sprigs

1 Place the chicken, garlic, grated ginger, egg white and cornstarch in a food processor, and process into a smooth paste. Stir in the pistachios, and season well with salt and pepper.

2 Place the sesame seeds in a bowl. Form the chicken mixture into 20 balls between the palms of the hands and roll in the sesame seeds to coat them completely.

3 Heat a wok and add the oil. When the oil is hot, stir-fry the chicken bites in batches, turning regularly until golden. Drain on paper towels and keep warm.

4 To make the dipping sauce, combine the hoisin and chili sauces in a small bowl.

5 Place the chicken bites on a serving platter and garnish with shredded ginger, chopped pistachios and dill. Serve with the dipping sauce.

Spicy Chicken Canapés

These little cocktail sandwiches have a spicy filling, finished with different flavors of toppings.

Makes 18
generous ½ cup finely chopped cooked chicken
2 scallions, finely chopped
2 tablespoons chopped red bell pepper
6 tablespoons Curry Mayonnaise
5 slices white bread
1 tablespoon paprika
1 tablespoon chopped fresh parsley
2 tablespoons chopped salted peanuts

1 Mix the chicken with the chopped scallions and red pepper and half the curry mayonnaise.

2 Spread the mixture on both sides of three of the bread slices and sandwich with the remaining bread, pressing them together. Spread the remaining curry mayonnaise on top and cut into 1½-inch circles using a plain cutter.

3 Dip into paprika, chopped parsley or chopped nuts and arrange on a serving platter.

Curry Mayonnaise

Makes about 1¼ cups
2 egg yolks
1 teaspoon French mustard
3–4 tablespoons curry paste
⅔ cup extra virgin olive oil
⅔ cup peanut or sunflower oil
2 teaspoons white wine vinegar
salt and freshly ground black pepper

1 Place the egg yolks, mustard and curry paste in a food processor and blend smoothly.
2 Add the olive oil a little at a time while the processor is running. When the mixture is thick, add the remainder of the oil in a slow, steady stream. Add the vinegar and season to taste with salt and pepper.

Chicken & Avocado Mayonnaise

You need forks or spoons to eat this appetizer, so don't be tempted to pass it around as finger food.

Serves 4
2 tablespoons mayonnaise
1 tablespoon fromage frais
2 garlic cloves, crushed
scant 1 cup chopped cooked chicken
1 large ripe but firm avocado
2 tablespoons lemon juice
salt and freshly ground black pepper
nacho chips or tortilla chips, to serve

1 Combine the mayonnaise, fromage frais, garlic and seasoning to taste in a small bowl. Stir in the chopped chicken.

2 Peel, pit and chop the avocado and immediately toss in the lemon juice, then stir gently into the chicken mixture. Taste and adjust the seasoning as necessary. Chill until required.

3 Serve in small dishes, with nacho or tortilla chips as scoops.

Cook's Tip
This mixture also makes a great, chunky filling for sandwiches or pita bread. Alternatively, serve it as a main-course salad, heaped on a base of mixed salad leaves.

Chicken Cigars

These small, crispy rolls can be served warm as canapés with a drink before a meal, or as a first course with a crisp, colorful salad.

Serves 4
10-ounce package phyllo pastry
3 tablespoons olive oil
fresh flat-leaf parsley, to garnish

For the filling
12 ounces ground chicken
1 egg, beaten
½ teaspoon ground cinnamon
½ teaspoon ground ginger
2 tablespoons raisins
1 tablespoon olive oil
1 small onion, finely chopped
salt and freshly ground
 black pepper

1 To make the filling, combine all the ingredients, except the oil and onion, in a bowl. Heat the oil in a large frying pan and cook the onion until tender. Let cool, then stir into the chicken mixture.

2 Preheat the oven to 350°F. Once the phyllo pastry package has been opened, keep the pastry covered at all times with a damp dish towel. Work fast, as the pastry dries out very quickly when exposed to the air. Unravel the pastry and cut into 4 × 10-inch strips.

3 Take one strip (cover the remainder), brush with a little oil and place a small spoonful of the filling about ½ inch from the end.

4 To encase the filling, fold the sides inward to a width of 2 inches and roll into a cigar shape. Place on a greased baking sheet and brush with oil. Bake for 20–25 minutes, until golden brown and crisp. Garnish with parsley and serve.

Eggplant with Sesame Chicken

Sweet, delicate-tasting, small eggplant are stuffed with seasoned chicken and deep-fried in a crispy sesame seed coating.

Serves 4
6 ounces chicken, breast or
 thigh, skinned
1 scallion, green part only,
 finely chopped
1 tablespoon dark soy sauce
1 tablespoon mirin or
 sweet sherry

½ teaspoon sesame oil
¼ teaspoon salt
4 small eggplant,
 about 4 inches long
1 tablespoon sesame seeds
all-purpose flour, for dusting
vegetable oil, for deep-frying

For the dipping sauce
¼ cup dark soy sauce
¼ cup dashi or vegetable stock
3 tablespoons mirin or
 sweet sherry

1 Remove the chicken meat from the bone and grind it finely in a food processor. Add the scallion, soy sauce, mirin or sherry, sesame oil and salt.

2 Make four slits in each eggplant, leaving them joined at the stem. Spoon the ground chicken mixture into the eggplant, opening them slightly to accommodate the mixture. Dip the fat end of each stuffed eggplant in the sesame seeds, then dust in flour. Set aside.

3 To make the dipping sauce, combine the soy sauce, dashi or stock and mirin or sherry. Pour into a shallow serving bowl and set aside.

4 Heat the vegetable oil in a deep-fat fryer to 385°F. Fry the eggplant, two at a time, for 3–4 minutes. Lift out using a slotted spoon onto paper towels to drain. Serve hot, accompanied by the dipping sauce.

Chicken with Lemon & Garlic

This succulent dish is simplicity itself to cook and will disappear from the serving plates even more quickly.

Serves 4
8 ounces chicken breast
   fillets, skinned
2 tablespoons olive oil

1 shallot, finely chopped
4 garlic cloves, finely chopped
1 teaspoon paprika
juice of 1 lemon
2 tablespoons chopped
   fresh parsley
salt and freshly ground
   black pepper
lemon wedges, to serve
flat-leaf parsley, to garnish

1 Sandwich the chicken breast fillets between two sheets of plastic wrap or waxed paper. Beat with a rolling pin until the fillets are about ¼ inch thick, then cut into strips about ½ inch wide.

2 Heat the oil in a large frying pan. Stir-fry the chicken strips with the shallot, garlic and paprika over high heat for about 3 minutes, until lightly browned and cooked through.

3 Add the lemon juice and parsley with salt and pepper to taste. Serve hot with lemon wedges, garnished with flat-leaf parsley.

Variation
Try using strips of turkey breast instead for this dish.

Nutty Chicken Balls

Serve these as a first course with the lemon sauce, or make into smaller balls and serve on toothpicks as canapés with drinks.

Serves 4
2 ounces boneless chicken
½ cup pistachios, finely chopped
1 tablespoon lemon juice
2 eggs, beaten
all-purpose flour, for shaping
¾ cup blanched
   chopped almonds

generous 1 cup dried
   bread crumbs
oil, for greasing
salt and freshly ground
   black pepper

For the lemon sauce
⅔ cup Chicken Stock
1 cup cream cheese
1 tablespoon lemon juice
1 tablespoon chopped
   fresh parsley
1 tablespoon snipped
   fresh chives

1 Skin the chicken and grind or chop finely. Mix with salt and pepper to taste, plus the pistachios, lemon juice and 1 of the beaten eggs.

2 Shape into 16 small balls using floured hands (use a spoon as a guide, so that all the balls are roughly the same size). Roll the balls in the remaining beaten egg and coat with the almonds first and then the dried bread crumbs, pressing on firmly. Chill until ready to cook.

3 Preheat the oven to 375°F. Place the chicken balls on a greased baking sheet and bake for about 15 minutes or until golden brown and crisp.

4 To make the lemon sauce, gently heat the chicken stock and cream cheese together in a pan, whisking until smooth. Add the lemon juice, herbs and seasoning to taste. Serve hot with the chicken balls.

Chicken Kofta with Paneer

This rather unusual appetizer looks most elegant when served in small individual karahis.

Serves 6

1 pound boneless chicken, skinned and cubed
1 teaspoon crushed garlic
1 teaspoon grated fresh ginger root
1 1/2 teaspoons ground coriander
1 1/2 teaspoons chili powder
1/2 teaspoon ground fenugreek
1/4 teaspoon ground turmeric
1 teaspoon salt
2 tablespoons chopped cilantro
2 fresh green chiles, chopped
2 1/2 cups water
corn oil, for frying
1 dried red chile, crushed (optional), and fresh mint sprigs, to garnish

For the paneer mixture

1 medium onion, sliced
1 red bell pepper, seeded and cut into strips
1 green bell pepper, seeded and cut into strips
6 ounces paneer, cubed
1 cup corn kernels

1 Put the chicken, garlic, spices, salt, cilantro, chiles and water into a medium saucepan. Bring slowly to a boil over medium heat and cook until all the liquid has evaporated.

2 Remove from heat and let cool slightly. Put the mixture in a food processor or blender and process for 2 minutes, stopping once or twice to loosen the mixture with a spoon or spatula.

3 Scrape the mixture into a large mixing bowl using a wooden spoon. Taking a little of the mixture at a time, shape it into small even-size balls using your hands. You should be able to make about 12 koftas.

4 Heat 1/2 inch oil in a karahi or deep, round frying pan over high heat. Turn the heat down slightly and drop the koftas carefully into the oil. Move them around gently to ensure that they cook evenly.

5 When the koftas are lightly browned, remove them from the oil with a slotted spoon and drain on paper towels. Set aside.

6 Reheat the oil still remaining in the karahi and flash-fry all the ingredients for the paneer mixture. This should take about 3 minutes over high heat.

7 Divide the paneer mixture evenly between six small individual karahis, if using. Add two koftas to each serving and garnish with crushed red chile, if using, and mint sprigs.

> **Cook's Tip**
> Paneer is a smooth white cheese available at Asian food stores and some supermarkets.

Buffalo-style Chicken Wings

A fiery-hot fried chicken recipe, said to have originated in the town of Buffalo, New York, after which it is named. Serve it with traditional blue-cheese dip and celery sticks.

Makes 48

24 plump chicken wings, tips removed
vegetable oil, for frying
6 tablespoons butter
1/4 cup hot pepper sauce, or to taste
1 tablespoon white or cider vinegar
salt

For the blue-cheese dip

4 ounces blue cheese, such as Danish blue
1/2 cup mayonnaise
1/2 cup sour cream
2–3 scallions, finely chopped
1 garlic clove, finely chopped
1 tablespoon white or cider vinegar
salad greens, to garnish
celery stalks, to serve

1 To make the dip, use a fork to mash the blue cheese gently against the side of a bowl. Add the mayonnaise, sour cream, scallions, garlic and vinegar, and stir together until well blended. Chill until ready to serve.

2 Using kitchen scissors or a sharp knife, cut each wing in half at the joint to make 48 pieces in all.

3 In a large saucepan or wok, heat 2 inches of oil until hot but not smoking. Fry the chicken wing pieces in small batches for 8–10 minutes, until crisp and golden, turning once. Drain on paper towels. Season with salt to taste and arrange in a bowl.

4 In a small saucepan over medium-low heat, melt the butter. Stir in the hot pepper sauce and vinegar, and immediately pour onto the chicken, tossing to combine. Serve the wings hot, garnished with salad greens and accompanied by the blue-cheese dip and celery stalks.

Bon-bon Chicken with Sesame Sauce

For this popular Szechuan Chinese dish the chicken meat is tenderized by being beaten with a stick (called a *bon*)—hence its name.

Serves 6–8
1 chicken, about 2¼ pounds
5 cups water
1 tablespoon sesame oil
shredded cucumber, to garnish

For the sauce
2 tablespoons light soy sauce
1 teaspoon sugar
1 tablespoon finely
  chopped scallions
1 teaspoon red chili oil
½ teaspoon ground
  Szechuan peppercorns
1 teaspoon white sesame seeds
2 tablespoons sesame paste or
  2 tablespoons peanut butter
  creamed with a little
  sesame oil

1 Clean the chicken well. In a wok or saucepan, bring the water to a rolling boil, add the chicken, reduce the heat and cook, covered, for 40–45 minutes. Remove the chicken from the pan and immerse in cold water to cool.

2 After at least 1 hour, remove the chicken from the water and drain; dry well with paper towels and brush on a coating of sesame oil. Carve the meat off the legs, wings and breast, and pull the meat off the rest of the bones.

3 On a flat work surface, pound the meat with a rolling pin, then tear it into shreds with your fingers.

4 To make the sauce, combine all the ingredients in a bowl, reserving a little chopped scallions for the garnish.

5 Place the shredded chicken in a serving dish and arrange the cucumber around the edge. Pour the sauce onto the chicken, garnish with the reserved scallions and serve.

Lettuce Parcels

This popular "assemble-it-yourself" treat is based on a recipe from Hong Kong. The filling—an imaginative blend of textures and flavors—is served with crisp lettuce leaves, which are used as wrappers.

Serves 6
2 chicken breast fillets, about
  12 ounces total weight
4 Chinese dried mushrooms,
  soaked for 30 minutes in warm
  water to cover

vegetable oil, for stir-frying and
  deep-frying
2 garlic cloves, crushed
6 canned water chestnuts, drained
  and thinly sliced
2 tablespoons light soy sauce
1 teaspoon Szechuan peppercorns,
  dry-fried and crushed
4 scallions, finely chopped
1 teaspoon sesame oil
2 ounces cellophane noodles
salt and freshly ground
  black pepper
1 crisp head of lettuce and
  ¼ cup hoisin sauce, to serve

1 Remove the skin from the chicken fillets, pat dry and set aside. Cut the chicken into thin strips. Drain the soaked mushrooms. Cut off and discard the mushroom stems; slice the caps finely and set aside.

2 Heat 2 tablespoons of the oil in a wok or large frying pan. Add the garlic, then add the chicken and stir-fry until the pieces are cooked through and no longer pink.

3 Add the sliced mushrooms, water chestnuts, soy sauce and peppercorns. Toss for 2–3 minutes, then taste and add salt and pepper if necessary. Stir in half of the scallions and the sesame oil. Remove from heat and set aside.

4 Heat the oil for deep-frying to 375°F. Cut the chicken skin into strips, deep-fry until very crisp and drain on paper towels. Add the noodles to the hot oil and deep-fry until crisp. Transfer to a plate lined with paper towels.

5 Crush the noodles and place in a serving dish. Top with the chicken skin, chicken and vegetable mixture and the remaining scallions. Wash the lettuce leaves, pat dry and arrange on a large platter.

6 Toss the chicken and noodles to mix. Invite guests to take one or two lettuce leaves, spread the inside with hoisin sauce and add a spoonful of filling, turning in the sides of the leaves and rolling them into a parcel. The parcels are traditionally eaten in the hand.

Cook's Tip
Szechuan peppercorns are wild red peppers from Szechuan province in China. They are more aromatic but less hot than either white or black peppercorns, yet give a unique flavor.

Chicken Croquettes

These tasty bites are a great way to "stretch" a small amount of chicken to make an appetizer for four people.

Serves 4
2 tablespoons butter
$\frac{1}{4}$ cup all-purpose flour
$\frac{2}{3}$ cup milk
I tablespoon olive oil
I chicken breast fillet with skin, about 3 ounces, diced
I garlic clove, finely chopped
I small egg, beaten
I cup fresh white bread crumbs
vegetable oil, for deep-frying
salt and freshly ground black pepper
flat-leaf parsley, to garnish
lemon wedges, to serve

I Melt the butter in a small saucepan. Add the flour and cook over low heat, stirring, for I minute. Gradually beat in the milk to make a smooth, very thick sauce. Cover with a lid and remove from heat.

2 Heat the olive oil in a frying pan and cook the chicken with the garlic for 5 minutes, until the chicken is lightly browned and cooked through.

3 Transfer the contents of the frying pan to a food processor and process until finely chopped. Stir into the sauce. Add plenty of salt and pepper to taste, then let cool completely.

4 Shape the chicken mixture into eight small sausages using moistened hands. Dip each one in beaten egg and then in bread crumbs.

5 Heat the oil in a heavy pan or deep-fat fryer. It is ready when a cube of bread tossed into the oil sizzles on the surface. Deep-fry the croquettes in the oil for 4 minutes or until crisp and golden. Drain on paper towels.

6 Pile the croquettes onto a serving plate, garnish with flat-leaf parsley and serve with lemon wedges.

Chicken Goujons

Serve as a first course for eight people or as a filling main course for four.

Serves 4–8
4 chicken breast fillets, skinned
3 cups fresh bread crumbs
I teaspoon ground coriander
2 teaspoons ground paprika
$\frac{1}{2}$ teaspoon ground cumin
3 tablespoons all-purpose flour
2 eggs, beaten
oil, for deep-frying
salt and freshly ground black pepper
lemon wedges and cilantro sprigs, to garnish

For the dip
$1\frac{1}{4}$ cups plain yogurt
2 tablespoons lemon juice
$\frac{1}{4}$ cup chopped cilantro
$\frac{1}{4}$ cup chopped fresh parsley

I Divide the chicken breasts into two natural fillets. Place them between two sheets of plastic wrap and, using a rolling pin, flatten each one to a thickness of $\frac{1}{4}$ inch. Cut on the diagonal into 1-inch strips.

2 Mix the bread crumbs with the spices and seasoning in a bowl. Place the flour and beaten eggs in separate bowls.

3 Toss the chicken fillet pieces (goujons) in the flour, keeping them separate. Dip the goujons into the beaten egg and finally coat in the bread crumb mixture.

4 To make the dip, thoroughly combine all the ingredients and season to taste. Pour into a serving bowl and chill.

5 Heat the oil in a heavy pan or deep-fat fryer. It is ready when a cube of bread tossed into the oil sizzles on the surface. Fry the goujons in batches until golden and crisp. Drain on paper towels and keep warm in the oven.

6 Arrange the goujons on a warmed serving plate and garnish with lemon wedges and sprigs of cilantro. Serve with the dip.

Chicken Roulades

These attractive chicken rolls, stuffed with a nutty spinach filling, make an impressive hot first course for a dinner party.

Makes 4

4 chicken thighs, boned
  and skinned
4 ounces chopped
  frozen spinach
1 tablespoon butter
2 tablespoons pine nuts

pinch of grated nutmeg
½ cup fresh white bread crumbs
4 strips bacon
2 tablespoons olive oil
⅔ cup white wine or
  Chicken Stock
2 teaspoons cornstarch
2 tablespoons light cream
1 tablespoon snipped
  fresh chives
salt and freshly ground
  black pepper
salad leaves, to garnish

1 Preheat the oven to 350°F. Place the chicken thighs between plastic wrap and flatten with a rolling pin.

2 Put the spinach and butter into a saucepan, heat gently until the spinach has defrosted, then increase the heat and cook rapidly, stirring occasionally, until all the moisture has evaporated. Add the pine nuts, seasoning, nutmeg and bread crumbs.

3 Divide the spinach mixture between the chicken pieces and roll up neatly. Wrap a strip of bacon around each piece and secure with string.

4 Heat the oil in a large frying pan and brown the roulades all over. Drain through a slotted spoon and place in a shallow, ovenproof dish.

5 Pour in the wine or stock, cover and bake for 15–20 minutes or until tender. Transfer the chicken to a serving plate and remove the string. Strain the cooking liquid into a saucepan. Mix the cornstarch into a thin, smooth paste with a little cold water and add to the juices in the pan, along with the cream. Bring to a boil to thicken, stirring constantly. Adjust the seasoning and add the chives. Pour the sauce around the chicken and serve with a garnish of salad leaves.

Mini Spring Rolls

Eat these light, crispy parcels with your fingers. If you like slightly spicier food, sprinkle them with a little cayenne pepper before serving.

Makes 20

1 fresh green chile
½ cup vegetable oil
1 small onion, finely chopped
1 garlic clove, crushed
3 ounces cooked chicken breast

1 small carrot, cut into
  fine matchsticks
1 scallion, thinly sliced
1 small red bell pepper, seeded
  and cut into fine matchsticks
1 ounce bean sprouts
1 teaspoon sesame oil
4 large sheets phyllo pastry
1 small egg white,
  lightly beaten
fresh chives, to garnish (optional)
light soy sauce, to serve

1 Carefully remove the seeds from the chile and chop finely, wearing rubber gloves to protect your hands, if necessary.

2 Heat a wok or heavy frying pan, then add 2 tablespoons of the vegetable oil. When hot, add the onion, garlic and chile. Stir-fry for 1 minute.

3 Slice the chicken thinly, then add to the wok and stir-fry over high heat, stirring constantly, until browned.

4 Add the carrot, scallion and red pepper, and stir-fry for 2 minutes. Add the bean sprouts, stir in the sesame oil, then remove from heat and let cool.

5 Cut each sheet of phyllo pastry into five short strips. Place a small amount of filling at one end of each strip, then fold in the long sides and roll up the pastry to make a neat parcel. Seal and glaze the parcels with the egg white, then chill, uncovered, for 15 minutes before frying.

6 Wipe out the wok with paper towels, heat it again and add the remaining vegetable oil. When the oil is hot, fry the rolls in batches until crisp and golden brown. Drain on paper towels and keep warm. Serve garnished with chives, if desired, accompanied by light soy sauce for dipping.

Chicken & Sticky Rice Balls

These balls can either be steamed or deep-fried. The fried versions are crunchy and are excellent for serving at drinks parties.

Makes about 30
1 pound ground chicken
1 egg
1 tablespoon tapioca
4 scallions, finely chopped
2 tablespoons chopped cilantro
2 tablespoons fish sauce
pinch of sugar
8 ounces cooked sticky rice
banana leaves
oil, for brushing
freshly ground black pepper
shredded carrot, strips of red bell
    pepper and snipped chives,
    to garnish
sweet chili sauce, to serve

1 In a bowl, combine the chicken, egg, flour, scallions and cilantro. Mix and season with fish sauce, sugar and pepper.

2 Spread the cooked sticky rice on a large plate or flat tray.

3 Place 1 teaspoon of the chicken mixture on the bed of rice. With damp hands, roll and shape the mixture in the rice to make a ball about the size of a walnut. Repeat using the rest of the chicken mixture and rice.

4 Line a bamboo steamer with banana leaves and lightly brush them with oil. Place the chicken balls on the leaves, spacing them well apart to prevent them from sticking together. Steam over high heat for about 10 minutes or until cooked.

5 Remove the balls from the steamer and arrange on serving plates. Garnish with shredded carrot, red pepper strips and snipped chives. Serve with sweet chili sauce for dipping.

Cook's Tip
Sticky rice, also known as glutinous rice, has a very high starch content. It is so called because the grains stick together when it is cooked. It is very popular in Thailand and can be eaten both as a savory and as a sweet dish.

San Francisco Chicken Wings

A mouthwatering dish that reflects the influence of Chinese immigrants on American cuisine.

Serves 8
5 tablespoons soy sauce
1 tablespoon light brown sugar
1 tablespoon rice vinegar
2 tablespoons dry sherry
juice of 1 orange
2-inch strip orange zest
1 star anise
1 teaspoon cornstarch
1/4 cup water
1 tablespoon grated fresh
    ginger root
1 tablespoon crushed garlic
1/4–1 teaspoon chili sauce
24 chicken wings, about
    3–3 1/2 pounds, tips removed
salad leaves and chives,
    to garnish

1 Preheat the oven to 400°F. Combine the soy sauce, brown sugar, vinegar, sherry, orange juice and zest, and star anise in a saucepan. Bring to a boil over medium heat.

2 Combine the cornstarch and water in a small bowl and stir until blended. Add to the boiling soy sauce mixture, stirring well. Boil for 1 minute, stirring constantly.

3 Remove the soy sauce mixture from heat and stir in the ginger, garlic and chili sauce.

4 Arrange the chicken wings, in a single layer, in a large ovenproof dish. Pour over the soy sauce mixture and stir thoroughly to coat the wings evenly.

5 Bake the wings for 30–40 minutes, until tender and browned, basting occasionally. Serve hot or warm, garnished with salad leaves and chives.

Turkey Sticks with Sour Cream Dip

Crisp morsels of turkey with a quick-to-prepare dip.

salt and freshly ground black pepper

Serves 4

12 ounces turkey breast fillet, skinned
1 cup fine fresh bread crumbs
1/4 teaspoon paprika
1 small egg, lightly beaten

For the sour cream dip

3 tablespoons sour cream
1 tablespoon ready-made Tomato Sauce
1 tablespoon mayonnaise

1 Preheat the oven to 375°F. Cut the turkey into strips. In a bowl, mix the bread crumbs and paprika, and season with salt and pepper. Put the beaten egg into another bowl.

2 Dip the turkey strips into the egg, then into the bread crumbs, turning until evenly coated. Place on a greased baking sheet.

3 Cook the turkey at the top of the oven for 20 minutes, until crisp and golden. Turn once during the cooking time.

4 To make the dip, combine all the ingredients and season to taste. Serve the turkey sticks accompanied by the dip.

Basic Pasta Dough

1 3/4 cups all-purpose flour
pinch of salt
2 eggs
2 teaspoons cold water

1 Sift the flour and salt onto a work surface. Make a well in the center. Break the eggs and add the water into the well.

2 Using a fork, beat the eggs gently together, then draw in the flour to make a thick paste.
3 Use your hands to mix into a firm dough.
4 Knead the dough for 5 minutes, until smooth. Wrap the pasta in plastic wrap and let rest for 20–30 minutes.

Pasta Bonbons

These little pasta parcels are filled with a turkey stuffing.

2–3 fresh sage leaves, chopped
2 anchovy fillets, drained

Serves 4–6

1 batch of Basic Pasta Dough
all-purpose flour, for dusting
1 egg white, beaten
salt and freshly ground black pepper

For the filling

1 small onion, finely chopped
1 garlic clove, crushed
2/3 cup Chicken Stock
8 ounces ground turkey

For the sauce

2/3 cup Chicken Stock
7 ounces cream cheese
1 tablespoon lemon juice
1 teaspoon sugar
2 tomatoes, peeled, seeded and finely diced
1/2 red onion, finely chopped
6 small cornichons (pickled gherkins), sliced

1 To make the filling, put the onion, garlic and stock into a saucepan. Cover and simmer for 5 minutes. Uncover and boil for 5 minutes or until the stock has reduced to 2 tablespoons.

2 Add the turkey and stir until it is no longer pink. Add the sage and anchovies, and season. Cook, uncovered, for 5 minutes, until all the liquid has been absorbed. Let cool.

3 Divide the pasta dough in half. Roll into thin sheets and cut into 3 1/2 x 2 1/2-inch rectangles. Lay on a lightly floured dish towel. Repeat with the remaining dough. Place a teaspoon of the filling on the center of each rectangle, brush around the meat with egg white and roll up the pasta, pinching in the ends. Transfer to a floured dish towel and let rest for 1 hour.

4 To make the sauce, put the stock, cream cheese, lemon juice and sugar into a saucepan. Heat gently and whisk until smooth. Add the tomatoes, onion and cornichons. Keep warm.

5 Cook the pasta bonbons in a large pan of boiling, salted water for 5 minutes. Remove with a slotted spoon, drain well and serve immediately with the sauce poured on top.

Chicken Liver Salad

An inspired combination of flavors and textures: warm, succulent livers; cool, refreshing grapefruit; smooth, rich avocado and crisp salad leaves.

Serves 4

mixed salad leaves, e.g. frisée and
    oakleaf lettuce or radicchio
1 avocado, peeled, pitted
    and diced
2 pink grapefruit, segmented
12 ounces chicken livers

2 tablespoons olive oil
1 garlic clove, crushed
salt and freshly ground
    black pepper
fresh chives, to garnish
crusty bread, to serve

For the dressing

2 tablespoons lemon juice
¼ cup olive oil
½ teaspoon whole-grain mustard
½ teaspoon honey
1 tablespoon snipped
    fresh chives

1 To make the dressing, put all the ingredients into a screw-top jar with salt and pepper, and shake vigorously to emulsify. Taste and adjust the seasoning as necessary.

2 Wash the salad leaves and spin dry. Arrange attractively on a serving plate with the avocado and grapefruit.

3 Dry the chicken livers on paper towels and remove any unwanted pieces. Cut the larger livers in half and leave the smaller ones whole.

4 Heat the oil in a large frying pan. Stir-fry the livers and garlic briskly until the livers are brown all over but still slightly pink on the inside. Season with salt and pepper. Remove the livers from the pan using a slotted spoon and drain briefly on paper towels.

5 Place the warm livers on the salad and spoon on the dressing. Garnish with snipped fresh chives and serve immediately with crusty bread.

Chicken Liver, Bacon & Tomato Salad

Warm salads are especially welcome during the autumn months when the evenings are growing shorter and a little cooler.

Serves 4

8 ounces young spinach,
    stems removed
1 frisée lettuce

7 tablespoons peanut oil
6 ounces bacon, cut into strips
3 ounces day-old bread, crusts
    removed and cut into
    short fingers
1 pound chicken livers, trimmed
4 ounces cherry tomatoes
salt and freshly ground
    black pepper

1 Wash the salad leaves and spin dry. Place in a salad bowl. Heat ¼ cup of the oil in a large frying pan. Add the bacon and cook for 3–4 minutes or until crisp and brown. Remove the bacon with a slotted spoon and drain on paper towels.

2 Fry the bread fingers in the bacon-flavored oil, tossing them until crisp and golden. Drain the croutons on paper towels.

3 Heat the remaining oil in the frying pan, add the chicken livers and fry briskly for 2–3 minutes. They should be colored on the outside but still slightly pink in the middle. Arrange the livers on the salad leaves and add the bacon, croutons and tomatoes. Season, toss and serve immediately.

French Vinaigrette

French vinaigrette is appreciated for its simplicity.

Makes about ½ cup

6 tablespoons extra virgin
    olive oil
1 tablespoon white wine vinegar
1 teaspoon French mustard
pinch of sugar

1 Place the olive oil and vinegar in a screw-top jar.
2 Add the mustard and sugar. Replace the lid and shake well.

Pan-fried Chicken Liver Salad

The hot dressing includes vin santo, a sweet dessert wine from Tuscany, but this is not essential—any dessert wine will do, or a sweet or cream sherry.

Serves 4

3 ounces baby spinach leaves
3 ounces oakleaf lettuce leaves
5 tablespoons olive oil
1 tablespoon butter
8 ounces chicken livers, trimmed and thinly sliced
3 tablespoons vin santo
2–3 ounces Parmesan cheese, shaved into curls
salt and freshly ground black pepper

1 Wash the spinach and lettuce, and spin dry. Tear the leaves into a large bowl, season with salt and pepper to taste, and toss gently to mix.

2 Heat 2 tablespoons of the oil with the butter in a large, heavy frying pan. When foaming, add the chicken livers and toss over medium to high heat for 5 minutes or until the livers are browned on the outside but still pink in the center. Remove from heat.

3 Remove the livers from the pan using a slotted spoon, drain them on paper towels, then place on top of the salad.

4 Return the pan to medium heat, add the remaining oil and the vin santo, and stir until sizzling.

5 Pour the hot dressing over the spinach and livers, and toss to coat. Transfer the salad to a serving bowl and sprinkle on the Parmesan shavings. Serve immediately.

Warm Chicken Salad with Shallots & Snowpeas

Succulent cooked chicken pieces are combined with vegetables in a lightly spiced chili dressing.

Serves 6

2 ounces mixed salad leaves
2 ounces baby spinach leaves
2 ounces watercress
2 tablespoons chili sauce
2 tablespoons dry sherry
1 tablespoon light soy sauce
1 tablespoon ketchup
2 teaspoons olive oil
8 shallots, finely chopped
1 garlic clove, crushed
12 ounces chicken breast fillet, skinned and cut into thin strips
1 red bell pepper, seeded and sliced
6 ounces snowpeas, trimmed
14-ounce can baby corn, drained and halved
10 ounces cooked brown rice
salt and freshly ground black pepper
fresh flat-leaf parsley sprig, to garnish

1 Wash the salad leaves and spinach, and spin dry. Arrange the salad leaves and the spinach, tearing up any large ones, on a serving dish. Add the watercress and toss to mix.

2 In a small bowl, combine the chili sauce, sherry, soy sauce and ketchup. Set aside.

3 Heat the oil in a large, nonstick frying pan or wok. Add the shallots and garlic, and stir-fry over medium heat for 1 minute.

4 Add the sliced chicken to the pan and stir-fry for another 4–5 minutes, until the chicken pieces are nearly cooked.

5 Add the red pepper, snowpeas, corn and cooked rice, and stir-fry for 2–3 minutes.

6 Pour in the chili sauce mixture and stir-fry for 2–3 minutes, until hot and bubbling. Season to taste. Spoon the chicken mixture onto the salad leaves, toss together and serve immediately, garnished with a sprig of flat-leaf parsley.

Warm Chicken Salad with Sesame & Cilantro Dressing

This salad needs to be served warm to make the most of the wonderful sesame, lemon and cilantro flavorings.

Serves 6

4 medium chicken breast
 fillets, skinned
8 ounces snowpeas
2 heads decorative lettuce,
 e.g. oakleaf
3 carrots, cut into small
 matchsticks

generous 2 cups button
 mushrooms, sliced
6 strips bacon, fried
 and chopped
1 tablespoon chopped cilantro
 leaves, to garnish

For the dressing
½ cup lemon juice
2 tablespoons whole-grain mustard
1 cup olive oil
5 tablespoons sesame oil
1 teaspoon coriander
 seeds, crushed

1 To make the dressing, combine all the ingredients in a bowl, beating well to blend. Place the chicken breasts in a shallow dish and pour on half the dressing. Chill overnight, and chill the remaining dressing also.

2 Cook the snowpeas for 2 minutes in boiling water, then cool under cold running water to stop them from cooking any more, so they remain crisp.

3 Wash and dry the lettuces. Tear the leaves into small pieces and place in a large bowl. Add the snowpeas, carrots, mushrooms and bacon, and toss to mix thoroughly. Divide among individual serving dishes.

4 Broil the chicken until cooked through, then slice on the diagonal into quite thin pieces. Divide between the bowls of salad and sprinkle some dressing on top. Combine quickly, sprinkle cilantro on each bowl and serve.

Chicken Salad with Cranberry Dressing

The unusual fruity dressing lifts this deceptively simple salad to a higher plane.

Serves 4
4 chicken breast fillets, about
 1½ pounds total weight
1¼ cups Chicken Stock or a
 mixture of stock and
 dry white wine
fresh herb sprigs
7 ounces mixed salad leaves
½ cup chopped walnuts
 or hazelnuts

For the dressing
2 tablespoons olive oil
1 tablespoon walnut or
 hazelnut oil
1 tablespoon raspberry or
 red wine vinegar
2 tablespoons cranberry relish
salt and freshly ground
 black pepper

1 Skin the chicken breast fillets. Pour the stock, or stock and wine mixture, into a large, shallow saucepan. Add the herbs and bring the liquid to the simmering point. Add the chicken and poach for about 15 minutes, until cooked through. Alternatively, leave the skin on the breasts and broil or roast them until tender, then remove the skin.

2 Wash and dry the salad leaves and arrange them on four plates. Slice each chicken breast neatly, keeping the slices together, then place each breast on top of a portion of salad, fanning the slices out slightly.

3 To make the dressing, place all the ingredients in a screw-top jar and shake vigorously.

4 Spoon a little dressing on each salad and sprinkle with the chopped walnuts or hazelnuts. Serve.

Lemon & Tarragon Chicken Salad

Warm cooked chicken is tossed with salad leaves as soon as it comes out of the pan.

Serves 4
4 chicken breast fillets, skinned
 and cut into strips
4 strips bacon, chopped (optional)
1 tablespoon oil
5 teaspoons chopped
 fresh tarragon
juice of 1 lemon
mixed salad leaves, washed
French Dressing
salt and freshly ground
 black pepper

1 Cook the chicken and bacon, if using, in the oil with half the tarragon for about 5 minutes, until lightly browned. Add the lemon juice, season to taste and cook for about 5 more minutes.

2 Meanwhile, put the salad leaves in a large bowl, add a little French dressing, and toss. Stir the remaining tarragon into the chicken and add to the salad bowl. Serve immediately.

Warm Chicken Salad with Hazelnut Dressing

This quickly prepared, warm salad combines pan-fried chicken and spinach with a light, nutty dressing.

Serves 4
3 tablespoons olive oil
2 tablespoons hazelnut oil
1 tablespoon white wine vinegar
1 garlic clove, crushed
1 tablespoon chopped fresh
　mixed herbs
8 ounces baby spinach leaves
9 ounces cherry tomatoes, halved
1 bunch scallions, chopped
2 chicken breast fillets, skinned
　and cut into pieces
salt and freshly ground
　black pepper

1 Place 2 tablespoons of the olive oil, the hazelnut oil, vinegar, garlic and chopped herbs in a small bowl or pitcher and whisk together until thoroughly mixed. Set aside.

2 Wash and dry the spinach leaves and trim any long stalks. Place the spinach in a large serving bowl with the tomatoes and scallions, and toss together to mix.

3 Heat the remaining olive oil in a frying pan, add the chicken and stir-fry over high heat for 7–10 minutes, until the chicken is cooked, tender and lightly browned.

4 Sprinkle the cooked chicken pieces on the salad, give the dressing a quick whisk to blend, then drizzle it on the salad and gently toss all the ingredients together. Season to taste with salt and pepper, and serve immediately

> **Variation**
> You could substitute walnut oil for the hazelnut oil and endive for the spinach leaves.

Peanut Chicken Salad in a Pineapple Boat

This beautiful dish would be a great centerpiece at a celebration meal.

2 small ripe pineapples
8 ounces cooked chicken breast
　fillet, cut into bite-size pieces
2 celery stalks, diced
2 ounces scallions, chopped
8 ounces seedless green grapes
6 tablespoons salted peanuts,
　coarsely chopped

For the dressing
6 tablespoons smooth
　peanut butter
1/2 cup mayonnaise
2 tablespoons cream or milk
1 garlic clove, finely chopped
1 teaspoon mild curry powder
1 tablespoon apricot jam
salt and freshly ground
　black pepper
fresh mint sprigs, to garnish

1 Make four pineapple boats (see box) from the pineapples. Cut the flesh removed from the boats into bite-size pieces.

2 Combine the pineapple flesh, cooked chicken, celery, scallions and grapes in a bowl.

3 To make the dressing, put all the ingredients in another bowl and mix with a wooden spoon or whisk until evenly blended. Season with salt and pepper. (The dressing will be thick at this point, but will be thinned by the juices from the pineapple.)

4 Add the dressing to the pineapple and chicken mixture. Fold together gently but thoroughly.

5 Divide the chicken salad among the pineapple boats. Sprinkle the chopped peanuts on top before serving, garnished with mint sprigs.

Making a Pineapple Boat

1 Trim off any browned ends from the green leaves of the crown. Trim the stalk end if necessary. Using a long, sharp knife, cut the pineapple lengthwise in half, through the crown. Cut a thin slice from the underside of each "boat" so it has a flat surface and will not rock.
2 Using a small sharp knife, cut straight across the top and bottom of the central core in each pineapple half.

3 Cut lengthwise at a slant on either side of the core. This will cut out the core in a V-shape.
4 Using a curved, serrated grapefruit knife, cut out and reserve the flesh from each half.

Orange Chicken Salad

For this delicious dish the rice is cooked with thinly pared orange zest for a more intense flavor.

Serves 4
3 large seedless oranges
6 ounces long-grain rice
2 cups water
2/3 cup French Dressing, made with
  red wine vinegar and a mixture
  of olive and vegetable oils
2 teaspoons Dijon mustard
1/2 teaspoon sugar
1 pound cooked chicken, diced
3 tablespoons snipped
  fresh chives
3 ounces cashews, toasted
salt and freshly ground
  black pepper
cucumber slices and chives,
  to garnish

1 Thinly peel 1 orange, taking only the colored part of the zest and leaving the white pith.

2 Combine the orange zest, rice and water in a saucepan. Add a pinch of salt. Bring to a boil, cover and cook over very low heat for 15–18 minutes or until the rice is tender and all the water has been absorbed.

3 Peel all the oranges and separate the segments, reserving the juice. Add the orange juice to the French dressing, then add the Dijon mustard and sugar and whisk to combine well. Taste and add more salt and freshly ground black pepper if needed.

4 When the rice is cooked, remove it from heat and cool slightly, uncovered. Discard the orange zest.

5 Turn the rice into a serving bowl and add half of the dressing. Toss well and let cool completely.

6 Add the cooked chicken, the chives, cashews and orange segments to the rice with the remaining dressing. Toss gently. Serve at room temperature, garnished with cucumber slices and chives.

Chicken & Fruit Salad

An ideal party dish, as the chickens may be cooked in advance and the salad finished on the day itself. Serve with warm garlic bread.

Serves 8
4 fresh tarragon or
  rosemary sprigs
2 3 1/2-pound chickens
5 tablespoons softened butter
2/3 cup Chicken Stock
2/3 cup white wine
1 cup walnut pieces
1 small cantaloupe
1 pound seedless grapes or
  pitted cherries
salt and freshly ground
  black pepper
mixed lettuce, to serve

For the dressing
2 tablespoons tarragon vinegar
1/2 cup light olive oil
2 tablespoons chopped mixed
  fresh herbs, e.g. parsley, mint
  and tarragon

1 Preheat the oven to 400°F. Put the sprigs of tarragon or rosemary inside the chickens and season. Tie the chickens in a neat shape with string. Spread them with 1/4 cup of the butter, place in a roasting pan and add the stock. Cover loosely with aluminum foil and roast for about 1 1/2 hours, basting twice, until browned and the juices run clear. Remove the chickens from the roasting pan and let cool.

2 Add the wine to the juices in the pan. Boil until syrupy. Strain and cool. Heat the remaining butter in a frying pan and fry the walnuts until lightly browned. Drain on paper towels and cool. Scoop the melon into balls. Joint the chickens.

3 To make the dressing, whisk the vinegar and oil together with a little salt and pepper. Remove all the fat from the cooled chicken juices and add these to the dressing with the herbs.

4 Wash and spin dry the lettuce and arrange on a serving platter. Put the chicken pieces on top and sprinkle on the grapes or cherries and the melon. Spoon on the dressing, sprinkle with the walnuts and serve.

Chinese-style Chicken Salad

A spicy peanut sauce accompanies this salad of crunchy vegetables and tender chicken.

Serves 4

4 chicken breast fillets,
    about 6 ounces each
1/4 cup dark soy sauce
pinch of Chinese five
    spice powder
good squeeze of lemon juice
1/2 cucumber, peeled and cut
    into matchsticks
1 teaspoon salt
3 tablespoons sunflower oil

2 tablespoons sesame oil
1 tablespoon sesame seeds
2 tablespoons dry sherry
2 carrots, cut into matchsticks
8 scallions, shredded
scant 1/2 cup bean sprouts

For the sauce

1/4 cup crunchy
    peanut butter
2 teaspoons lemon juice
2 teaspoons sesame oil
1/4 teaspoon hot chili powder
1 scallion, finely chopped

1 Put the chicken portions into a large saucepan and just cover with water. Add 1 tablespoon of the soy sauce, the Chinese five spice powder and lemon juice. Cover and bring to a boil, then simmer for about 20 minutes.

2 Meanwhile, place the cucumber matchsticks in a colander, sprinkle with the salt and cover with a plate with a weight on top. Let drain for 30 minutes—set the colander in a bowl or on a deep plate to catch the drips.

3 Lift out the poached chicken with a draining spoon and set aside until cool enough to handle. Remove and discard the skin, and roll the chicken lightly with a rolling pin to loosen the fibers. Slice into thin strips and reserve.

4 Heat the oils in a large frying pan or wok. Add the sesame seeds, fry for 30 seconds and then stir in the remaining soy sauce and the sherry. Add the carrots and stir-fry for 2–3 minutes, until tender. Remove from heat and reserve.

5 Rinse the cucumber well, pat dry with paper towels and place in a bowl. Add the shredded scallions, bean sprouts, cooked carrots, pan juices and shredded chicken, and combine. Transfer to a shallow dish. Cover and chill for about 1 hour, turning the mixture in the juices once or twice.

6 To make the sauce, cream the peanut butter with the lemon juice, sesame oil and chili powder, adding a little hot water to form a paste, then stir in the chopped scallion. Arrange the chicken mixture on a serving dish and serve with the peanut sauce.

Tangy Chicken Salad

This fresh and lively dish is bursting with the flavors of Thailand. It is ideal for an appetizer or light lunch.

Serves 4–6

4 chicken breast fillets, skinned
2 garlic cloves, crushed and
    roughly chopped
2 tablespoons soy sauce
2 tablespoons vegetable oil
1/2 cup coconut milk
2 tablespoons fish sauce
juice of 1 lime
2 tablespoons sugar

1 head lettuce
4 ounces water chestnuts, sliced
2 ounces cashews, toasted
4 shallots, finely sliced
4 kaffir lime leaves, finely sliced
1 lemongrass stalk, finely sliced
1 teaspoon chopped galangal
1 large red fresh chile, seeded
    and thinly sliced
2 scallions, thinly sliced
10–12 mint leaves, torn
cilantro sprigs and sliced
    red chiles, to garnish

1 Trim the chicken breasts of any excess fat and put them in a large, shallow dish. Rub with the garlic, soy sauce and 1 tablespoon of the oil. Let marinate for 1–2 hours.

2 Broil or pan-fry the chicken for 3–4 minutes on both sides or until cooked. Remove from heat and set aside to cool.

3 In a small saucepan, heat the coconut milk, fish sauce, lime juice and sugar. Stir until all of the sugar has dissolved and then remove from heat. Wash and dry the lettuce.

4 Cut the cooked chicken into strips and combine in a bowl with the water chestnuts, cashews, shallots, kaffir lime leaves, lemongrass, galangal, red chile, scallions and mint leaves. Pour on the coconut dressing, toss and mix well.

5 Spread out the lettuce leaves on a large serving platter or individual plates. Arrange the chicken salad on top, garnish with sprigs of cilantro and sliced red chiles, and serve.

Chicken & Pasta Salad

This is a delicious way to use up leftover cooked chicken and makes a really filling meal.

Serves 4
2 cups tricolored pasta twists
2 tablespoons bottled pesto sauce
1 tablespoon olive oil

1 beefsteak tomato
8 ounces cooked green beans
12 pitted black olives
12 ounces cooked chicken, cubed
salt and freshly ground
    black pepper
fresh basil, to garnish

1 Cook the pasta in plenty of boiling salted water according to the package instructions until *al dente*. Drain, rinse in plenty of cold running water, then drain again.

2 Put the pasta in a large bowl and stir in the pesto sauce and olive oil, mixing well.

3 Peel the tomato: place it in boiling water for about 10 seconds and then into cold water to loosen the skin, which you can then slip off easily. Cut the tomato into small cubes. Cut the beans into 1½-inch lengths.

4 Add the tomato and beans to the pasta with the olives and seasoning to taste. Add the cubed chicken. Toss gently together and transfer to a serving platter. Garnish with basil and serve.

Penne Salad with Chicken & Bell Peppers

A rainbow-hued salad that tastes as good as it looks.

Serves 4
3 cups penne
3 tablespoons olive oil
1½ cups cooked chicken,
    cut into bite-size pieces
1 small red bell pepper, seeded
    and diced
1 small yellow bell pepper, seeded
    and diced
½ cup pitted green olives
4 scallions, chopped
3 tablespoons mayonnaise
1 teaspoon Worcestershire sauce
1 tablespoon wine vinegar
salt and freshly ground
    black pepper

1 Cook the pasta in a large pan of boiling salted water according to the package instructions until *al dente*.

2 Drain and rinse under cold water. Drain again well and transfer to a large bowl.

3 Toss with the olive oil and let cool completely.

4 Combine all the remaining ingredients, then mix into the pasta and serve immediately.

Chicken & Broccoli Salad

Gorgonzola makes a tangy dressing that goes well with both chicken and broccoli. Serve this salad for lunch or a light supper.

Serves 4
6 ounces broccoli, divided into
    small florets
2 cups farfalle
2 large cooked chicken breasts

salt and freshly ground
    black pepper
fresh sage leaves, to garnish

For the dressing
3½ ounces Gorgonzola cheese
1 tablespoon white wine vinegar
¼ cup extra virgin olive oil
½–1 teaspoon finely chopped
    fresh sage

1 Cook the broccoli florets in a large saucepan of boiling salted water for 3 minutes. Remove with a slotted spoon and rinse under cold running water, then spread out on paper towels to drain and dry.

2 Add the farfalle to the broccoli cooking water, then bring back to a boil and cook according to the package instructions until *al dente*. When it is cooked, drain the pasta into a colander, rinse well under cold running water until cold, then let drain and dry, shaking the colander occasionally.

3 Remove the skin from the cooked chicken breasts and cut the meat into bite-size pieces.

4 To make the dressing, put the cheese in a large bowl and mash with a fork, then whisk in the wine vinegar, followed by the oil, chopped sage, and salt and pepper to taste.

5 Add the pasta, chicken and broccoli to the bowl. Toss well, then taste and adjust the seasoning as necessary. Serve garnished with sage leaves.

Dijon Chicken Salad

An attractive and elegant dish to serve for lunch with herb and garlic bread.

Serves 4
4 chicken breast fillets, skinned
mixed salad leaves, e.g. frisée and
   oakleaf lettuce or radicchio,
   to serve

For the marinade
2 tablespoons Dijon mustard
3 garlic cloves, crushed
1 tablespoon grated onion
1/4 cup white wine

For the mustard dressing
2 tablespoons tarragon
   wine vinegar
1 teaspoon Dijon mustard
1 teaspoon honey
6 tablespoons olive oil
salt and freshly ground
   black pepper

1 To make the marinade, combine all the ingredients in a shallow glass or earthenware dish that is large enough to hold the chicken in a single layer.

2 Add the chicken to the marinade and turn several times to coat completely. Cover with plastic wrap and chill overnight.

3 Preheat the oven to 375°F. Transfer the chicken and the marinade to an ovenproof dish, cover with aluminum foil and bake for about 35 minutes or until tender. Remove from the oven and let cool in the liquid.

4 To make the mustard dressing, put all the ingredients into a screw-top jar and shake vigorously to emulsify. (This can be made several days in advance and stored in the refrigerator.)

5 Slice the chicken thinly, fan out the slices and arrange on a serving dish with the salad leaves. Spoon on some of the mustard dressing and serve.

French Chicken Salad

A light first course for eight people or a substantial main course for four, this is served with large, crisp, garlic-flavored croutons.

Serves 8
3 1/2-pound free-range chicken
1 1/4 cups white wine and
   water, mixed
24 slices French bread,
   1/4-inch thick
1 garlic clove, peeled
8 ounces green beans
4 ounces young spinach leaves
2 celery stalks, thinly sliced

2 scallions, thinly sliced
2 sun-dried tomatoes, chopped
fresh chives and parsley,
   to garnish

For the vinaigrette
2 tablespoons red wine vinegar
6 tablespoons olive oil
1 tablespoon whole-grain mustard
1 tablespoon honey
2 tablespoons chopped mixed
   fresh herbs, e.g. thyme, parsley
   and chives
2 teaspoons finely chopped capers
salt and freshly ground
   black pepper

1 Preheat the oven to 375°F. Put the chicken in a casserole with the wine and water. Roast for 1 1/2 hours, until tender. Remove from the oven and let cool in the liquid. Discard the skin and bones and cut the flesh into small pieces.

2 To make the vinaigrette, put all the ingredients into a screw-top jar and shake vigorously to emulsify.

3 Toast the French bread under the broiler or in the oven until dry and golden brown, then lightly rub with the peeled garlic clove.

4 Trim the green beans, cut into 2-inch lengths and cook in boiling water for a few minutes, until just tender. Drain and rinse under cold running water.

5 Wash the spinach thoroughly and spin dry. Remove the stalks and tear the leaves into small pieces. Arrange on a serving platter with the celery, beans, scallions, chicken and tomatoes. Spoon on the vinaigrette. Arrange the toasted croutons on top, garnish with chives and parsley, and serve the salad immediately.

Broiled Chicken Salad with Lavender & Sweet Herbs

Lavender may seem like an odd salad ingredient, but its delightful scent has a natural affinity with orange, sweet garlic and other wild herbs. The inclusion of polenta makes this salad both filling and delicious.

Serves 4

4 chicken breast fillets
3¾ cups light Chicken Stock
1½ cups fine polenta
    or cornmeal
¼ cup butter
1 pound young spinach
6 ounces lamb's lettuce

8 fresh lavender sprigs
8 small tomatoes, halved
salt and freshly ground
    black pepper

For the lavender marinade

6 fresh lavender flowers
2 teaspoons finely grated
    orange zest
2 garlic cloves, crushed
2 teaspoons honey
2 tablespoons olive oil
2 teaspoons chopped fresh thyme
2 teaspoons chopped
    fresh marjoram

1 To make the marinade, strip the lavender flowers from the stems and combine with the orange zest, garlic, honey and a pinch of salt. Add the olive oil and herbs. Slash the chicken deeply, spread the mixture on the chicken and let marinate in a cool place for at least 20 minutes.

2 To make the polenta, bring the chicken stock to a boil in a heavy saucepan. Add the meal in a steady stream, stirring constantly for 2–3 minutes until thick. Turn the cooked polenta out into a wide 1-inch-deep buttered pan and let cool.

3 Heat the broiler to medium. (If using a grill, let the embers settle to a steady glow.) Broil the chicken for about 15 minutes, turning once.

4 Cut the polenta into 1-inch cubes, using a wet knife. Heat the butter in a large frying pan and fry the polenta until golden, turning once.

5 Wash and dry the salad leaves, then divide among four large plates. Slice each chicken breast and lay on the salad. Place the polenta on the salad, arrange the sprigs of lavender and tomatoes decoratively on top, season and serve.

> **Cook's Tip**
> Be sure to use culinary lavender, not that sold by the cosmetics industry, as that will have been treated and will not be edible.

Maryland Salad

Grilled chicken, corn, bacon, bananas and watercress combine here in a sensational main-course salad. Serve with baked potatoes and a pat of butter.

Serves 4

4 chicken breast fillets
oil, for brushing
8 ounces bacon
4 ears of corn
3 tablespoons softened butter

4 ripe bananas, peeled and
    halved
4 firm tomatoes, halved
1 head escarole or
    butterhead lettuce
1 bunch watercress
salt and freshly ground
    black pepper

For the dressing

5 tablespoons peanut oil
1 tablespoon white wine vinegar
2 teaspoons maple syrup
2 teaspoons mild mustard

1 Season the chicken fillets, brush with oil and grill or broil for 15 minutes, turning once. Broil the bacon for 8–10 minutes or until crisp.

2 Bring a large saucepan of salted water to a boil. Shuck and trim the corn, or leave the husks on if desired. Boil for 20 minutes. For extra flavor, brush with butter and brown on the grill.

3 Grill or broil the bananas and tomatoes for 6–8 minutes. You can brush these with butter too, if desired.

4 To make the dressing, combine the oil, vinegar, maple syrup and mustard with 1 tablespoon water in a screw-top jar and shake well to emulsify.

5 Wash and dry the salad leaves. Place in a large bowl, pour on the dressing and toss to coat thoroughly.

6 Distribute the salad leaves among four large plates. Slice the chicken and arrange on the leaves with the bacon, banana, corn and tomatoes. Serve immediately.

Coronation Chicken

A dish that never fails to please, this was invented for the coronation of Queen Elizabeth II.

Serves 8
1/2 lemon
5-pound chicken
I onion, quartered
I carrot, quartered
I large bouquet garni
8 black peppercorns, crushed
salt
watercress sprigs, to garnish

For the sauce
I tablespoon butter
I small onion, chopped
I tablespoon curry paste
I tablespoon tomato paste
1/2 cup red wine
I bay leaf
juice of 1/2 lemon, or more
    to taste
2–3 tablespoons apricot jam
1 1/4 cups mayonnaise
1/2 cup whipping cream, whipped
freshly ground black pepper

1 Put the lemon half in the chicken cavity, then place the chicken in a saucepan that it just fits in. Add the vegetables, bouquet garni, peppercorns and salt.

2 Add enough water to come two-thirds of the way up the chicken, bring to a boil, then cover and cook gently for 1 1/2 hours or until the chicken juices run clear.

3 Transfer the chicken to a large bowl, pour in the cooking liquid and let cool. When cold, lift the chicken from the liquid, discard the skin and bones and chop into bite-size pieces.

4 To make the sauce, heat the butter in a saucepan and cook the onion until soft. Add the curry paste, tomato paste, wine, bay leaf and lemon juice, and cook for 10 minutes. Add the jam, heat gently, stirring until it is incorporated, then remove the pan from heat. Strain the sauce and let it cool.

5 Beat the cooled sauce into the mayonnaise. Fold in the whipped cream. Add salt and pepper to taste, plus a little more lemon juice if needed. Stir in the chicken and serve garnished with watercress.

Swiss Cheese, Chicken & Tongue Salad with Apple & Celery

The rich, sweet flavors of this salad marry well with the tart, peppery nature of watercress. A minted lemon dressing combines to freshen the overall effect. Serve with warm new potatoes.

Serves 4
2 chicken breast fillets, skinned
1/2 chicken boullion cube
8 ounces sliced ox tongue or ham,
    1/4 inch thick
8 ounces Gruyère cheese
I red leaf lettuce
I butterhead lettuce
I bunch watercress

2 green-skinned apples, cored
    and sliced
3 celery stalks, sliced
1/4 cup sesame seeds, toasted
salt, freshly ground black pepper
    and grated nutmeg

For the dressing
5 tablespoons peanut or
    sunflower oil
I teaspoon sesame oil
3 tablespoons lemon juice
2 teaspoons chopped fresh mint
3 drops Tabasco sauce

1 Place the chicken breasts in a shallow saucepan, cover with 1 1/4 cups water, add the 1/2 boullion cube and bring to a boil. Put the lid on the pan and simmer for 15 minutes. Drain, reserving the stock for another occasion, then cool the chicken under cold running water.

2 To make the dressing, put all the ingredients into a screw-top jar and shake vigorously. Cut the chicken, tongue and cheese into strips. Moisten with a little dressing and set aside.

3 Wash and dry the salad leaves and place in a large bowl. Add the apple and celery. Pour in some dressing and toss to coat thoroughly.

4 Distribute the salad leaves among four large plates. Pile the chicken, tongue and cheese in the center, and sprinkle on the toasted sesame seeds. Season with salt, freshly ground black pepper and grated nutmeg, and serve.

Chicken, Vegetable & Chili Salad

This Vietnamese salad is full of surprising textures and flavors. Serve it as a light lunch dish or for supper with crusty French bread.

Serves 4
8 ounces Chinese cabbage
2 carrots, cut into matchsticks
1/2 cucumber, cut into matchsticks
2 fresh red chiles, seeded and cut
    into thin strips
1 small onion, sliced into thin rings
4 pickled gherkins, sliced, plus
    3 tablespoons of the liquid
1/2 cup peanuts,
    lightly ground
8 ounces cooked chicken,
    thinly sliced
1 garlic clove, crushed
1 teaspoon sugar
2 tablespoons cider or
    white wine vinegar
salt

1 Thinly slice the Chinese cabbage and spread out on a large board with the carrot and cucumber matchsticks. Sprinkle the vegetables with salt and set aside for 15 minutes.

2 In a bowl, mix together the chiles and onion rings, and add the sliced gherkins and ground peanuts. Transfer the salted vegetables to a colander, rinse well with cold water and pat dry with paper towels.

3 Put the vegetables in a salad bowl and add the chili mixture and cooked chicken. In a small pitcher or bowl, mix the gherkin liquid with the garlic, sugar and vinegar. Pour on the salad and toss lightly, then serve immediately.

Cook's Tip
Add a little more cider or white wine vinegar to the dressing if a sharper taste is desired.

Hot-&-Sour Chicken Salad

Another salad from Vietnam, in which deliciously spiced chicken is served hot on crisp vegetables.

Serves 4–6
2 chicken breast fillets, skinned
1 small fresh red chile, seeded
    and finely chopped
1/2-inch piece fresh ginger root,
    peeled and finely chopped
1 garlic clove, crushed
1 tablespoon crunchy
    peanut butter
2 tablespoons chopped cilantro
1 teaspoon sugar
1/2 teaspoon salt
1 tablespoon rice or white
    wine vinegar
1/4 cup vegetable oil
2 teaspoons fish sauce (optional)
1/2 cup bean sprouts
1 head Chinese cabbage,
    roughly shredded
2 medium carrots, cut
    into matchsticks
1 red onion, cut into thin rings
2 large pickled gherkins, sliced

1 Slice the chicken thinly, place in a shallow bowl and set aside.

2 Grind the chile, ginger and garlic in a mortar with a pestle. Add the peanut butter, cilantro, sugar and salt. Add the vinegar, 2 tablespoons of the oil and the fish sauce, if using. Combine well.

3 Cover the chicken with the spice mixture and let marinate for at least 2–3 hours.

4 Heat the remaining oil in a wok or frying pan. Add the chicken and cook for 10–12 minutes, tossing occasionally.

5 Arrange the bean sprouts, Chinese cabbage, carrots, onion and gherkins on a serving platter or individual plates and place the chicken on top. Pour on the pan juices and serve immediately.

Turkey, Rice & Apple Salad

A flavorful, healthy and crunchy salad to use up leftover turkey and fruit during the holiday festivities.

Serves 8

1¼ cups brown rice
⅓ cup wild rice
2 red-skinned apples, quartered, cored and chopped
2 celery stalks, coarsely sliced
4 ounces seedless grapes
3 tablespoons lemon or orange juice
⅔ cup thick mayonnaise
12 ounces cooked turkey, chopped
salt and freshly ground black pepper
frisée lettuce leaves, to serve

1 Cook the brown and wild rice together in plenty of boiling salted water for about 30 minutes or until tender. Rinse under cold running water and drain thoroughly.

2 Transfer the rice to a large bowl and add the apples, celery and grapes. In another bowl, beat the lemon or orange juice into the mayonnaise, season with salt and pepper, and pour over the rice, mixing thoroughly.

3 Add the cooked turkey and mix well to coat completely with the mayonnaise.

4 Arrange the lettuce on the bottom and around the sides of a large serving dish. Spoon the turkey and rice mixture on top and serve immediately.

> **Cook's Tip**
> This is a good choice for a summer buffet party, but keep the salad in the refrigerator until ready to serve.

Wild Rice & Turkey Salad

An attractive fanned pear garnish complements this salad, which is tossed in a walnut oil dressing.

Serves 4

scant 1 cup wild rice, boiled or steamed
2 celery stalks, thinly sliced
2 ounces scallions, chopped
1½ cups small button mushrooms, quartered
1 pound cooked turkey breast, diced
½ cup French Dressing made with walnut oil
1 teaspoon fresh thyme leaves
2 pears, peeled, halved and cored
¼ cup walnut pieces, toasted
fresh parsley sprigs, to garnish

1 Combine the cooled cooked wild rice with the celery, scallions, mushrooms and turkey in a bowl.

2 Add the dressing and thyme leaves to the salad, and toss to mix.

3 Thinly slice the pear halves lengthwise without cutting through the stem end and spread the slices like a fan.

4 Divide the salad among four plates. Arrange a fanned pear half alongside each salad and sprinkle with walnuts. Garnish with parsley sprigs and serve.

Cooking Wild Rice

Although called "rice," this is actually an aquatic grass. Its deliciously nutty flavor and firm, chewy texture make it a perfect complement to many meat and poultry dishes. It is also an excellent partner for vegetables such as zucchini and mushrooms. It can be cooked like white rice, by boiling or steaming, and needs only about 20 minutes more cooking time.

Apricot Duck Breasts with Bean Sprout Salad

The duck stays beautifully moist when cooked on a grill.

Serves 4

4 plump duck breasts, with skin
1 small red onion, thinly sliced
½ cup dried apricots
1 tablespoon honey
1 teaspoon sesame oil
2 teaspoons ground star anise
salt and freshly ground
   black pepper

For the salad
½ head Chinese cabbage,
   finely shredded
3 cups bean sprouts
2 scallions, shredded

For the dressing
1 tablespoon light soy sauce
1 tablespoon peanut oil
1 teaspoon sesame oil
1 teaspoon honey

1 Place a duck breast, skin-side down, on a board and cut a long slit down one side, cutting not quite through, to form a large pocket. Tuck some slices of onion and apricots inside the pocket and press the breast firmly back into shape. Secure with a metal skewer. Repeat with the other breasts.

2 Combine the honey and sesame oil, and brush onto the duck. Sprinkle on the ground star anise and season with salt and pepper.

3 To make the salad, combine the shredded Chinese cabbage, bean sprouts and scallions in a bowl.

4 To make the dressing, put all the ingredients in a screw-top jar with salt and pepper to taste and shake vigorously. Toss into the salad, mixing well.

5 Cook the duck on a medium-hot grill for 12–15 minutes, turning once, until golden brown on the outside and cooked through. Divide the salad among four plates, place a duck breast on top of each portion and serve immediately.

Warm Duck Salad with Orange

The distinct, sharp flavors of radicchio, curly chicory and fresh oranges are perfect foils for the rich taste of duck. Serve with steamed new potatoes for an elegant main course.

Serves 4

2 duck breast fillets
2 oranges
curly chicory, radicchio and lamb's
   lettuce leaves
2 tablespoons medium-dry sherry
2–3 teaspoons dark soy sauce
salt

1 Rub the skin of the duck breast fillets with salt and then slash the skin several times with a sharp knife.

2 Heat a heavy, cast-iron frying pan and fry the duck breasts, skin-side down at first, for 20–25 minutes, turning once, until the skin is well browned and the flesh is cooked through. Transfer to a plate to cool slightly and pour off the excess fat from the pan, leaving behind the meat juices.

3 Peel the oranges. Separate the oranges into segments and use a sharp knife to remove all the pith, working over a small bowl to catch the juice.

4 Wash and dry the salad leaves and arrange in a wide, shallow serving bowl.

5 Heat the cooking juices remaining in the pan and stir in 3 tablespoons of the reserved orange juice. Bring to a boil over medium heat, and add the sherry and then just enough soy sauce to give a piquant, spicy flavor.

6 Cut the duck into thin slices and arrange on the salad with the orange segments. Pour on the warm dressing and serve immediately.

Chicken Teriyaki

A bowl of boiled rice is the ideal accompaniment to this Japanese-style chicken dish.

Serves 4
1 pound chicken breast
   fillet, skinned
watercress, to garnish

For the marinade
1 teaspoon sugar
1 tablespoon sake
1 tablespoon dry sherry
2 tablespoons dark soy sauce
grated zest of 1 orange

1 Thinly slice the chicken fillets.

2 To make the marinade, combine the sugar, sake, sherry, soy sauce and orange zest in a small bowl, stirring until the sugar has dissolved.

3 Place the chicken in another bowl, pour on the marinade and let marinate for 15 minutes.

4 Heat a wok or heavy frying pan, add the chicken and marinade and stir-fry for 4–5 minutes. Serve garnished with watercress.

Cook's Tip
Make sure the marinade is brought to a boil and cooked for 4–5 minutes, because it has been in contact with raw chicken.

Lemon Chicken Stir-fry

It is essential to prepare all the ingredients before you begin so they are ready to cook. This dish can then be cooked in minutes.

Serves 4
4 chicken breast fillets, skinned
1 tablespoon light soy sauce
5 tablespoons cornstarch
1 bunch scallions
1 lemon
1 garlic clove, crushed
1 tablespoon sugar
2 tablespoons sherry
⅔ cup Chicken Stock
¼ cup olive oil
salad leaves, to serve

1 Divide each chicken breast into two natural fillets. Place each between two sheets of plastic wrap and flatten to a thickness of ¼ inch with a rolling pin. Cut into 1-inch strips across the grain of the fillets. Put the chicken into a bowl with the soy sauce and toss to coat. Sprinkle on ¼ cup cornstarch to coat each piece.

2 Trim the roots off the scallions and cut diagonally into ½-inch pieces. With a swivel peeler, remove the lemon zest in thin strips, without cutting into the white pith, and cut into fine shreds. Squeeze the juice from the lemon into a small bowl. Have ready the garlic, sugar, sherry, stock, lemon juice and remaining cornstarch blended to a thin paste with water.

3 Heat the oil in a wok or large, heavy frying pan and cook the chicken very quickly in small batches for 3–4 minutes, until lightly colored. Remove and keep warm while frying the rest of the chicken. Remove the final batch of chicken.

4 Add the scallions and garlic to the pan and cook for 2 minutes. Add the sugar, sherry, stock and cornstarch paste and bring to a boil, stirring until thickened. Add more sherry or stock if the sauce seems a little too thick.

5 Return the chicken to the pan and stir until it is evenly covered with sauce. Reheat for 2 more minutes. Serve immediately on a bed of salad leaves.

Glazed Chicken with Cashews

Hoisin sauce lends a sweet yet slightly hot note to this chicken dish, while cashews add a pleasing contrast of texture.

Serves 4

¾ cup cashews
1 red bell pepper
1 pound chicken breast
   fillet, skinned
3 tablespoons peanut oil
4 garlic cloves, finely chopped
2 tablespoons rice wine or
   medium-dry sherry
3 tablespoons hoisin sauce
2 teaspoons sesame oil
5–6 scallions, green parts only, cut
   into 1-inch lengths
cooked rice or noodles, to serve

1 Heat a wok or heavy frying pan until hot, add the cashews and stir-fry over low to medium heat for 1–2 minutes, until golden brown. Remove from heat and set the cashews aside.

2 Halve the red pepper and remove the seeds. Slice the pepper and chicken into finger-length strips.

3 Heat the wok again until hot, add the oil and swirl it around. Add the garlic and let it sizzle in the oil for a few seconds. Add the red pepper and chicken, and stir-fry for 2 minutes.

4 Add the rice wine or sherry and hoisin sauce. Continue to stir-fry until the chicken is tender and all the ingredients are evenly glazed.

5 Stir in the sesame oil, reserved toasted cashews and the scallion tips. Serve immediately with rice or noodles.

> **Variation**
> *Use blanched almonds instead of cashews if you prefer.*

Yellow Chicken

A super-fast version of an all-time Chinese favorite stir-fry.

Serves 4

2 tablespoons oil
¾ cup salted cashews
4 scallions
1 pound chicken breast fillet
5½-ounce jar yellow bean sauce
cooked rice, to serve

1 Heat 1 tablespoon of the oil in a wok or frying pan and fry the cashews until browned. Remove from the pan with a slotted spoon and set aside.

2 Roughly chop the scallions. Skin and thinly slice the chicken fillets. Heat the remaining oil and cook the scallions and chicken for 5–8 minutes, until the meat is browned all over and cooked.

3 Return the nuts to the pan and pour on the jar of sauce. Stir well and cook gently until hot. Serve immediately, accompanied by cooked rice.

> **Cook's Tip**
> *Yellow bean sauce is made from salted, fermented yellow soybeans crushed with sugar and flour to make a thick paste. It is available at supermarkets and Chinese food stores.*

Stir-fried Chicken with Pineapple

An Indonesian-inspired dish in which pineapple adds an extra dimension to chicken and the usual stir-fry flavorings.

Serves 4–6
1¼ pounds chicken breast fillet
2 tablespoons cornstarch
¼ cup sunflower oil
1 garlic clove, crushed
2-inch piece fresh ginger root, peeled and cut into matchsticks
1 small onion, thinly sliced
1 fresh pineapple, peeled, cored and cubed, or 15-ounce can pineapple chunks in natural juice
2 tablespoons dark soy sauce
1 bunch scallions, white bulbs left whole, green tops sliced
salt and freshly ground black pepper

1 Skin the chicken fillets and slice thinly on the diagonal. Toss the strips of chicken in the cornstarch with a little seasoning.

2 Heat the oil in a wok or heavy frying pan and stir-fry the chicken for 5–8 minutes, until lightly browned and cooked through. Lift the chicken out of the wok using a slotted spoon and keep warm.

3 Reheat the oil and sauté the garlic, ginger and onion until soft but not browned. Add the fresh pineapple and ½ cup water, if using, or the canned pineapple pieces together with their juice.

4 Stir in the soy sauce and return the chicken to the pan to heat through. Taste and adjust the seasoning as necessary.

5 Stir in the whole scallion bulbs and half of the sliced green tops. Toss well together and then turn the chicken stir-fry onto a serving platter. Serve garnished with the remaining sliced green scallion tops.

Thai Chicken & Vegetable Stir-fry

An all-in-one main course that needs only boiled or steamed rice as an accompaniment.

Serves 4
2 tablespoons sunflower oil
1 lemongrass stalk, thinly sliced
½-inch piece fresh ginger root, peeled and chopped
1 large garlic clove, chopped
10 ounces lean chicken, thinly sliced
½ red bell pepper, seeded and sliced
½ green bell pepper, seeded and sliced
4 scallions, chopped
2 medium carrots, cut into matchsticks
¾ cup fine green beans
2 tablespoons oyster sauce
pinch of sugar
salt and freshly ground black pepper
¼ cup salted peanuts, lightly crushed, and cilantro leaves, to garnish
cooked rice, to serve

1 Heat the oil in a wok or heavy frying pan over high heat. Add the lemongrass, ginger and garlic, and stir-fry for 30 seconds, until lightly browned.

2 Add the chicken and stir-fry for 2 minutes. Then add the vegetables and stir-fry for 4–5 minutes, until the chicken is cooked and the vegetables are almost cooked.

3 Stir in the oyster sauce, sugar and seasoning to taste, and stir-fry for another minute to mix and blend well.

4 Serve immediately, sprinkled with the peanuts and cilantro leaves, and accompanied by rice.

Variations
If lemongrass is unavailable, you can substitute the thinly pared and chopped zest of ½ lemon, although the citrus flavor will not be as intense. Make this quick supper dish a little hotter by adding more fresh ginger root, if desired.

Chinese Chicken with Cashews

The roasted cashews provide additional proteins as well as extra texture and flavor to this dish.

Serves 4

4 chicken breast fillets, about
  6 ounces each, skinned and
  cut into strips
3 garlic cloves, crushed
¼ cup soy sauce
2 tablespoons cornstarch
8 ounces dried egg noodles
3 tablespoons peanut or
  sunflower oil
1 tablespoon sesame oil
1 cup cashews, roasted
6 scallions, cut into 2-inch pieces
  and halved lengthwise
scallion curls and a little chopped
  red chile, to garnish

1 Place the chicken in a bowl with the garlic, soy sauce and cornstarch, and mix until the chicken is well coated. Cover and chill for about 30 minutes.

2 Meanwhile, bring a large saucepan of water to a boil and add the egg noodles. Turn off the heat and let stand for 5 minutes. Drain well and reserve.

3 Heat the oils in a wok or large, heavy frying pan and add the chilled chicken and marinade juices. Stir-fry over high heat for 3–4 minutes or until the chicken is golden brown all over.

4 Add the cashews and scallions to the pan, and stir-fry for 2–3 minutes.

5 Add the drained noodles and stir-fry for another 2 minutes. Toss well to mix everything thoroughly. Serve immediately, garnished with scallion curls and chopped red chile.

Stir-fried Rice Noodles with Chicken & Shrimp

This Thai recipe combines chicken with shrimp and has the characteristic sweet, sour and salty flavors.

Serves 4

8 ounces dried flat rice noodles
½ cup water
¼ cup fish sauce
1 tablespoon sugar
1 tablespoon fresh lime juice
1 teaspoon paprika
pinch of cayenne pepper
3 tablespoons oil
2 garlic cloves, finely chopped
1 chicken breast fillet, skinned
  and finely sliced
8 shrimp, peeled, deveined
  and cut in half
1 egg
2 ounces roasted peanuts,
  coarsely crushed
3 scallions, cut into
  short lengths
¾ cup bean sprouts
cilantro leaves and lime wedges,
  to garnish

1 Place the rice noodles in a large bowl, cover with warm water and soak for 30 minutes until soft. Drain well. Combine the water, fish sauce, sugar, lime juice, paprika and cayenne in a small bowl. Set aside until needed.

2 Heat the oil in a wok or heavy frying pan. Add the garlic and sauté for 30 seconds until it starts to brown. Stir in the chicken and shrimp, and stir-fry for 3–4 minutes, until cooked.

3 Push the chicken and shrimp mixture to the sides of the wok. Break the egg into the center, then quickly stir to break up the yolk, and cook over medium heat until lightly scrambled.

4 Add the noodles and the fish sauce mixture to the wok. Add half the crushed peanuts and cook, stirring frequently, until the noodles are soft and most of the liquid has been absorbed.

5 Add the scallions and half of the bean sprouts. Cook, stirring for 1 more minute. Spoon onto a serving platter. Sprinkle on the remaining peanuts and bean sprouts. Garnish with cilantro and lime wedges, and serve.

Shredded Chicken with Celery

The tender chicken breast makes a fine contrast with the crisp texture of the celery, and the red chiles add color and flavor.

Serves 4

10 ounces chicken breast
   fillet, skinned
1 teaspoon salt
½ egg white, lightly beaten
2 teaspoons cornstarch

about 2 cups vegetable oil
1 celery heart, thinly shredded
1–2 fresh red chiles, seeded and
   thinly shredded
1 scallion, thinly shredded
few strips of fresh ginger root,
   peeled and thinly shredded
1 teaspoon light brown sugar
1 tablespoon Chinese rice wine or
   dry sherry
few drops of sesame oil

1 Using a sharp knife, thinly shred the chicken. Place in a bowl and add a pinch of the salt and the egg white. Mix the cornstarch into a thin paste with a little water and add to the bowl, stirring well to coat.

2 Heat the oil in a wok or heavy frying pan until warm, add the chicken and stir to separate the shreds. When the chicken turns white, remove with a slotted spoon and drain on paper towels. Keep warm.

3 Pour all but 2 tablespoons of the oil from the wok. Add the celery, chiles, scallion and ginger, and stir-fry for 1 minute.

4 Return the chicken to the wok and add the remaining salt, sugar and rice wine or sherry. Stir-fry for 1 minute, then add the sesame oil. Serve immediately.

Cook's Tip
Sesame oil is not often used for frying in Chinese cooking. It is usually added toward the end of the cooking time to provide extra flavor.

Chicken with Chinese Vegetables

Shiitake mushrooms, bamboo shoots and snowpeas combine with chicken in this tasty stir-fry.

Serves 4

8–10 ounces chicken, boned
   and skinned
1 teaspoon salt
½ egg white, lightly beaten
2 teaspoons cornstarch
¼ cup vegetable oil
6–8 small dried shiitake
   mushrooms, soaked in water
   and drained

4 ounces canned sliced bamboo
   shoots, drained
4 ounces snowpeas, trimmed
1 scallion, cut into
   short sections
few small pieces of fresh
   ginger root, peeled
1 teaspoon light brown sugar
1 tablespoon light soy sauce
1 tablespoon Chinese rice wine
   or dry sherry
few drops of sesame oil

1 Using a sharp knife, cut the chicken into thin slices, each about the size of an oblong postage stamp. Place in a bowl and mix with a pinch of the salt and the egg white. Mix the cornstarch into a thin paste with a little water and add to the bowl.

2 Heat a wok or heavy frying pan and add the oil. When the oil is hot, add the chicken and stir-fry over medium heat for about 30 seconds, then remove with a slotted spoon and drain on paper towels. Keep warm.

3 Add the mushrooms, bamboo shoots, snowpeas, scallion and ginger to the wok, and stir-fry over high heat for about 1 minute.

4 Return the chicken to the wok, and add the remaining salt and the sugar. Blend, then add the soy sauce and rice wine or sherry. Stir a few more times. Sprinkle with the sesame oil and serve immediately.

Chicken with Snowpeas & Cilantro

Delicate and fresh-tasting snowpeas are excellent in stir-fries and also give additional color to paler ingredients, such as chicken.

Serves 4
4 chicken breast fillets, skinned
8 ounces snowpeas
vegetable oil, for deep-frying
1 tablespoon vegetable oil
3 garlic cloves, finely chopped
1-inch piece fresh ginger root,
    freshly grated
5–6 scallions, cut into
    1 1/2 -inch lengths
2 teaspoons sesame oil
2 tablespoons chopped cilantro
salt
cooked rice, to serve

For the marinade
1 teaspoon cornstarch
1 tablespoon light soy sauce
1 tablespoon medium-dry sherry
1 tablespoon vegetable oil

For the sauce
1 teaspoon cornstarch
2–3 teaspoons dark soy sauce
1/2 cup Chicken Stock
2 tablespoons oyster sauce

1 Cut the chicken into strips about 1/2 × 1 1/2 inches and place in a wide, shallow dish. To make the marinade, blend the cornstarch and soy sauce in a small bowl. Stir in the sherry and oil. Pour onto the chicken, turning the pieces to coat them evenly, and set aside for 30 minutes.

2 Trim the snowpeas and plunge into a pan of boiling salted water. Bring back to a boil, then drain and refresh under cold running water.

3 To make the sauce, combine the cornstarch, soy sauce, stock and oyster sauce in a bowl. Set aside.

4 Heat the oil in a deep-fat fryer. Drain the chicken strips and fry, in batches if necessary, for about 30 seconds, until brown. Remove using a slotted spoon and drain on paper towels.

5 Heat 1 tablespoon oil in a wok or heavy frying pan and add the garlic and ginger. Stir-fry for 30 seconds. Add the snowpeas and stir-fry for 1–2 minutes. Transfer to a plate and keep warm.

6 Heat another 1 tablespoon oil in the wok, add the scallions and stir-fry for 1–2 minutes. Add the chicken and stir-fry for 2 minutes. Pour in the sauce, reduce the heat and cook until it thickens and the chicken is cooked through.

7 Return the snowpeas to the wok, and stir in the sesame oil and chopped cilantro. Serve with rice.

Variation
If snowpeas are not available you could use broccoli or green beans.

Fu-yung Chicken

Because the egg whites (*Fu-yung* in Chinese) mixed with milk are deep-fried, they have prompted some rather imaginative cooks to refer to this dish as "deep-fried milk!"

Serves 4
6 ounces chicken breast fillet
1 teaspoon salt
4 egg whites, lightly beaten
1 tablespoon cornstarch

2 tablespoons milk
vegetable oil, for deep-frying
1 lettuce heart, separated
    into leaves
about 1/2 cup Chicken Stock
1 tablespoon Chinese rice wine
    or dry sherry
1 tablespoon peas
few drops of sesame oil
1 teaspoon very finely chopped
    ham, to garnish

1 Finely grind the chicken meat and place in a bowl. Add a pinch of the salt and the egg whites. Mix the cornstarch into a thin paste with a little water and add to the bowl with the milk. Blend well until smooth.

2 Heat the oil in a very hot wok, but before the oil gets too hot, gently spoon the chicken mixture into the oil in batches. Do not stir, otherwise it will spatter. Stir the oil from the bottom of the wok so that the chicken pieces rise to the surface. Remove the chicken as soon as the color turns bright white. Drain.

3 Pour off the excess oil, leaving about 1 tablespoon in the wok. Add the lettuce leaves and remaining salt, and stir-fry for 1 minute. Add the stock and bring to a boil.

4 Return the chicken to the wok, add the rice wine or sherry and peas, and blend well. Sprinkle with the sesame oil, garnish with the ham and serve.

Pasta with Chicken Livers

Chicken livers and bacon seem made for each other in this surprisingly rich-tasting dish. If orecchiette pasta is unavailable, use another medium-size pasta.

Serves 4
8 ounces chicken livers
2 tablespoons olive oil
2 garlic cloves, crushed
6 ounces bacon, roughly chopped
14-ounce can chopped tomatoes
⅔ cup Chicken Stock
1 tablespoon tomato paste
1 tablespoon dry sherry
2 tablespoons chopped fresh
    mixed herbs, e.g. parsley,
    rosemary and basil
12 ounces dried orecchiette
salt and freshly ground
    black pepper
Parmesan cheese shavings,
    to serve

1 Trim the chicken livers and cut into bite-size pieces. Heat the olive oil in a sauté pan and fry the livers for 3–4 minutes, until lightly browned.

2 Add the garlic and bacon to the pan, and fry until golden brown. Add the tomatoes, chicken stock, tomato paste, sherry, herbs and seasoning.

3 Bring to a boil and simmer gently, uncovered, for about 5 minutes, until the sauce has thickened.

4 Meanwhile, cook the pasta in boiling salted water for about 12 minutes or according to the package instructions, until *al dente*. Drain well, then toss in the sauce. Serve hot, sprinkled with Parmesan cheese shavings.

Cook's Tip
You'll find orecchiette, a dried pasta shaped like ears—it means "little ears"—at most large supermarkets.

Noodles with Eggplant & Chicken Livers

A modern pasta recipe with an unusual and tasty sauce.

Serves 4
2 large eggplant,
    about 12 ounces each
2 garlic cloves
1 large onion
6–8 tablespoons oil
1¼-pound crushed tomatoes
1 cup boiling water
12 ounces flat noodles
10 ounces chicken livers
salt and freshly ground
    black pepper
chopped flat-leaf parsley,
    to garnish

1 Peel and dice the eggplant. Crush the garlic and roughly chop the onion.

2 Put half the oil in a frying pan and sauté the onion for about 1 minute. Add the garlic and cook until the onion starts to brown. Transfer to a plate.

3 Add the remaining oil to the pan and heat. Add the eggplant and cook briskly, turning occasionally, until browned.

4 Return the onion to the pan, and add the tomatoes, boiling water and seasoning. Simmer for 30 minutes.

5 Preheat the broiler. Cook the noodles in boiling salted water or according to the package instructions until *al dente*. Meanwhile, broil the chicken livers on oiled aluminum foil for 3–4 minutes on each side. Snip into strips.

6 Drain the noodles and arrange on serving plates. Spoon on the eggplant sauce and top with the chicken livers. Serve immediately, garnished with flat-leaf parsley.

Conchiglie with Chicken Livers & Herbs

Fresh sage and flat-leaf parsley are a superb foil to chicken livers, here cooked in a tasty sauce and tossed with pasta shells.

Serves 4

4 tablespoons butter
4 ounces pancetta or lean bacon, diced
9 ounces chicken livers, trimmed and diced
2 garlic cloves, crushed
2 teaspoons chopped fresh sage
12 ounces conchiglie
⅔ cup dry white wine
4 ripe Italian plum tomatoes, peeled and diced
1 tablespoon chopped fresh flat-leaf parsley
salt and freshly ground black pepper

1 Melt half the butter in a medium frying pan or saucepan, add the pancetta or bacon and fry over medium heat for a few minutes, until lightly colored but not crisp.

2 Add the chicken livers, garlic, half the sage and plenty of pepper. Increase the heat and toss the livers for about 5 minutes, until they change color all over but remain slightly pink in the center.

3 Meanwhile, bring a large saucepan of salted water to a boil, add the pasta and cook according to the package instructions until *al dente*.

4 Pour the wine over the chicken livers in the pan and let it sizzle, then lower the heat and simmer gently for 5 minutes.

5 Add the remaining butter to the pan. As soon as it has melted, add the tomatoes, toss to mix, then add the remaining sage and the parsley. Stir well. Taste and add salt if needed.

6 Drain the pasta and turn it into a warmed bowl. Pour on the sauce and toss well. Serve immediately.

Penne with Chicken & Cheese

Broccoli, garlic and Gorgonzola cheese form a great partnership with strips of chicken.

Serves 4

8 ounces broccoli, divided into small florets
¼ cup butter
2 chicken breast fillets, skinned and cut into thin strips
2 garlic cloves, crushed
12 ounces penne
½ cup dry white wine
scant 1 cup heavy cream
3½ ounces Gorgonzola cheese, rind removed and finely diced
salt and freshly ground black pepper
grated Parmesan cheese, to serve

1 Plunge the broccoli into a saucepan of boiling salted water. Bring back to a boil and boil for 2 minutes, then drain in a colander and refresh under cold running water.

2 Melt the butter in a large frying pan or saucepan, add the chicken and garlic, with salt and pepper to taste, and stir well. Cook over medium heat for 3 minutes.

3 Meanwhile, bring a large saucepan of salted water to a boil, add the pasta and cook according to the package instructions until *al dente*.

4 Pour the wine and cream onto the chicken mixture in the pan, stir to mix, then simmer, stirring occasionally, for about 5 minutes, until the sauce has reduced and thickened. Add the broccoli, increase the heat, toss to heat it through and mix it with the chicken. Taste and adjust the seasoning as necessary. Drain the pasta and add it to the sauce. Stir in the Gorgonzola and toss well. Serve with grated Parmesan.

> **Variation**
> *Use leeks instead of broccoli if desired. Cook them with the chicken.*

Pappardelle with Chicken & Mushrooms

Rich and creamy, this is a good supper party dish.

Serves 4

½ ounces dried porcini
    mushrooms
¾ cup warm water
2 tablespoons butter
1 garlic clove, crushed
1 small handful fresh flat-leaf
    parsley, coarsely chopped

1 small leek, chopped
½ cup dry white wine
1 cup Chicken Stock
12 ounces pappardelle
2 chicken breast fillets, skinned
    and cut into thin strips
7 tablespoons mascarpone cheese
salt and freshly ground
    black pepper
fresh basil leaves, to garnish

1 Put the dried mushrooms in a bowl. Pour in the warm water and let soak for 15–20 minutes. Transfer into a fine sieve set over a bowl and squeeze the mushrooms with your hands to release as much liquid as possible. Chop the mushrooms finely and set aside the strained soaking liquid until needed.

2 Melt the butter in a medium frying pan, and add the mushrooms, garlic, parsley and leek, with salt and pepper to taste. Cook over low heat, stirring frequently, for about 5 minutes, then pour in the wine and stock, and bring to a boil. Lower the heat and simmer for about 5 minutes or until reduced and thickened.

3 Meanwhile, bring a large saucepan of salted water to a boil, adding the reserved soaking liquid. Add the pasta and cook according to the package instructions until *al dente*.

4 Add the chicken to the sauce and simmer for 5 minutes or until just tender. Add the mascarpone a spoonful at a time, stirring well after each addition, then add one or two spoonfuls of the water used for cooking the pasta.

5 Drain the pasta and transfer it to a warmed large bowl. Add the chicken and sauce, and toss well. Serve immediately, topped with the basil leaves.

Farfalle with Chicken & Cherry Tomatoes

Quick to prepare and easy to cook, this colorful dish is full of flavor.

Serves 4

12 ounces chicken breast fillet,
    skinned and cut into bite-
    size pieces
¼ cup Italian dry vermouth
2 teaspoons chopped
    fresh rosemary
1 tablespoon olive oil

1 onion, finely chopped
3½-ounce piece Italian
    salami, diced
12 ounces farfalle
1 tablespoon balsamic vinegar
14 ounces cherry tomatoes
good pinch of crushed dried
    red chiles
salt and freshly ground
    black pepper
fresh rosemary sprigs, to garnish

1 Put the pieces of chicken in a large bowl, pour in the dry vermouth and sprinkle with half the chopped rosemary, and salt and pepper to taste. Stir well and set aside.

2 Heat the oil in a large frying pan or saucepan, add the onion and salami, and cook over medium heat for about 5 minutes, stirring frequently.

3 Meanwhile, bring a large saucepan of salted water to a boil, add the pasta and cook according to the package instructions until *al dente*.

4 Add the chicken and vermouth to the onion and salami, increase the heat to high and cook for 3 minutes or until the chicken is white on all sides. Sprinkle in the balsamic vinegar. Add the cherry tomatoes and crushed dried red chiles. Stir well and simmer for a few more minutes. Taste and adjust the seasoning as necessary.

5 Drain the pasta and add it to the sauce. Add the remaining chopped rosemary, and toss to mix the pasta and sauce together. Serve immediately in warmed bowls, garnished with the rosemary sprigs.

Tagliatelle with Chicken & Herb Sauce

A rich, creamy dish made with vermouth and fromage frais, this just needs a simple green salad accompaniment.

Serves 4

2 tablespoons olive oil
1 red onion, cut into wedges
12 ounces tagliatelle
1 garlic clove, chopped
12 ounces chicken, diced
1¼ cups dry vermouth
3 tablespoons chopped fresh
   mixed herbs
⅔ cup fromage frais
salt and freshly ground
   black pepper
shredded fresh mint, to garnish

1 Heat the oil in a large frying pan and sauté the onion for 5–7 minutes, until softened and the layers separate.

2 Bring a large saucepan of salted water to a boil, add the tagliatelle and cook according to the package instructions.

3 Add the garlic and chicken to the frying pan and cook for 10 minutes, stirring occasionally, until the chicken is browned all over and cooked through.

4 Pour the vermouth onto the chicken, bring to a boil and boil rapidly until reduced by about half.

5 Stir in the mixed herbs, fromage frais and seasoning, and heat through gently, but do not boil.

6 Drain the pasta thoroughly and toss it with the sauce to coat. Serve immediately, garnished with shredded fresh mint.

> **Cook's Tip**
> If you don't want to use vermouth, use dry white wine instead. Orvieto and frascati are two Italian wines that are ideal to use in this sauce.

Penne with Chicken & Ham Sauce

A meal in itself, this colorful pasta sauce is perfect for a midweek lunch or dinner.

Serves 4

12 ounces penne
2 tablespoons butter
1 onion, chopped
1 garlic clove, chopped
1 bay leaf
scant 2 cups dry white wine
⅔ cup crème fraîche
1½ cups cooked chicken, skinned,
   boned and diced
⅔ cup cooked lean ham, diced
1 cup Gouda cheese, grated
1 tablespoon chopped fresh mint
salt and freshly ground
   black pepper
finely shredded fresh mint,
   to garnish

1 Bring a large saucepan of salted water to a boil, add the pasta and cook according to the instructions on the package until *al dente*.

2 Heat the butter in a large frying pan and gently sauté the onion for 10 minutes, until softened.

3 Add the garlic, bay leaf and wine, and bring to a boil. Boil rapidly until reduced by half. Remove the bay leaf, then stir in the crème fraîche and return to a boil.

4 Add the chicken, ham and cheese, and simmer for 5 minutes, stirring occasionally, until heated through. Add the chopped mint and seasoning to taste.

5 Drain the pasta thoroughly and transfer it to a large warmed serving bowl. Add the sauce, toss to coat well, then serve, garnished with shredded mint.

Pasta Spirals with Chicken & Tomato Sauce

A recipe for a speedy supper—serve this dish with a mixed bean salad.

Serves 4

1 tablespoon olive oil
1 onion, chopped
1 carrot, chopped
1 garlic clove, chopped
14-ounce can chopped tomatoes
1 tablespoon tomato paste
2/3 cup Chicken Stock
12 ounces pasta spirals (fusilli)
2 ounces sun-dried tomatoes in olive oil, drained weight
8 ounces boneless chicken, diagonally sliced
salt and freshly ground black pepper
fresh mint sprigs, to garnish

1 Heat the oil in a large frying pan, and cook the onion and carrot for 5 minutes, stirring occasionally.

2 Stir the garlic, canned chopped tomatoes, tomato paste and stock into the onion and carrot, and bring to a boil. Simmer for 10 minutes, stirring occasionally.

3 Bring a large saucepan of salted water to a boil, add the pasta spirals and cook according to the package instructions until *al dente*.

4 Pour the sauce into a food processor or blender and process until smooth. Return the sauce to the pan.

5 Chop the sun-dried tomatoes and stir into the sauce along with the chicken. Bring back to a boil, then simmer for 10 minutes, until the chicken is cooked. Season to taste.

6 Drain the pasta thoroughly and toss it in the sauce. Serve immediately, garnished with fresh mint.

Pasta with Chicken & Sausage Sauce

A lovely meaty sauce with a strong tomato flavor coating farfalle (small bow-shaped pasta).

Serves 4

3 tablespoons olive oil
1 pound chicken breast fillet, skinned and cut into 1/2-inch pieces
3 small spicy cooked sausages, cut diagonally into 1/2-inch slices
6 scallions, cut diagonally into 1/4-inch lengths
10 sun-dried tomatoes in oil, drained and chopped
1 cup canned chopped tomatoes
1 medium zucchini, cut diagonally into 1/4-inch slices
12 ounces farfalle
salt and freshly ground black pepper

1 Heat the olive oil in a frying pan. Add the chicken and sausage pieces with a little salt and pepper, and cook for about 10 minutes, until browned. Using a slotted spoon, remove the chicken and sausage from the pan, and drain on paper towels.

2 Add the scallions and sun-dried tomatoes to the pan, and cook for about 5 minutes, until softened.

3 Stir in the canned tomatoes and cook for about 5 minutes, until thickened, stirring occasionally.

4 Add the zucchini, and return the chicken and sausage to the pan. Cook for 5 more minutes, until the zucchini is just tender and the meat is heated through. Taste and adjust the seasoning as necessary.

5 Bring a large saucepan of salted water to a boil, add the farfalle and cook according to the package instructions until *al dente*. Drain the pasta thoroughly, and toss with the chicken and sausage sauce. Serve immediately.

Italian Chicken

The chicken is finished in a sauce of tomatoes, black olives, garlic and herbs, with added zing from some ready-made red pesto, and served on a bed of noodles.

Serves 4

2 tablespoons all-purpose flour
4 chicken portions (legs, breasts
    or quarters)
2 tablespoons olive oil
I onion, chopped
2 garlic cloves, chopped
I red bell pepper, seeded
    and chopped

I 4-ounce can
    chopped tomatoes
2 tablespoons red pesto sauce
4 sun-dried tomatoes in oil,
    drained and chopped
⅔ cup Chicken Stock
I teaspoon dried oregano
8 black olives, pitted
salt and freshly ground
    black pepper
chopped fresh basil and whole
    basil leaves, to garnish
cooked tagliatelle, to serve

I Place the flour and seasoning in a plastic bag. Add the chicken pieces and shake well until coated. Heat the oil in a flameproof casserole, add the chicken and brown quickly. Remove using a slotted spoon and set aside.

2 Lower the heat and add the onion, garlic and red pepper, and cook for 5 minutes. Stir in the canned chopped tomatoes, red pesto sauce, sun-dried tomatoes, stock and oregano, and bring to a boil.

3 Return the sautéed chicken portions to the casserole, season lightly, cover and simmer for 30–35 minutes or until the chicken is cooked.

4 Add the olives and simmer for another 5 minutes. Transfer to a warmed serving dish, sprinkle with the chopped basil and garnish with whole basil leaves. Serve hot with tagliatelle.

Chicken with Mushrooms

Serve on a dish surrounded with nutty brown rice or tagliatelle verde. White wine or brandy may be used to deglaze the pan instead of dry sherry.

Serves 4

4 large chicken breast
    fillets, skinned
3 tablespoons olive oil

I onion, thinly sliced
I garlic clove, crushed
3 cups button mushrooms,
    quartered
2 tablespoons dry sherry
I tablespoon lemon juice
⅔ cup light cream
salt and freshly ground
    black pepper
fresh parsley, to garnish

I Divide each chicken breast into two natural fillets. Place the fillets between two sheets of plastic wrap and flatten to a thickness of ¼ inch with a rolling pin. Cut into I-inch diagonal strips.

2 Heat 2 tablespoons of the oil in a large frying pan and cook the onion and garlic gently until tender.

3 Add the mushrooms and cook for another 5 minutes. Remove the vegetables from the pan and keep warm.

4 Increase the heat. Add the remaining oil and stir-fry the chicken very quickly, in small batches, for 3–4 minutes, until lightly colored. Season each batch with a little salt and pepper. Remove and keep warm while cooking the rest of the chicken.

5 Add the sherry and lemon juice to the pan and quickly return the chicken, onions, garlic and mushrooms, stirring well to coat.

6 Stir in the cream and bring to just below the boiling point. Adjust the seasoning to taste. Serve immediately, garnished with parsley.

Cannelloni al Forno

A lighter alternative to the usual beef-filled, béchamel-coated version, this recipe uses chicken breast.

Serves 4–6

generous 3 cups chopped cooked
   chicken breast fillet
3 cups mushrooms
2 garlic cloves, crushed
2 tablespoons chopped fresh
   flat-leaf parsley
I tablespoon chopped
   fresh tarragon
I egg, beaten
fresh lemon juice
12–18 cannelloni tubes
butter, for greasing
scant 2 cups Fresh Tomato Sauce
²⁄₃ cup grated Parmesan cheese
I fresh flat-leaf parsley sprig,
   to garnish
salt and freshly ground
   black pepper

I Preheat the oven to 400°F. Place the cooked chicken in a food processor and process until finely ground. Transfer to a bowl.

2 Place the mushrooms, garlic, parsley and tarragon in the food processor, and process until finely ground.

3 Beat the mushroom mixture into the chicken with the egg. Stir in salt, pepper and lemon juice to taste.

4 Bring a large saucepan of salted water to a boil, add the cannelloni and cook according to the package instructions.

5 Place the chicken mixture in a piping bag with a large plain nozzle. Use this to fill each tube of cannelloni.

6 Lay the filled cannelloni tightly together in a single layer in a buttered, shallow, ovenproof dish. Spoon on the tomato sauce and sprinkle with Parmesan cheese. Bake for 30 minutes or until brown and bubbling. Serve garnished with a sprig of parsley.

Chicken Lasagne

Based on the Italian beef lasagne, this dish will be popular with the whole family.

Serves 8

2 tablespoons olive oil
2 pounds ground chicken
8 ounces bacon, chopped
2 garlic cloves, crushed
I pound leeks, sliced
8 ounces carrots, diced
2 tablespoons tomato paste
scant 2 cups Chicken Stock
12 sheets (no need to precook)
   lasagne verde
salt and freshly ground
   black pepper
green salad, to serve

For the cheese sauce

¹⁄₄ cup butter
¹⁄₂ cup all-purpose flour
2¹⁄₂ cups milk
I cup grated aged
   Cheddar cheese
¹⁄₄ teaspoon dry English mustard

I Heat the oil in a large, flameproof casserole and brown the ground chicken and bacon briskly, separating the pieces with a wooden spoon. Add the garlic, leeks and carrots, and cook for 5 minutes, until softened. Add the tomato paste, stock and seasoning. Bring to a boil, cover and simmer for 30 minutes.

2 To make the sauce, melt the butter in a saucepan, add the flour and gradually blend in the milk, stirring until smooth. Bring to a boil, stirring constantly until thickened, and simmer for 3 minutes. Add half the cheese, the mustard and season to taste.

3 Preheat the oven to 375°F. Layer the chicken mixture, lasagne and half the cheese sauce in a 12¹⁄₂-cup ovenproof dish, starting and finishing with a layer of chicken.

4 Pour the remaining half of the cheese sauce on top to cover, sprinkle with the remaining grated cheese and bake for I hour or until bubbling and lightly browned on top. Serve with green salad.

Smoked Chicken, Yellow Bell Pepper & Sun-dried Tomato Pizzettes

Smoked chicken is now widely available at supermarkets and makes a special topping for these small pizzas.

Serves 4
2 tablespoons olive oil, plus extra for greasing
4 ready-made 4–5-inch pizza crusts
2 yellow bell peppers, seeded and cut into thin strips
¼ cup sun-dried tomato paste
6 ounces sliced smoked chicken or turkey, chopped
6 ounces mozzarella cheese, cubed
2 tablespoons chopped fresh basil
salt and freshly ground black pepper

1 Preheat the oven to 425°F. Grease two baking sheets and place two pizza crusts on each one, spaced well apart.

2 Heat half of the oil in a frying pan and stir-fry the peppers for 3–4 minutes.

3 Brush the pizza crusts generously with the sun-dried tomato paste. Arrange the smoked chicken or turkey and yellow peppers evenly on top.

4 Sprinkle on the mozzarella cheese and basil. Season with salt and pepper.

5 Drizzle on the remaining oil and bake for 15–20 minutes, until crisp and golden. Serve immediately.

> **Variation**
> *For a vegetarian pizza with a similar smoky taste, omit the chicken, roast or broil the yellow peppers and remove the skins before using, and replace the mozzarella with Bavarian smoked cheese.*

Chicken, Shiitake Mushroom & Cilantro Pizza

The addition of shiitake mushrooms adds an earthy flavor to this colorful pizza, while fresh red chile adds a hint of spiciness.

Serves 3–4
¼ cup olive oil
12 ounces chicken breast fillet, skinned and cut into thin strips
1 bunch scallions, sliced
1 fresh red chile, seeded and chopped
1 red bell pepper, seeded and cut into thin strips
3 ounces fresh shiitake mushrooms, wiped and sliced
3–4 tablespoons chopped cilantro
1 ready-made 10–12-inch pizza crust
5 ounces mozzarella cheese
salt and freshly ground black pepper

1 Preheat the oven to 425°F. Heat 2 tablespoons of the olive oil in a wok or large frying pan. Add the chicken, scallions, chile, red pepper and mushrooms, and stir-fry over high heat for 2–3 minutes, until the chicken is firm but still slightly pink inside. Season to taste.

2 Pour off any excess oil, then set aside the chicken mixture to cool. Stir the cilantro into the cooled chicken mixture.

3 Brush the pizza crust with 1 tablespoon of the oil. Spoon on the chicken mixture and drizzle on the remaining olive oil.

4 Grate the mozzarella cheese and sprinkle it evenly on the pizza. Bake on an oiled baking sheet for 15–20 minutes, until crisp and golden. Serve immediately.

> **Variation**
> *Other flavorful fresh mushrooms, such as chestnut, chanterelle or field mushrooms, could be used instead of the shiitake.*

Chicken Liver Kebabs

These may be broiled and served with rice and broccoli or grilled outdoors and served with salad and baked potatoes.

Serves 4

4 ounces bacon
12 ounces chicken
  livers, trimmed
12 large pitted prunes
12 cherry tomatoes
8 button mushrooms
2 tablespoons olive oil
mixed green salad, to serve

1 Cut each strip of bacon in half, wrap a piece around each chicken liver and secure in position with wooden toothpicks.

2 Wrap the pitted prunes around the cherry tomatoes.

3 Thread the bacon-wrapped livers onto metal skewers with the prune-wrapped tomatoes and the mushrooms. Brush with oil. Cook under a preheated broiler for 5 minutes on each side. Alternatively, cover the tomatoes and prunes with a strip of aluminum foil to protect them and cook on a hot grill for 5 minutes on each side.

4 Remove the toothpicks from the livers. Serve the kebabs immediately on warmed plates, accompanied by a mixed green salad.

Cook's Tip
Light the grill 30–45 minutes before you intend to cook. The coals will be at the right temperature when they are glowing and covered with a thin layer of grayish-white ash.

Chicken, Bacon & Corn Kebabs

Don't wait for warm weather to have kebabs. If you are serving them to children, remember to remove the skewers first.

Serves 4
2 ears corn
8 thick strips bacon
8 brown cap mushrooms, halved
2 small chicken breast fillets
2 tablespoons sunflower oil
1 tablespoon lemon juice
1 tablespoon maple syrup
salt and freshly ground
  black pepper
green salad, to serve

1 Cook the corn in boiling water until tender, then drain and cool. Stretch the bacon strips with the back of a heavy knife and cut each in half. Wrap a piece of bacon around each half mushroom.

2 Cut both the corn and chicken into eight equal pieces. Combine the oil, lemon juice, maple syrup and seasoning, and brush liberally on the chicken.

3 Thread the corn, bacon-wrapped mushrooms and chicken pieces alternately on metal skewers and brush all over with the lemon dressing.

4 Broil the kebabs under a preheated broiler for 8–10 minutes, turning them once and basting occasionally with any extra dressing. Serve hot with a crisp green salad.

Cook's Tip
Made from the sap of a North American tree, pure maple syrup is expensive, but its flavor is vastly superior to blended varieties.

Sweet-&-Sour Kebabs

This marinade contains sugar and will burn very easily, so grill the kebabs slowly, turning often. Serve with harlequin rice.

Serves 2
2 chicken breast fillets, skinned
8 pickling onions or 2 medium
  onions, peeled
4 strips bacon
3 firm bananas
1 red bell pepper, seeded and diced
flat-leaf parsley sprig, to garnish

For the marinade
2 tablespoons soft brown sugar
1 tablespoon Worcestershire
  sauce
2 tablespoons lemon juice
salt and freshly ground
  black pepper

1 To make the marinade, combine ingredients in a bowl. Cut each chicken breast into four pieces, add to the marinade, cover and refrigerate for at least 4 hours or preferably overnight.

2 Blanch the onions in boiling water for 5 minutes and drain. If using medium onions, quarter them after blanching.

3 Cut each strip of bacon in half. Peel the bananas and cut each into three pieces. Wrap a strip of bacon around each piece of banana.

4 Thread the bacon-wrapped banana pieces onto metal skewers with the chicken pieces, onions and pepper pieces. Brush with the marinade.

5 Grill over low coals or cook under a preheated broiler for 15 minutes, turning and basting frequently with the marinade. Garnish with parsley and serve.

Cook's Tip
Pour boiling water onto the small onions and then drain, to make peeling easier.

Citrus Kebabs

A piquant orange, lemon and mint marinade with a hint of cumin makes these kebabs special.

Serves 4
4 chicken breast fillets, skinned
fresh mint sprigs and orange,
  lemon or lime slices, to garnish
salad leaves, to serve

For the marinade
finely grated zest and juice of
  ½ orange
finely grated zest and juice of
  ½ small lemon or lime
2 tablespoons olive oil
2 tablespoons honey
2 tablespoons chopped fresh mint
¼ teaspoon ground cumin
salt and freshly ground
  black pepper

1 Cut the chicken into 1-inch cubes. To make the marinade, combine the ingredients in a bowl. Add the chicken cubes and let marinate for at least 2 hours.

2 Thread the chicken pieces onto metal skewers and grill over low coals or broil under a preheated broiler for 15 minutes, basting with the marinade and turning frequently.

3 Serve the kebabs on a bed of salad leaves, garnished with mint sprigs and orange, lemon or lime slices.

Harlequin Rice

This is a delicious and colorful accompaniment to kebabs.

Serves 4
2 tablespoons olive oil
generous 1 cup
  cooked rice
1 cup cooked peas
1 small red bell pepper, diced
salt and freshly ground
  black pepper

1 Heat the oil in a frying pan and add the rice, peas and diced red pepper.
2 Season to taste with salt and pepper. Stir until heated through, then serve immediately.

Chicken, Banana & Pineapple Kebabs

Here, fruit and a sweet-sharp marinade help keep the chicken wonderfully moist during cooking.

Serves 4
4 boned chicken thighs, skinned and cubed
½ small fresh pineapple
2 firm bananas
fresh orange segments and bay leaves, to garnish
cooked rice, to serve

For the marinade
3 tablespoons sunflower oil
1 tablespoon honey
1 teaspoon whole-grain mustard
1 teaspoon crushed coriander seeds
grated zest and juice of 1 orange
4 cardamom pods

1 To make the marinade, combine the oil, honey, mustard, coriander seeds and orange zest and juice in a shallow dish. Crush the cardamom pods and stir in the seeds.

2 Add the prepared chicken cubes to the dish and turn to coat them all over with the marinade. Then cover the dish and let marinate in the refrigerator for at least 2 hours.

3 Just before cooking, core the pineapple and cut it into neat wedges, leaving the skin on. Peel and slice the bananas. Add the pineapple wedges and banana slices to the marinade and turn them over to coat them thoroughly.

4 Drain the chicken, pineapple and banana, reserving the marinade. Thread alternately onto eight metal skewers.

5 Broil the kebabs on a rack under a preheated broiler, turning occasionally and brushing them with the reserved marinade, for about 15 minutes, until the chicken is golden and cooked through. Serve the kebabs on a bed of rice, garnished with fresh orange segments and bay leaves.

Chicken with Herb & Ricotta Stuffing

These little chicken drumsticks are full of flavor, and the stuffing and bacon help to keep them moist and tender.

Serves 4
¼ cup ricotta cheese
1 garlic clove, crushed
3 tablespoons mixed chopped fresh herbs, e.g. chives, flat-leaf parsley and mint
2 tablespoons fresh brown bread crumbs
8 chicken drumsticks
8 strips bacon
1 teaspoon whole-grain mustard
1 tablespoon sunflower oil
salt and freshly ground black pepper

1 Combine the ricotta cheese, garlic, herbs and bread crumbs. Season well with salt and pepper.

2 Carefully loosen the skin of each drumstick and spoon a little of the herb stuffing underneath, smoothing the skin back over firmly, but gently.

3 Wrap a strip of bacon around the wide end of each drumstick, to hold the skin in place over the stuffing while it is cooking.

4 Combine the mustard and oil, and brush on the chicken. Cook on a medium-hot grill, or under a preheated broiler, for about 25 minutes, turning occasionally, until the juices run clear and not pink when the flesh is pierced with the point of a knife. Serve immediately.

Cook's Tip
Ricotta is a creamy white cheese from Italy, widely available at supermarkets.

Broiled Poussins with Citrus Glaze

This recipe is suitable for many kinds of small birds, including squabs and partridges, provided they are young and tender.

Serves 4
2 poussins, about 1½ pounds each
¼ cup butter, softened
2 tablespoons olive oil
2 garlic cloves, crushed
½ teaspoon dried thyme
¼ teaspoon cayenne pepper
grated zest and juice of 1 lemon
grated zest and juice of 1 lime
2 tablespoons honey
salt and freshly ground
   black pepper
fresh dill, to garnish
tomato salad, to serve

1 Using kitchen scissors or poultry shears, cut along both sides of the backbone of each bird; remove and discard. Cut the birds in half along the breast bone, then use a rolling pin to flatten them.

2 Beat the butter in a small bowl, then beat in 1 tablespoon of the olive oil, the garlic, thyme, cayenne, salt and pepper, half the lemon and lime zest and 1 tablespoon each of the lemon and lime juice.

3 Using your fingertips, carefully loosen the skin of each poussin breast. Using a round-bladed knife, spread the butter mixture evenly between the skin and breast meat.

4 Preheat the broiler and line a broiler pan with aluminum foil. In a small bowl, combine the remaining olive oil, lemon and lime juices, zest and the honey. Place the bird halves, skin-side up, in the broiler pan and brush with the juice mixture.

5 Broil for 10–12 minutes, basting once or twice with the juices. Turn over and broil for 7–10 minutes, basting once, or until the juices run clear when the thigh is pierced with a knife. Serve with tomato salad, garnished with dill.

Grilled Spatchcocked Poussins

These little, herb-marinated chickens can be cooked under the broiler, but taste best if they are grilled over charcoal.

Serves 4
2 large or 4 small poussins
fresh herbs, to garnish
mixed salad leaves, to serve

For the marinade
⅔ cup olive oil
1 onion, grated
1 garlic clove, crushed
1 tablespoon chopped fresh mint
1 tablespoon chopped fresh
   flat-leaf parsley
1 tablespoon chopped cilantro
1–2 teaspoons ground cumin
1 teaspoon paprika
pinch of cayenne pepper

1 Tuck the wings of each poussin under the body and remove the wishbone. Turn the birds over and cut along each side of the backbone using kitchen scissors or poultry shears, then remove and discard.

2 Push down on each bird to break the breast bone. Keeping the bird flat, push a skewer through the wings and breast. Push another skewer through the thighs.

3 To make the marinade, blend together all the ingredients in a bowl. Spread the marinade on both sides of the poussins. Place in a large, shallow dish, cover with plastic wrap and marinate for at least 4 hours or overnight.

4 Prepare a grill or preheat the broiler. Cook the poussins for 25–35 minutes, turning occasionally and brushing with the marinade. If broiling, cook under a medium broiler about 3 inches from heat, for 25–35 minutes or until cooked through, turning and basting occasionally.

5 When the birds are cooked, cut them in half. Garnish with herbs and serve immediately with salad leaves.

Chicken Wings Teriyaki-style

This simple, Asian glaze can be used with any cut of chicken or with fish.

Serves 4

1 garlic clove, crushed
3 tablespoons soy sauce
2 tablespoons dry sherry
2 teaspoons honey
2 teaspoons grated fresh
  ginger root
1 teaspoon sesame oil
12 chicken wings
1 tablespoon sesame
  seeds, toasted

1 Place the garlic, soy sauce, sherry, honey, ginger and sesame oil in a large bowl and beat with a fork to mix evenly. Add the chicken wings and toss thoroughly to coat in the marinade. Cover and let sit in the refrigerator for 30 minutes or longer.

2 Cook the wings on a fairly hot grill for 20–25 minutes, turning occasionally and brushing with the remaining marinade. Sprinkle with the toasted sesame seeds and serve hot.

Sticky Ginger Chicken

A quick, tasty way of cooking chicken drumsticks.

Serves 4

2 tablespoons lemon juice
2 tablespoons light brown sugar
1 teaspoon grated fresh
  ginger root
2 teaspoons soy sauce
8 chicken drumsticks, skinned
freshly ground black pepper

1 Combine the juice, sugar, ginger, soy sauce and pepper. Slash the chicken drumsticks, then toss the chicken in the glaze.

2 Cook under a hot broiler, turning occasionally and brushing with the glaze, until the chicken is golden and the juices run clear, not pink, when it is pierced.

Spanish Chicken

A colorful, one-pot dish, ideal for a weekday supper when you are craving something a little unusual.

Serves 8

2 tablespoons all-purpose flour
2 teaspoons ground paprika
1/2 teaspoon salt
16 chicken drumsticks
1/4 cup olive oil
5 cups Chicken Stock
1 onion, finely chopped
2 garlic cloves, crushed
2 1/4 cups long-grain rice
2 bay leaves
1 1/2 cups diced cooked ham
1 cup pimento-stuffed green olives
1 green bell pepper, seeded
  and diced
2 14-ounce cans chopped
  tomatoes, with their juice
fresh flat-leaf parsley, to garnish

1 Preheat the oven to 350°F. Shake together the flour, paprika and salt in a plastic bag, add the chicken drumsticks and toss to coat.

2 Heat the oil in a large frying pan and, working in batches, brown the chicken slowly on both sides. Remove from the pan, drain on paper towels and keep warm.

3 Meanwhile, in a large saucepan, bring the stock to a boil and add the onion, garlic, rice and bay leaves. Lower the heat and simmer for 10 minutes.

4 Remove the pan from heat and add the ham, olives, green pepper and canned tomatoes with their juice. Transfer to a shallow, ovenproof dish.

5 Arrange the chicken on top, cover and bake for 30–40 minutes or until the chicken and rice are tender. Add a little more stock during the cooking time if necessary to prevent the dish from drying out.

6 Remove and discard the bay leaves. Taste and adjust the seasoning as necessary. Serve the drumsticks on top of the rice, garnished with flat-leaf parsley.

Crispy Chicken with Garlicky Rice

Chicken wings cooked until they are really tender have a surprising amount of meat on them, and make a very economical supper for a crowd of youngsters. Provide lots of paper towels or napkins for sticky fingers.

Serves 4
1 large onion, chopped
2 garlic cloves, crushed
2 tablespoons sunflower oil
scant 1 cup patna or basmati rice
1½ cups hot Chicken Stock
2 teaspoons finely grated lemon zest
2 tablespoons chopped fresh mixed herbs
8–12 chicken wings
½ cup all-purpose flour
salt and freshly ground black pepper
Fresh Tomato Sauce, to serve

1 Preheat the oven to 400°F. Sauté the onion and garlic in the oil in a large, ovenproof casserole until golden. Add the rice and toss until well coated in oil.

2 Stir in the stock, lemon zest and herbs, and bring to a boil. Cover and cook in the middle of the oven for 40–50 minutes. Stir the rice once or twice during cooking.

3 Meanwhile, dry the chicken wings with paper towels. Season the flour with salt and pepper, and use to coat the wings thoroughly, dusting off any excess.

4 Place the chicken wings in a small roasting pan and cook in the top of the oven for 30–40 minutes, turning once, until crisp and golden brown all over.

5 Serve the rice and the chicken wings together with fresh tomato sauce.

Jambalaya

A popular Southern classic, this is a wonderful mix of flavors. Everything is cooked together in the same pan, so you have less clean-up time after you enjoy a great meal.

Serves 6
2 tablespoons vegetable oil
4 chicken breast fillets, skinned and cut into chunks
1 pound cooked spicy sausage, sliced
1 cup cubed smoked ham
1 large onion, chopped
2 celery stalks, chopped
2 green bell peppers, seeded and chopped
3 garlic cloves, crushed
1 cup canned chopped tomatoes
2 cups Chicken Stock
1 teaspoon cayenne pepper
1 fresh thyme sprig, chopped, or ¼ teaspoon dried thyme
2 flat-leaf parsley sprigs
1 bay leaf
1⅔ cups rice
salt and freshly ground black pepper
4 scallions, finely chopped

1 Heat the oil in a large, heavy frying pan. Add the chicken chunks and sausage slices, and cook for about 5 minutes, until well browned. Stir in the ham cubes and cook for 5 more minutes.

2 Add the onion, celery, peppers, crushed garlic, tomatoes, chicken stock, cayenne pepper, fresh or dried thyme, parsley and bay leaf to the frying pan. Bring to a boil, stirring constantly.

3 Stir in the rice, and salt and pepper to taste. When the liquid returns to a boil, reduce the heat and cover the pan tightly. Simmer for 10 minutes.

4 Remove the pan from heat and, without removing the lid, set aside for 20 minutes to let the rice finish cooking.

5 Discard the bay leaf. Sprinkle the chopped scallions on top of the jambalaya just before serving.

Yogurt Chicken & Rice

An unusual Middle Eastern dish in which marinated chicken is layered between flavored and plain rice.

Serves 6
3 tablespoons butter
3–3½-pound chicken
1 large onion, chopped
1 cup Chicken Stock
2 eggs
2 cups plain yogurt
2–3 saffron threads, dissolved in 1 tablespoon boiling water
1 teaspoon ground cinnamon
2¼ cups basmati rice
3 ounces zereshk or dried cranberries
salt and freshly ground black pepper
herb salad, to serve

1 Melt 2 tablespoons of the butter, and cook the chicken and onion for 4–5 minutes, until the onion is softened and the chicken browned. Add the stock, salt and pepper, and bring to a boil. Reduce the heat and simmer for about 45 minutes or until the chicken is cooked and the stock reduced by half.

2 Skin and bone the chicken. Cut the flesh into large pieces and place in a large bowl. Reserve the stock.

3 In a bowl, beat the eggs and blend with the yogurt. Add the saffron water and cinnamon, and season with salt and pepper. Pour onto the chicken and let marinate for up to 2 hours.

4 Cook the rice in a large saucepan of boiling salted water for 5 minutes, then reduce the heat and simmer very gently for 10 minutes, until half cooked. Drain, rinse in lukewarm water and drain again.

5 Transfer the chicken from the yogurt mixture to another bowl and mix half the rice into the yogurt mixture.

6 Preheat the oven to 325°F and grease a large 4-inch deep ovenproof dish.

7 Place the rice and yogurt mixture in the bottom of the dish, arrange the chicken pieces in a layer on top and then add the plain rice. Sprinkle with the zereshk or cranberries.

8 Mix the remaining butter with the reserved chicken stock and pour over the rice. Cover tightly with aluminum foil and bake for 35–45 minutes.

9 Let the dish cool for a few minutes. Place on a cold, damp cloth, which will help lift the rice from the bottom of the dish, then run a knife around the edges of the dish. Place a large flat plate over the dish, invert and turn out. You should have a rice "cake" that can be cut into wedges. Serve hot with an herb salad.

> **Cook's Tip**
> Zereshk is a small sour berry that grows on trees by the water in the warmer part of Iran. It is traditionally served with Persian rice dishes.

Risotto with Chicken

Smooth, mild and almost creamy—few dishes can equal a good risotto when it is made with the best ingredients in the traditional Italian way.

Serves 4
2 tablespoons olive oil
8 ounces chicken breast fillet, skinned and cut into 1-inch cubes
1 onion, finely chopped
1 garlic clove, finely chopped
¼ teaspoon saffron threads, soaked in a little hot water
2 ounces prosciutto, cut into thin strips
2¼ cups risotto rice, preferably arborio
½ cup dry white wine
7½ cups simmering chicken stock
2 tablespoons butter (optional)
⅓ cup grated Parmesan cheese, plus extra to serve
salt and freshly ground black pepper
fresh flat-leaf parsley, to garnish

1 Heat the oil in a wide, heavy pan over medium-high heat. Add the chicken cubes and cook, stirring, until they start to turn white.

2 Reduce the heat to low and add the finely chopped onion, garlic, saffron and its soaking water and prosciutto. Cook, stirring, until the onion is soft. Stir in the rice. Sauté for 1–2 minutes, stirring constantly.

3 Add the wine and bring to a boil. Simmer gently until almost all the wine is absorbed.

4 Add the simmering stock, a ladleful at a time, and cook, stirring continuously, until the rice is just tender and the risotto creamy. Let each ladleful of stock be almost completely absorbed before you add the next.

5 Add the butter, if using, and Parmesan cheese, and stir in well. Season with salt and pepper to taste. Serve the risotto hot, sprinkled with a little more Parmesan and garnished with flat-leaf parsley.

Seville Chicken

This Spanish dish incorporates oranges and almonds, favorite ingredients in Seville, where the orange and almond trees are a familiar and wonderful sight.

Serves 4

1 orange
all-purpose flour, for dusting
8 chicken thighs
3 tablespoons olive oil
1 large Spanish onion,
   roughly chopped
2 garlic cloves, crushed

1 red bell pepper, seeded
   and sliced
1 yellow bell pepper, seeded
   and sliced
4 ounces chorizo sausage, sliced
½ cup sliced almonds
generous 1 cup brown
   basmati rice
2½ cups Chicken Stock
14-ounce can chopped tomatoes
¾ cup white wine
generous pinch of dried thyme
salt and freshly ground
   black pepper
fresh thyme sprigs, to garnish

1 Pare a thin strip of zest from the orange and set it aside. Peel the orange, then cut it into segments, working over a bowl to catch the juice.

2 Place some flour in a plastic bag and season with salt and pepper. Put the chicken thighs into the bag and shake to coat well. Dust off any excess.

3 Heat the oil in a large frying pan and fry the chicken pieces on both sides until nicely browned. Transfer to a plate. Add the onion and garlic to the pan and sauté for 4–5 minutes, until the onion begins to brown. Add the red and yellow peppers, and cook, stirring occasionally, until slightly softened.

4 Add the chorizo, stir-fry for a few minutes, then add the almonds and rice. Cook, stirring, for 1–2 minutes.

5 Pour in the chicken stock, tomatoes and wine, and add the reserved strip of orange zest and the thyme. Season well. Bring to the simmering point, stirring, then return the chicken pieces to the pan.

6 Cover tightly and cook over very low heat for 1–1¼ hours until the rice and chicken are tender. Just before serving, add the orange segments and let heat through briefly. Garnish with fresh thyme and serve.

Cook's Tip
Cooking times for this dish will depend largely on the heat. If the rice seems to be drying out too quickly, add a little more stock or wine and reduce the heat. If, after 40 minutes or so, the rice is still barely cooked, increase the heat a little. Make sure the rice is kept below the liquid (the chicken can lie on the surface) and stir occasionally if it seems to be cooking unevenly.

Chicken Pilaf

The French marmite pot is ideal for this recipe. The tall sides slant inward, reducing evaporation and ensuring that the rice cooks slowly without becoming dry.

Serves 3–4

15–20 dried chanterelle
   mushrooms
1–2 tablespoons olive oil
1 tablespoon butter

4 thin strips bacon, chopped
3 chicken breast fillets, skinned
   and cut into thin slices
4 scallions, sliced
generous 1 cup basmati rice
scant 2 cups hot Chicken Stock
salt and freshly ground
   black pepper

1 Preheat the oven to 350°F. Soak the mushrooms for 10 minutes in warm water. Drain, reserving the liquid. Slice the mushrooms, discarding the stems.

2 Heat the olive oil and butter in a frying pan. Fry the bacon for 2–3 minutes. Add the chicken and stir-fry until the pieces are golden brown all over. Transfer the chicken and bacon mixture to a bowl using a slotted spoon.

3 Briefly sauté the mushrooms and scallions in the fat remaining in the pan, then add them to the chicken pieces.

4 Add the rice to the pan, with a little more olive oil if necessary. Stir-fry for 2–3 minutes. Spoon the rice into an earthenware pot or casserole.

5 Pour the hot chicken stock and reserved mushroom liquid over the rice in the pot or casserole. Stir in the reserved chicken and mushroom mixture, and season.

6 Cover with a double piece of aluminum foil and secure with a lid. Cook the pilaf in the oven for 30–35 minutes, until the rice is tender. Serve hot.

Caribbean Peanut Chicken

Peanut butter adds a richness to this dish, as well as a delicious depth of flavor all of its own.

Serves 4
4 boneless chicken breast fillets, skinned and cut into thin strips
generous 1 cup white long-grain rice
1 tablespoon butter, plus extra for greasing
2 tablespoons peanut oil
1 onion, finely chopped
2 tomatoes, peeled, seeded and chopped
1 fresh green chile, seeded and sliced

¼ cup smooth peanut butter
scant 2 cups Chicken Stock
lemon juice, to taste
salt and freshly ground black pepper
lime wedges and fresh flat-leaf parsley sprigs, to garnish

For the marinade
1 tablespoon sunflower oil
1–2 garlic cloves, crushed
1 teaspoon chopped fresh thyme
5 teaspoons medium curry powder
juice of ½ lemon

1 To make the marinade, combine all the ingredients in a large bowl. Stir in the chicken and cover loosely with plastic wrap. Set aside in a cool place for 2–3 hours.

2 Meanwhile, cook the rice in a large saucepan of boiling salted water until tender. Drain well and transfer to a generously buttered casserole.

3 Preheat the oven to 350°F. Heat 1 tablespoon of the oil and the butter in a flameproof casserole, and cook the chicken pieces for 4–5 minutes, until evenly browned. Add more oil if necessary.

4 Transfer the chicken to a plate. Add the onion to the flameproof casserole and sauté for 5–6 minutes, until lightly browned, adding more oil if necessary. Stir in the chopped tomatoes and chile. Cook over low heat for 3–4 minutes, stirring occasionally. Remove from heat.

5 Mix the peanut butter with the chicken stock. Stir into the tomato and onion mixture, then return the chicken. Add the lemon juice and seasoning to taste, and spoon the mixture onto the rice in the other casserole.

6 Cover and bake for 15–20 minutes or until piping hot. Use a large spoon to toss the rice with the chicken mixture. Serve immediately, garnished with lime wedges and fresh parsley sprigs.

Cook's Tip
If the casserole is not large enough to let you toss the rice with the chicken mixture before serving, invert a large, deep plate over the casserole, turn both over and toss the mixture on the plate.

Joloff Chicken & Rice

A famous West African dish.

Serves 4
2¼-pound chicken, cut into 4–6 pieces
2 garlic cloves, crushed
1 teaspoon dried thyme
2 tablespoons vegetable oil
14-ounce can chopped tomatoes
1 tablespoon tomato paste

1 onion, chopped
scant 2 cups Chicken Stock or water
2 tablespoons dried shrimp, ground
1 fresh green chile, seeded and finely chopped
1¾ cups long-grain rice

1 Rub the chicken with the garlic and thyme, and set aside. Heat the oil in a large saucepan until cloudy and then add the chopped tomatoes, tomato paste and onion. Cook over medium-high heat for about 15 minutes, until the tomatoes are well reduced, stirring frequently.

2 Reduce the heat a little, add the chicken pieces and stir well to coat. Cook for 10 minutes, stirring, then add the stock or water, the ground dried shrimp and the chile. Bring to a boil and simmer for 5 minutes, stirring occasionally.

3 Put the rice in a separate saucepan. Scoop 1¼ cups of the sauce into a measuring cup, dilute to a scant 2 cups and stir into the rice. Cook, covered, until the liquid is absorbed, place a piece of aluminum foil on top of the rice, cover the pan with a lid and cook over low heat for 20 minutes, until the rice is cooked; add more water if necessary.

4 Transfer the chicken pieces to a warmed serving plate. Simmer the sauce until reduced by half. Pour onto the chicken and serve with the rice.

Cook's Tip
Dried shrimp are available at specialty African, Caribbean and Asian food stores

Chicken & Vegetable Tagine

This lightly spiced Moroccan stew is traditionally served with couscous, but rice alone makes an equally delicious accompaniment if couscous is not available.

Serves 4

2 tablespoons peanut oil
4 chicken breast fillets, skinned
   and cut into large pieces
I large onion, chopped
2 garlic cloves, crushed
I small parsnip, cut into
   I-inch pieces
I small turnip, cut into
   ³/₄-inch pieces
3 carrots, cut into
   I¹/₂-inch pieces
4 tomatoes, chopped
I cinnamon stick
4 cloves
I teaspoon ground ginger
I bay leaf

¹/₄–¹/₂ teaspoon cayenne pepper
I¹/₂ cups Chicken Stock
14-ounce can chickpeas, drained
I red bell pepper,
   seeded and sliced
5 ounces green beans, halved
I piece preserved lemon peel,
   thinly sliced
20–30 pitted brown or
   green olives
salt

For the rice and couscous

3 cups Chicken Stock
generous I cup long-grain rice
²/₃ cup couscous
3 tablespoons chopped cilantro

I Heat half of the oil in a large, flameproof casserole and cook the chicken pieces for a few minutes until evenly browned. Transfer to a plate.

2 Heat the remaining oil and cook the onion, garlic, parsnip, turnip and carrots together over medium heat for 4–5 minutes, until the vegetables are lightly flecked with brown, stirring frequently. Lower the heat, cover and sweat the vegetables for 5 more minutes, stirring occasionally.

3 Add the tomatoes, cook for a few minutes, then add the cinnamon stick, cloves, ginger, bay leaf and cayenne. Cook for 1–2 minutes. Pour in the chicken stock and add the chickpeas. Return the browned chicken pieces to the casserole and season with salt. Cover and simmer for 25 minutes.

4 Meanwhile, to make the rice and couscous accompaniment, bring the chicken stock to a boil in a large saucepan. Add the rice and simmer for about 5 minutes, until almost tender. Remove the pan from heat, stir in the couscous, cover tightly and set aside for about 5 minutes.

5 When the vegetables in the tagine are almost tender, stir in the red pepper slices and green beans, and simmer for 10 minutes. Add the preserved lemon peel and olives, stir well and cook for 5 more minutes or until the vegetables are perfectly tender.

6 Stir the chopped cilantro into the rice and couscous mixture, and pile it onto a plate. Serve the chicken tagine in the traditional dish, if you have one, or in the casserole.

Chicken Paella

There are many variations on this basic recipe. Any seasonal vegetables can be added, as can mussels and other seafood. Serve straight from the pan.

Serves 4

4 chicken legs (thighs
   and drumsticks)
¹/₄ cup olive oil
I large onion, finely chopped
I garlic clove, crushed

I teaspoon ground turmeric
4 ounces chorizo sausage
generous I cup long-grain rice
2¹/₂ cups Chicken Stock
4 tomatoes, peeled, seeded
   and chopped
I red bell pepper,
   seeded and sliced
I cup frozen peas
salt and freshly ground
   black pepper

I Preheat the oven to 350°F. Cut the chicken legs in half through the joint.

2 Heat the oil in a 12-inch paella pan or large, flameproof casserole and brown the chicken pieces on both sides. Add the onion and garlic, and stir in the turmeric. Cook for 2 minutes.

3 Slice the sausage and add to the pan, with the rice and stock. Bring to a boil and season to taste. Cover and bake for 15 minutes.

4 Remove the pan from the oven and add the chopped tomatoes, sliced red pepper and frozen peas. Return to the oven and cook for another 10–15 minutes or until the chicken is tender and the rice has absorbed the stock. Serve hot.

Cook's Tip
There are many varieties of chorizo, a well-known Spanish sausage. They are all made from pork and incorporate paprika, which gives them their typical coloring. They are all quite spicy, and some are very hot.

Chicken Stroganov

This is based on the classic Russian dish, usually made with fillet of beef. Serve with rice to which chopped celery, scallions and parsley have been added.

Serves 4

4 chicken breast fillets, skinned
3 tablespoons olive oil
1 large onion, thinly sliced
3 cups mushrooms, sliced
1¼ cups sour cream
salt and freshly ground
    black pepper
1 tablespoon chopped fresh
    parsley, to garnish
cooked rice, chopped celery,
    scallions and parsley,
    to serve

1 Divide each chicken breast into two natural fillets, place between two sheets of plastic wrap and flatten each to a thickness of ¼ inch with a rolling pin. Slice on the diagonal into 1-inch strips.

2 Heat 2 tablespoons of the oil in a large frying pan and cook the onion slowly until soft but not colored.

3 Add the mushrooms and cook until golden brown. Remove the vegetables from the pan and keep warm.

4 Increase the heat, add the remaining oil to the pan and cook the chicken very quickly, in small batches, for 3–4 minutes, until lightly colored. Remove each batch and keep warm while cooking the rest of the chicken.

5 Return all the chicken, onion and mushrooms to the pan, and season with salt and pepper to taste. Stir in the sour cream and bring to a boil. Sprinkle with chopped parsley and serve immediately.

Cook's Tip
If sour cream is not available, fresh heavy cream may be used, "soured" with the juice of ½ lemon.

Chicken Piri-piri

A classic Portuguese dish based on a hot sauce made from Angolan chiles, this is popular wherever there are Portuguese communities, and is often served in southern Africa.

Serves 4

4 chicken breasts
2–3 tablespoons olive oil
1 large onion, finely sliced
2 carrots, cut into thin strips
1 large or 2 small parsnip(s), cut
    into thin strips
1 red bell pepper, seeded
    and sliced
1 yellow bell pepper, seeded
    and sliced
4 cups Chicken Stock
3 tomatoes, peeled, seeded
    and chopped
generous dash of piri-piri sauce
1 tablespoon tomato paste
½ cinnamon stick
1 fresh thyme sprig, plus extra
    to garnish
1 bay leaf
1½ cups white long-grain rice
1 tablespoon lime or lemon juice
salt and freshly ground
    black pepper

1 Preheat the oven to 350°F. Rub the chicken skin with a little salt and pepper. Heat 2 tablespoons of the oil in a large frying pan and brown the chicken portions on all sides. Transfer to a plate.

2 Add some more oil to the pan, if necessary, and sauté the onion for 2–3 minutes, until slightly softened. Add the carrots, parsnip(s) and red and yellow peppers, stir-fry for a few minutes, then cover and sweat for 4–5 minutes, until quite soft.

3 Pour in the chicken stock and add the tomatoes, piri-piri sauce, tomato paste and cinnamon stick. Stir in the thyme and bay leaf. Season to taste and bring to a boil. Using a ladle, spoon off 1¼ cups of the liquid and set aside in a small pan.

4 Put the rice in the bottom of a casserole. Using a slotted spoon, scoop the vegetables out of the frying pan and spread them on the rice. Arrange the chicken pieces on top. Pour on the spicy chicken stock from the frying pan, cover the casserole tightly and bake for about 45 minutes, until both the rice and chicken are completely tender.

5 Meanwhile, heat the reserved chicken stock, adding a few more drops of piri-piri sauce and the lime or lemon juice.

6 To serve, spoon the chicken and rice onto warmed serving plates and garnish with thyme. Serve the sauce separately or poured over the chicken.

Cook's Tip
Piri-piri sauce can be obtained at specialty food stores, or use Tabasco sauce as an alternative.

Chicken Korma with Saffron Rice

Mild and fragrant, this dish is, quite understandably, an old favorite.

Serves 4

¾ cup sliced almonds
1 tablespoon ghee or butter
about 1 tablespoon sunflower oil
1½ pounds chicken breast fillet, skinned and cut into bite-size pieces
1 onion, chopped
4 green cardamom pods
2 garlic cloves, crushed
2 teaspoons ground cumin
1 teaspoon ground coriander
1 cinnamon stick
good pinch of chili powder
1¼ cups canned coconut milk
¾ cup Chicken Stock

1 teaspoon tomato paste (optional)
5 tablespoons light cream
1–2 tablespoon fresh lime or lemon juice
2 teaspoons grated lime or lemon zest
1 teaspoon garam masala
salt and freshly ground black pepper

For the saffron rice
1½ cups basmati rice
3 cups Chicken Stock
generous pinch of saffron threads, crushed, then soaked in hot water

1 Dry-fry the sliced almonds in a small frying pan until pale golden. Transfer about two thirds of the almonds to a plate and continue to dry-fry the remainder until they are slightly deeper in color. Transfer the darker almonds to a separate plate and set them aside for the garnish. Let the paler almonds cool, then grind them in a spice mill or coffee grinder.

2 Heat the ghee or butter and oil in a wok or large frying pan and fry the chicken pieces, in batches if necessary, until evenly browned. Transfer to a plate.

3 Add a little more oil to the pan if necessary and sauté the onion for 2 minutes, then stir in the cardamom pods and garlic, and sauté for 3–4 more minutes, until the onion is lightly flecked with brown. Stir in the ground almonds, the cumin, coriander, cinnamon stick and chili powder, and cook for 1 minute. Stir in the coconut milk, chicken stock and tomato paste, if using.

4 Bring to the simmering point, then return the chicken to the pan and season. Cover and cook over low heat for 10 minutes, until the chicken is tender. Set aside, covered.

5 Place the rice in a saucepan with the stock and saffron water. Bring to a boil over medium heat, then cover tightly and cook over low heat for 10 minutes or according to the instructions on the package, until the rice is just tender.

6 Just before the rice is ready, reheat the korma until it is simmering gently. Stir in the cream, the citrus juice and zest, and the garam masala. Taste and season as necessary. Pile the rice into a warmed serving dish and spoon the korma into a separate dish. Garnish with the reserved browned almonds. Serve immediately.

Chicken & Bean Risotto

Brown rice, red kidney beans, corn and broccoli make this a filling and nutritious meal-in-a-pot using only a small amount of chicken.

Serves 4–6

1 onion, chopped
2 garlic cloves, crushed
1 fresh red chile, seeded and finely chopped
2½ cups mushrooms, sliced
2 celery stalks, chopped
generous 1 cup long-grain brown rice
scant 2 cups Chicken Stock

⅔ cup white wine
14-ounce can red kidney beans
8 ounces chicken breast fillet, skinned and diced
7-ounce can corn kernels
¾ cup golden raisins
6 ounces small broccoli florets
2–3 tablespoons chopped fresh mixed herbs
salt and freshly ground black pepper

1 Put the onion, garlic, chile, mushrooms, celery, rice, stock and wine in a saucepan. Cover, bring to a boil, lower the heat and simmer for 15 minutes.

2 Rinse and drain the kidney beans. Stir the chicken, kidney beans, corn and golden raisins into the pan. Cook for another 20 minutes, until almost all the liquid has been absorbed.

3 Cook the broccoli in a separate saucepan of boiling salted water for 5 minutes, then drain.

4 Stir the broccoli and chopped herbs into the risotto, season to taste and serve immediately.

Variation
Replace the kidney beans with another type of canned beans, such as black-eyed peas or cannellini.

Chicken in Cashew Sauce

This chicken dish has a deliciously thick and nutty sauce, and it is best served with plain boiled rice.

Serves 4
2 medium onions
2 tablespoons tomato paste
$\frac{1}{2}$ cup cashews
$1\frac{1}{2}$ teaspoons garam masala
1 teaspoon crushed garlic
1 teaspoon chili powder
1 tablespoon lemon juice
$\frac{1}{4}$ teaspoon ground turmeric
1 teaspoon salt
1 tablespoon plain low-fat yogurt
1 tablespoon corn oil
2 tablespoons chopped cilantro
1 tablespoon golden raisins
1 pound skinless boneless
   chicken, cubed
$2\frac{1}{2}$ cups button mushrooms
$1\frac{1}{4}$ cups water

1 Cut the onions into quarters, place in a food processor or blender and process for about 1 minute.

2 Add the tomato paste, cashews, garam masala, garlic, chili powder, lemon juice, turmeric, salt and yogurt to the onions. Process for another 1–1$\frac{1}{2}$ minutes.

3 In a heavy saucepan, heat the oil, lower the heat to medium and pour in the spice mixture from the food processor. Fry for about 2 minutes, lowering the heat if necessary.

4 Add half the chopped cilantro, the golden raisins and chicken, and continue to stir-fry for another 1 minute.

5 Add the mushrooms, pour in the water and bring to a simmer. Cover the saucepan and cook over low heat for about 10 minutes.

6 After this time, check to see that the chicken is cooked through and the sauce is thick. Cook for a little longer if necessary. Serve, garnished with the remaining chopped cilantro.

Fragrant Chicken Curry

In this dish, the mildly spiced sauce is thickened using lentils rather than the traditional onions fried in ghee.

Serves 4
$\frac{1}{3}$ cup red lentils
2 tablespoons mild curry powder
2 teaspoons ground coriander
1 teaspoon cumin seeds
2 cups vegetable stock
8 chicken thighs, skinned
8 ounces fresh spinach, shredded
   or frozen spinach, thawed and
   well drained
1 tablespoon chopped cilantro
salt and freshly ground
   black pepper
cilantro, to garnish
boiled white or brown basmati
   rice and poppadums,
   to serve

1 Rinse the lentils under cold running water. Put into a large, heavy saucepan with the curry powder, ground coriander, cumin seeds and stock.

2 Bring to a boil, then lower the heat. Cover and simmer gently for 10 minutes.

3 Add the chicken and spinach to the lentils. Re-cover and simmer gently for another 40 minutes or until the chicken has cooked.

4 Stir in the chopped cilantro and season to taste. Serve, garnished with cilantro sprigs, accompanied by rice and poppadums.

Chicken in Green Almond Sauce

The sauce in this Mexican dish, deliciously thickened with ground almonds, is given its beautiful color by cilantro, green bell pepper and tomatillos.

Serves 6

3–3½-pound chicken, cut into
    serving portions
2 cups Chicken Stock
1 onion, chopped
1 garlic clove, chopped

2 cups cilantro, coarsely chopped
1 green bell pepper, seeded
    and chopped
1 jalapeño chile, seeded
    and chopped
10-ounce can tomatillos
1 cup ground almonds
2 tablespoons corn oil
salt
cilantro, to garnish
cooked rice, to serve

1 Put the chicken into a flameproof casserole or pan. Pour in the stock, bring to a simmer, cover and cook for 45 minutes until tender. Drain the stock into a measuring cup and set aside.

2 Put the onion, garlic, cilantro, green pepper, chile, tomatillos with their juice and the almonds in a food processor. Purée fairly coarsely.

3 Heat the oil in a frying pan, add the almond mixture and cook over low heat, stirring, for 3–4 minutes. Scrape the mixture into the casserole or pan with the chicken.

4 Add water to the stock to make 2 cups (if necessary). Stir it into the casserole or pan. Mix gently and simmer just long enough to blend the flavors and heat the chicken pieces through. Add salt to taste. Serve immediately, garnished with cilantro and accompanied by rice.

> **Cook's Tip**
> If the color of the sauce seems a little pale, add 2–3 outer leaves of dark green Romaine lettuce. Cut out the central veins, chop the leaves and add to the food processor.

Moroccan Chicken Couscous

This spicy chicken dish is served on a fragrant bed of couscous.

Serves 4
For the chicken
1 tablespoon butter
1 tablespoon sunflower oil
4 chicken portions
2 onions, finely chopped
2 garlic cloves, crushed
½ teaspoon ground cinnamon
¼ teaspoon ground ginger
¼ teaspoon ground turmeric
2 tablespoons orange juice
2 teaspoons honey

salt
fresh mint sprigs, to garnish

For the couscous
2 cups couscous
2 teaspoons sugar
2 tablespoons sunflower oil
½ teaspoon ground cinnamon
pinch of grated nutmeg
1 tablespoon orange
    blossom water
2 tablespoons golden raisins
½ cup chopped blanched
    almonds
3 tablespoons chopped
    pistachios

1 Heat the butter and oil in a large pan and add the chicken portions, skin-side down. Fry for 3–4 minutes, until the skin is golden, then turn over. Add the onions, garlic, spices and a pinch of salt. Pour in the orange juice and 1¼ cups water. Cover and bring to a boil, then reduce the heat and simmer for about 30 minutes.

2 Meanwhile, place the couscous with 1 teaspoon salt in a bowl and cover with 1½ cups water. Stir once and let stand for 5 minutes. Stir in the sugar, 1 tablespoon of the oil, the cinnamon, nutmeg, orange blossom water and golden raisins.

3 Heat the remaining oil in a pan and lightly fry the almonds until golden. Stir into the couscous with the pistachios. Line a steamer with waxed paper and spoon in the couscous. Steam over the chicken for 10 minutes.

4 Remove the steamer. Stir the honey into the chicken liquid and boil for 3–4 minutes. Spoon the couscous onto a warmed serving platter. Top with the chicken and sauce. Garnish and serve.

Chicken & Rice Omelet

These quickly cooked omelets are a favorite with children, topped with ketchup.

Serves 4

4 ounces boneless chicken thigh, skinned and diced

7 teaspoons butter

I small onion, chopped

1/4 cup chopped carrot

2 shiitake mushrooms, stems removed and chopped

I tablespoon finely chopped fresh parsley

2 1/4 cups freshly boiled rice

2 tablespoons ketchup

6 large eggs

1/4 cup milk

salt and freshly ground black or white pepper

ketchup and fresh parsley sprigs, to garnish

I Season the chicken. Melt 1 1/2 teaspoons of the butter in a frying pan. Sauté the chopped onion for I minute, then add the chicken and cook until it is white and cooked. Add the carrot pieces and mushrooms, stir-fry until soft over medium heat, then add the chopped parsley. Set aside and clean the frying pan.

2 Melt another 1 1/2 teaspoons of the butter in the frying pan, add the rice and stir well. Mix in the fried ingredients and ketchup, adding salt and pepper to taste. Keep warm.

3 Beat the eggs lightly in a bowl, add the milk, 1/2 teaspoon salt and pepper to taste. Melt I teaspoon of the butter in an omelet pan over medium heat. Pour in a quarter of the egg mixture and stir it briefly with a fork, then let set for I minute. Top with a quarter of the rice mixture. Fold the omelet over the rice and slide it to the edge of the pan to shape it into a cylinder. Do not cook the omelet too much.

4 Invert the omelet onto a warmed plate, cover with a sheet of paper towel and press neatly into a rectangular shape. Cook another three omelets from the remaining ingredients. Serve with ketchup on top, garnished with parsley.

Chicken Cakes with Teriyaki Sauce

These little chicken cakes, about the size of small meatballs, are cooked with a glaze and garnished with scallions.

Serves 4

14 ounces ground chicken

I small egg

1/4 cup grated onion

1 1/2 teaspoons sugar

1 1/2 teaspoons soy sauce

cornstarch, for coating

1/2 bunch scallions, finely shredded

I tablespoon oil

For the teriyaki sauce

2 tablespoons sake or dry white wine

2 tablespoons sugar

2 tablespoons mirin

2 tablespoons soy sauce

I Mix the ground chicken with the egg, grated onion, sugar and soy sauce until the ingredients are thoroughly combined and well bound together. This process takes about 3 minutes, until the mixture is quite sticky. Shape the mixture into 12 small, flat, round cakes and dust them lightly all over with cornstarch.

2 Soak the shredded scallions in cold water for 5 minutes and drain well.

3 Heat the oil in a frying pan. Place the chicken cakes in the pan in a single layer, and cook over medium heat for 3 minutes. Turn the chicken cakes and cook for 3 minutes on the second side.

4 To make the teriyaki sauce, combine all the ingredients in a bowl. Pour the sauce into the frying pan and turn the chicken cakes until they are evenly glazed. Move or gently shake the pan constantly to prevent the sauce from burning.

5 Arrange the chicken cakes on a warmed serving plate and top with the scallion shreds. Serve immediately.

Chicken Lollipops

These tasty stuffed wings can be served hot or cold. They can be prepared and frozen in advance.

Makes 12
12 large chicken wings
3 cups dried bread crumbs
2 tablespoons sesame seeds
2 eggs, beaten
oil, for deep-frying

For the filling
1 teaspoon cornstarch
¼ teaspoon salt
½ teaspoon fresh thyme leaves
pinch of freshly ground
   black pepper

1 Remove the wing tips and discard or use them for making stock. Skin the second joint sections, removing the two small bones, and reserve the meat for the filling.

2 To make the filling, place all the ingredients in a bowl and add the reserved chicken meat. Mix well.

3 Holding the large end of the bone on the third section of the wing and using a sharp knife, cut the skin and flesh off the bone, scraping down and pulling the meat over the small end, forming a pocket. Repeat this process with the remaining wing sections.

4 Fill the tiny pockets with the filling. Mix the bread crumbs and the sesame seeds together. Place the bread crumb mixture and the beaten eggs in separate dishes.

5 Brush the meat with beaten egg and roll in the bread crumb mixture to cover. Chill and repeat to give a second layer, forming a thick coating. Chill until ready to fry.

6 Preheat the oven to 350°F. Heat 2 inches oil in a heavy pan until hot but not smoking, or the bread crumbs will burn. Gently fry two or three lollipops at a time until golden brown, remove and drain on paper towels. Complete the cooking for 15–20 minutes or until tender. Serve hot or cold.

Pan-fried Honey Chicken Drumsticks

Flavored with a sweet marinade before frying, these drumsticks are served with a wine sauce.

Serves 4
½ cup honey
juice of 1 lemon
2 tablespoons soy sauce
1 tablespoon sesame seeds
½ teaspoon fresh or dried
   thyme leaves
12 chicken drumsticks
¾ cup all-purpose flour
3 tablespoons butter
   or margarine
3 tablespoons vegetable oil
½ cup white wine
½ cup Chicken Stock
salt and freshly ground
   black pepper
fresh flat-leaf parsley, to garnish

1 In a large bowl, combine the honey, lemon juice, soy sauce, sesame seeds and thyme. Add the chicken drumsticks and mix to coat them well. Let marinate in a cool place for 2 hours or more, turning occasionally.

2 Mix ½ teaspoon each of salt and pepper with the flour in a shallow bowl. Drain the drumsticks, reserving the marinade. Roll them in the seasoned flour to coat all over.

3 Heat the butter or margarine with the oil in a large, heavy frying pan. When hot and sizzling, add the drumsticks and brown on all sides. Reduce the heat to medium-low and cook for 12–15 minutes, until the chicken is done.

4 Check that the chicken is cooked through by piercing the thickest part with a fork: the juices should run clear. Remove the drumsticks from the pan, place on a serving platter and keep hot.

5 Pour off most of the fat from the pan. Add the white wine, chicken stock and reserved marinade, and stir well to mix in the cooking juices on the bottom of the pan. Bring to a boil and simmer until reduced by half. Season to taste, then spoon the sauce onto the drumsticks and serve, garnished with flat-leaf parsley.

Chicken with Sweet Potatoes

Sweet potatoes are still an undervalued vegetable. A dish like this, in which they are baked with chicken and finished with an orange and ginger glaze, shows them at their best.

Serves 6

grated zest and juice of 1 large
   navel orange
6 tablespoons soy sauce
1-inch piece fresh ginger root,
   peeled and finely grated
1/4 teaspoon pepper
2 1/2 pounds chicken portions
1/2 cup all-purpose flour
3 tablespoons corn oil
2 tablespoons butter
   or margarine
2 pounds sweet potatoes, peeled
   and cut into 1-inch pieces
3 tablespoons light brown sugar
steamed broccoli, to serve

1 In a plastic bag, combine the orange zest and juice, soy sauce, ginger and pepper. Add the chicken pieces. Put the bag in a mixing bowl (this will keep the chicken immersed in the marinade) and seal. Let marinate in the refrigerator overnight.

2 Preheat the oven to 425°F. Drain the chicken, reserving the marinade. Coat the chicken with flour, shaking off any excess.

3 Heat 2 tablespoons of the oil in a frying pan. Add the chicken pieces and brown on all sides. Remove from the pan and drain.

4 Put the remaining oil and the butter or margarine in a 12 × 9-inch ovenproof dish. Briefly heat in the oven.

5 Put the potato pieces in the bottom of the dish, tossing well to coat with the butter and oil. Arrange the chicken portions in a single layer on top of the potatoes. Cover with aluminum foil and bake for 40 minutes.

6 Mix the reserved marinade with the brown sugar. Remove the foil from the baking dish and pour the marinade mixture onto the chicken and potatoes. Bake, uncovered, for about 20 minutes, until the chicken and potatoes are cooked through and tender. Serve with steamed broccoli.

Golden Chicken

One of those rare dishes that is better cooked in advance and reheated. The chicken (preferably an old boiling fowl and not a young roaster) cooks in its own rich gravy. Letting it cool helps in the removal of any fat and improves the flavor.

Serves 5–6

1–2 tablespoons oil
5 1/2-pound chicken
2 tablespoons all-purpose flour
1/2 teaspoon paprika
2 1/2 cups boiling water
salt and freshly ground
   black pepper
cooked rice and broccoli, to serve

1 Preheat the oven to 325°F. Heat the oil in a large, flameproof casserole and sauté the chicken slowly on all sides until the skin is brown. A boiling fowl is fatter, so you should prick the skin with a fork on the back and legs to release the fat as the chicken cooks.

2 Transfer the chicken to a plate and sprinkle the flour on the oil remaining in the casserole, adding a little more if necessary, to make a paste. Add the paprika and seasoning, and gradually pour in the boiling water, stirring constantly to make a thick sauce. When the sauce is simmering, replace the chicken, spoon some of the sauce on top and cover tightly with a sheet of aluminum foil and then the lid.

3 Cook in the center of the oven for about 1 hour and then turn the chicken over. Continue cooking for about 2 hours or until the chicken is tender (a roaster will cook much quicker than a boiler). Add a little extra boiling water if the sauce appears to be drying up.

4 When the meat on the legs is tender, the chicken is done. Let cool, then pour the gravy into a bowl. When it is cold, chill in the refrigerator until the fat solidifies into a pale layer on top. Remove with a spoon.

5 Joint the chicken, place in a clean pan and pour in the cold gravy. Reheat thoroughly and serve with rice and broccoli.

Pan-fried Chicken with Pesto

Pan-fried chicken, served with warm pesto, makes a deliciously quick main course. Serve with rice noodles and braised mixed vegetables.

Serves 4
1 tablespoon olive oil
4 chicken breast fillets, skinned
fresh basil leaves, to garnish
braised baby carrots and celery,
   to serve

For the pesto
6 tablespoons olive oil
½ cup pine nuts
⅔ cup grated
   Parmesan cheese
1 cup fresh basil leaves
¼ cup fresh parsley
2 garlic cloves, crushed
salt and freshly ground
   black pepper

1 Heat the 1 tablespoon oil in a frying pan. Add the chicken fillets and cook gently for 15–20 minutes, turning several times, until tender, lightly browned and thoroughly cooked.

2 Meanwhile, to make the pesto, place the olive oil, pine nuts, Parmesan cheese, basil, parsley, garlic and salt and pepper to taste in a blender or food processor, and process until smooth and well mixed.

3 Remove the chicken from the pan, cover and keep hot. Reduce the heat slightly, then add the pesto to the pan and cook gently, stirring constantly, for a few minutes until the pesto has warmed through.

4 Pour the warm pesto over the chicken, then garnish with basil leaves and serve with braised baby carrots and celery.

Succulent Fried Chicken

Crisp-coated deep-fried chicken, tender and succulent within, is justifiably popular.

Serves 4
1 cup milk
1 egg, beaten
1¼ cups all-purpose flour
1 teaspoon paprika
8 chicken portions
oil, for deep-frying
salt and freshly ground
   black pepper
lemon wedges and fresh flat-
   leaf parsley, to garnish

1 Mix the milk with the beaten egg in a shallow dish. On a sheet of waxed paper, combine the flour, paprika, salt and pepper.

2 One at a time, dip the chicken portions in the egg mixture and turn them to coat all over. Then dip them in the flour and shake off any excess.

3 Deep-fry in hot oil for 25–30 minutes, turning the pieces so they brown and cook evenly. Drain well on paper towels and serve very hot, garnished with lemon wedges and parsley.

Chicken Bitki

A Polish dish, in which finely chopped chicken and mushrooms are formed into small sausage shapes and fried. You could use guinea fowl to mimic the flavor of Polish chicken.

Makes 12
1 tablespoon butter, melted
1½ cups flat mushrooms,
   finely chopped

1 cup fresh white bread crumbs
12 ounces chicken breast fillet,
   skinned and finely chopped
2 eggs, separated
¼ teaspoon grated nutmeg
2 tablespoons all-purpose flour
3 tablespoons oil
salt and freshly ground
   black pepper
green salad and grated pickled
   beets, to serve

1 Melt the butter in a pan and cook the mushrooms for 5 minutes, until they are soft and all the juices have evaporated. Set aside to cool.

2 Combine the bread crumbs, chicken, egg yolks, nutmeg, salt and pepper and mushrooms in a bowl.

3 In a clean bowl, whisk the egg whites until stiff. Stir half into the chicken mixture, then fold in the remainder.

4 Shape the mixture into 12 even sausages, about 3 inches long and 1 inch wide. Roll in the flour to coat.

5 Heat the oil in a frying pan and fry the bitki for 10 minutes, turning until evenly golden brown and cooked through. Serve hot with a green salad and pickled beets.

> **Cook's Tip**
> It is always better to use freshly grated nutmeg rather than ready ground because the essential oils that give it its flavor are very volatile.

Layered Chicken & Mushroom Potato Casserole

A delicious and moist combination of chicken, vegetables and gravy in a simple, one-dish meal topped with crunchy slices of potato.

Serves 4–6
1 tablespoon olive oil
4 large chicken breast fillets, cut into chunks
1 leek, finely sliced into rings
¼ cup butter
¼ cup all-purpose flour
2 cups milk
1 teaspoon whole-grain mustard
1 carrot, very finely diced
3 cups button mushrooms, finely sliced
2 pounds potatoes, finely sliced
salt and freshly ground black pepper

1 Preheat the oven to 350°F. Heat the oil in a large saucepan and cook the chicken for 5 minutes, until browned. Add the leek and sauté for another 5 minutes.

2 Add half the butter to the pan and let it melt. Then sprinkle on the flour and stir in the milk. Cook over low heat until thickened, then stir in the mustard. Add the carrots with the mushrooms. Season with salt and pepper.

3 Line the bottom of a 7½-cup ovenproof dish with potato slices. Spoon on one third of the chicken mixture. Cover with another layer of potatoes. Repeat the layering, finishing with a layer of potatoes. Top with the remaining butter.

4 Bake for 1½ hours, covering with aluminum foil after 30 minutes' cooking time. Serve hot.

> **Cook's Tip**
> *The liquid from the mushrooms keeps the chicken moist, and the potatoes help to mop up any excess juices.*

Chicken with Potato Dumplings

Poached chicken breasts in a creamy sauce topped with light herb and potato dumplings make a delicate yet hearty meal.

Serves 6
1 onion, chopped
1¼ cups vegetable stock
½ cup white wine
4 large chicken breasts
1¼ cups light cream
1 tablespoon chopped fresh tarragon
salt and freshly ground black pepper

For the dumplings
8 ounces potatoes, boiled and mashed
1¼ cups suet
1 cup self-rising flour
2 tablespoons chopped mixed fresh herbs
¼ cup water

1 Place the onion, stock and wine in a deep-sided frying pan. Add the chicken and simmer for 20 minutes, covered. Remove the chicken from the stock, cut into chunks and reserve.

2 Strain the stock and discard the onion. Reduce the stock by one third over high heat. Stir in the cream and tarragon, and simmer until just thickened. Stir in the chicken and season. Spoon the mixture into a 3¾-cup ovenproof dish. Preheat the oven to 375°F.

3 To make the dumplings, combine the ingredients in a bowl with salt and pepper, and stir in the water to make a soft dough. Divide into six and shape into balls with floured hands.

4 Place on top of the chicken mixture and bake uncovered for 30 minutes, until the dumplings are browned and cooked through. Serve immediately.

> **Cook's Tip**
> *Do not reduce the sauce too much before it is cooked in the oven, as the dumplings absorb quite a lot of the liquid.*

Chicken with Cajun Sauce

Real Cajun sauce must start with a Cajun roux.

Serves 4
1 cup all-purpose flour
3½-pound chicken, cut into
   8 portions
1 cup buttermilk
vegetable oil, for frying
salt and freshly ground
   black pepper
fresh parsley sprigs, to garnish

For the sauce
½ cup lard or vegetable oil
generous ½ cup all-purpose flour
2 onions, chopped
2–3 celery stalks, chopped
1 large green bell pepper,
   seeded and chopped
2 garlic cloves, finely chopped
1 cup passata
scant 2 cups red wine or
   Chicken Stock
8 ounces tomatoes, peeled
   and chopped
2 bay leaves
1 tablespoon brown sugar
1 teaspoon grated orange zest
½ teaspoon cayenne pepper

1 To make the sauce, melt the lard and stir in the flour. Cook over low heat, stirring, for 15–20 minutes or until golden brown.

2 Add the onions, celery, green pepper and garlic and cook, stirring, until softened. Stir in the remaining sauce ingredients and season. Bring to a boil, then simmer for 1 hour or until the sauce is rich and thick. Stir occasionally.

3 Meanwhile, prepare the chicken. Put the flour in a plastic bag and season. Dip each piece of chicken in buttermilk, then dredge in the flour. Set aside for 20 minutes.

4 Heat 1 inch oil in a frying pan. Fry the chicken pieces, turning once, for 30 minutes, until deep golden and cooked. Drain on paper towels. Add them to the sauce, garnish and serve.

Persian Chicken

A sauce flavored with cinnamon, saffron and lemon juice makes this simple dish quite special.

Serves 4
1 tablespoon oil
4 chicken portions
1 large onion, chopped
3 garlic cloves, finely chopped

1 teaspoon ground cinnamon
2–3 saffron threads, soaked in
   1 tablespoon boiling water
2 tablespoons lemon juice
2 cups water
salt and freshly ground
   black pepper
cooked rice, yogurt and salad,
   to serve

1 Heat the oil in a large saucepan or flameproof casserole and sauté the chicken portions until golden. Remove from the pan and set aside.

2 Add the onion to the pan and sauté gently over medium heat for about 5 minutes, stirring frequently, until softened and golden, then add the garlic and cook briefly.

3 Stir in the cinnamon, saffron, lemon juice and seasoning. Return the chicken to the pan, add the water and bring to a boil over medium heat.

4 Reduce the heat, cover and simmer for 30–45 minutes until the chicken is cooked and the sauce is reduced to ½ cup. Serve with rice, yogurt and salad.

Cook's Tip
Cinnamon is the dried rolled bark of a tropical tree. It is available in sticks, which are difficult to grind, and ready ground.

Thyme & Lime Chicken

Scallion-stuffed chicken thighs are coated in butter infused with lime juice, thyme and garlic.

Serves 4

8 chicken thighs
2 tablespoons chopped
scallion
1 teaspoon dried or chopped
fresh thyme
2 garlic cloves, crushed
juice of 1 lime
6 tablespoons melted butter
salt and freshly ground
black pepper
lime slices, chopped scallions and
cilantro sprigs, to garnish
cooked rice, to serve

1 Put the chicken thighs in an ovenproof dish skin-side down and, using a sharp knife, make a slit lengthwise along each thigh bone. Mix the scallions with a little salt and pepper, and press the mixture into the slits.

2 Combine the thyme, garlic, lime juice and all but 2 tablespoons of the melted butter in a small bowl, and spoon a little onto each chicken thigh.

3 Spoon the remaining melted butter on top. Cover the chicken loosely with plastic wrap and let marinate in a cool place for several hours or overnight in the refrigerator.

4 Preheat the oven to 375°F. Remove the plastic wrap from the chicken and cover the dish with aluminum foil. Bake the chicken for 1 hour, then remove the foil and cook for a few more minutes to brown. Serve hot, garnished with lime, scallions and cilantro, and accompanied by rice.

> **Cook's Tip**
> *You may need to use two limes, depending on their size and juiciness. Or, for a less sharp flavor, use lemons instead.*

Palava Chicken

A variation of a popular Ghanaian dish, which was originally made from fish. In Sierra Leone, peanut butter is often added.

Serves 4

1½ pounds chicken breast
fillet, skinned
2 garlic cloves, crushed
2 tablespoons butter
or margarine
2 tablespoons vegetable oil
1 onion, finely chopped
4 tomatoes, peeled and chopped
2 tablespoons peanut butter
2½ cups Chicken Stock or water
1 fresh thyme sprig or
1 teaspoon dried thyme
8 ounces frozen leaf spinach,
thawed and chopped
1 fresh chile, seeded and chopped
salt and freshly ground
black pepper
boiled yams, to serve

1 Cut the chicken fillets into thin slices, place in a bowl and stir in the garlic and a little salt and pepper. Melt the butter or margarine in a large frying pan and fry the chicken over medium heat, turning once or twice to brown evenly. Transfer to a plate, using a slotted spoon, and set aside.

2 Heat the oil in a large saucepan, and cook the onion and tomatoes over high heat for 5 minutes, until soft. Reduce the heat, add the peanut butter and half of the stock or water, and blend together well.

3 Cook for 4–5 minutes, stirring constantly to prevent the peanut butter from burning, then add the remaining stock or water, the thyme, spinach, chile and seasoning. Stir in the chicken slices and cook over medium heat for 10–15 minutes, until the chicken is cooked through. Pour into a warmed serving dish and serve with boiled yams.

> **Cook's Tip**
> *If you have time, fresh spinach adds a fresher flavor. Egusi— ground melon seed—can be used instead of peanut butter.*

Pan-fried Chicken

The essence of this dish is to cook it quickly over high heat, and it therefore works best with small amounts. To serve four people, double the amount and either cook in batches or use two pans.

Serves 2
2 chicken breast fillets, skinned
1 small fresh red or green chile,
    seeded and finely sliced
2 garlic cloves, finely sliced
3 scallions, sliced
4–5 thin slices fresh ginger root
½ teaspoon ground coriander
½ teaspoon ground cumin
2 tablespoons olive oil
1½ tablespoons lemon juice
2 tablespoons pine nuts
1 tablespoon raisins (optional)
oil, for frying
1 tablespoon chopped cilantro
1 tablespoon chopped fresh mint
salt and freshly ground
    black pepper
sprigs of fresh mint and lemon
    wedges, to garnish
cooked rice or couscous, to serve

1 Cut the chicken fillets lengthwise into three or four thin slices. Place in a shallow bowl. Blend together the chile, garlic, scallions, spices, olive oil, lemon juice, pine nuts and raisins, if using. Season, then pour onto the chicken pieces, stirring to coat. Cover with plastic wrap and set in a cool place for 1–2 hours.

2 Lift the chicken out of the dish, reserving the marinade. Brush a heavy frying pan with oil, and heat. Add the chicken slices and stir-fry over fairly high heat for 3–4 minutes, until the chicken is browned on all sides. Add the reserved marinade and continue to cook over high heat for 6–8 minutes, until the chicken is cooked through.

3 Reduce the heat, stir in the herbs, cook for 1 minute, then garnish and serve.

Hunter's Chicken

This traditional Italian dish sometimes has strips of green bell pepper in the sauce for extra color and flavor instead of mushrooms.

Serves 4
¼ cup dried porcini mushrooms
2 tablespoons olive oil
1 tablespoon butter
4 chicken portions, on the
    bone, skinned
1 large onion, thinly sliced
14-ounce can chopped tomatoes
⅔ cup red wine
1 garlic clove, crushed
leaves of 1 fresh rosemary sprig,
    finely chopped
1½ cups fresh field mushrooms,
    thinly sliced
salt and freshly ground
    black pepper
fresh rosemary sprigs, to garnish
creamed potatoes or polenta,
    to serve

1 Put the porcini in a bowl, add 1 cup warm water and let soak for 20–30 minutes. Remove from the liquid and squeeze the porcini over the bowl. Strain the liquid and reserve. Finely chop the porcini.

2 Heat the oil and butter in a large, flameproof casserole until foaming. Add the chicken and sauté over medium heat for 5 minutes or until golden. Drain on paper towels.

3 Add the onion and porcini to the pan. Cook gently, stirring frequently, for 3 minutes, until the onion has softened but not browned. Stir in the chopped tomatoes, wine and reserved mushroom soaking liquid, then add the crushed garlic and chopped rosemary, with salt and pepper to taste. Bring to a boil, stirring constantly.

4 Return the chicken to the casserole and turn to coat with the sauce. Cover and simmer gently for 30 minutes.

5 Add the fresh mushrooms and stir well to mix into the sauce. Continue simmering gently for 10 minutes or until the chicken is tender. Taste and adjust the seasoning as necessary. Transfer to a warmed serving dish and garnish with rosemary. Serve hot, with creamed potatoes or polenta, if desired.

Country Chicken Sauté

Chicken in a bacon, mushroom and wine sauce.

Serves 4
1 cup chopped bacon
2 teaspoons oil
3½-pound chicken, cut into
    8 portions
seasoned flour, for coating
3 cups mushrooms, quartered
butter
3 tablespoons dry white wine
1 cup Chicken Stock

1 Cook the bacon in the oil until lightly colored. Remove and reserve.

2 Dredge the chicken in seasoned flour and fry until evenly browned. Remove and set aside.

3 Add the mushrooms and butter to the pan, and sauté until softened. Return the bacon and chicken, and add the wine and stock. Bring to a boil, cover and cook over low heat for 20–25 minutes or until the chicken is tender.

Stoved Chicken

"Stoved" is derived from the French étouffer—to cook in a covered pot— and originates from the Franco/Scottish "Alliance" of the 17th century.

Serves 4

2 pounds potatoes, cut into
    ¼-inch slices
2 large onions, thinly sliced
1 tablespoon chopped
    fresh thyme
2 tablespoons butter
1 tablespoon oil
2 strips bacon, chopped
4 large chicken portions, halved
1 bay leaf, plus extra to garnish
2½ cups Chicken Stock
salt and freshly ground
    black pepper

1 Preheat the oven to 300°F. Make a layer of half the potato slices in the bottom of a casserole. Cover with half the onions. Sprinkle with half the thyme and season well.

2 Heat the butter and oil in a large frying pan, add the bacon and chicken, and fry until browned. Transfer the chicken and bacon to the casserole. Reserve the fat in the pan.

3 Sprinkle the remaining thyme and some seasoning on the chicken, and add the bay leaf. Cover with the remaining onion, followed by a final layer of potatoes. Sprinkle with seasoning.

4 Pour the stock into the casserole, brush the potatoes with the reserved fat, then cover tightly and bake for about 2 hours, until the chicken is tender.

5 Preheat the broiler. Uncover the casserole, place under the broiler and cook until the slices of potato are beginning to brown and crisp. Serve hot, garnished with bay leaves.

Cook's Tip
Instead of buying large chicken joints and cutting them in half, choose either chicken thighs or drumsticks—or use a mixture of the two.

Chicken with Mushrooms & Tomatoes

Quickly cooked on the stove, this dish lends itself to endless variation and reheats well.

Serves 4

¼ cup all-purpose flour
2¼ pounds chicken portions
1 tablespoon olive oil
3 small onions or large
    shallots, sliced
1½ cups mushrooms, quartered
1 garlic clove, crushed
¼ cup dry white wine
½ cup Chicken Stock
12 ounces tomatoes, peeled,
    seeded and chopped, or 1 cup
    canned chopped tomatoes
salt and freshly ground
    black pepper
fresh flat-leaf parsley sprig,
    to garnish

1 Put the flour into a plastic bag, and season with salt and pepper. One at a time, drop the chicken portions into the bag and shake to coat with flour. Tap off the excess.

2 Heat the oil in a heavy, flameproof casserole. Fry the chicken over medium-high heat until golden brown, turning once. Transfer to a plate and keep warm.

3 Pour off all but 1 tablespoon of fat from the casserole. Add the onions or shallots, mushrooms and garlic. Cook until golden, stirring frequently.

4 Return the chicken to the casserole with any juices. Add the wine and bring to a boil, then stir in the stock and tomatoes. Bring back to a boil, reduce the heat, cover and simmer over low heat for about 20 minutes until the chicken is tender and the juices run clear when the thickest part of the meat is pierced with a knife.

5 Tilt the pan and skim off any fat that has risen to the surface. Taste the sauce and adjust the seasoning as necessary. Serve, garnished with flat-leaf parsley.

Burgundy Chicken

There are many versions of this traditional French dish, but this one is especially delicious. Serve it with warm French bread.

Serves 4
2 tablespoons olive oil
1 tablespoon butter
3½-pound chicken, cut into
  8 portions
4 ounces ham, cut into
  ¼-inch strips
4 ounces pearl onions, peeled
1½ cups button mushrooms
2 garlic cloves, crushed
2 tablespoons brandy
1 cup red wine
1¼ cups Chicken Stock
1 bouquet garni
1 tablespoon butter, blended with
  2 tablespoons all-purpose flour
salt and freshly ground
  black pepper
fresh parsley, to garnish
French bread, to serve

1 Preheat the oven to 325°F. Heat the oil and butter in a large flameproof casserole and brown the chicken portions on both sides.

2 Add the ham strips, peeled onions, mushrooms and garlic, and stir to mix.

3 Pour in the brandy and set it on fire. Add the red wine, stock, bouquet garni and seasoning. Cover and bake for about 1 hour.

4 Remove the chicken from the casserole and keep warm. Add the butter and flour mixture to the sauce and heat, stirring, on top of the stove until thickened. Taste and adjust the seasoning as necessary.

5 Return the chicken to the casserole and continue cooking for several minutes. Serve, garnished with parsley and accompanied by French bread.

Yassa Chicken

A specialty of Senegal, where instead of frying the chicken, they often broil it before adding it to the sauce. For a less tangy flavor, you can reduce the lemon juice.

Serves 4
⅔ cup lemon juice
¼ cup malt vinegar
3 onions, sliced
4 tablespoons peanut or
  vegetable oil
2¼ pounds chicken portions
1 fresh thyme sprig
1 fresh green chile, seeded and
  finely chopped
2 bay leaves
scant 2 cups Chicken Stock

1 Combine the lemon juice, vinegar, onions and 2 tablespoons of the oil in a bowl. Place the chicken in a shallow dish and pour in the lemon mixture. Cover with plastic wrap and let marinate for 3 hours.

2 Heat the remaining oil in a large frying pan and fry the chicken pieces for 4–5 minutes, until browned.

3 Add the marinated onions. Cook for 3 minutes, then add the marinade, thyme, chile, bay leaves and half the stock.

4 Cover the pan and simmer gently over medium heat for about 35 minutes, until the chicken is cooked through, adding the remaining stock as the sauce evaporates. Serve hot.

Chicken with Ham & Cheese

This tasty combination comes from the Emilia-Romagna region of Italy, where it is also prepared with veal.

Serves 4
4 small chicken breast
  fillets, skinned
seasoned flour
¼ cup butter
3–4 fresh sage leaves, plus extra
  to garnish
4 thin slices prosciutto crudo or
  cooked ham, cut in half
⅔ cup grated
  Parmesan cheese

1 Cut each chicken fillet in half lengthwise. Coat in the seasoned flour.

2 Heat the butter in a frying pan with the sage. Add the chicken and cook for 15 minutes over low heat until golden, turning as necessary.

3 Transfer to a flameproof dish or broiler pan. Place one piece of ham on each chicken fillet, and top with the Parmesan. Broil for 3–4 minutes or until the cheese has melted. Serve, garnished with sage.

Chicken Crêpes

A good way of using up leftover cooked chicken, these make a very quick and tasty lunch or supper dish if prepared with bought crêpes.

Serves 4

8 ounces cooked, boned chicken
2 tablespoons butter
1 small onion, finely chopped
¾ cup mushrooms,
　finely chopped
2 tablespoons all-purpose flour
⅔ cup Chicken Stock or milk
1 tablespoon chopped
　fresh parsley
8 small or 4 large
　cooked crêpes
oil, for brushing
2 tablespoons grated cheese
salt and freshly ground
　black pepper
watercress, to garnish

1 Remove the skin from the chicken and cut the meat into cubes. Set aside.

2 Heat the butter in a saucepan and gently cook the onion until tender. Add the mushrooms. Cook with the lid on for another 3–4 minutes.

3 Add the flour and then the stock or milk, stirring continuously. Boil to thicken and simmer for 2 minutes. Season with salt and pepper. Add the chicken and parsley.

4 Divide the filling equally between the crêpes, roll them up and arrange in a greased ovenproof dish. Preheat the broiler.

5 Brush the crêpes with a little oil and sprinkle with the cheese. Grill until browned. Serve garnished with watercress.

Cook's Tip
Homemade crêpes can be frozen, interleaved with waxed paper, in freezer bags. They thaw in minutes.

Chicken Crisp

Potato chips and grated cheese make a different—and super-quick—topping for this dish.

Serves 4

1 cup pasta shapes
6 ounces broccoli, cut into florets
¼ cup butter
1 red onion, thinly sliced
4 strips bacon, chopped
8 ounces chicken breast fillet,
　skinned and cut into chunks
¼ cup all-purpose flour
scant 2 cups milk
3 small packages plain
　potato chips
¾ cup cheese, grated
salt and freshly ground
　black pepper

1 Bring a large saucepan of salted water to a boil, add the pasta and cook according to the instructions on the package until *al dente*. Add the broccoli for the last 5 minutes of the cooking time. Drain well.

2 Meanwhile, melt the butter in a heavy saucepan and sauté the sliced onion until it begins to soften. Add the bacon and chicken, and fry gently until browned all over. Add the flour and mix well.

3 Remove the pan from heat and gradually mix in the milk. Season, return to the heat and bring to a boil, stirring constantly. Stir in the drained pasta and broccoli. Transfer the mixture to a shallow, heatproof dish.

4 Preheat the broiler. Cover the top of the mixture with the chips and sprinkle with the cheese. Put under the hot broiler for a few minutes, until the cheese has melted and is golden brown. Serve immediately.

Variation
If preferred, substitute flavored chips, such as cheese and onion or sour cream and chives, for the plain.

Chicken with Olives

Chicken breast fillets may be flattened for quick and even cooking. Here they are prepared with black olives and tomatoes.

Serves 4

4 chicken breast fillets, about
  5–6 ounces each, skinned
1/4 teaspoon cayenne pepper

5–7 tablespoons extra virgin
  olive oil
1 garlic clove, finely chopped
16–24 pitted black olives
6 ripe plum tomatoes, quartered
small handful of fresh basil leaves
salt

1 Place each chicken breast between two sheets of plastic wrap and pound with the flat side of a meat mallet or roll out with a rolling pin to flatten to about 1/2 inch thick. Season with salt and the cayenne pepper.

2 Heat 3–4 tablespoons of the olive oil in a large, heavy frying pan over medium-high heat. Add the chicken and cook for 4–5 minutes, until golden brown and just cooked, turning once. Transfer the chicken to warmed serving plates and keep warm.

3 Wipe out the frying pan and return to the heat. Add the remaining oil and sauté the garlic for 1 minute until golden and fragrant. Stir in the olives, cook for another minute, then stir in the tomatoes.

4 Shred the basil leaves and stir into the olive and tomato mixture, then spoon it over the chicken and serve immediately.

Cook's Tip
If the tomato skins are at all tough, remove them. Score the bottom of each tomato with a knife, then plunge them into boiling water for 45 seconds. Cool quickly in cold water. The skin should then peel off easily.

Chicken, Carrot & Leek Parcels

These intriguing parcels may sound a bit tricky for every-day cooking, but they take very little time to make and you can freeze them—ready to cook gently from frozen.

Serves 4

oil, for greasing
2 small leeks, sliced

4 chicken breast fillets
2 carrots, grated
4 pitted black olives, chopped
1 garlic clove, crushed
1–2 tablespoons olive oil
8 canned anchovy fillets, drained
salt and freshly ground
  black pepper
black olives and fresh herb sprigs,
  to garnish

1 Preheat the oven to 400°F. Prepare four sheets of waxed paper about 9 inches square and grease them.

2 Divide the leeks equally among the sheets of waxed paper, placing them near the edge. Season the chicken fillets well on both sides and place one on each pile of leeks.

3 Combine the carrots, olives, garlic and oil. Season lightly and place on top of the chicken portions. Top each with two of the anchovy fillets, then carefully wrap up each parcel, making sure the paper folds are secure and positioned underneath and that the carrot mixture is on top.

4 Bake for 20 minutes and serve hot, in the paper, garnished with black olives and fresh herb sprigs.

Cook's Tip
You can also wrap the chicken and vegetables in aluminum foil, but remove the foil before serving.

Mediterranean Chicken

This is the perfect after-work supper-party dish: it is quick to prepare and full of sunshiny flavors.

Serves 4
4 chicken breast portions, about
  1½ pounds total weight
1 cup cream cheese with garlic
  and herbs
1 pound zucchini
2 red bell peppers, seeded
1 pound plum tomatoes
4 celery stalks

about 3 tablespoons olive oil
10 ounces onions,
  roughly chopped
3 garlic cloves, crushed
8 sun-dried tomatoes,
  roughly chopped
1 teaspoon dried oregano
2 tablespoons balsamic vinegar
1 teaspoon paprika
salt and freshly ground
  black pepper
olive ciabatta or crusty bread,
  to serve

1 Preheat the oven to 375°F. Loosen the skin of each chicken portion, without removing it, to make a pocket. Divide the cheese into four pieces and push one quarter underneath the skin of each chicken portion in an even layer.

2 Cut the zucchini and peppers into similar-size chunky pieces. Quarter the tomatoes and slice the celery stalks.

3 Heat 2 tablespoons of the oil in a large, shallow, flameproof casserole. Cook the onions and garlic for 4 minutes, until they are soft and golden, stirring frequently.

4 Add the zucchini, peppers and celery to the casserole, and cook for another 5 minutes.

5 Stir in the tomatoes, sun-dried tomatoes, oregano and balsamic vinegar. Season well.

6 Place the chicken on top of the vegetables, drizzle on a little more olive oil, and season with salt and the paprika. Bake for 35–40 minutes or until the chicken is golden and cooked through. Serve with plenty of olive ciabatta or crusty bread to mop up the juices.

Stuffed Chicken Breasts

This dish consists of large chicken breasts filled with an herbed spinach mixture, then topped with butter and baked until mouth-wateringly tender.

Serves 6
4 ounces potatoes, diced
4 ounces spinach leaves,
  finely chopped
1 egg, beaten
2 tablespoons chopped cilantro
4 large chicken breasts

¼ cup butter
salt and freshly ground
  black pepper
cilantro sprigs, to garnish
fried mushrooms, to serve

For the sauce
14-ounce can
  chopped tomatoes
1 garlic clove, crushed
⅔ cup Chicken Stock
2 tablespoons chopped cilantro

1 Preheat the oven to 350°F. Boil the potatoes in a large saucepan of boiling water for 15 minutes or until tender. Drain, place in a large bowl and roughly mash.

2 Stir the spinach into the potato with the egg and cilantro. Season with salt and pepper to taste.

3 Cut almost all the way through the chicken breasts and open out to form a pocket in each. Spoon the filling into the center and fold the chicken back over again. Secure with toothpicks and place in a roasting pan. Dot with butter and cover with aluminum foil. Bake for 25 minutes. Remove the foil and cook for another 10 minutes, until the chicken is golden.

4 Meanwhile, to make the sauce, heat the tomatoes, garlic and stock in a saucepan. Boil rapidly for 10 minutes. Season and stir in the cilantro.

5 Remove the chicken from the oven and place on warmed serving plates with fried mushrooms. Pour on the sauce, garnish with cilantro and serve.

Koftas in Tomato Sauce

Delicious, lightly spiced chicken meatballs in a rich tomato sauce.

.

Serves 4

1½ pounds chicken
1 onion, grated
1 garlic clove, crushed
1 tablespoon chopped
   fresh parsley
½ teaspoon ground cumin
½ teaspoon ground coriander
1 egg, beaten
seasoned flour, for coating
¼ cup olive oil

salt and freshly ground
   black pepper
chopped fresh parsley, to garnish
cooked pasta and grated
   Parmesan cheese, to serve

For the tomato sauce

1 tablespoon butter
1 tablespoon all-purpose flour
scant 1 cup Chicken Stock
15-ounce can chopped tomatoes,
   with their juice
1 teaspoon sugar
¼ teaspoon dried mixed herbs

1 Preheat the oven to 350°F. Remove any skin and bone from the chicken, and grind or chop the meat finely.

2 Put the chicken in a bowl together with the onion, garlic, parsley, spices, seasoning and beaten egg. Combine thoroughly and shape into 1½-inch balls. Roll lightly in seasoned flour to coat.

3 Heat the oil in a frying pan and brown the balls in small batches. Remove and drain on paper towels.

4 To make the tomato sauce, melt the butter in a large saucepan. Add the flour, and then blend in the stock and tomatoes along with their juice. Add the sugar and herbs. Bring to a boil, cover and simmer for 10–15 minutes.

5 Place the chicken balls in a shallow, ovenproof dish and pour in the sauce. Cover and bake for 30–40 minutes.

6 Serve the koftas and sauce, garnished with parsley, accompanied by pasta plus grated Parmesan cheese.

Pasta with Turkey & Tomatoes

The flavor of the tomatoes is intensified by roasting and gives an extra boost to the dish, so it is worth taking the trouble to do this.

Serves 4

1½ pounds ripe but firm plum
   tomatoes, peeled and quartered
6 tablespoons olive oil
1 teaspoon dried oregano

12 ounces broccoli florets
1 small onion, sliced
1 teaspoon dried thyme
1 pound turkey breast
   fillet, cubed
3 garlic cloves, finely chopped
1 tablespoon lemon juice
3 cups dried pasta twists
salt and freshly ground
   black pepper

1 Preheat the oven to 400°F. Place the tomatoes in an ovenproof dish. Drizzle on 1 tablespoon of the oil, sprinkle on the oregano and season with salt. Bake for 30–40 minutes, until the tomatoes are just browned.

2 Meanwhile, bring a large pan of salted water to a boil. Add the broccoli and cook for about 5 minutes, until just tender. Drain and set aside.

3 Heat another 2 tablespoons of the oil in a large, nonstick frying pan. Add the onion, thyme, turkey and salt to taste. Cook over high heat for 5–7 minutes, stirring frequently, until the meat is cooked and beginning to brown. Add the garlic and cook for another minute, stirring frequently.

4 Remove from heat. Stir in the lemon juice and season with pepper. Set aside and keep warm.

5 Bring another large pan of salted water to a boil. Add the pasta and cook according to the package instructions until *al dente*. Drain and place in a large serving bowl. Toss the pasta with the remaining oil.

6 Add the broccoli to the turkey mixture and toss into the pasta. Stir the tomatoes gently into the pasta mixture. Serve immediately.

Spaghetti & Turkey in Cheese Sauce

An Italian-American recipe, this makes an excellent family meal. Serve it with a tossed green salad.

Serves 4–6
6 tablespoons butter
12 ounces turkey breast fillet, cut into thin strips
2 pieces bottled roasted bell pepper, drained, rinsed, dried and cut into thin strips

6 ounces spaghetti
½ cup all-purpose flour
3¾ cups hot milk
1⅓ cups grated Parmesan cheese
¼–½ teaspoon mustard powder
salt and freshly ground black pepper
salad leaves, to garnish

1 Melt about a third of the butter in a saucepan, add the turkey and sprinkle with a little salt and plenty of pepper. Toss the turkey over medium heat for about 5 minutes, until the meat turns white, then add the roasted pepper strips and toss to mix. Remove from the pan using a slotted spoon and set aside.

2 Preheat the oven to 350°F. Bring a large saucepan of salted water to a boil, add the pasta and cook according to the package instructions until *al dente*.

3 Meanwhile, melt the remaining butter over low heat in the pan in which the turkey was cooked. Sprinkle in the flour and cook, stirring, for 1–2 minutes. Increase the heat to medium.

4 Add the milk a little at a time, whisking vigorously. Bring to a boil and cook, stirring, until the sauce is smooth. Add two thirds of the grated Parmesan, then whisk in mustard, salt and pepper to taste. Remove from heat.

5 Drain the pasta and return it to the clean pan. Mix in half the cheese sauce, then spoon the mixture around the edge of an ovenproof dish. Stir the turkey mixture into the remaining cheese sauce and spoon into the dish. Sprinkle the remaining Parmesan on top and bake for 15–20 minutes, until the topping is just crisp. Serve hot with salad leaves.

Turkey with Yellow Bell Pepper Sauce

Turkey cutlets are wrapped around a garlicky cream-cheese filling and served with bell pepper purée.

Serves 4
2 tablespoons olive oil
2 large bell yellow peppers, seeded and chopped
1 small onion, chopped
1 tablespoon freshly squeezed orange juice

1¼ cups Chicken Stock
4 turkey cutlets
6 tablespoons cream cheese with garlic
12 fresh basil leaves
2 tablespoons butter
salt and freshly ground black pepper
cooked pasta and black olives, to serve

1 Heat half the oil in a frying pan and gently cook the peppers and onion until beginning to soften. Add the orange juice and stock, and cook until very soft.

2 Meanwhile, lay the turkey cutlets between two sheets of plastic wrap and beat with the side of a rolling pin to flatten.

3 Spread the cutlets with the cream cheese. Chop half the basil and sprinkle on top, then roll up, tucking in the ends like an envelope, and secure neatly with half a toothpick.

4 Heat the remaining oil and the butter in a frying pan and fry the turkey parcels for 7–8 minutes, turning them frequently, until golden and cooked.

5 Meanwhile, press the pepper mixture through a sieve, or blend until smooth, then strain back into the pan. Season to taste and warm through, or serve cold, with the turkey, accompanied by pasta, black olives and garnished with the remaining basil leaves.

Variation
Chicken breast fillets and plain cream cheese could be used instead of the turkey, if desired.

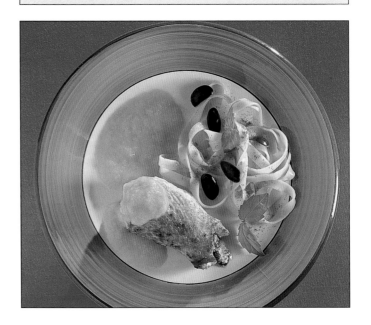

Stir-fried Turkey with Broccoli & Mushrooms

This is a really easy, tasty supper dish that works well with chicken too.

Serves 4

4 ounces broccoli florets
4 scallions
1 teaspoon cornstarch
3 tablespoons oyster sauce
1 tablespoon dark soy sauce
½ cup Chicken Stock
2 teaspoons lemon juice
3 tablespoons peanut oil

1 pound turkey steaks, cut into strips about ¼ × 2 inches
1 small onion, chopped
2 garlic cloves, crushed
2 teaspoons grated fresh ginger root
4 ounces fresh shiitake mushrooms, sliced
⅓ cup baby corn, halved lengthwise
1 tablespoon sesame oil
salt and freshly ground black pepper
egg noodles, to serve

1 Divide the broccoli florets into smaller sprigs and cut the stalks into thin diagonal slices. Finely chop the white parts of the scallions and slice the green parts into thin shreds. In a bowl, blend together the cornstarch, oyster sauce, soy sauce, stock and lemon juice. Set aside.

2 Heat a wok until hot, add 2 tablespoons of the peanut oil and swirl it around. Add the turkey and stir-fry for about 2 minutes, until golden and crispy at the edges. Remove the turkey from the wok and keep warm.

3 Add the remaining oil and stir-fry the onion, garlic and ginger for about 1 minute. Increase the heat, add the broccoli, mushrooms and corn, and stir-fry for 2 minutes.

4 Return the turkey to the wok, then add the sauce with the chopped scallion whites and seasoning. Cook, stirring, for about 1 minute, until the sauce has thickened. Stir in the sesame oil. Serve immediately on a bed of egg noodles with the finely shredded scallion greens on top.

Turkey Rolls with Gazpacho Sauce

This Spanish-style recipe uses quick-cooking turkey steaks, which are served with a refreshing sauce made from raw mixed vegetables.

Serves 4

4 turkey breast steaks
1 tablespoon red pesto or tomato paste
4 chorizo sausages

For the gazpacho sauce

1 green bell pepper, seeded and chopped
1 red bell pepper, seeded and chopped
3-inch piece cucumber
1 medium-size tomato
1 garlic clove
3 tablespoons olive oil
1 tablespoon red wine vinegar
salt and freshly ground black pepper

1 To make the gazpacho sauce, place the peppers, cucumber, tomato, garlic, 2 tablespoons of the oil and the vinegar in a food processor, and process until almost smooth. Season to taste with salt and pepper, and set aside.

2 If the turkey breast steaks are quite thick, place them between two sheets of plastic wrap and beat them with the side of a rolling pin, to flatten them slightly.

3 Spread the pesto or tomato paste on the turkey and then place a chorizo on each piece and roll up firmly.

4 Slice the rolls thickly and thread them onto skewers, piercing them through the spiral. Cook on a medium-hot grill or under a preheated broiler for 10–12 minutes, brushing with remaining oil and turning once. Serve with the gazpacho sauce.

> **Cook's Tip**
> If using wooden skewers, soak them in cold water for 30 minutes to prevent them from charring.

Turkey Scaloppine with Lemon & Sage

For this Italian-inspired dish, turkey is marinated in fresh lemon juice with sage, then coated in bread crumbs and fried quickly.

Serves 4

4 turkey breast steaks, about
  6 ounces each
1 tablespoon grated lemon zest
1 tablespoon chopped fresh or
  1 teaspoon dried sage
$\frac{1}{4}$ cup lemon juice
6 tablespoons vegetable oil
1 cup fine dry bread crumbs
salt and freshly ground
  black pepper
fresh sage leaves and lemon
  slices, to garnish
steamed new potatoes and
  zucchini, to serve

1 Place each turkey steak between two sheets of plastic wrap and beat with the side of a rolling pin until about $\frac{1}{4}$ inch thick. Sprinkle with salt and pepper.

2 In a small bowl, combine the lemon zest, sage, lemon juice and 2 tablespoons of the oil. Stir well to mix.

3 Arrange the turkey scaloppine, in one layer, in one or two shallow dish(es). Divide the lemon mixture between the scaloppine and rub in well. Let marinate for 20 minutes.

4 Heat the remaining oil in a frying pan. Dredge the turkey scaloppine in the bread crumbs, shaking off the excess. Fry for about 2 minutes on each side, until golden brown.

5 Garnish with sage leaves and lemon slices, and serve with new potatoes and zucchini.

Variation
For a delicious alternative, substitute fresh tarragon leaves for the sage.

Turkey Meat Loaf

Bursting with the Mediterranean flavors of green bell pepper, onion, garlic, sun-dried tomatoes, pine nuts and herbs, this makes an especially good midweek supper.

Serves 4

1 tablespoon olive oil
1 onion, chopped
1 green bell pepper, seeded and
  finely chopped
1 garlic clove, finely chopped
1 pound ground turkey
1 cup fresh white bread crumbs
1 egg, beaten
$\frac{1}{2}$ cup pine nuts
12 sun-dried tomatoes in oil,
  drained and chopped
$\frac{1}{3}$ cup milk
2 teaspoons chopped fresh or
  $\frac{1}{2}$ teaspoon dried rosemary
1 teaspoon fennel seeds
$\frac{1}{2}$ teaspoon dried oregano
salt and freshly ground
  black pepper
salad, to serve

1 Preheat the oven to 375°F. Heat the oil in a frying pan. Add the onion, green pepper and garlic, and cook over low heat for 8–10 minutes, stirring frequently, until the vegetables are just softened. Remove from heat and let cool.

2 Place the ground turkey in a large bowl. Add the onion mixture and all the remaining ingredients and stir until thoroughly combined.

3 Transfer to an $8\frac{1}{2} \times 4\frac{1}{2}$-inch loaf pan, packing down firmly. Bake for about 1 hour, until golden brown. Serve with salad.

Turkey Spirals

These little spirals are very simple to make and an excellent way to pep up plain turkey.

Serves 4

4 thinly sliced turkey breast
  steaks, about $3\frac{1}{2}$ ounces each
4 teaspoons tomato paste
$\frac{1}{2}$ cup large basil leaves
1 garlic clove, crushed
1 tablespoon milk
2 tablespoons whole-wheat flour
salt and freshly ground
  black pepper
passata or Fresh Tomato Sauce
  and pasta with fresh basil,
  to serve

1 Place the turkey steaks between two sheets of plastic wrap and flatten slightly with a rolling pin. Spread each steak with tomato paste, then top with a few basil leaves, a little crushed garlic, and salt and pepper. Roll up firmly around the filling and secure with a toothpick. Brush with milk and sprinkle with flour to coat lightly.

2 Cook under a medium-hot broiler for 15–20 minutes, turning occasionally. Serve hot, sliced, with passata or fresh tomato sauce and pasta, sprinkled with fresh basil leaves.

Turkey Crêpes

These quick and easy crêpes are filled with a turkey and apple mixture.

Serves 4

For the filling
2 tablespoons oil
1 pound ground turkey
2 tablespoons snipped
   fresh chives
2 green apples, cored
   and diced
1/4 cup all-purpose flour
3/4 cup Chicken Stock
salt and freshly ground
   black pepper

For the crêpes
1 cup all-purpose flour
pinch of salt
1 egg, beaten
1 1/4 cups milk
oil, for frying
lightly cooked snowpeas,
   to serve

For the sauce
1/4 cup cranberry sauce
1/4 cup Chicken Stock
1 tablespoon honey
1 tablespoon cornstarch

1 To make the filling, heat the oil and fry the turkey for 5 minutes. Add the chives and apples, and then the flour. Stir in the stock and seasoning. Bring to a boil, stirring, lower the heat and simmer for 20 minutes, stirring occasionally.

2 To make the crêpes, sift the flour into a bowl with the salt. Make a well in the center and drop in the egg. Beat it in gradually with the milk to form a smooth batter.

3 Heat the oil in a 5-inch omelet pan. Pour off the oil, add one quarter of the batter and cook for 2–3 minutes. Turn the pancake over and cook for another 2 minutes. Make three more in the same way, adding more oil to the pan.

4 To make the sauce, heat the cranberry sauce, stock and honey in a pan. Mix the cornstarch with 4 teaspoons water, stir it into the sauce and bring to a boil, stirring until clear.

5 Lay the crêpes on a cutting board, spoon the filling into the center and fold around the filling. Place on a plate and spoon on the sauce. Serve with snowpeas.

Turkey Breasts with Tomato Salsa

Turkey can lack flavor, but this is a great way of turning it into a tasty meal with a minimum of fat or fuss.

Serves 4
4 turkey breast fillets, about
   6 ounces each, skinned
2 tablespoons lemon juice
2 tablespoons olive oil
1/2 teaspoon ground cumin
1/2 teaspoon dried oregano
salt and freshly ground
   black pepper
salad greens, to serve

For the salsa
1 fresh green chile
1 pound tomatoes, seeded
   and chopped
7-ounce can corn
   kernels, drained
3 scallions, chopped
1 tablespoon finely chopped
   fresh parsley
2 tablespoons finely chopped
   cilantro
2 tablespoons lemon juice
3 tablespoons olive oil

1 Place the turkey fillets between two sheets of plastic wrap and beat with a meat mallet or the side of a rolling pin until thin. Blend the lemon juice, oil, cumin, oregano and pepper in a shallow dish. Add the turkey and turn to coat. Cover and let stand for at least 2 hours, or chill overnight.

2 To make the salsa, roast the chile over a gas flame, holding it with tongs, until charred on all sides. (Alternatively, char the skin under the broiler.) Let cool for 5 minutes. Wearing rubber gloves, carefully rub off the charred skin. For a less fiery salsa, discard the seeds. Chop the chile finely and place in a bowl. Add all the remaining salsa ingredients to the chile, plus salt to taste, and stir well until mixed thoroughly. Set aside.

3 Remove the turkey breast fillets from the marinade. Season lightly on both sides with salt to taste.

4 Heat a heavy ridged frying pan. When hot, add the turkey breasts and cook for about 3 minutes, until browned. Turn and cook the meat on the other side for another 3–4 minutes, until cooked through. Serve immediately with the salsa and salad greens.

Turkey Surprise Packages

Let diners open their own parcels and savor the aroma to the full.

Serves 4
2 tablespoons chopped
   fresh parsley
4 turkey breast steaks, about
   5–6 ounces each
8 strips bacon

2 scallions, cut into
   thin strips
2 ounces fennel, cut into thin strips
1 carrot, cut into thin strips
1 small celery stalk, cut into
   thin strips
grated zest and juice of 1 lemon
salt and freshly ground
   black pepper
lemon wedges, to serve

1 Sprinkle parsley on each turkey breast steak and pat it into the meat using your hands. Wrap 2 strips of bacon around each one.

2 Preheat the oven to 375°F. Cut four 12-inch circles out of baking parchment or waxed paper and put a turkey breast just off center on each one.

3 Arrange the vegetable strips on top of the steaks, sprinkle on the lemon zest and juice, and season well with salt and pepper.

4 Fold the paper over the turkey and vegetables and, starting at one side, twist and fold the paper edges together. Work your way around the semicircle, to seal the edges of the parcel together neatly.

5 Place the parcels in a roasting pan and cook for 35–45 minutes or until the turkey is cooked and tender. Serve the packages with lemon wedges for squeezing.

Cook's Tip
The cut surfaces of fennel will turn brown very quickly when exposed to the air. If you have to cut the fennel in advance of using, drop it in a bowl of water acidulated with a little lemon juice.

Turkey Croquettes

A crisp patty of flavorful smoked turkey mixed with mashed potatoes and scallions and rolled in bread crumbs, served with a tangy tomato sauce.

Serves 4
1 pound potatoes, diced
3 eggs
2 tablespoons milk
6 ounces smoked turkey bacon,
   finely chopped
2 scallions, thinly sliced

2 cups fresh white bread crumbs
vegetable oil, for deep-frying
salt and freshly ground
   black pepper

For the sauce
1 tablespoon olive oil
1 onion, finely chopped
14-ounce can tomatoes, drained
2 tablespoons tomato paste
1 tablespoon chopped
   fresh parsley

1 Boil the potatoes in salted water for 20 minutes or until tender. Drain and return the pan to low heat to make sure all the excess water evaporates.

2 Mash the potatoes with 2 of the eggs and the milk. Season well with salt and pepper. Stir in the turkey and scallions. Chill for 1 hour.

3 Meanwhile, to make the sauce, heat the oil in a frying pan and sauté the onion for 5 minutes, until softened. Add the tomatoes and tomato paste, stir and simmer for 10 minutes. Stir in the parsley, season with salt and pepper, and keep the sauce warm until needed.

4 Beat the remaining egg and place in a dish. Place the bread crumbs in a separate dish. Divide the potato mixture into eight portions. Shape each one into a sausage shape and dip into the beaten egg and then into the bread crumbs, shaking off any excess.

5 Heat the vegetable oil in a deep-fat fryer to 330°F and deep-fry the croquettes for 5 minutes or until golden and crisp. Drain on paper towels. Serve with the sauce.

Duck Breasts with Pineapple & Ginger

For this Chinese dish, use the boneless duck breasts that are widely available or alternatively use a whole bird, saving the legs for another meal and using the carcass to make stock.

Serves 2–3

4 scallions, chopped
2 duck breast fillets, skinned
1 tablespoon light soy sauce
8-ounce can pineapple rings
5 tablespoons water
4 pieces drained Chinese preserved ginger in syrup, plus 3 tablespoons syrup from the jar
2 tablespoons cornstarch, mixed into a thin paste with a little water
¼ each red and green bell pepper, seeded and cut into thin strips
salt and freshly ground black pepper
cooked thin egg noodles, baby spinach and green beans, to serve

1 Select a shallow bowl that will fit into your steamer and that will accommodate the duck breasts side by side. Spread out the chopped scallions in the bowl, arrange the duck breasts on top and cover with nonstick baking paper. Set the steamer over boiling water and cook the duck for about 1 hour or until tender. Remove the duck from the steamer and let cool.

2 Cut the duck into thin slices. Place on a plate and moisten with a little of the cooking juices from the steaming bowl. Strain the remaining juices into a small saucepan and set aside. Cover the duck slices with the baking paper or aluminum foil and keep warm.

3 Drain the pineapple rings, reserving 5 tablespoons of the juice. Add this to the reserved cooking juices, with the measured water. Stir in the ginger syrup, soy sauce, then stir in the cornstarch paste and cook, stirring, until thickened. Season to taste.

4 Cut the pineapple and ginger into attractive shapes. Put the cooked noodles, baby spinach and green beans on a plate, add slices of duck and top with the pineapple, ginger and pepper strips. Pour on the sauce and serve.

Duck Breasts with Orange Sauce

A simple variation on the classic dish using a whole roast duck—and much quicker to prepare.

Serves 4

4 duck breasts
1 tablespoon sunflower oil
2 oranges
⅔ cup orange juice
1 tablespoon port
2 tablespoons Seville orange marmalade
1 tablespoon butter
1 teaspoon cornstarch
salt and freshly ground black pepper
sautéed potatoes and steamed green beans, to serve

1 Season the duck breast skin. Heat the oil in a frying pan over medium heat and add the duck breasts, skin-side down. Cover and cook for 3–4 minutes, until lightly browned. Turn the breasts over, lower the heat slightly and cook uncovered for 5–6 minutes.

2 Peel the skin and pith from the oranges. Working over a bowl to catch any juice, slice either side of the membranes to release the orange segments, then set aside with the juice.

3 Remove the duck breasts from the pan using a slotted spoon, drain on paper towels and keep warm in the oven while making the sauce. Drain off the fat from the pan.

4 Add the segmented oranges, all but 2 tablespoons of the orange juice, the port and the orange marmalade to the pan. Bring to a boil and then reduce the heat slightly. Whisk small pats of the butter into the sauce and season to taste.

5 Blend the cornstarch with the reserved orange juice, pour into the pan and stir until slightly thickened. Add the duck breasts and cook gently for about 3 minutes. Arrange the sliced breasts on warmed plates and pour on the sauce. Serve with sautéed potatoes and steamed green beans.

Duck & Ginger Chop Suey

Chicken can also be used in this recipe, but duck gives a richer contrast of flavors.

Serves 4
2 duck breasts, about
  6 ounces each
3 tablespoons sunflower oil
1 small egg, lightly beaten
1 garlic clove
¾ cup bean sprouts
2 slices fresh ginger root,
  cut into matchsticks

2 teaspoons oyster sauce
2 scallions, cut
  into matchsticks
salt and freshly ground
  black pepper

For the marinade
1 tablespoon honey
2 teaspoons rice wine
2 teaspoons light soy sauce
2 teaspoons dark soy sauce

1 Remove the skin and fat from the duck, cut the breasts into thin strips and place in a bowl. To make the marinade, combine the ingredients in a bowl. Pour the marinade onto the duck, cover and refrigerate overnight.

2 Next day, make the omelet. Heat a small frying pan and add 1 tablespoon of the oil. When the oil is hot, pour in the egg and swirl it around into an even layer. When the omelet is cooked, remove it from the pan, let it cool, then cut into strips. Drain the duck and discard the marinade.

3 Bruise the garlic with the flat side of a knife blade. Heat a wok or large frying pan, then add 2 teaspoons of the oil. When the oil is hot, add the garlic and sauté for 30 seconds, pressing it to release the flavor. Discard. Add the bean sprouts with seasoning and stir-fry for 30 seconds. Transfer to a heated dish, draining off any liquid.

4 Heat the wok again and add the remaining oil. When the oil is hot, stir-fry the duck for 3 minutes, until cooked. Add the ginger and oyster sauce, and stir-fry for another 2 minutes. Add the bean sprouts, egg strips and scallions, stir-fry briefly and serve immediately.

Stir-fried Crispy Duck

This stir-fry would be delicious wrapped in flour tortillas or steamed Chinese pancakes, served with a little extra warm plum sauce.

Serves 2
10–12 ounce duck
  breast fillets
2 tablespoons all-purpose flour
¼ cup oil
1 bunch scallions, halved
  lengthwise and cut into
  2-inch strips

2½ cups green cabbage,
  finely shredded
8-ounce can water chestnuts,
  drained and sliced
½ cup unsalted
  cashews
4 ounces cucumber, cut
  into strips
3 tablespoons plum sauce
1 tablespoon light soy sauce
salt and freshly ground
  black pepper
sliced scallions, to garnish

1 Trim the skin and a little of the fat off the duck and thinly slice the meat. Season the flour well and use it to coat each piece of duck.

2 Heat the oil in a wok or large frying pan and cook the duck over high heat until golden and crisp. Keep stirring to prevent the duck from sticking. Remove using a slotted spoon and drain on paper towels. You may need to cook the duck in batches.

3 Add the scallions to the pan and cook for 2 minutes. Stir in the shredded cabbage and cook for 5 minutes or until softened and golden.

4 Return the duck to the pan with the water chestnuts, cashews and cucumber. Stir-fry for 2 minutes.

5 Add the plum sauce and soy sauce with plenty of seasoning, and heat for 2 minutes. Serve piping hot, garnished with sliced scallions.

Chicken & Curry Mayonnaise Sandwich

A very useful and appetizing way of using leftover pieces of chicken.

Makes 2
4 slices whole-grain bread
2 tablespoons softened butter
4 ounces cooked chicken, sliced
I bunch watercress, trimmed

For the curry mayonnaise
1/2 cup ready-made mayonnaise
2 teaspoons concentrated curry paste
1/2 teaspoon lemon juice
2 teaspoons sieved apricot jam

I To make the curry mayonnaise, put all the ingredients in a bowl and mix thoroughly. Chill until needed.

2 Spread the bread with butter and arrange the chicken on two of the slices. Spread curry mayonnaise on the chicken slices.

3 Arrange sprigs of watercress on top, cover with the remaining bread and press lightly together. Cut in half and serve.

Variation
For an alternative spicy mayonnaise, add I teaspoon English mustard, I teaspoon Worcestershire sauce and a dash of Tabasco sauce to the ready-made mayonnaise.

Asian Chicken Sandwich

This filling is also good served in warmed pita bread—just cut the chicken into small cubes before brushing with the soy mixture, broil on skewers and serve warm.

Makes 2
6 ounces chicken breast fillet, skinned
I tablespoon soy sauce
I teaspoon honey
I teaspoon sesame oil
I garlic clove, crushed
4 slices white bread
1/4 cup peanut sauce
I ounce bean sprouts
I ounce red bell pepper, seeded and finely sliced

I Place the chicken breast in a heatproof dish or roasting pan. Combine the soy sauce, honey, sesame oil and garlic. Brush on the chicken breast.

2 Broil the chicken for 3–4 minutes on each side until cooked through, then slice thinly.

3 Spread two slices of the white bread with some of the peanut sauce.

4 Lay the chicken on the sauce-covered bread.

5 Spread a little more sauce on the chicken.

6 Sprinkle on the bean sprouts and red pepper, and sandwich together with the remaining slices of bread. Serve.

Cook's Tip
For homemade peanut sauce, stir together I seeded and ground fresh red chile, 2 tablespoons coconut milk and 4 ounces crunchy peanut butter over low heat until thick and smooth. Stir in I teaspoon brown sugar, I teaspoon lemon juice and salt to taste. Set aside to cool.

Chicken & Pesto Baked Potatoes

Although it is usually served with pasta, pesto can also give a wonderful lift to many other dishes. Here, it is combined with chicken and yogurt to make a tasty topping for baked potatoes.

Serves 4

4 baked potatoes, pricked
2 chicken breast fillets
I cup plain yogurt
I tablespoon pesto sauce
fresh basil sprigs, to garnish

I Preheat the oven to 400°F. Bake the potatoes for about 1¼ hours or until they are soft on the inside when tested with a skewer.

2 About 20 minutes before the potatoes are ready, cook the chicken breasts, leaving the skin on so that the flesh remains moist. Either bake the breasts in a dish alongside the potatoes in the oven or cook them on a rack under a medium-hot preheated broiler.

3 Stir together the yogurt and pesto in a small bowl. Skin the chicken breasts and cut them into slices.

4 When the potatoes are cooked through, cut them open. Fill the potatoes with the chicken slices, top with the yogurt sauce, garnish with basil and serve.

Variation
This filling would work equally well with sweet potatoes. Bake them in the same way until soft on the inside.

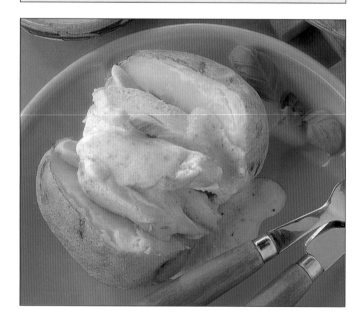

Fried Chicken

This is Japanese-style fried chicken, flavored with ginger. It may be cooked with or without its skin, according to personal preference.

Serves 4

8 boneless chicken thighs
oil, for deep-frying
scant ½ cup cornstarch,
*   for coating*
salad leaves, to serve

For the marinade
2-ounce piece fresh ginger root
¼ cup sake or dry white wine
¼ cup soy sauce

I To make the marinade, peel and grate the ginger, and squeeze it over a bowl to extract its juice. Add the sake or white wine and the soy sauce.

2 Cut the chicken thighs into four chunks and add to the marinade, rubbing it in well with your hands. Set aside in a cool place for 30 minutes.

3 Heat the oil slowly to 330–340°F. Lift the chicken out of the marinade and pat dry on paper towels. Dust generously with cornstarch. When the oil is hot, lower in the chicken pieces. To maintain the oil temperature, do not add too many chicken pieces at once. Deep-fry the chicken pieces for 4–5 minutes, until crisp, golden and cooked through. Remove the chicken from the pan.

4 Halve one chicken piece to make sure it is cooked inside. Drain the rest of the chicken on paper towels, then serve hot or cold, with salad.

Cook's Tip
Use Japanese rather than Chinese soy sauce for a more authentic flavor.

Hot Turkey Sandwich

A generous open sandwich that can be made with leftover roast turkey breast, served with a delicious hot mushroom gravy.

Serves 4

4 tablespoons butter
    or margarine
1/2 small onion, finely chopped
3 cups button mushrooms,
    quartered
1 1/4 pounds roast turkey breast
2 cups thick turkey gravy
4 thick slices whole-wheat bread
fresh parsley sprigs, to garnish

1 Melt half the butter or margarine in a frying pan. Add the onion and cook for 5 minutes, until softened.

2 Add the mushrooms and cook for about 5 minutes, stirring occasionally, until the moisture they render has evaporated.

3 Meanwhile, skin the turkey breast and carve the meat into four thick slices.

4 In a saucepan, heat up the turkey gravy. Stir in the onion and mushroom mixture.

5 Spread the slices of bread with the remaining butter or margarine. Set a slice on each of four plates and top with the turkey slices. Pour the mushroom gravy onto the turkey and serve hot, garnished with parsley.

Variation
If desired, the sandwich bread may be toasted and buttered.

Chinese Duck in Pita

This recipe is based on Chinese crispy duck, but uses duck breast instead of whole duck. After 15 minutes' cooking, the duck breast will still have a pinkish tinge. If you like it well-done, leave it in the oven for another 5 minutes.

Makes 2

1 duck breast, about 6 ounces
3 scallions
3-inch piece cucumber
2 round pita breads
2 tablespoons hoisin sauce
radish chrysanthemum and
    scallion tassel, to garnish

1 Preheat the oven to 425°F. Skin the duck breast, place the skin and breast separately on a rack in a roasting pan and bake for 10 minutes.

2 Remove the skin from the oven, cut into pieces and return to the oven with the breast for another 5 minutes.

3 Meanwhile, cut the scallions and cucumber into fine shreds about 1 1/2 inches long.

4 Heat each pita bread in the oven for a few minutes until puffed up, then split in half to make a pocket. Slice the duck breast thinly.

5 Stuff the duck breast into the pita bread with a little scallion, cucumber, crispy duck skin and some hoisin sauce. Serve, garnished with a radish chrysanthemum and scallion tassel.

Variation
Use Chinese chives instead of scallions and plum sauce instead of hoisin.

Traditional Roast Chicken

Serve with bacon rolls, chipolata sausages, gravy and stuffing balls or Bread Sauce.

Serves 4
3½-pound chicken
4 strips bacon
2 tablespoons butter
salt and freshly ground
   black pepper

For the prune and nut stuffing
2 tablespoons butter
½ cup chopped
   pitted prunes
½ cup chopped walnuts
1 cup fresh bread crumbs
1 egg, beaten
1 tablespoon chopped
   fresh parsley
1 tablespoon snipped fresh chives
2 tablespoons sherry or port

For the gravy
2 tablespoons all-purpose flour
1¼ cups Chicken Stock or
   vegetable cooking water

1 Preheat the oven to 375°F. To make the stuffing, combine all the ingredients in a bowl and season well. Stuff the neck end of the chicken quite loosely, allowing room for the bread crumbs to swell during cooking. (Any remaining stuffing can be shaped into small balls and fried.) Tuck the neck skin under the bird to secure the stuffing and hold in place with the wing tips or sew with thread or fine strips.

2 Place in a roasting pan and cover with the bacon. Spread with the butter, cover loosely with aluminum foil and roast for about 1½ hours, until the juices run clear when the thickest part of the thigh is pierced with a knife or skewer. Baste with the juices in the roasting pan three or four times during cooking.

3 Remove any trussing string and transfer to a serving plate. Cover with the foil and let rest while making the gravy. Carefully spoon off the fat from the juices in the roasting pan. Blend the flour into the juices and cook gently until golden brown. Add the stock or vegetable water and bring to a boil, stirring until thickened. Adjust the seasoning to taste, then strain the gravy into a pitcher or gravy boat. Serve with the chicken.

Honey Roast Chicken

A delicious variation on the classic roast chicken, this is filled with a bacon and mushroom stuffing and basted with honey and brandy.

Serves 4
3½-pound chicken
2 tablespoons honey
1 tablespoon brandy
5 teaspoons all-purpose flour
⅔ cup Chicken Stock
green beans, to serve

For the stuffing
2 shallots, chopped
4 strips bacon, chopped
¾ cup button mushrooms,
   quartered
1 tablespoon butter
   or margarine
2 thick slices white bread, diced
1 tablespoon chopped
   fresh parsley
salt and freshly ground
   black pepper

1 To make the stuffing, gently fry the shallots, bacon and mushrooms in a frying pan for 5 minutes, then transfer to a bowl. Pour off all but 2 tablespoons of bacon fat from the pan. Add the butter or margarine to the pan and fry the bread until golden brown. Add the bread to the bacon mixture. Stir in the parsley, and salt and pepper to taste. Let cool.

2 Preheat the oven to 350°F. Pack the stuffing into the neck end of the chicken and truss with string. Transfer the chicken to a roasting pan that just holds it.

3 Mix the honey with the brandy. Brush half of the mixture over the chicken. Roast for about 1 hour and 20 minutes, until the juices run clear when the thickest part of the thigh is pierced with a skewer or knife. Baste the chicken frequently with the remaining honey mixture during roasting.

4 Transfer the chicken to a warmed serving platter. Cover with aluminum foil and set aside. Strain the cooking juices into a degreasing pitcher. Set aside to let the fat rise, then pour off the fat. Stir the flour into the sediment in the roasting pan. Add the cooking juices and the chicken stock. Boil rapidly until the gravy has thickened, stirring constantly to prevent lumps from forming. Pour into a gravy boat and serve with the chicken and green beans.

Roast Chicken with Fresh Herbs & Garlic

A smaller chicken can also be roasted in this way.

Serves 4

4-pound chicken or
  4 small poussins
finely grated zest and juice of
  1 lemon
1 garlic clove, crushed
2 tablespoons olive oil
2 fresh thyme sprigs
2 fresh sage sprigs
6 tablespoons unsalted
  butter, softened
salt and freshly ground
  black pepper

1 Season the chicken or poussins well with salt and pepper. Combine the lemon zest and juice, garlic and olive oil and pour over the chicken. Let marinate for at least 2 hours in a nonmetallic dish.

2 When the chicken has marinated, preheat the oven to 450°F. Place the herbs in the cavity of the bird and smear the butter on the skin. Season well.

3 Roast the chicken for 10 minutes, then turn the oven down to 375°F. Baste the chicken well and then roast for another 1½ hours, until the juices run clear when the thickest part of the thigh is pierced with a skewer or knife. Let rest for 10–15 minutes before carving to serve.

Bread Sauce

Smooth and surprisingly delicate, this old-fashioned sauce is traditionally served with roast chicken, turkey and various game birds.

Serves 6

1 small onion
4 cloves
1 bay leaf
1¼ cups milk
2 cups fresh
  white bread crumbs
1 tablespoon butter
1 tablespoon light cream
salt and freshly ground
  black pepper

1 Peel the onion and stick the cloves into it. Put it into a saucepan with the bay leaf and milk. Bring to a boil, then remove from heat and set aside for 15–20 minutes.

2 Remove the bay leaf and onion. Return to the heat and stir in the bread crumbs. Simmer for 4–5 minutes or until thick and creamy. Stir in the butter and cream, then season to taste.

Roast Chicken with Lemon & Herbs

For this French roasting method, a well-flavored chicken is essential—use a free-range or corn-fed bird if possible.

Serves 4

3-pound chicken
1 unwaxed lemon, halved
small bunch of fresh thyme sprigs
1 bay leaf
1 tablespoon butter, softened
4–6 tablespoons Chicken Stock
  or water
salt and freshly ground
  black pepper

1 Preheat the oven to 400°F. Season the chicken inside and out with salt and pepper.

2 Squeeze the juice of one lemon half and then place the juice, the squeezed lemon half, the thyme and bay leaf in the chicken cavity. Tie the legs with string and rub the breast with butter.

3 Place the chicken on a rack in a roasting pan. Squeeze on the juice of the other lemon half. Roast the chicken for 1 hour, basting two or three times, until the juices run clear when the thickest part of the thigh is pierced with a knife or skewer.

4 Pour the juices from the cavity into the roasting pan and transfer the chicken to a carving board. Cover loosely with aluminum foil and let rest for 10–15 minutes before carving.

5 Skim off the fat from the cooking juices. Add the stock or water and boil over medium heat, scraping the bottom of the pan, until slightly reduced. Strain and serve with the chicken.

Cook's Tip
Be sure to save the carcasses of roast poultry for stock. Freeze them until you have several, then simmer with aromatic vegetables, herbs and water.

Olive Oil Roast Chicken with Mediterranean Vegetables

Eggplant, red bell pepper, fennel, garlic and potatoes are roasted in the chicken juices until they are meltingly tender.

Serves 4

4-pound chicken
⅔ cup extra virgin olive oil
½ lemon
few sprigs of fresh thyme
1 pound small new potatoes
1 eggplant, cut into 1-inch cubes
1 red bell pepper, seeded and quartered
1 fennel bulb, trimmed and quartered
8 large garlic cloves, unpeeled
coarse salt and freshly ground black pepper

1 Preheat the oven to 400°F. Rub the chicken all over with some of the olive oil and season with pepper. Place the lemon half inside the bird, with a sprig or two of thyme. Put the chicken, breast-side down, in a large roasting pan. Roast for about 30 minutes.

2 Remove the chicken from the oven and season with salt. Turn the chicken right side up and baste with the juices from the pan. Surround the bird with the potatoes, roll them in the juices and return the pan to the oven to continue roasting.

3 After 30 minutes, add the eggplant, red pepper, fennel and garlic. Drizzle on the remaining oil and season. Add any remaining thyme. Return to the oven and cook for 30–50 more minutes, turning the vegetables occasionally.

4 To find out if the chicken is cooked, push the tip of a sharp knife or skewer into the thickest part of the thigh: if the juices run clear, it is done. The vegetables should be tender and just beginning to brown.

5 Serve the chicken and vegetables from the pan, or transfer the vegetables to a serving dish, joint the chicken and place it on top. Serve the skimmed juices in a gravy boat.

Roast Chicken Stuffed with Forest Mushrooms

Use a free-range bird for this dish, and let its flavor mingle with the aroma of woodland mushrooms.

Serves 4

2 tablespoons unsalted butter, plus extra for basting and to finish the gravy
1 shallot, chopped
8 ounces wild mushrooms, e.g. chanterelles, cèpes, bay boletus, and oyster, trimmed and chopped
¾ cup fresh white bread crumbs
2 egg yolks
4-pound chicken
½ celery stalk, chopped
½ small carrot, chopped
3 ounces potato, peeled and chopped
1 cup Chicken Stock, plus extra if required
2 teaspoons wine vinegar
salt and freshly ground black pepper
fresh parsley sprigs, to garnish
roast potatoes and carrots, to serve

1 Preheat the oven to 425°F. Melt the butter in a saucepan and gently sauté the shallot. Add half of the mushrooms and cook for 2–3 minutes, until the juices run. Remove from heat and stir in the bread crumbs, seasoning and egg yolks. Spoon the stuffing into the neck of the chicken, enclose and fasten the skin on the underside with a skewer.

2 Rub the chicken with some butter and season. Put the celery, carrot, potato and remaining mushrooms in a roasting pan. Place the chicken on top, add the stock and roast for 1¼ hours or until the juices run clear when the thickest part of the thigh is pierced with a knife or skewer.

3 Transfer the chicken to a carving board, then process the vegetables and mushrooms. Pour the mixture back into the pan and heat gently, adjusting the consistency with chicken stock, if necessary. Taste and adjust the seasoning, then add the vinegar and a pat of butter, and stir briskly. Pour the sauce into a pitcher or gravy boat. Serve the chicken with roast potatoes and carrots, garnished with parsley and accompanied by the sauce.

Roast Chicken with Celeriac

Celeriac mixed with chopped bacon, onion and herbs makes a moist and tasty stuffing.

Serves 4

3½-pound chicken
1 tablespoon butter
celery leaves and parsley,
   to garnish

For the stuffing
1 pound celeriac, chopped
2 tablespoons butter
3 strips bacon, chopped

1 onion, finely chopped
leaves from 1 fresh thyme
   sprig, chopped
leaves from 1 small fresh tarragon
   sprig, chopped
2 tablespoons chopped
   fresh parsley
1½ cups fresh
   brown bread crumbs
dash of Worcestershire sauce
1 egg, beaten
salt and freshly ground
   black pepper

1 To make the stuffing, cook the celeriac in boiling water until tender. Drain well and chop finely.

2 Heat the butter in a saucepan, and gently cook the bacon and onion until the onion is soft. Stir in the celeriac and herbs, and cook, stirring occasionally, for 2–3 minutes. Meanwhile, preheat the oven to 400°F.

3 Remove the pan from heat and stir in the bread crumbs, Worcestershire sauce, seasoning and enough egg to bind. Use to stuff the neck end of the chicken. Season the bird's skin, then rub with the butter.

4 Roast the chicken, basting occasionally with the juices, for 1¼–1½ hours, until the juices run clear when the thickest part of the thigh is pierced with a skewer or knife.

5 Turn off the oven, prop the door open slightly and let the chicken rest for 10–15 minutes before carving and serving, garnished with celery leaves and parsley.

Roast Chicken with Herb & Orange Bread Stuffing

Tender roast chicken scented with orange and herbs, served with gravy.

Serves 4–6
2 onions
2 tablespoons butter, plus extra
2½ cups soft white bread crumbs
2 tablespoons chopped fresh
   mixed herbs
grated zest of 1 orange
3½-pound chicken with giblets

1 carrot, sliced
1 bay leaf
1 fresh thyme sprig
3¾ cups water
1 tablespoon tomato paste
2 teaspoons cornstarch, mixed
   into a thin paste with
   1 tablespoon cold water
salt and freshly ground
   black pepper
chopped fresh thyme, to garnish

1 Preheat the oven to 400°F. Finely chop one of the onions. Melt the butter in a pan and add the chopped onion. Cook for 3–4 minutes, until soft. Stir in the bread crumbs, chopped mixed herbs and orange zest. Season well.

2 Remove the giblets and put aside. Wash the neck end of the chicken and dry with paper towels. Spoon in the stuffing, then rub a little butter into the breast and season it well. Put the chicken into a roasting pan and bake for 20 minutes, then reduce the heat to 350°F and cook for another hour or until the juices run clear when the thickest part of the thigh is pierced with a knife or skewer.

3 Put the giblets, the remaining onion, the carrot, bay leaf, thyme and water into a large saucepan. Bring to a boil, then simmer while the chicken is roasting.

4 Place the chicken on a warmed serving platter and let rest. Skim the fat off the cooking juices, strain the juices and stock into a pan, and discard the giblets and vegetables. Simmer for about 5 minutes. Whisk in the tomato paste. Whisk the cornstarch paste into the gravy and cook for 1 minute. Season and serve with the chicken, garnished with chopped thyme.

Stuffed Roast Masala Chicken

At one time this dish was cooked only in Indian palaces.

Serves 4–6
1 envelope saffron powder
½ teaspoon grated nutmeg
1 tablespoon warm milk
3-pound chicken
6 tablespoons ghee or
   melted butter
½ cup dry, shredded coconut,
   toasted
steamed carrots, to serve

For the stuffing
3 medium onions, finely chopped
2 fresh green chiles, chopped
scant ½ cup golden raisins
½ cup ground almonds
½ cup dried apricots, soaked in
   water until soft
3 hard-boiled eggs, coarsely chopped
salt

For the masala
4 scallions, chopped
2 garlic cloves, crushed
1 teaspoon five-spice powder
4–6 green cardamom pods
½ teaspoon ground turmeric
1 teaspoon freshly ground
   black pepper
2 tablespoons plain yogurt
5 tablespoons hot water

1 Preheat the oven to 350°F. Mix the saffron, nutmeg and milk. Brush the inside of the chicken with the mixture and spread some under the skin.

2 Heat 4 tablespoons of the ghee or butter in a frying pan and fry the chicken all over. Remove from the pan and keep warm.

3 To make the stuffing, sauté the onions, chiles and golden raisins for 2–3 minutes in the same ghee or butter. Remove from heat, let cool, then mix in the ground almonds, apricots, chopped eggs and salt, and use to stuff the chicken.

4 To make the masala, heat the remaining ghee or butter in a pan and gently fry all the ingredients except the water for 2–3 minutes. Add to the water in a roasting pan.

5 Place the chicken on the masala, and roast for 1 hour. Remove the chicken, set aside and keep warm. Return the masala to the pan and cook until reduced. Pour onto the chicken. Sprinkle with toasted coconut and serve with carrots.

Roast Chicken with Almonds

In this Moroccan dish the chicken is stuffed with a mixture of couscous, nuts and fruit.

Serves 4
3½-pound chicken
pinch of ground ginger
pinch of ground cinnamon
pinch of saffron, dissolved in
   2 tablespoons boiling water
2 onions, chopped
1¼ cups Chicken Stock
3 tablespoons sliced almonds
1 tablespoon all-purpose flour
salt and freshly ground
   black pepper
lemon wedges and cilantro,
   to garnish

For the stuffing
⅓ cup couscous
½ cup Chicken Stock
1½ tablespoons butter
1 shallot, finely chopped
½ small apple, peeled, cored
   and chopped
5 teaspoons sliced almonds
2 tablespoons ground almonds
2 tablespoons chopped cilantro
good pinch of paprika
pinch of cayenne pepper

1 Preheat the oven to 350°F. To make the stuffing, place the couscous in a bowl, bring the chicken stock to a boil and pour it onto the couscous. Stir with a fork and set aside for 10 minutes for the couscous to swell.

2 Meanwhile, melt the butter in a small frying pan and sauté the shallot for 2–3 minutes, until soft. Fluff up the couscous, and stir in the shallot and all the butter from the pan. Add the remaining stuffing ingredients, season and stir well.

3 Loosely push the couscous mixture into the neck end of the chicken and truss the bird neatly.

4 Blend the ginger and cinnamon with the saffron water. Rub the chicken with salt and pepper, and then pour on the saffron water.

5 Place the chicken in a small roasting pan or dish so that it fits snugly. Spoon the chopped onions and stock around the edge, and then cover the dish with aluminum foil, pinching the foil around the edges of the dish firmly so that the chicken sits in a foil "tent."

6 Cook for 1¼ hours, then increase the temperature to 400°F. Transfer the chicken to a plate and strain the cooking liquid into a pitcher, reserving the chopped onions. Place the chicken back in the roasting pan with the onions, baste with a little of the cooking liquid and sprinkle on the almonds.

7 Return to the oven and cook for about 30 minutes, until the chicken is golden brown and the juices run clear when the thickest part of the thigh is pierced with a knife or skewer.

8 Pour off the fat from the reserved cooking juices and pour into a small saucepan. Blend the flour with 2 tablespoons cold water, stir into the pan with the cooking juices and heat gently, stirring to make a smooth sauce. Garnish the chicken with lemon wedges and cilantro, and serve with the sauce.

Sunday Roast Chicken

As you might expect, rum features in the glaze for this Caribbean-style roast.

Serves 6
3½-pound chicken
1 teaspoon paprika
1 teaspoon dried thyme
½ teaspoon dried tarragon
1 teaspoon garlic powder
1 tablespoon lemon juice
2 tablespoons honey
3 tablespoons dark rum
melted butter, for basting
1¼ cups Chicken Stock
salt and freshly ground
    black pepper
lime quarters and herbs,
    to garnish

1 Place the chicken in a roasting pan and sprinkle with the paprika, thyme, tarragon, garlic powder and salt and pepper. Rub the mixture all over the chicken, lifting the skin and spreading the seasoning underneath it too. Cover the chicken loosely with plastic wrap and let marinate in a cool place for at least 2 hours or preferably overnight in the refrigerator.

2 Preheat the oven to 375°F. Blend together the lemon juice, honey and rum, and pour over and under the skin of the chicken, rubbing it in well.

3 Spoon the melted butter onto the chicken, then roast for 1½–2 hours or until the juices run clear when the thickest part of the thigh is pierced with a skewer or knife.

4 Transfer the chicken to a warmed serving platter and let rest while you make the gravy. Pour the juices from the roasting pan into a small saucepan. Add the stock and simmer over low heat for 10 minutes or until reduced. Adjust the seasoning and pour into a pitcher. Serve with the chicken, garnished with lime quarters and herbs.

Cook's Tip
Extra herbs and rum can be used to make a richer, tastier gravy, if desired.

Harissa-spiced Roast Chicken

The spices and fruit in the stuffing give this chicken an unusual flavor.

Serves 4–5
3½-pound chicken
2–4 tablespoons garlic oil
a few bay leaves
2 teaspoons honey
2 teaspoons tomato paste
¼ cup lemon juice
⅔ cup Chicken Stock
½–1 teaspoon harissa

For the stuffing
2 tablespoons butter
1 onion, chopped
1 garlic clove, crushed
1½ teaspoons ground cinnamon
½ teaspoon ground cumin
1⅓ cups dried fruit, soaked for
    several hours or overnight in
    water to cover
¼ cup blanched almonds,
    finely chopped
salt and freshly ground
    black pepper

1 To make the stuffing, melt the butter in a saucepan. Add the onion and garlic, and cook gently for 5 minutes, until soft. Add the cinnamon and cumin and cook, stirring, for 2 minutes. Drain the dried fruit, chop it roughly and add to the stuffing with the almonds. Season with salt and pepper, and cook for 2 minutes more. Transfer to a bowl and let cool.

2 Preheat the oven to 400°F. Stuff the neck of the chicken with the fruit mixture, reserving any excess. Brush the garlic oil onto the chicken. Place the chicken in a roasting pan, tuck in the bay leaves and roast for 1–1¼ hours, basting occasionally, until the juices run clear when the thickest part of the thigh is pierced with a knife or skewer.

3 Transfer the chicken to a carving board. Pour off any excess fat from the roasting pan. Stir the honey, tomato paste, lemon juice, stock and harissa into the juices in the roasting pan. Add salt to taste. Bring to a boil, lower the heat and simmer for 2 minutes, stirring frequently.

4 Reheat any excess stuffing. Carve the chicken, pour the sauce into a small bowl and serve with the stuffing and chicken.

East African Roast Chicken

Smothered in a generous layer of butter combined with spices, herbs and coconut milk, this chicken is left to stand overnight so the flavors can mingle.

Serves 6
4-pound chicken
2 tablespoons softened butter, plus extra for basting
3 garlic cloves, crushed
1 teaspoon freshly ground black pepper
1 teaspoon ground turmeric
½ teaspoon ground cumin
1 teaspoon dried thyme
1 tablespoon finely chopped cilantro
¼ cup thick coconut milk
¼ cup medium-dry sherry
1 teaspoon tomato paste
salt and chili powder
cilantro leaves, to garnish

1 Remove the giblets from the chicken, if necessary, rinse out the cavity and pat the skin dry.

2 Put the butter and all the remaining ingredients in a bowl and combine well to form a thick paste.

3 Gently ease the skin of the chicken away from the flesh and rub the flesh generously with the herb and butter mixture. Rub more of the mixture onto the skin, legs and wings of the chicken and into the neck cavity.

4 Place the chicken in a roasting pan, cover loosely with aluminum foil and let marinate overnight in the refrigerator.

5 Preheat the oven to 375°F. Cover the chicken with clean foil and roast for 1 hour, then turn the chicken over and baste with the pan juices. Cover again with foil and cook for 30 minutes.

6 Remove the foil and place the chicken breast-side up. Rub with a little extra butter and roast for another 10–15 minutes, until the juices run clear when the thickest part of the thigh is pierced with a skewer or knife and the skin is golden brown. Let the chicken rest for 10–15 minutes in a warm place before serving, garnished with cilantro leaves.

Spicy Roast Chicken

Roasting chicken like this in an oven that has not been preheated produces a particularly crispy skin.

Serves 4
3½-pound chicken
juice of 1 lemon
4 garlic cloves, finely chopped
1 tablespoon each cayenne pepper, paprika and dried oregano
2 teaspoons olive oil
salt and freshly ground black pepper
cilantro sprigs, to garnish
sliced mixed peppers, to serve

1 Using a sharp knife or poultry shears, remove the backbone from the chicken. Turn it breast-side up. With the heel of your hand, press down firmly to break the breastbone and open the chicken out flat like a book. Insert a skewer through the chicken, at the thighs, to keep it flat during cooking.

2 Place the chicken in a shallow dish and pour in the lemon juice. Place the garlic, cayenne, paprika, oregano, black pepper and oil in a small bowl and mix well. Rub evenly on the surface of the chicken.

3 Cover the chicken and let marinate for 2–3 hours at room temperature, or chill the chicken overnight and then return to room temperature before roasting.

4 Season both sides of the chicken with salt and place it, skin-side up, in a shallow roasting pan.

5 Put the pan in a cold oven and set the temperature to 400°F. Roast for about 1 hour, until the chicken is done, basting with the juices in the pan. To test whether the chicken is cooked, prick the thickest part of the flesh with a skewer or knife: the juices that run out should be clear. Serve the chicken hot, garnished with cilantro sprigs and accompanied by mixed peppers.

Moroccan Roast Chicken

Ideally this chicken should
be cooked whole,
Moroccan-style, on a spit
over hot charcoal. However,
it is still excellent roasted in
a hot conventional oven and
can be cooked whole, halved
or in quarters.

Serves 4–6
4-pound chicken
2 small shallots

1 garlic clove
1 fresh parsley sprig
1 cilantro sprig
1 teaspoon salt
1½ teaspoons paprika
pinch of cayenne pepper
1–1½ teaspoons ground cumin
about 3 tablespoons butter
½–1 lemon (optional)
sprigs of parsley or cilantro,
    to garnish

1 Remove the chicken giblets if necessary and rinse out the
cavity with cold running water. Pat dry with paper towels.
Unless cooking it whole, cut the chicken in half or into quarters
using poultry shears or a sharp knife.

2 Place the shallots, garlic, herbs, salt and spices in a food
processor or blender and process until the shallots are finely
chopped. Add the butter and process to make a smooth paste.

3 Thoroughly rub the paste on the skin of the chicken and then
let it stand for 1–2 hours.

4 Preheat the oven to 400°F and place the chicken in a
roasting pan. If using, quarter the lemon and place one or two
quarters around the chicken pieces (or in the body cavity if the
chicken is whole) and squeeze a little juice on the skin. Roast
for 1–1¼ hours (2–2¼ hours for a whole bird), until the juices
run clear when the thickest part of the thigh is pierced with a
skewer or knife. Baste occasionally during cooking with the
juices in the roasting pan. If the skin starts to brown too quickly,
cover the chicken loosely with aluminum foil or waxed paper.

5 Let the chicken stand for 10–15 minutes, covered in foil,
before carving. Serve, garnished with parsley or cilantro.

Chicken with 40 Cloves of Garlic

This recipe is not as
alarming as it sounds. Long,
slow cooking makes the
garlic soft, fragrant and
sweet, and the delicious
flavor permeates the
chicken meat.

Serves 4–6
½ lemon
fresh rosemary sprigs
3½–4-pound chicken
4 or 5 whole garlic bulbs
¼ cup olive oil
salt and freshly ground
    black pepper
steamed fava beans and scallions,
    to serve

1 Preheat the oven to 375°F. Place the lemon half and the
rosemary sprigs in the chicken. Separate three or four of the
garlic bulbs into cloves and remove the papery husks, but do
not peel. Slice the top off the remaining garlic bulb.

2 Heat the oil in a large, flameproof casserole. Add the chicken,
turning it in the hot oil to coat the skin completely. Season with
salt and pepper, and add all the garlic.

3 Cover the casserole with a sheet of aluminum foil, then the
lid, to seal in the steam and the flavor. Cook for 1–1¼ hours,
until the chicken juices run clear when the thickest part of the
thigh is pierced with a skewer or knife.

4 Serve the chicken with the garlic, accompanied by steamed
fava beans and scallions.

Cook's Tip
*Make sure that each guest receives an equal portion of garlic.
The idea is to mash the garlic into the pan juices to make an
aromatic sauce.*

Chicken Breasts with Burnt Almond Stuffing

Bread crumbs are often the basis of stuffings, but this Jewish dish uses crunchy vegetables and matzo meal.

Serves 4
4 fat scallions
2 carrots
2 celery stalks
2 tablespoons oil

¼ cup sliced almonds
1¼ cups Chicken Stock
6 tablespoons medium-ground
 matzo meal
4 chicken breasts with skin
salt and freshly ground
 black pepper
fresh dill sprigs, to garnish
mixed salad, to serve

1 Preheat the oven to 375°F. Slice the onions and chop the carrots and celery. Heat the oil in a frying pan and sauté the almonds until they are light brown. Remove with a slotted spoon and set aside. Add the chopped vegetables to the pan and sauté over medium heat for a few minutes.

2 Add the seasoning and pour in half of the stock. Cook over high heat until the liquid is slightly reduced and the vegetables are just moist. Mix in the matzo meal and the sautéed almonds.

3 Ease the skin off the chicken breasts on one side and press some of the stuffing underneath each one. Press the skin back over the stuffing and slash the skin to stop it from curling up. Arrange the breasts in a roasting pan.

4 Roast the chicken breasts, skin-side up, for 20–30 minutes or until the meat is tender and white. The skin should be crisp and brown.

5 Keep the chicken warm while you make the gravy. Pour the remaining stock into the roasting pan and, over medium heat, stir in any chicken juices or remaining bits of stuffing. Bring to a boil and then strain into a pitcher. Serve with a mixed salad and garnish with fresh dill sprigs.

Chicken Roulé

Relatively easy to prepare, this recipe uses ground beef as a filling. It is rolled in chicken spread with a creamy garlic cheese that will melt in your mouth.

Serves 4
4 chicken breast fillets,
 about 4 ounces each
4 ounces ground beef

2 tablespoons chopped
 fresh chives
1 cup cream cheese with garlic
2 tablespoons honey
salt and freshly ground
 black pepper
cooked green beans and
 mushrooms, to serve

1 Preheat the oven to 375°F. Place the chicken breasts between two pieces of plastic wrap and beat with a meat mallet or rolling pin until ¼ inch thick and joined together.

2 Place the ground beef in a large saucepan. Cook for 3 minutes, stirring constantly to break up the clumps, then add the fresh chives and seasoning. Remove from heat and let cool.

3 Place the chicken on a board and spread with the cream cheese. Top with the ground beef mixture. Carefully roll up the chicken to form a sausage shape.

4 Brush with honey and place in a roasting pan. Cook for 1 hour. Remove from the pan and slice thinly. Serve with freshly cooked green beans and mushrooms.

Cook's Tip
Chives are one of the classic four fine herbes and have a subtle oniony flavor. They are best snipped with kitchen scissors, rather than chopped—and this is an easier method of preparing them too. The attractive, round pink flowers are also edible and make an interesting garnish.

Chicken in a Tomato Coat

This roasted chicken keeps deliciously moist as it cooks in its red "jacket."

Serves 4–6
3½–4-pound chicken
1 small onion
pat of butter
5 tablespoons Fresh
 Tomato Sauce

2 tablespoons chopped mixed fresh
 herbs, e.g. parsley, tarragon, sage,
 basil and marjoram, or
 2 teaspoons dried mixed herbs
small glass of dry white wine
2–3 small tomatoes, sliced
olive oil
a little cornstarch (optional)
salt and freshly ground
 black pepper

1 Preheat the oven to 375°F. Wash and wipe the chicken dry, and place in a roasting pan. Place the onion, the pat of butter and some seasoning inside the chicken.

2 Spread most of the tomato sauce on the chicken, and sprinkle with half the herbs and some seasoning. Pour the wine into the roasting pan.

3 Cover with aluminum foil, then roast for 1½ hours, basting occasionally. Remove the foil, spread with the remaining sauce and the sliced tomatoes, and drizzle with oil. Continue cooking for another 20–30 minutes, until the chicken juices run clear when the thickest part of the thigh is pierced with a skewer or knife.

4 Remove the chicken from the oven and let rest for 10–15 minutes. Sprinkle with the remaining herbs, then carve into portions. Serve with the juices from the roasting pan, thickened with a little cornstarch, if desired.

Cook's Tip
Whenever possible, buy sun-ripened tomatoes, which have a sweeter and more concentrated flavor than those grown under glass. Plum tomatoes are ideal for cooking, as they are much less watery than standard varieties.

Cold Sliced Roast Chicken

Cooking the chestnut stuffing under the skin keeps the breast meat succulent and creates an attractive striped effect when the chicken is carved. An excellent dish for a buffet.

Serves 6–8
2 onions, cut in half
2–3 tablespoons vegetable oil

1¼ cups fresh
 white bread crumbs
¾ cup unsweetened chestnut
 purée
4½-pound chicken
salt and freshly ground
 black pepper
fresh flat-leaf parsley, to garnish
lettuce leaves and potato salad,
 to serve

1 Chop 1 of the onions finely. Heat half of the vegetable oil in a small frying pan and sauté the chopped onion until golden. Stir in ½ cup boiling water, take the pan off the heat and let stand for 5 minutes to let some of the liquid be absorbed.

2 Mix the bread crumbs and chestnut purée with the onion and any liquid in the pan. Season well. Let cool completely.

3 Preheat the oven to 425°F. Wipe the chicken well with paper towels, inside and out, and carefully slide your hand under the skin on the breast to ease it away from the meat. Press the stuffing underneath the skin all over the breast.

4 Brush a roasting pan with the remaining oil and put in the chicken, breast-side down, with the remaining onion. Roast for 1 hour, basting occasionally and pouring off any excess liquid.

5 Turn the chicken over and continue to roast for another 15 minutes or until the juices run clear when the thickest part of the thigh is pierced with a skewer or knife. Cover the top with a strip of aluminum foil if it looks too brown.

6 When the chicken is cooked, let it cool before cutting downward into slices. Garnish with flat-leaf parsley, and serve with lettuce leaves and potato salad.

Crispy Roast Spring Chickens

These small birds, roasted with a honey glaze, are delicious either hot or cold. One bird is sufficient for two servings.

Serves 4
2 2-pound chickens
2 tablespoons honey
2 tablespoons sherry
1 tablespoon vinegar
salt and freshly ground
    black pepper
salad greens and lime wedges,
    to garnish

1 Preheat the oven to 350°F. Tie the birds into shape and place on a wire rack over the sink. Pour on boiling water to plump the flesh, then pat dry with paper towels.

2 To make the honey glaze, combine the honey, sherry and vinegar together in a small bowl, and brush over the birds. Season well.

3 Place the rack in a roasting pan and cook for 45–55 minutes, basting with the glaze until crisp and golden brown. Garnish with salad greens and lime wedges, and serve hot or cold.

Basic Herb Stuffing

This simple herb stuffing is suitable for all poultry.

1 small onion, finely chopped
1 tablespoon butter
2 cups fresh
    white bread crumbs
1 tablespoon chopped
    fresh parsley
1 teaspoon dried mixed herbs
1 egg, beaten
salt and freshly ground
    black pepper

1 Sauté the onion in the butter until tender. Set aside to cool.
2 Add to the remaining ingredients and mix thoroughly. Season well with salt and pepper.

Middle Eastern Spring Chickens

This dish is widely enjoyed in Lebanon and Syria. The stuffing is a delicious blend of meat, nuts and rice.

Serves 6–8
2 2¼-pound chickens
about 1 tablespoon butter
plain yogurt and salad, to serve

For the stuffing
3 tablespoons oil
1 onion, chopped
1 pound ground lamb
¾ cup almonds, chopped
¾ cup pine nuts
1½ cups cooked rice
salt and freshly ground
    black pepper

1 Preheat the oven to 350°F. To make the stuffing, heat the oil in a large frying pan and sauté the onion over low heat until slightly softened. Add the ground lamb and cook over medium heat for 4–8 minutes, until well browned, stirring frequently. Set aside.

2 Heat a small, heavy pan over medium heat and dry-fry the almonds and pine nuts for 2–3 minutes, until golden, shaking the pan frequently.

3 Combine the meat mixture, almonds, pine nuts and cooked rice. Season to taste with salt and pepper. Spoon the stuffing mixture into the body cavities of the chickens. (Cook any leftover stuffing separately in a greased ovenproof dish.) Rub the chickens all over with the butter.

4 Place the chickens in a large roasting pan, cover with aluminum foil and bake for 45–60 minutes. After about 30 minutes, remove the foil and baste the chickens with the cooking juices.

5 Continue roasting without the foil until the chickens are cooked through: the juices will run clear when the thickest part of the thigh is pierced with a skewer or knife. Serve the chickens, cut into portions, with yogurt and a salad.

French-style Pot-roast Poussins

Small, young chickens are cooked with tender baby vegetables in a wine-enriched stock—the perfect early summer meal.

Serves 4

1 tablespoon olive oil
1 onion, sliced
1 large garlic clove, sliced
⅓ cup diced bacon
2 poussins, just under
    1 pound each
2 tablespoons melted butter
2 baby celery hearts, quartered
8 baby carrots
2 small zucchini, cut
    into chunks
8 small new potatoes
2½ cups
    Chicken Stock
⅔ cup dry white wine
1 bay leaf
2 fresh thyme sprigs
2 fresh rosemary sprigs
1 tablespoon butter, softened
1 tablespoon all-purpose flour
salt and freshly ground
    black pepper
fresh herbs, to garnish

1 Preheat the oven to 375°F. Heat the oil in a large, flameproof casserole and add the onion, garlic and bacon. Sauté for 5–6 minutes, until the onions have softened. Brush the poussins with a little of the melted butter and season well. Place on top of the onion mixture and arrange the prepared vegetables around them. Pour the chicken stock and wine around the birds, and add the herbs.

2 Cover, cook for 20 minutes, then remove the lid and brush the birds with the remaining melted butter. Cook for another 25–30 minutes, until golden.

3 Transfer the poussins to a warmed serving platter and cut each in half. Remove the vegetables with a draining spoon and arrange them around the birds. Cover with aluminum foil and keep warm.

4 Discard the herbs from the cooking juices. In a bowl, mix the softened butter and flour to form a paste. Bring the cooking liquid to a boil and then whisk in spoonfuls of the paste until thickened. Season the sauce, and serve with the poussins and vegetables, garnished with herbs.

Baby Chickens with Cranberry Sauce

Fresh cranberries make a delicious sauce for these simply roasted poussins.

Serves 4

4 poussins, with giblets (optional),
    about 1 pound each
3 tablespoons butter
    or margarine
1 onion, quartered
¼ cup port
¾ cup Chicken Stock
2 tablespoons honey
1¼ cups cranberries
salt and freshly ground
    black pepper
cooked new potatoes and broccoli,
    to serve

1 Preheat the oven to 450°F. Smear the poussins on all sides with 2 tablespoons of the butter or margarine. Arrange them, on their sides, in a roasting pan in which they will fit comfortably. Sprinkle them with salt and pepper. Add the onion quarters to the pan. Chop the giblets and livers, if using, and arrange them around the poussins.

2 Roast for 20 minutes, basting frequently. Turn the poussins onto their other sides and roast for 20 more minutes, basting often. Turn them breast up and continue roasting for about 15 minutes, until they are cooked through. Transfer to a warmed serving dish. Cover with aluminum foil and set aside.

3 Skim any fat off the juices in the roasting pan. Put the pan over medium heat and bring the juices to a boil. Add the port and bring back to a boil, stirring well to dislodge any particles sticking to the bottom of the pan.

4 Strain the sauce into a small saucepan. Add the chicken stock, return to a boil and boil until reduced by half. Stir in the honey and cranberries. Simmer for about 3 minutes, until the cranberries pop.

5 Remove the pan from heat and swirl in the remaining butter or margarine. Season to taste, pour the sauce into a pitcher or gravy boat and serve with the poussins, accompanied by new potatoes and broccoli.

Poussins with Bulghur Wheat & Vermouth

These young birds are filled with a bulghur wheat and nut stuffing laced with vermouth, and served with a medley of roast vegetables finished with a vermouth glaze.

Serves 4
⅓ cup bulghur wheat
⅔ cup dry white vermouth
¼ cup olive oil
I large onion, finely chopped
2 carrots, finely chopped

¾ cup pine nuts, chopped
I teaspoon celery seeds
4 poussins
3 red onions, quartered
4 baby eggplant, halved
4 patty pan squashes
12 baby carrots
3 tablespoons corn syrup
salt and freshly ground
    black pepper

I Preheat the oven to 400°F. Put the bulghur wheat in a heatproof bowl, pour in half the vermouth and cover with boiling water. Set aside.

2 Heat half the oil in a large, shallow frying pan. Add the onion and carrots, and cook for 10 minutes, then remove the pan from heat and stir in the pine nuts, celery seeds and the well-drained bulghur wheat.

3 Stuff the poussins with the bulghur wheat mixture. Place them in a roasting pan, brush with oil and sprinkle with salt and pepper. Roast for 45–55 minutes, until the juices run clear when the thickest part of the thigh is pierced with a skewer or knife.

4 Meanwhile, spread out the red onions, eggplant, patty pans and baby carrots in a single layer on a baking sheet.

5 Mix the corn syrup with the remaining vermouth and oil in a small bowl. Season with salt and pepper to taste. Brush the corn syrup mixture on the vegetables and roast for 35–45 minutes, until golden. Cut each poussin in half and serve immediately with the roasted vegetables.

Poussins with Raisin-walnut Stuffing

This easy-to-prepare traditional American dish offers something different for a midweek supper.

Serves 4
I cup port
⅔ cup raisins
I tablespoon walnut oil
I cup mushrooms,
    finely chopped
I large celery stalk,
    finely chopped

I small onion, chopped
I cup fresh bread crumbs
½ cup chopped walnuts
I tablespoon each chopped fresh
    basil and parsley or
    2 tablespoons chopped
    fresh parsley
½ teaspoon dried thyme
6 tablespoons butter, melted
4 poussins
salt and freshly ground
    black pepper
salad and vegetables, to serve

I Preheat the oven to 350°F. In a small bowl, combine the port and raisins, and let soak for 20 minutes.

2 Meanwhile, heat the oil in a nonstick frying pan. Add the mushrooms, celery and onion, and cook over low heat for 8–10 minutes, until softened. Let cool slightly.

3 Drain the raisins, reserving the port. Combine the raisins, bread crumbs, walnuts, basil (if using), parsley and thyme in a bowl. Stir in the onion mixture and 4 tablespoons of the melted butter. Add salt and pepper to taste.

4 Fill the cavity of each bird with the stuffing mixture. Do not pack too tightly. Tie the legs together, looping the tail with string to enclose the stuffing securely.

5 Brush the birds with the remaining butter and place in a roasting pan just large enough to hold them comfortably. Pour in the reserved port. Roast, basting occasionally, for about I hour or until the juices run clear when the thickest part of the thigh is pierced with a skewer or knife. Serve immediately, pouring some of the pan juices over each bird. Accompany with salad and vegetables.

Baked Poussins

The important factor in this recipe is a good, long marinating time before cooking, which lets the spicy yogurt mixture penetrate and the flavors to permeate the birds.

Serves 4

2 cups plain yogurt
¼ cup olive oil
1 large onion, grated
2 garlic cloves, crushed
½ teaspoon paprika
2–3 saffron threads, soaked in 1 tablespoon boiling water
juice of 1 lemon
4 poussins, halved
oil, for greasing
salt and freshly ground black pepper
Romaine lettuce salad, to serve

1 In a bowl, blend together the plain yogurt, olive oil, grated onion, crushed garlic, paprika, saffron threads with their soaking water and lemon juice, and season to taste with salt and freshly ground black pepper.

2 Place the poussin halves in a shallow dish and pour on the yogurt mixture, ensuring that they are well coated, spreading with the back of a spoon or your fingers. Cover and let marinate overnight in a cool place or for at least 4 hours in the refrigerator.

3 Preheat the oven to 350°F. Arrange the poussins in a greased ovenproof dish and bake for 30–45 minutes, basting frequently until cooked. Serve with a Romaine lettuce salad.

> **Cook's Tip**
> The poussins can also be grilled outdoors, which makes them, if anything, even more delicious.

Parmesan Chicken Casserole

The tomato sauce may be made the day before and left to cool. Serve with crusty bread and salad.

Serves 4

4 chicken breast fillets, skinned
¼ cup all-purpose flour
3 tablespoons olive oil
salt and freshly ground black pepper

For the tomato sauce

1 tablespoon olive oil
1 onion, finely chopped
1 celery stalk, finely chopped
1 red bell pepper, seeded and diced
1 garlic clove, crushed
1 4-ounce can chopped tomatoes, with their juice
⅔ cup Chicken Stock
1 tablespoon tomato paste
2 teaspoons sugar
1 tablespoon chopped fresh basil
1 tablespoon chopped fresh parsley

To assemble

8 ounces mozzarella cheese, sliced
¼ cup grated Parmesan cheese
2 tablespoons fresh bread crumbs

1 To make the tomato sauce, heat the oil in a frying pan. Add the onion, celery, red pepper and garlic, and cook gently until tender. Add the tomatoes with their juice, the stock, tomato paste, sugar and herbs. Season and bring to a boil. Simmer for 30 minutes until thick, stirring occasionally.

2 Divide each chicken fillet into two natural pieces, place between sheets of plastic wrap and flatten to a thickness of ¼ inch with a rolling pin or meat mallet. Season the flour with salt and pepper. Toss the chicken breasts in the flour to coat, shaking to remove the excess.

3 Preheat the oven to 350°F. Heat the oil in a large frying pan and cook the chicken quickly in batches for 3–4 minutes, until colored.

4 To assemble, layer the chicken pieces in an ovenproof dish with the cheeses and thick tomato sauce, finishing with a layer of cheese and bread crumbs on top. Bake, uncovered, for 20–30 minutes or until golden brown. Serve immediately.

Crunchy Stuffed Chicken Breasts

These can be prepared ahead of time as long as the stuffing is quite cold before it is spooned into the "pockets." It is an ideal dish for entertaining.

Serves 4

4 chicken breast fillets
2 tablespoons butter
I garlic clove, crushed
I tablespoon Dijon mustard
cooked vegetables, to serve

For the stuffing

I tablespoon butter
I bunch scallions, sliced
3 tablespoons fresh bread crumbs
2 tablespoons pine nuts
I egg yolk
I tablespoon chopped
    fresh parsley
salt and freshly ground
    black pepper
¼ cup grated cheese

For the topping

2 strips bacon, finely chopped
I cup fresh bread crumbs
I tablespoon grated
    Parmesan cheese
I tablespoon chopped
    fresh parsley

I Preheat the oven to 400°F. First, make the stuffing. Heat the butter in a heavy frying pan and cook the scallions, stirring occasionally, until soft. Remove from heat and let cool for a few minutes. Add the remaining ingredients and mix thoroughly.

2 To make the topping, fry the chopped bacon until crisp, then drain well on paper towels. Place the bread crumbs, grated Parmesan cheese and parsley in a bowl, and add the bacon. Mix thoroughly to combine.

3 Carefully cut a pocket in each chicken breast, using a sharp knife. Divide the stuffing into fourths and use to fill the pockets. Transfer the chicken breasts to a buttered ovenproof dish.

4 Melt the remaining butter, mix it with the crushed garlic and mustard, and brush liberally on the chicken. Press on the topping and bake, uncovered, for 30–40 minutes or until tender. Serve with vegetables.

Oven-fried Chicken

An easy way of cooking "fried" chicken with a crisp bread crumb coating—once it is in the oven, you can turn your attention to preparing the rest of the meal without any worries.

Serves 4

4 large chicken portions
½ cup all-purpose flour
½ teaspoon salt
¼ teaspoon black pepper
I egg
2 tablespoons water
2 tablespoons finely chopped
    mixed fresh herbs, e.g. parsley,
    basil and thyme
I cup fresh bread crumbs
¾ cup grated
    Parmesan cheese
oil, for greasing
lemon wedges, to serve

I Preheat the oven to 400°F. Rinse the chicken portions and pat dry with paper towels.

2 Combine the flour, salt and pepper on a large plate and stir with a fork to mix. Coat the chicken portions on all sides with the seasoned flour and shake off the excess.

3 Sprinkle a little water onto the chicken portions and coat again lightly with the seasoned flour.

4 Beat the egg with 2 tablespoons water in a shallow dish and stir in the herbs. Combine the bread crumbs and grated Parmesan cheese on a plate.

5 Dip the chicken portions into the egg mixture, turning to coat them evenly, then roll in the bread crumbs, patting them on with your fingertips to help them stick.

6 Place the chicken portions in a greased shallow roasting pan or ovenproof dish large enough to hold them in one layer. Bake for 20–30 minutes until thoroughly cooked and golden brown. Serve immediately, with lemon wedges for squeezing.

Chicken Baked in a Salt Crust

This unusual dish is extremely simple to make. Once it is cooked, you just break off the salt crust to reveal the wonderfully tender, golden-brown chicken within.

Serves 4
bunch of mixed fresh herbs, e.g. rosemary, thyme, marjoram and parsley
3½-pound corn-fed chicken
about 7 cups coarse sea salt
1 egg white
1–2 whole garlic bulbs, baked for 1 hour, to serve

1 Preheat the oven to 375°F. Stuff the herbs into the chicken cavity, then truss the chicken.

2 Combine the sea salt and egg white until all the salt crystals are moistened. Select a roasting pan into which the chicken will fit neatly, then line it with a large double layer of aluminum foil. Spread a thick layer of moistened salt in the foil-lined pan and place the chicken on top. Cover with the remaining salt and press into a neat shape, over and around the chicken, making sure it is completely enclosed.

3 Bring the foil edges up and over the chicken to enclose it and bake for 1½ hours. Remove from the oven and let rest for 10 minutes.

4 Carefully lift the foil package from the container and open it. Break the salt crust to reveal the chicken inside. Brush any traces of salt from the bird, then serve with baked whole garlic bulbs. Each clove can be slipped from its skin and eaten with a bite of chicken.

Cook's Tip
Sea salt is available in the form of whole crystals and coarsely or finely ground. Coarsely ground salt works best here.

Roast Turkey

A classic roast, served with stuffing balls, chipolata sausages and gravy. Roast potatoes and Brussels sprouts are the traditional accompaniments.

Serves 8
10-pound turkey, with giblets (thawed overnight if frozen)
1 large onion, peeled and stuck with 6 whole cloves
¼ cup butter, softened
10 chipolata sausages
salt and freshly ground black pepper

For the stuffing
8 ounces bacon, chopped
1 large onion, finely chopped
1 pound pork sausagemeat
⅓ cup rolled oats
2 tablespoons chopped fresh parsley
2 teaspoons dried mixed herbs
1 large egg, beaten
½ cup dried apricots, finely chopped

For the gravy
2 tablespoons all-purpose flour
scant 2 cups giblet stock

1 Preheat the oven to 400°F. To make the stuffing, cook the bacon and onion gently in a pan until the bacon is crisp and the onion tender. Transfer to a large bowl and mix in all the remaining stuffing ingredients. Season to taste.

2 Stuff the neck end of the turkey, tuck the flap of skin under and secure it with a small skewer or stitch it with thread. Reserve any remaining stuffing.

3 Put the whole onion, studded with cloves, in the body cavity of the turkey and tie the legs together. Weigh the stuffed bird and calculate the cooking time; allow 15 minutes per 1 pound plus 15 extra minutes. Place the turkey in a large roasting pan.

4 Spread the turkey with the butter and season it with salt and pepper. Cover it loosely with aluminum foil and cook it for 30 minutes. Baste the turkey with the pan juices. Then lower the oven temperature to 350°F and cook for the remainder of the calculated time (about 3½ hours for a 10-pound bird). Baste it every 30 minutes or so. Remove the foil from the turkey for the last hour of cooking and baste it.

5 Using wet hands, shape the remaining stuffing into small balls or pack it into a greased ovenproof dish. Cook for 20 minutes or until golden brown and crisp.

6 About 20 minutes before the end of the cooking time, place the chipolatas in an ovenproof dish and put them in the oven.

7 The turkey is cooked if the juices run clear when the thickest part of the thigh is pierced with a skewer or knife. Transfer it to a serving plate, cover with foil and let it stand for 10–15 minutes before carving. To make the gravy, spoon off the fat from the roasting pan, leaving the meat juices. Blend in the flour and cook for 2 minutes. Gradually stir in the stock and bring to a boil. Check the seasoning and pour into a pitcher or gravy boat. Remove the skewer or thread from the bird and pour any juices into the gravy. To serve, surround the turkey with the chipolata sausages and stuffing balls.

Roast Duckling with Honey

A sweet-and-sour orange sauce is the perfect foil for this rich-tasting Polish duck recipe, and frying the orange zest intensifies the flavor.

Serves 4

5-pound duckling
½ teaspoon ground allspice
1 orange
1 tablespoon sunflower oil
2 tablespoons all-purpose flour
⅔ cup duck or Chicken Stock
2 teaspoons red wine vinegar
1 tablespoon honey
salt and freshly ground
    black pepper
watercress and thinly pared
    orange zest, to garnish

1 Preheat the oven to 425°F. Using a fork, pierce the duckling all over, except the breast, so that the fat runs out during cooking.

2 Rub all over the skin of the duckling with ground allspice and sprinkle with salt and pepper to season, pressing into the surface of the bird.

3 Put the duckling on a rack over a roasting pan and cook for about 20 minutes. Then reduce the oven temperature to 375°F and cook for another 2 hours.

4 Meanwhile, thinly pare the zest from the orange and cut into very fine strips. Heat the oil in a pan and gently fry the orange zest for 2–3 minutes. Squeeze the juice from the orange and set aside.

5 Transfer the duckling to a warmed serving dish and keep warm. Drain off all but 2 tablespoons fat from the pan, sprinkle in the flour and stir well.

6 Stir in the stock, vinegar, honey, orange juice and zest. Bring to a boil, stirring constantly. Simmer for 2–3 minutes and season to taste. Pour into a serving bowl or pitcher.

7 Serve the duckling garnished with watercress and thinly pared orange zest and accompanied by the sauce.

Roast Wild Duck with Juniper

Wild duck should be served slightly underdone or the meat will be very tough.

Serves 2

1 tablespoon juniper berries, fresh
    if possible
1 wild duck (preferably a mallard)
2 tablespoons butter, softened
3 tablespoons gin
½ cup duck or Chicken Stock
½ cup whipping cream
salt and freshly ground
    black pepper
watercress, to garnish

1 Preheat the oven to 450°F. Reserve a few juniper berries for garnishing and put the remainder in a heavy plastic bag. Crush coarsely with a rolling pin.

2 Wipe the duck with damp paper towels. Tie the legs with string, then spread the butter on the duck. Season and press the crushed juniper berries onto the skin.

3 Place the duck in a roasting pan and roast for 20–25 minutes, basting occasionally; it is ready if the juices run clear when the thickest part of the thigh is pierced with a knife. Pour the juices from the cavity into the roasting pan and transfer the duck to a carving board. Cover loosely with aluminum foil and let stand for 10–15 minutes.

4 Skim off as much fat as possible from the roasting pan, leaving as much of the juniper as possible, and place the pan over medium-high heat. Add the gin and stir, scraping the sediment from the bottom and bring to a boil. Cook until the liquid has almost evaporated, then add the stock and boil to reduce by half. Add the cream and boil for 2 minutes or until the sauce thickens slightly. Strain into a small saucepan and keep warm.

5 Carve the legs from the duck and separate the thighs from the drumsticks. Remove the breasts and arrange the duck in a warmed serving dish. Pour on a little sauce, sprinkle with the reserved juniper berries and garnish with watercress. Pass the rest of the sauce separately in a pitcher or gravy boat.

Wild Duck Roasted with Morels & Madeira

Wild duck has a rich, autumnal flavor that combines well with stronger-tasting mushrooms.

Serves 4

2 2¼-pound mallards (dressed and barded weight)
4 tablespoons unsalted butter
5 tablespoons Madeira or sherry
1 medium onion, halved and sliced
½ celery stalk, chopped
1 small carrot, chopped
10 large dried morel mushrooms
3 cups assorted mushrooms, trimmed and sliced
2½ cups Chicken Stock, boiling
1 fresh thyme sprig
2 teaspoons wine vinegar
salt and freshly ground black pepper
fresh parsley sprigs and carrots, to garnish

1 Preheat the oven to 375°F and season the ducks with salt and pepper. Melt half of the butter in a heavy frying pan. Add the ducks and brown the birds evenly. Transfer them to a shallow dish.

2 Heat the sediment in the pan, pour in the Madeira or sherry and bring to a boil, stirring constantly and scraping the bottom to deglaze the pan. Pour this liquid onto the birds and set the dish aside.

3 Heat the remaining butter in a large, flameproof casserole and add the onion, celery and carrot. Place the birds on top (reserve the Madeira or sherry) and cook for 40 minutes.

4 Tie all the mushrooms in an 18-inch square of muslin. Add the stock, the Madeira or sherry from the frying pan, the thyme and the muslin bag to the casserole. Cover and return to the oven for 40 minutes.

5 Transfer the birds to a warmed serving platter, remove and discard the thyme and set the mushrooms aside. Process the braising liquid in a food processor or blender and pour it back into the casserole. Break open the muslin bag and stir the mushrooms into the sauce. Add the vinegar, season to taste and heat through gently.

6 Garnish the ducks with parsley and carrots. Pass the Madeira or sherry sauce separately in a pitcher or gravy boat.

> **Cook's Tip**
> Mallard is the most popular wild duck, although there are substitutes. Ask your butcher to choose for you.

Duckling Jubilee

This East European dish partners roast duck with a lightly spiced apricot sauce.

Serves 4

4½-pound duckling
¼ cup chopped fresh parsley
1 lemon, quartered
3 carrots, sliced
2 celery stalks, sliced
1 onion, roughly chopped
salt and freshly ground black pepper
apricots and sage flowers, to garnish

For the sauce
15-ounce can apricots in syrup
¼ cup sugar
2 teaspoons mustard
¼ cup apricot jam
1 tablespoon lemon juice
2 teaspoons grated lemon zest
¼ cup orange juice
¼ teaspoon each ground ginger and ground coriander
4–5 tablespoons brandy

1 Preheat the oven to 425°F. Clean the duck well and pat dry with paper towels. Season the skin liberally. Combine the parsley, lemon, carrots, celery and onion in a bowl, then spoon this mixture into the cavity of the duck.

2 Cook the duck for 45 minutes on a rack set over a roasting pan. Baste the duck occasionally with its juices. Remove the duck from the oven and prick the skin well. Return it to the oven, reduce the temperature to 350°F and cook for another 1–1½ hours or until golden brown, tender and crisp.

3 Meanwhile, to make the sauce, put the apricots and their syrup, the sugar and mustard in a food processor or blender. Add the jam and process until smooth.

4 Pour the apricot mixture into a pan and stir in the lemon juice and zest, orange juice and spices. Bring to a boil, add the brandy and cook for another 1–2 minutes. Remove from heat and adjust the seasoning. Pour into a pitcher or gravy boat.

5 Discard the fruit, vegetables and herbs from inside the duck and arrange the bird on a serving platter. Garnish with fresh apricots and sage flowers. Serve the sauce separately.

Roast Goose with Apples

The apples are filled with a hazelnut, raisin and orange stuffing and roasted around the bird.

Serves 6

scant 1 cup raisins
grated zest and juice of 1 orange
2 tablespoons butter
1 onion, finely chopped
¾ cup hazelnuts, chopped
3 cups fresh white bread crumbs
1 tablespoon honey
1 tablespoon chopped
    fresh marjoram
2 tablespoons chopped
    fresh parsley
6 red apples
1 tablespoon lemon juice
10–11-pound young goose
salt and freshly ground
    black pepper
fresh herbs, to garnish
orange wedges, red cabbage and
    green beans, to serve

1 Preheat the oven to 425°F. Put the raisins in a bowl and pour in the orange juice. Melt the butter in a frying pan and sauté the onions for 5 minutes. Add the nuts and cook for 4–5 minutes or until beginning to brown. Add the onion and nuts to the raisins with 1 cup of the bread crumbs, the orange zest, honey, herbs and seasoning. Mix well.

2 Remove the apple cores to leave a ¾-inch hole. Make a shallow cut horizontally around the middle of each apple. Brush the cut and the cavity with the lemon juice. Pack the center of each apple with nut and raisin stuffing, reserving the remainder.

3 Mix the remaining bread crumbs into the leftover stuffing and place in the bird's cavity. Close with a small skewer. Place the goose in a roasting pan and prick the skin with a skewer. Roast for 30 minutes, then reduce the temperature to 350°F and cook for another 3 hours or until the juices run clear when the thickest part of the thigh is pierced with a skewer or knife. Pour off the excess fat from time to time.

4 Bake the apples around the goose for the last 30–40 minutes of its cooking time. Rest the goose for 10–15 minutes before carving. Garnish with fresh herbs and serve with the stuffed apples, orange wedges, red cabbage and green beans.

Roast Goose with Caramelized Apples & Port & Orange Gravy

Choose a young goose with a pliable breast bone.

Serves 8

10–12-pound goose,
    with giblets
salt and freshly ground
    black pepper

For the apple and nut stuffing

1 cup prunes
⅔ cup port
1½ pounds apples, peeled,
    cored and cubed
1 large onion, chopped
4 celery stalks, sliced
1 tablespoon dried mixed herbs

finely grated zest of 1 orange
1 goose liver, chopped
1 pound pork sausagemeat
1 cup chopped pecans or walnuts
2 eggs

For the caramelized apples

¼ cup butter
¼ cup red currant jelly
2 tablespoons red wine vinegar
8 small apples, peeled and cored

For the gravy

2 tablespoons all-purpose flour
2½ cups giblet stock
juice of 1 orange

1 To make the stuffing, soak the prunes in the port the day before serving. Then pit and cut each into four pieces, reserving the port. Mix with all the remaining stuffing ingredients and season. Moisten with half the reserved port.

2 Preheat the oven to 400°F. Stuff the neck end of the goose, tucking the flap of skin under and securing it with a small skewer. Remove the excess fat from the cavity and pack it with the stuffing. Tie the legs together to hold them in place.

3 Weigh the stuffed goose and calculate the cooking time: allow 15 minutes per 1 pound. Put the bird on a rack in a roasting pan and rub the skin with salt. Prick the skin all over.

4 Roast the goose for 30 minutes, then reduce the oven temperature to 350°F and roast for the remaining cooking time. Pour off any fat produced during cooking into a bowl. The goose is cooked if the juices run clear when the thickest part of the thigh is pierced with a skewer or knife. Pour a little cold water on the breast to crisp the skin.

5 Meanwhile, to make the caramelized apples, melt the butter with the red currant jelly and vinegar in a small roasting pan or shallow ovenproof dish. Put in the apples, baste them well and cook for 15–20 minutes. Baste halfway through the cooking time. Do not overcook them, or they will collapse.

6 Lift the goose onto a serving dish and let it stand for 10–15 minutes before carving. Pour off the excess fat from the roasting pan, leaving any sediment in the bottom. To make the gravy, stir the flour into the sediment and cook gently until golden brown, then blend in the stock. Bring to a boil, add the remaining reserved port, the orange juice and seasoning. Simmer for 2–3 minutes. Strain into a pitcher or gravy boat. Surround the goose with the caramelized apples, spoon on the red currant glaze and serve with the gravy.

Roast Pheasant with Port

Roasting young pheasants in foil keeps the flesh particularly tender and moist.

Serves 4
oil, for brushing
2 hen pheasants, about
   1½ pounds each
¼ cup unsalted butter, softened
8 fresh thyme sprigs
2 bay leaves
6 strips bacon
1 tablespoon all-purpose flour
¾ cup game or Chicken Stock,
   plus more if needed
1 tablespoon red currant jelly
3–4 tablespoons port
freshly ground black pepper

1 Preheat the oven to 450°F. Line a large roasting pan with a sheet of strong aluminum foil large enough to enclose the pheasants. Lightly brush the foil with oil.

2 Wipe the pheasants with damp paper towels and remove any extra fat or skin. Using your fingertips, carefully loosen the skin of the breasts. Spread the butter between the skin and breast meat of each bird. Tie the legs securely with string, then place the thyme sprigs and a bay leaf on the breast of each bird. Lay bacon strips on the breasts, place the birds in the foil-lined pan and season with pepper. Bring together the long ends of the foil, fold over securely to enclose, then seal the ends.

3 Roast the birds for 20 minutes, then reduce the oven temperature to 375°F and cook for another 40 minutes. Uncover the birds and roast for 10–15 more minutes or until they are browned and the juices run clear when the thickest part of the thigh is pierced with a knife or skewer. Transfer the birds to a board and let stand, covered with clean foil, for 10–15 minutes before carving.

4 Pour the juices from the foil into the roasting pan and skim off any fat. Sprinkle in the flour and cook over medium heat, stirring, until smooth. Whisk in the stock and red currant jelly, and bring to a boil. Simmer until the sauce thickens slightly, adding more stock if needed, then stir in the port and adjust the seasoning to taste. Strain and serve with the pheasants.

Pheasant in Green Pipian Sauce

An unusual and delicious way of cooking pheasant, Mexican-style, that keeps it wonderfully moist.

Serves 4
2 pheasants
2 tablespoons corn oil
generous 1 cup pepitas
   (Mexican pumpkin seeds)
1 tablespoon achiote
   (annatto) seeds
1 onion, finely chopped
2 garlic cloves, chopped
10-ounce can tomatillos
   (Mexican green tomatoes)
2 cups Chicken Stock
salt and freshly ground
   black pepper
cilantro, to garnish

1 Preheat the oven to 350°F. Using a large, sharp knife or poultry shears, cut the pheasants in half lengthwise and season well with salt and pepper. Heat the oil in a large frying pan and sauté the pheasant pieces until lightly browned on all sides. Lift out of the pan, drain and arrange, skin-side up, in a single layer in a roasting pan. Set aside.

2 Grind the pepitas finely in a nut grinder or a food processor. Shake through a sieve into a bowl. Grind the achiote seeds, add them to the bowl and set aside.

3 Place the onion, garlic, tomatillos and their juice into a food processor and purée. Pour into a saucepan. Add the pepita mixture, stir in the stock and simmer over very low heat for 10 minutes. Do not let the mixture boil, as it will separate. Remove from heat and let cool.

4 Pour the sauce onto the pheasant halves. Bake for 40 minutes or until tender, basting occasionally with the sauce. Garnish with cilantro and serve.

Cook's Tip
Achiote is a typical ingredient in the Yucatán. There is no substitute. Look for it at Caribbean and tropical markets.

Chicken, Barley & Apple Casserole

Barley is underrated as a casserole ingredient these days: it is nutritious and makes a really tasty and filling meal.

Serves 4

1 tablespoon sunflower oil
1 large onion, sliced
1 garlic clove, crushed
3 carrots, cut into sticks
2 celery stalks, thickly sliced

⅔ cup pearl barley
4 chicken breast fillets, skinned
3 cups Chicken Stock
1 bay leaf
few sprigs each of fresh thyme
   and marjoram, plus extra
   to garnish
3 apples

1 Heat the oil in a flameproof casserole and sauté the onion for about 5 minutes, until soft. Stir in the garlic, carrots and celery, and continue to cook over low heat for another 5 minutes.

2 Stir in the pearl barley, then add the chicken breast fillets, stock and herbs. Bring to a boil, lower the heat, cover the casserole and cook gently for 1 hour.

3 Core the apples and slice them thickly. Add to the casserole, replace the lid and cook for 15 more minutes or until the apples are just tender but not mushy.

4 Divide the barley, vegetables and cooking juices among four warmed plates and arrange the chicken on top. Garnish with fresh herbs and serve.

Cook's Tip
You can also cook the casserole in a preheated 375°F oven. The timing is the same. Chicken thighs can be substituted for breast fillets—they are not as "meaty" but are a good value for the money.

Country Cider Casserole

Root vegetables, chopped bacon and prunes all bring flavor to the wonderful cider gravy in this filling chicken dish.

Serves 4

2 tablespoons all-purpose flour
4 boneless chicken breasts
2 tablespoons butter
1 tablespoon vegetable oil
15 baby onions

4 strips bacon, chopped
2 teaspoons Dijon mustard
scant 2 cups dry cider
3 carrots, chopped
2 parsnips, chopped
12 prunes, pitted
1 fresh rosemary sprig
1 bay leaf
salt and freshly ground
   black pepper
mashed potatoes, to serve

1 Preheat the oven to 325°F. Place the flour and seasoning in a plastic bag, add the chicken and shake until coated. Set aside.

2 Heat the butter and oil in a flameproof casserole. Add the onions and bacon, and fry over medium heat for 4 minutes, until the onions have softened. Remove from the pan with a slotted spoon and set aside.

3 Add the floured chicken breasts to the oil in the casserole and fry until they are browned all over, then spread a little of the mustard on top of each breast.

4 Return the onions and bacon to the casserole. Pour in the cider and add the carrots, parsnips, prunes, rosemary and bay leaf. Season well. Bring to a boil, then cover and transfer to the oven. Cook for about 1½ hours, until the chicken is tender.

5 Remove the rosemary sprig and bay leaf, and serve the chicken hot with creamy mashed potatoes.

Chicken in Creamed Horseradish

The piquant flavor of the horseradish sauce gives this quick dish a sophisticated and unusual taste. If you are using fresh horseradish, halve the amount.

Serves 4
2 tablespoons olive oil
4 chicken portions
2 tablespoons butter
2 tablespoons all-purpose flour
scant 2 cups Chicken Stock
2 tablespoons horseradish sauce
1 tablespoon chopped
   fresh parsley
salt and freshly ground
   black pepper
mashed potatoes and lightly
   cooked green beans, to serve

1 Heat the oil in a large, flameproof casserole and gently brown the chicken portions on both sides over medium heat. Remove the chicken from the casserole and keep warm.

2 Wipe out the casserole, then add the butter and let it melt. Stir in the flour and gradually blend in the stock. Bring to a boil, stirring constantly.

3 Add the horseradish sauce and season with salt and pepper. Return the chicken to the casserole, cover and simmer for 30–40 minutes or until tender.

4 Transfer to a serving dish and sprinkle with the chopped parsley. Serve with mashed potatoes and green beans.

Cook's Tip
Fresh horseradish requires very careful handling, as the volatile mustard oils given off when it is peeled and grated irritate the mucous membranes and the eyes, causing them to water. Dried flaked horseradish root is a safer substitute.

Chicken with Tomatoes & Honey

An easy-to-make Moroccan-style dish served with a sprinkling of toasted almonds and sesame seeds.

Serves 4
2 tablespoons sunflower oil
2 tablespoons butter
4 chicken quarters or 1 whole
   chicken, quartered
1 onion, grated or very
   finely chopped
1 garlic clove, crushed
1 teaspoon ground cinnamon
good pinch of ground ginger
3½ pounds tomatoes, peeled,
   seeded and roughly chopped
2 tablespoons honey
½ cup blanched almonds
1 tablespoon sesame seeds
salt and freshly ground
   black pepper
corn bread, to serve

1 Heat the oil and butter in a large, flameproof casserole. Add the chicken pieces and cook over medium heat for about 3 minutes, until the chicken is lightly browned.

2 Add the onion, garlic, cinnamon, ginger, tomatoes and seasoning. Heat gently until the tomatoes begin to bubble.

3 Lower the heat, cover and simmer very gently for 1 hour, stirring and turning the chicken occasionally, until it is completely cooked through. Transfer the chicken pieces to a plate and set aside.

4 Increase the heat and cook the tomatoes until the sauce is reduced to a thick purée, stirring frequently. Stir in the honey, cook for a minute, then return the chicken to the pan and cook for 2–3 minutes to heat through. Dry-fry the almonds and sesame seeds or toast under the broiler until golden.

5 Transfer the chicken and sauce to a warmed serving dish, and sprinkle with the almonds and sesame seeds. Serve with corn bread.

Chicken Kdra with Chickpeas & Almonds

A kdra is a type of Moroccan tagine. The almonds in this recipe are precooked until soft, adding an interesting texture and flavor to the chicken.

Serves 4

¾ cup blanched almonds
scant ½ cup chickpeas, soaked in
 water overnight
4 part-boned chicken
 breasts, skinned
¼ cup butter
½ teaspoon saffron
2 Spanish onions, thinly sliced
3¾ cups Chicken Stock
1 small cinnamon stick
¼ cup chopped fresh flat-leaf
 parsley, plus extra to garnish
lemon juice, to taste
salt and freshly ground
 black pepper

1 Place the almonds in a saucepan of water and simmer for 1½–2 hours, until fairly soft. Drain and set aside.

2 Cook the chickpeas for 1–1½ hours, until soft. Drain, then place in a bowl of cold water and rub with your fingers to remove the skins. Discard the skins and drain.

3 Place the chicken breasts in a flameproof casserole together with the butter, half of the saffron, salt and plenty of black pepper. Heat gently, stirring, until the butter has melted.

4 Add the onions and stock, bring to a boil and then add the chickpeas and cinnamon stick. Cover and cook very gently for 45–60 minutes, until the chicken is completely tender.

5 Transfer the chicken to a serving plate and keep warm. Bring the sauce to a boil and simmer until well reduced, stirring frequently. Remove and discard the cinnamon stick. Add the cooked almonds, the parsley and remaining saffron to the sauce, and cook for another 2–3 minutes. Sharpen the sauce with a little lemon juice, then pour onto the chicken and serve, garnished with extra parsley.

Chicken with Preserved Lemon & Olives

This is one of the most famous Moroccan dishes. You must use preserved lemon, as fresh lemon simply doesn't have the mellow flavor needed.

Serves 4

2 tablespoons olive oil
1 Spanish onion, chopped
3 garlic cloves
½-inch piece fresh ginger root,
 grated, or ½ teaspoon
 ground ginger
½–1 teaspoon ground cinnamon
pinch of saffron
4 chicken quarters, preferably
 breasts, halved if desired
3 cups Chicken Stock
2 tablespoons chopped cilantro
2 tablespoons chopped
 fresh parsley
1 preserved lemon
⅔ cup Moroccan tan olives
salt and freshly ground
 black pepper
lemon wedges and cilantro sprigs,
 to garnish

1 Heat the oil in a large, flameproof casserole and sauté the onion for 6–8 minutes over medium heat, until lightly golden, stirring occasionally.

2 Crush the garlic and blend with the ginger, cinnamon, saffron and seasoning. Stir into the pan and fry for 1 minute. Add the chicken pieces and fry over medium heat for 2–3 minutes, until lightly browned. Add the stock, cilantro and parsley, bring to a boil, then cover and simmer very gently for 45 minutes.

3 Rinse the preserved lemon under cold water, discard the flesh and cut the peel into small pieces. Stir into the pan with the olives and simmer for another 15 minutes, until the chicken is very tender.

4 Transfer the chicken to a plate and keep warm. Bring the sauce to a boil and cook for 3–4 minutes, until reduced and fairly thick. Pour onto the chicken and serve, garnished with lemon wedges and cilantro sprigs.

Chicken Fricassée Forestier

The term fricassée is used to describe a light stew, usually of chicken that is first sautéed in butter. The accompanying sauce can vary, but here wild mushrooms and bacon provide a rich flavor.

Serves 4

3 chicken breasts, sliced
4 tablespoons unsalted butter
1 tablespoon vegetable oil
4 ounces bacon, cut into pieces
5 tablespoons dry sherry or white wine
1 medium onion, chopped
4½ cups assorted wild mushrooms, such as chanterelles, bay boletus, horns of plenty, chicken of the woods, and closed field mushrooms, trimmed and sliced
3 tablespoons all-purpose flour
2½ cups Chicken Stock
2 teaspoons lemon juice
¼ cup chopped fresh parsley
salt and freshly ground black pepper
boiled rice, carrots and baby corn, to serve

1 Season the chicken with pepper. Heat half of the butter with the oil in a large, heavy frying pan or flameproof casserole, and brown the chicken and bacon pieces. Transfer to a shallow dish and pour off any excess fat.

2 Return the pan to the heat and brown the sediment. Pour in the sherry or wine and stir to deglaze the pan. Pour the sherry or wine liquid onto the chicken and wipe the pan clean.

3 Sauté the onion in the remaining butter until golden brown. Add the mushrooms and cook, stirring frequently, for 6–8 minutes, until their juices begin to run. Stir in the flour, then remove from heat. Gradually add the chicken stock and stir well until the flour is completely absorbed.

4 Add the reserved chicken and bacon with the sherry or wine juices, return to the heat and stir to thicken. Simmer for 10–15 minutes and then add the lemon juice, parsley and seasoning. Serve with boiled rice, carrots and baby corn.

Coq au Vin

This classic French dish was originally made with an old rooster, marinated and then slowly braised until tender.

Serves 4

3½–4-pound chicken, cut into portions
1½ tablespoons olive oil
8 ounces baby onions
1 tablespoon butter
3 cups mushrooms, quartered if large
2 tablespoons all-purpose flour
3 cups dry red wine
1 cup Chicken Stock, or more to cover
1 bouquet garni
salt and freshly ground black pepper

1 Pat the chicken pieces dry and season with salt and pepper. Place in a large, heavy frying pan, skin-side down, and cook over medium-high heat for 10–12 minutes or until golden brown. Transfer to a plate.

2 Meanwhile, heat the oil in a large, flameproof casserole over medium-low heat, add the onions and cook, covered, until evenly browned, stirring frequently.

3 Wipe the frying pan clean and melt the butter in it over medium heat. Add the mushrooms and sauté, stirring, until golden brown.

4 Sprinkle the onions in the casserole with flour and cook for 2 minutes, stirring frequently, then add the wine and boil for 1 minute, stirring. Add the chicken, mushrooms, stock and bouquet garni. Bring to a boil, reduce the heat to very low and simmer, covered, for 45–50 minutes, until the chicken is tender and the juices run clear when the thickest part of the meat is pierced with a skewer or knife.

5 Transfer the chicken pieces and vegetables to a plate. Strain the cooking liquid, skim off the fat and return the liquid to the pan. Boil to reduce by one third, then return the chicken and vegetables to the casserole and simmer for 3–4 minutes to heat through. Serve immediately.

Chicken with Chianti

Together the robust, full-flavored Italian red wine and red pesto give this sauce a rich color and almost spicy flavor, while the grapes add a delicious touch of sweetness.

Serves 4
3 tablespoons olive oil
4 part-boned chicken
   breasts, skinned
1 medium red onion
2 tablespoons red pesto
1¼ cups Chianti
1¼ cups water
4 ounces red grapes, halved
   lengthwise and seeded
   if necessary
salt and freshly ground
   black pepper
fresh parsley leaves, to garnish
arugula salad, to serve

1 Heat 2 tablespoons of the oil in a large frying pan, add the chicken breasts and sauté over medium heat for about 5 minutes, until they have changed color on all sides. Remove using a slotted spoon and drain on paper towels.

2 Cut the onion in half, through the root. Trim off the root, then slice the onion halves lengthwise to create thin wedges.

3 Heat the remaining oil in the pan, add the onion wedges and red pesto, and cook gently, stirring constantly, for about 3 minutes, until the onion is softened, but not browned.

4 Add the Chianti and water to the pan, and bring to a boil, stirring. Return the chicken to the pan and season with salt and pepper to taste.

5 Reduce the heat, then cover the pan and simmer gently for about 20 minutes or until the chicken is tender and cooked through, stirring occasionally.

6 Add the grapes to the pan and cook over low to medium heat until heated through. Taste the sauce and adjust the seasoning as necessary. Serve the chicken hot, garnished with parsley and accompanied by the arugula salad.

Chicken Casserole with Spiced Figs

A Spanish recipe which, rather unusually, combines chicken with succulent figs.

Serves 4
⅔ cup sugar
½ cup white
   wine vinegar
1 lemon slice
1 cinnamon stick
1 pound fresh figs
½ cup medium sweet white wine
pared zest of ½ lemon
3½-pound chicken, cut into
   eight portions
2 ounces lardons, or thick bacon
   cut into strips
1 tablespoon olive oil
¼ cup Chicken Stock
salt and freshly ground
   black pepper

1 Put the sugar, vinegar, lemon slice and cinnamon stick in a pan with ½ cup water. Bring to a boil, then simmer for 5 minutes. Add the figs, cover and simmer for 10 minutes. Remove from heat, cover and let stand for 3 hours.

2 Preheat the oven to 350°F. Drain the figs and place in a bowl. Add the wine and lemon zest. Season the chicken with salt and pepper.

3 In a large frying pan, cook the lardons or bacon strips until the fat melts and they turn golden. Transfer to a shallow, ovenproof dish, leaving any fat in the pan. Add the oil to the pan and brown the chicken pieces all over.

4 Drain the figs, adding the wine to the chicken in the frying pan. Boil until the sauce has reduced and is syrupy. Transfer the contents of the frying pan to the ovenproof dish and cook uncovered, for about 20 minutes.

5 Add the figs and chicken stock, cover and return to the oven for another 10 minutes. Taste and adjust the seasoning as necessary. Serve hot.

Chicken with Lemons & Olives

A real Mediterranean chicken dish, enhanced with two ingredients particularly associated with the region.

Serves 4
½ teaspoon ground cinnamon
½ teaspoon ground turmeric
3½-pound chicken
2 tablespoons olive oil
1 large onion, thinly sliced
2-inch piece fresh ginger root, peeled and grated
2½ cups Chicken Stock
2 preserved lemons or limes, cut into wedges
¾ cup pitted brown olives
1 tablespoon honey
¼ cup chopped cilantro
salt and freshly ground black pepper
cilantro sprigs, to garnish

1 Preheat the oven to 375°F. Mix the ground cinnamon and turmeric in a bowl with a little salt and pepper, and rub all over the chicken skin to give an even coating.

2 Heat the oil in a shallow frying pan and fry the chicken on all sides until golden. Transfer the chicken to an ovenproof dish.

3 Add the onion to the pan and sauté for 3 minutes. Stir in the ginger and stock, and bring just to a boil. Pour over the chicken, cover with a lid and bake for 30 minutes.

4 Remove the chicken from the oven and add the preserved lemons or limes, brown olives and honey. Bake, uncovered, for another 45 minutes, until the chicken is tender.

5 Stir in the chopped cilantro and season to taste. Garnish with cilantro sprigs and serve immediately.

> **Cook's Tip**
> Preserved lemons (or limes) will provide the most authentic flavor to this dish, but if they are unavailable, you can substitute fresh ones.

Chicken with Chorizo

The addition of chorizo sausage and sherry gives a warm, interesting flavor to this simple Spanish casserole. Serve with rice or boiled potatoes.

Serves 4
1 medium chicken, jointed, or 4 chicken legs, halved
2 teaspoons ground paprika
¼ cup olive oil
2 small onions, sliced
6 garlic cloves, thinly sliced
5 ounces chorizo sausage, sliced
14-ounce can chopped tomatoes
12–16 bay leaves
5 tablespoons medium sherry
salt and freshly ground black pepper
boiled rice or potatoes, to serve

1 Preheat the oven to 375°F. Coat the chicken pieces in the paprika, making sure that they are evenly covered, then season with salt. Heat the olive oil in a frying pan and fry the chicken until brown.

2 Transfer to an ovenproof dish. Add the onions to the pan and sauté quickly. Add the garlic and sliced chorizo, and fry for about 2 minutes.

3 Add the tomatoes, 2 of the bay leaves and the sherry, and bring to a boil. Pour onto the chicken and cover with a lid. Bake for 45 minutes.

4 Remove the lid and season to taste. Cook for another 20 minutes, until the chicken is tender and golden. Serve with rice or potatoes, garnished with bay leaves.

> **Variation**
> For a Portuguese version of this dish, substitute linguica for the chorizo and white port for the sherry.

Chicken, Leek & Bacon Casserole

A moist whole chicken, braised on a bed of leeks and bacon, and topped with a creamy tarragon sauce.

Serves 4–6

1 tablespoon vegetable oil
2 tablespoons butter
3½-pound chicken
8 ounces bacon
1 pound leeks
1 cup Chicken Stock
1 cup heavy cream
1 tablespoon chopped
  fresh tarragon
salt and freshly ground
  black pepper

1 Preheat the oven to 350°F. Heat the oil and melt the butter in a large, flameproof casserole. Add the chicken and cook it, breast-side down, for 5 minutes, until golden. Remove from the casserole and set aside.

2 Dice the bacon and add to the casserole. Cook for 4–5 minutes until golden. Trim the leeks, cut them into 1-inch pieces and add to the bacon. Cook for 5 minutes, until the leeks begin to brown.

3 Return the chicken to the casserole, placing it on top of the bacon and leeks. Cover and put in the oven. Cook for 1½ hours or until the juices run clear when the thickest part of the thigh is pierced with a skewer or knife.

4 Remove the chicken, bacon and leeks from the casserole and keep warm. Skim the fat from the juices. Pour in the stock and cream, and bring to a boil. Cook for 4–5 minutes, until slightly reduced and thickened.

5 Stir in the tarragon and seasoning to taste. Carve the chicken and serve with the bacon, leeks and a little sauce.

Chicken with Red Cabbage

Cooked together like this with red wine, both chicken and cabbage are melt-in-your-mouth tender.

Serves 4

¼ cup butter
4 large chicken portions, halved
1 onion, chopped
1¼ pounds red cabbage,
  finely shredded
4 juniper berries, crushed
12 cooked chestnuts
½ cup red wine
salt and freshly ground
  black pepper
sprigs of fresh thyme, to garnish

1 Heat the butter in a heavy, flameproof casserole, add the chicken pieces and cook over medium heat until lightly browned. Transfer to a plate.

2 Add the onion to the casserole and sauté gently until soft and light golden brown. Stir the cabbage and juniper berries into the casserole, season and cook over medium heat for 6–7 minutes, stirring once or twice.

3 Stir in the chestnuts, then tuck the chicken pieces under the cabbage so that they are on the bottom of the casserole. Pour in the red wine.

4 Cover and cook gently for about 40 minutes, until the chicken juices run clear when the thickest part of a portion is pierced with a skewer or knife and the cabbage is very tender. Adjust the seasoning to taste and serve garnished with thyme.

Variation
You could substitute pheasant or partridge for the chicken in this recipe. Even older birds will remain pleasantly moist, and red cabbage is a traditional accompaniment to game.

Chicken Thighs with Lemon & Garlic

Versions of this classic dish can be found in Spain and Italy, although this particular recipe is of French origin.

Serves 4

2½ cups Chicken Stock
20 large garlic cloves
2 tablespoons butter
1 tablespoon olive oil
8 chicken thighs
1 lemon, peeled, pith removed and thinly sliced
2 tablespoons all-purpose flour
⅔ cup dry white wine
salt and freshly ground black pepper
chopped fresh parsley or basil, to garnish
boiled new potatoes or rice, to serve

1 Put the stock into a pan and bring to a boil. Add the garlic cloves, cover and simmer gently for 40 minutes. Strain the stock, reserving the garlic, and set aside.

2 Heat the butter and oil in a sauté or frying pan, add the chicken thighs and cook gently on all sides until golden. Transfer them to an ovenproof dish. Preheat the oven to 375°F.

3 Distribute the reserved garlic and the lemon slices among the chicken pieces. Add the flour to the fat in the pan in which the chicken was browned and cook, stirring, for 1 minute. Add the wine, stirring constantly and scraping the bottom of the pan, then add the stock. Cook, stirring, until the sauce has thickened and is smooth. Season with salt and pepper to taste.

4 Pour the sauce on the chicken, cover and cook for 40–45 minutes. If a thicker sauce is needed, lift out the chicken pieces and reduce the sauce by boiling it rapidly until it reaches the desired consistency.

5 Sprinkle the chopped parsley or basil on the chicken and serve with boiled new potatoes or rice.

Mediterranean Chicken with Turnips

Turnips are popular in all parts of the Mediterranean, and teamed with poultry in a casserole they make a substantial meal.

Serves 4

2 tablespoons sunflower oil
8 chicken thighs or 4 chicken portions
4 small turnips
2 onions, chopped
2 garlic cloves, crushed
6 tomatoes, peeled and chopped
1 cup tomato juice
1 cup Chicken Stock
½ cup white wine
1 teaspoon paprika
good pinch of cayenne pepper
20 black olives, pitted
½ lemon, cut into wedges
salt and freshly ground black pepper
couscous, to serve

1 Preheat the oven to 325°F. Heat 1 tablespoon of the oil in a large frying pan and fry the chicken until lightly browned. Peel the turnips and cut into julienne strips.

2 Transfer the chicken to a large casserole. Add the remaining oil to the frying pan and sauté the onions and garlic for 4–5 minutes, until lightly golden brown, stirring occasionally.

3 Add the turnips and stir-fry for 2–3 minutes. Add the tomatoes, tomato juice, stock, wine, paprika, cayenne and seasoning. Bring to a boil. Pour onto the chicken. Stir in the olives and lemon wedges.

4 Cover tightly and cook for 1–1¼ hours, until the chicken is tender. Adjust the seasoning to taste. Serve on a bed of couscous.

> **Cook's Tip**
> *This dish is especially tasty made with French turnips, which have a very delicate flavor. Young turnips do not require peeling, and their pale purple and white skins will enhance the appearance of the dish.*

Chicken, Pepper & Bean Stew

This colorful and filling one-pot meal needs only crusty bread to serve.

Serves 4–6
4-pound chicken, cut
   into portions
paprika
2 tablespoons olive oil
2 tablespoons butter
2 onions, chopped
½ each green and yellow bell
   pepper, seeded and chopped
2 cups peeled, chopped, fresh or
   canned plum tomatoes

1 cup white wine
2 cups Chicken Stock or water
3 tablespoons chopped
   fresh parsley
½ teaspoon Tabasco sauce
1 tablespoon Worcestershire
   sauce
2 7-ounce cans corn
4 ounces fava beans
   (fresh or frozen)
3 tablespoons all-purpose flour
salt and freshly ground
   black pepper
fresh parsley sprigs, to garnish

1 Rinse the chicken and pat dry. Sprinkle lightly with salt and a little paprika. Heat the oil with the butter in a flameproof casserole over medium-high heat. Add the chicken pieces and fry until golden brown on all sides (cook in batches, if necessary). Remove from the pan and set aside.

2 Reduce the heat and cook the onions and peppers for 8–10 minutes, until softened. Increase the heat, then add the tomatoes and their juice, the wine, stock or water, parsley, Tabasco and Worcestershire sauces. Stir and bring to a boil.

3 Return the chicken to the pan, pushing it into the sauce. Cover and simmer for 30 minutes, stirring occasionally. Stir in the corn and beans, partly cover and cook for 30 minutes.

4 Tilt the pan and skim off the surface fat. Mix the flour with a little water in a small bowl to make a paste. Stir in about ¾ cup of the hot sauce from the pan into the flour mixture and then stir into the stew and mix well. Cook for 5–8 more minutes, stirring occasionally. Taste the stew and adjust the seasoning as necessary. Serve in shallow soup dishes or large bowls, garnished with parsley sprigs.

Chicken & Eggplant Khoresh

This Persian dish is often served on festive occasions in its country of origin and is believed to have been a favorite of kings.

Serves 4
about 4 tablespoons oil
1 whole chicken or 4 large
   chicken portions
1 large onion, chopped
2 garlic cloves, crushed

1 4-ounce can chopped tomatoes
1 cup water
3 eggplant, sliced
3 bell peppers, preferably red,
   green and yellow, seeded
   and sliced
2 tablespoons lemon juice
1 tablespoon ground cinnamon
salt and freshly ground
   black pepper
cooked rice, to serve

1 Heat 1 tablespoon of the oil in a large saucepan or flameproof casserole and fry the chicken or chicken portions for about 10 minutes, turning to brown on all sides. Add the onion and cook for another 4–5 minutes, until the onion is golden brown.

2 Add the garlic, the chopped tomatoes and their liquid, water and seasoning. Bring to a boil, then reduce the heat, cover the pan and simmer gently for 10 minutes.

3 Meanwhile, heat the remaining oil and cook the eggplant, in batches, until lightly golden. Transfer to a plate with a slotted spoon. Add the peppers to the pan and cook for a few minutes, until slightly softened.

4 Place the eggplant on the chicken or chicken portions and then add the peppers. Sprinkle on the lemon juice and cinnamon, then cover and continue cooking over low heat for about 45 minutes or until the chicken is cooked (the juices should run clear when the thickest part of the thigh is pierced with a skewer or knife).

5 Transfer the chicken to a serving plate, and spoon the eggplant and peppers around the edge. Reheat the sauce if necessary, adjust the seasoning and pour onto the chicken. Serve with rice.

Chicken with Herbs & Lentils

Parsley, marjoram and thyme lend their flavors to this dish, which is served topped with delicious garlic butter.

Serves 4

4-ounce piece thick bacon or pork belly, chopped
I large onion, sliced
4 chicken portions
scant 2 cups Chicken Stock
I bay leaf
2 sprigs fresh parsley
2 sprigs fresh marjoram
2 sprigs fresh thyme
I cup green or brown lentils
salt and freshly ground black pepper
2–4 tablespoons garlic butter, to serve

I Fry the bacon or pork gently in a large, heavy flameproof casserole until all the fat runs out and the meat begins to brown. Add the onion and cook for another 2 minutes. Remove the bacon or pork and onion from the casserole using a slotted spoon and set aside.

2 Preheat the oven to 375°F. Add the chicken portions to the fat remaining in the casserole and cook for about 10 minutes, until lightly brown all over. Remove from the casserole and set aside.

3 Return the bacon or pork and onions to the casserole. Stir in the stock, bay leaf, the stalks and some of the leafy parts of the parsley, marjoram and thyme (keep some herb sprigs for the garnish), and the lentils. Season to taste.

4 Place the browned chicken portions on top of the lentils. Sprinkle with seasoning and some of the herbs. Cover the casserole and cook for about 40 minutes.

5 Serve with a pat of garlic butter on each portion of chicken and a few of the remaining herb sprigs sprinkled on top.

Winter Chicken with Root Vegetables

A casserole of wonderfully tender chicken, root vegetables and lentils, finished with crème fraîche, mustard and tarragon.

Serves 4

12 ounces onions
12 ounces trimmed leeks
8 ounces carrots
I pound rutabaga
2 tablespoons oil
4 chicken portions, about 2 pounds total weight
½ cup green lentils
2 cups Chicken Stock
1¼ cups apple juice
2 teaspoons cornstarch
3 tablespoons crème fraîche
2 teaspoons whole-grain mustard
2 tablespoons chopped fresh tarragon
salt and freshly ground black pepper
fresh tarragon sprigs, to garnish

I Preheat the oven to 375°F. Roughly chop the onions, leeks, carrots and rutabaga into similar-size pieces.

2 Heat the oil in a large, flameproof casserole. Season the chicken portions with salt and pepper, and fry them until golden. Drain on paper towels.

3 Add the onions to the casserole and cook for 5 minutes, stirring, until they begin to soften and color. Add the leeks, carrots, rutabaga and lentils, and stir over medium heat for 2 minutes.

4 Return the chicken to the casserole. Add the stock, apple juice and seasoning. Bring to a boil and cover. Cook for 50 minutes to 1 hour or until the chicken is tender.

5 Place the casserole over medium heat. Blend the cornstarch with 2 tablespoons water and add to the casserole with the crème fraîche, mustard and tarragon. Adjust the seasoning. Simmer gently for about 2 minutes, stirring. Serve, garnished with tarragon sprigs.

Chicken with Shallots

Shallots are cooked whole in this casserole, which makes the most of their superb, mild onion flavor.

Serves 4

3-pound chicken or
  4 chicken portions
seasoned flour, for coating
2 tablespoons sunflower oil
2 tablespoons butter
⅔ cup bacon, chopped
2 garlic cloves
scant 2 cups red wine
1 bay leaf
2 fresh thyme sprigs
9 ounces shallots
1½ cups button mushrooms,
  halved if large
2 teaspoons all-purpose flour
salt and freshly ground
  black pepper

1 Preheat the oven to 350°F. If using a whole chicken, cut into four or eight pieces. Place the seasoned flour in a plastic bag, add the chicken pieces and shake to coat.

2 Heat half the oil and half the butter in a flameproof casserole and fry the bacon and garlic for 3–4 minutes. Add the chicken and cook until lightly browned. Add the wine, bay leaf and thyme, and bring to a boil. Cover and cook for 1 hour.

3 Boil the shallots in salted water for 10 minutes. Heat the remaining oil in a small frying pan and sauté the shallots for 3–4 minutes, until beginning to brown. Add the mushrooms and cook for another 2–3 minutes.

4 Stir the shallots and mushrooms into the chicken casserole, and cook for another 8–10 minutes. Using a fork, blend the flour with the remaining butter to make a thick paste.

5 Transfer the chicken, shallots and mushrooms to a serving dish and keep warm. Bring the liquid to a boil, then add small pieces of the flour paste, stirring vigorously after each addition. When the sauce is thick, either pour it onto the chicken pieces or return the chicken to the casserole, and serve.

Old-fashioned Chicken Fricassée

A fricassée is a classic dish in which poultry is first seared in fat, then braised with liquid until cooked. This recipe is finished with a little cream, but you can leave it out if desired.

Serves 4–6

2½–3-pound chicken, cut into
  portions
¼ cup butter
2 tablespoons vegetable oil
¼ cup all-purpose flour
1 cup dry white wine
3 cups Chicken Stock
1 bouquet garni
¼ teaspoon white pepper
3 cups button mushrooms,
  trimmed
1 teaspoon lemon juice
16–24 small white onions, peeled
½ cup water
1 teaspoon sugar
6 tablespoons whipping cream
salt
2 tablespoons chopped fresh
  parsley, to garnish

1 Wash the chicken pieces, then pat dry with paper towels. Melt half the butter with the oil in a large, heavy flameproof casserole over medium heat. Add half the chicken pieces and cook for 10 minutes, turning occasionally or until just golden in color. Transfer to a plate, then cook the remaining pieces in the same way.

2 Return the seared chicken pieces to the casserole. Sprinkle with the flour, turning the pieces to coat. Cook over low heat for about 4 minutes, turning occasionally.

3 Pour in the wine, bring to a boil and add the stock. Push the chicken pieces to one side and scrape the bottom of the casserole, stirring until well blended.

4 Bring the liquid to a boil, add the bouquet garni and season with a pinch of salt and the white pepper. Cover and simmer over medium heat for 25–30 minutes, until the chicken is tender and the juices run clear when the thickest part of the thigh is pierced with a knife or skewer.

5 Meanwhile, in a frying pan, heat the remaining butter over medium-high heat. Add the mushrooms and lemon juice, and cook for 3–4 minutes, until the mushrooms are golden, stirring.

6 Add the onions, water and sugar to the pan, swirling to dissolve the sugar. Simmer for about 10 minutes, until just tender. Transfer the onions and any juices to a bowl with the mushrooms and set aside.

7 When the chicken is cooked, transfer the pieces to a deep serving dish and cover with aluminum foil to keep warm. Discard the bouquet garni. Add any cooking juices from the vegetables to the casserole. Bring to a boil and cook, stirring frequently, until the sauce is reduced by half.

8 Whisk the cream into the sauce and cook for 2 minutes. Add the mushrooms and onions, and cook for another 2 minutes. Adjust the seasoning, then pour the sauce on the chicken, sprinkle with parsley and serve.

Country Chicken Casserole

Succulent chicken oven-cooked in a wine-enriched vegetable sauce is excellent with rice.

Serves 4

2 chicken breasts, skinned
2 chicken legs, skinned
2 tablespoons whole-wheat flour
1 tablespoon sunflower oil
1¼ cups Chicken Stock
1¼ cups white wine
2 tablespoons passata
1 tablespoon tomato paste
4 strips bacon, chopped
1 large onion, sliced
1 garlic clove, crushed
1 green bell pepper, seeded and sliced
3 cups button mushrooms
8 ounces carrots, sliced
1 bouquet garni
8 ounces frozen Brussels sprouts
1½ cups frozen petits pois
salt and freshly ground black pepper
chopped fresh parsley, to garnish
cooked rice, to serve

1 Preheat the oven to 350°F. Coat the chicken pieces with seasoned flour. Heat the oil in a large, flameproof casserole, add the chicken and cook until browned all over. Remove and keep warm.

2 Add any remaining flour to the pan and cook for 1 minute. Gradually stir in the stock and wine, then add the passata and tomato paste. Bring to a boil, stirring, then return the chicken to the casserole. Add the bacon, onion, garlic, green pepper, mushrooms, carrots and bouquet garni, and stir. Cover and bake for 1½ hours, stirring once or twice. Stir in the Brussels sprouts and petits pois, cover and cook for another 30 minutes.

3 Discard the bouquet garni. Season the casserole to taste. Garnish with parsley and serve immediately with rice.

> **Cook's Tip**
> Use fresh Brussels sprouts and peas if available, and use red wine instead of white for a change.

Chicken Stew with Blackberries & Lemon Balm

This unusual stew combines some wonderful flavors, and the inclusion of red wine and blackberries gives it a dramatic appearance.

Serves 4

4 chicken breasts, partly boned
2 tablespoons butter
1 tablespoon sunflower oil
¼ cup all-purpose flour
⅔ cup red wine
⅔ cup Chicken Stock
grated zest of ½ orange
1 tablespoon orange juice
3 sprigs fresh lemon balm, finely chopped, plus 1 sprig to garnish
⅔ cup heavy cream
1 egg yolk
⅔ cup blackberries, plus ⅓ cup, to garnish
salt and freshly ground black pepper

1 Preheat the oven to 350°F. Remove any skin from the chicken and season the meat with salt and pepper. Heat the butter and oil in a frying pan, add the chicken and fry to seal it all over, then transfer to a casserole.

2 Stir the flour into the frying pan, then gradually add the wine and stock, and bring to a boil, stirring constantly. Add the orange zest and juice, together with the chopped lemon balm. Pour over the chicken in the casserole. Cover and bake for about 40 minutes.

3 In a bowl, blend the cream with the egg yolk, add a little of the liquid from the casserole and mix well. Stir the mixture back into the casserole with the blackberries. Cover and cook for another 10–15 minutes.

4 Taste the casserole and adjust the seasoning as necessary. Serve, garnished with blackberries and lemon balm.

Chicken Ghiveci

A hearty Romanian stew of chicken with colorful vegetables and herbs.

Serves 6

¼ cup vegetable oil or melted lard
1 mild onion, thinly sliced
2 garlic cloves, crushed
2 red bell peppers, seeded and sliced
3½-pound chicken
6 tablespoons tomato paste
3 potatoes, diced
1 teaspoon chopped fresh rosemary
1 teaspoon chopped fresh marjoram
1 teaspoon chopped fresh thyme
3 carrots, cut into chunks
½ small celeriac, cut into chunks
½ cup dry white wine
2 zucchini, sliced
salt and freshly ground black pepper
chopped fresh rosemary and marjoram, to garnish
dark rye bread, to serve

1 Heat the oil or lard in a large, heavy flameproof casserole. Add the onion and garlic, and cook for 1–2 minutes, until soft. Add the red peppers.

2 Divide the chicken into six pieces, place in the casserole and brown gently on all sides for about 15 minutes.

3 Add the tomato paste, potatoes, herbs, carrots, celeriac and white wine. Season to taste with salt and pepper. Cook over low heat, covered, for another 40–50 minutes.

4 Add the zucchini slices 5 minutes before the end of the cooking time. Adjust the seasoning to taste. Garnish with the herbs and serve with dark rye bread.

> **Cook's Tip**
> If fresh herbs are unavailable, replace each with ½ teaspoon dried herbs.

Cassoulet

Based on the traditional French dish, this recipe is full of delicious flavors and makes a welcoming and warming meal.

Serves 6

1 pound chicken or duck breast fillet
8 ounces thick-cut pork bacon
1 pound Toulouse or garlic sausages
3 tablespoons oil
1 pound onions, chopped
2 garlic cloves, crushed
2 15-ounce cans cannellini beans, rinsed and drained
8 ounces carrots, roughly chopped
14-ounce can chopped tomatoes
1 tablespoon tomato paste
1 bouquet garni
2 tablespoons chopped fresh thyme
about 2 cups Chicken Stock
2 cups fresh white bread crumbs
salt and freshly ground black pepper
fresh thyme sprigs, to garnish (optional)

1 Preheat the oven to 325°F. Cut the chicken or duck breast and pork or bacon into large pieces. Twist the sausages and cut into short lengths.

2 Heat the oil in a large flameproof casserole. Add the meat and cook in batches until well browned. Remove from the pan using a slotted spoon and drain on paper towels.

3 Add the onions and garlic to the pan and cook for 3–4 minutes or until beginning to soften, stirring frequently. Stir in the beans, carrots, tomatoes, tomato paste, bouquet garni, thyme and seasoning. Return the meat to the casserole and mix until well combined with the vegetables. Add enough of the stock just to cover the meat and beans. Bring to a boil. Cover tightly and bake for 1 hour.

4 Remove the cassoulet from the oven, add a little more stock or water if necessary and remove the bouquet garni. Sprinkle on the bread crumbs and return to the oven, uncovered, for another 40 minutes. Garnish with fresh thyme sprigs, if using.

Chicken with Melting Onions & Beans

This substantial Bulgarian casserole is bursting with flavor, texture and color.

Serves 4–6

1½ cups dried kidney or other beans, soaked in water overnight
8–12 chicken portions, such as thighs and drumsticks
12 strips bacon
2 large onions, thinly sliced
1 cup dry white wine
½ teaspoon chopped fresh sage or oregano
½ teaspoon chopped fresh rosemary
generous pinch of grated nutmeg
⅔ cup sour cream
1 tablespoon chili powder or paprika
salt and freshly ground black pepper
fresh rosemary sprigs and lemon wedges, to garnish

1 Preheat the oven to 350°F. Drain the beans, place in a saucepan and cover with fresh cold water. Bring to a boil and boil rapidly for 20 minutes. Rinse and drain well. Trim the chicken pieces, and season with salt and pepper.

2 Arrange the bacon around the sides and bottom of an ovenproof dish. Sprinkle on half of the onion and then half the beans, followed by the remaining onion and then the remaining beans.

3 In a bowl, combine the wine with the fresh sage or oregano, the rosemary and nutmeg. Pour the mixture onto the onion and beans.

4 In another bowl, combine the sour cream and the chili powder or paprika. Toss the chicken in the sour cream mixture and place on top of the beans.

5 Cover the dish with aluminum foil and bake for 1¼–1½ hours, removing the foil for the last 15 minutes of the cooking time. Serve, garnished with rosemary sprigs and lemon wedges.

Chicken-in-a-Pot

A traditional Bulgarian way of cooking chicken slowly and evenly in its own juices.

Serves 6–8

8 chicken portions
6–8 firm ripe tomatoes, chopped
2 garlic cloves, crushed
3 onions, chopped
¼ cup oil or melted lard
1 cup Chicken Stock
2 bay leaves
2 teaspoons paprika
10 white peppercorns, bruised
handful of parsley, stalks reserved and leaves finely chopped
salt

1 Put the chicken, tomatoes and garlic in a flameproof casserole. Cover and cook gently for 10–15 minutes.

2 Add the remaining ingredients, except the parsley leaves, and stir well. Cover tightly and cook over very low heat, stirring occasionally, for 1¾–2 hours or until the chicken is tender. Five minutes before the end of the cooking time, stir in the parsley. Adjust the seasoning as necessary. Serve hot.

Chicken with Apricots

A deliciously fruity combination that is quick and easy.

Serves 4

4 chicken portions
seasoned flour
3 tablespoons olive oil
12 ounces dried apricots, soaked overnight
salt and freshly ground black pepper

1 Coat the chicken in the seasoned flour. Heat the oil and fry the chicken until browned on all sides. Remove from the pan.

2 Add any remaining flour to the pan. Cook, stirring for 1 minute. Gradually stir in the apricot soaking water and bring to a boil, stirring constantly. Return the chicken to the pan and add the apricots. Season to taste, cover and simmer for 45–50 minutes. Serve hot.

Individual Noodle Casseroles

Traditionally, in Japan, these individual chicken, leek and spinach casseroles are cooked in earthenware pots.

Serves 4

4 ounces boneless chicken thigh
½ teaspoon salt
½ teaspoon sake or dry
   white wine
½ teaspoon soy sauce
1 leek
4 ounces spinach, trimmed

11 ounces dried udon noodles or
   1¼ pounds fresh noodles
4 shiitake mushrooms,
   stems removed
4 small eggs
seven-flavor spice, to serve

For the soup

6 cups instant dashi
4½ teaspoons soy sauce
1 teaspoon salt
1 tablespoon mirin

1 Cut the chicken into small chunks and sprinkle with the salt, sake or wine and soy sauce. Cut the leek diagonally into 1¾-inch slices. Cook the spinach in a little water for 1–2 minutes, then drain and soak in cold water for 1 minute. Drain, squeeze lightly, then cut into 1½-inch lengths.

2 Cook the noodles. Boil dried udon noodles according to the package instructions, allowing 3 minutes less than the suggested cooking time. If using fresh udon noodles, place them in boiling water, disentangle them and then drain.

3 Bring the ingredients for the soup to a boil in a saucepan ''and add the chicken and leek. Skim, then cook for 5 minutes. Divide the udon noodles among four individual flameproof casseroles. Divide the soup, chicken and leeks among them. Place over medium heat, then divide the shiitake mushrooms among the casseroles.

4 Gently break an egg into each casserole. Cover and simmer for 2 minutes. Divide the spinach among the casseroles and simmer for 1 minute.

5 Serve immediately, standing the hot casseroles on plates or table mats. Sprinkle seven-flavor spice on the casseroles.

Filipino Chicken Pot

This nourishing dish is one of many taken to the Philippines by the Spanish in the 16th century.

Serves 4–6

3 chicken legs
1 tablespoon vegetable oil
12 ounces lean pork, diced
1 chorizo sausage,
   sliced (optional)
1 small carrot, roughly chopped
1 medium onion, roughly chopped
1 cup dried navy beans, soaked in
   water overnight
7½ cups water
1 garlic clove, crushed

2 tablespoons tomato paste
1 bay leaf
2 chicken bouillon cubes
12 ounces sweet potatoes or
   new potatoes, peeled
2 teaspoons chili sauce
2 tablespoons white wine vinegar
3 firm tomatoes, peeled, seeded
   and chopped
8 ounces Chinese cabbage,
   shredded
salt and freshly ground
   black pepper
3 scallions, shredded,
   to garnish
boiled rice, to serve

1 Divide the chicken drumsticks from the thighs. Chop off the narrow end of each drumstick and discard.

2 Heat the oil in a wok or large saucepan, add the chicken, pork, chorizo, if using, the carrot and onion, then brown evenly.

3 Drain and rinse the navy beans; drain again. Add to the chicken with the water, garlic, tomato paste and bay leaf. Bring to a boil and simmer for 2 hours.

4 Crumble in the chicken bouillon cubes, add the sweet or new potatoes and the chili sauce, then simmer for 15–20 minutes, until the potatoes are cooked.

5 Add the vinegar, tomatoes and Chinese cabbage, and simmer for 1–2 minutes. Season to taste with salt and pepper. The dish is intended to provide enough liquid to be served as a first-course broth. This is followed by a main course of the meat and vegetables, sprinkled with the shredded scallions. Serve with rice as an accompaniment.

Chicken with Lentils & Coconut

This delicious, tangy chicken stew comes from Kenya. The amount of lemon juice can be reduced, if you prefer a less sharp sauce.

Serves 4–6
6 chicken thighs or portions
½–¾ teaspoon ground ginger
¼ cup mung beans
¼ cup corn oil
2 onions, finely chopped
2 garlic cloves, crushed
5 tomatoes, peeled and chopped
1 fresh green chile, seeded and finely chopped
2 tablespoons lemon juice
1¼ cups coconut milk
1¼ cups water
1 tablespoon chopped cilantro
salt and freshly ground black pepper
cooked green vegetable and rice or chapatis, to serve

1 Season the chicken pieces with the ginger and a little salt and freshly ground pepper, and set aside in a cool place to let the spices penetrate the meat. Meanwhile, boil the mung beans in plenty of water for 35 minutes until soft, then mash well.

2 Heat the oil in a large saucepan over medium heat and fry the chicken pieces, in batches if necessary, until evenly browned. Transfer to a plate and set aside, reserving the oil and chicken juices in the pan.

3 In the same pan, sauté the onions and garlic for 5 minutes, then add the tomatoes and chile, and cook for another 1–2 minutes, stirring well.

4 Add the mashed mung beans, lemon juice and coconut milk to the pan. Simmer for 5 minutes, then add the chicken pieces and a little water if the sauce is too thick. Stir in the chopped cilantro and simmer for about 35 minutes, until the chicken is cooked through.

5 Taste and adjust the seasoning as necessary. Serve with a green vegetable and rice or chapatis.

Chicken with Pimientos

In this Mediterranean Jewish recipe, chicken is baked with sweet red bell peppers or pimientos.

Serves 6
4½-pound chicken
3 ripe tomatoes
2 large red bell peppers (pimientos)
4–6 tablespoons olive oil
1 large onion, sliced
2 garlic cloves, crushed
1 tablespoon sugar
salt and freshly ground black pepper
fresh flat-leaf parsley, to garnish
boiled rice and black olives, to serve

1 Preheat the oven to 375°F. Joint the chicken and cut into six pieces; set aside. Peel and chop the tomatoes, and seed and slice the red peppers.

2 Heat half of the oil in a large, heavy frying pan and sauté the onion, garlic and red peppers for 3 minutes. Transfer to an ovenproof dish.

3 Add the chicken pieces to the frying pan, with a little more oil if necessary, and fry until browned all over. Add to the vegetables in the dish.

4 Cook the tomatoes in the remaining oil for a few minutes. Add the sugar, seasoning and 1 tablespoon water, then spoon the mixture onto the chicken.

5 Bake, uncovered, for about 1 hour. Cover if the chicken is getting too brown. Halfway through, pour the juices into a pitcher and let stand.

6 Serve the chicken with boiled rice and black olives, garnished with flat-leaf parsley. Pour the fat off the juices in the pitcher, reheat and pass as extra gravy.

Leftover Turkey Casserole

A different way of using up cooked turkey—crisply coated and set in a golden baked batter.

Serves 6
½ cup corn oil
4 eggs
2 cups milk
1 cup all-purpose flour

1½ pounds boneless cooked
 turkey, cubed
½ cup thick plain yogurt
3 cups cornflakes, crushed
salt and freshly ground
 black pepper
steamed broccoli, carrots and
 celeriac, to serve

1 Preheat the oven to 425°F. Pour the oil into a 13 x 9-inch ovenproof dish and heat in the oven for about 10 minutes.

2 Meanwhile, beat the eggs in a mixing bowl. Add the milk. Sift in the flour, and add a little salt and pepper. Mix until the batter is smooth. Set aside.

3 Coat the turkey cubes in the yogurt, then roll in the crushed cornflakes to coat all over.

4 Remove the dish from the oven and pour in the prepared batter. Arrange the turkey pieces on top. Return to the oven and bake for 35–40 minutes, until the batter is set and golden. Serve hot with steamed broccoli, carrots and celeriac.

Cook's Tip
There are many different types of yogurt available. Greek yogurt, which may be made either from cow's or sheep's milk, is rich and creamy and is, therefore, ideally suited to this dish. Low-fat yogurt is less suitable, but natural, plain yogurt is perfectly satisfactory.

Turkey with Apples, Bay & Madeira

This casserole will win you many compliments without the worry of a complicated menu. The unusual and tasty apple garnish looks especially attractive.

Serves 4
1½ pounds turkey breast fillet,
 cut into ¾-inch slices
4 tablespoons butter
2 tart apples, peeled, cored
 and sliced
¼ cup Madeira

⅔ cup Chicken Stock
3 bay leaves, plus extra to garnish
2 teaspoons cornstarch
⅔ cup heavy cream
salt and freshly ground
 black pepper
steamed patty pan squashes,
 to serve

For the apple garnish
1 tablespoon butter
2 tart apples, peeled, cored
 and sliced
2 tablespoons Madeira

1 Preheat the oven to 350°F. Season the turkey. Melt 2 tablespoons of the butter in a frying pan and fry the meat to seal it. Transfer to a casserole.

2 Add the remaining butter to the pan with the sliced apples and cook over low heat for 1–2 minutes. Add the Madeira, stock and bay leaves to the pan and stir in. Simmer for another couple of minutes.

3 Pour the contents of the frying pan around the chicken in the casserole. Cover and bake for about 40 minutes.

4 Blend the cornstarch with a little of the cream into a smooth paste, then add the rest of the cream. Add this mixture to the casserole and bake for another 10 minutes to let the sauce thicken.

5 To make the apple garnish, melt the butter in a pan and sauté the apple slices over low heat. Add the Madeira and set it on fire. Once the flames have died down, continue to sauté the apples until they are lightly browned. Garnish the casserole with the apples and bay leaves and serve with the patty pan squashes.

Duck & Chestnut Casserole

Serve this casserole with a mixture of mashed potatoes and celeriac, to soak up the rich duck juices.

Serves 4–6

4½-pound duck
3 tablespoons olive oil
6 ounces small onions
2 ounces field mushrooms, sliced
1 cup shiitake mushrooms, sliced
1¼ cups red wine
1¼ cups beef stock
8 ounces canned, peeled, unsweetened chestnuts, drained
salt and freshly ground black pepper
mashed potatoes and celeriac, to serve
fresh parsley, to garnish

1 Joint the duck into 8 pieces. Heat the oil in a large frying pan and brown the duck pieces. Remove from the frying pan using a slotted spoon and set aside.

2 Add the onions to the pan and cook for about 10 minutes, until well browned.

3 Add the mushrooms and cook for a few more minutes. Deglaze the pan with the red wine and boil to reduce the volume by half. Meanwhile, preheat the oven to 350°F.

4 Pour the contents of the frying pan into a casserole and stir in the stock. Add the browned duck and the chestnuts, season well and bake for 1½ hours. Serve with mashed potatoes and celeriac, garnished with parsley.

Cook's Tip
Unlike some poultry, duck freezes well because its high fat content ensures that it retains its flavor and moisture when it is thawed. However, the flesh can easily be damaged, so check the packaging carefully before buying. Fresh duck is also available all year round.

Duck Stew with Olives

In this Provençal recipe, the sweetness of the onions counterbalances the saltiness of the olives.

Serves 6–8

2 3-pound ducks, quartered, or 8 duck leg quarters
8 ounces small onions
2 tablespoons all-purpose flour
1½ cups dry red wine
2 cups duck or Chicken Stock
1 bouquet garni
1 cup pitted green or black olives, or a combination
salt, if needed, and freshly ground black pepper

1 Put the duck pieces, skin-side down, in a large frying pan over medium heat and cook for 10–12 minutes, until well browned, turning to color evenly and cooking in batches if necessary. Pour off the fat from the pan.

2 Heat 1 tablespoon of the duck fat in a large, flameproof casserole. Add the onions and cook, covered, over medium-low heat until evenly browned, stirring frequently. Sprinkle with the flour and continue cooking, uncovered, for 2 minutes, stirring frequently.

3 Stir in the wine and bring to a boil, then add the duck pieces, stock and bouquet garni. Bring back to a boil, then reduce the heat to very low and simmer, covered, for about 40 minutes, stirring occasionally.

4 Rinse the olives in several changes of cold water. If they are very salty, put them into a saucepan, cover with water and bring to a boil, then drain and rinse. Add the olives to the casserole and continue cooking for another 20 minutes, until the duck is very tender.

5 Transfer the duck pieces, onions and olives to a plate. Strain the cooking liquid, skim off the fat and return the liquid to the pan. Boil to reduce by about one third, then adjust the seasoning and return the duck and vegetables to the casserole. Simmer gently to heat through before serving.

Traditional Chicken Pie

Chicken, vegetables and herbs in a creamy white sauce with a top crust of rich pastry: a perennial family favorite.

Serves 6

¼ cup butter
 or margarine
1 medium onion, chopped
3 carrots, cut into ½-inch dice
1 parsnip, cut into ½-inch dice
3 tablespoons all-purpose flour
1½ cups Chicken Stock
6 tablespoons medium sherry
6 tablespoons dry white wine
¾ cup whipping cream
1 cup frozen peas, thawed

12 ounces cooked chicken meat,
 in chunks
1 teaspoon dried thyme
1 tablespoon finely chopped
 fresh parsley
salt and freshly ground
 black pepper

For the pastry

1⅓ cups all-purpose flour, plus
 extra for dusting
½ teaspoon salt
½ cup lard or vegetable fat
2–3 tablespoons ice water
1 egg
2 tablespoons milk

1 To make the pastry, sift the flour and salt into a mixing bowl. Using a pastry blender, cut in the fat until the mixture resembles coarse bread crumbs. Sprinkle in the water, 1 tablespoon at a time, tossing lightly with a fork until the dough forms a ball. Dust with flour, wrap and chill until required.

2 Preheat the oven to 400°F. Heat half of the butter or margarine in a saucepan. Add the onion, carrots and parsnip, and cook for about 10 minutes, until softened. Remove the vegetables from the pan using a slotted spoon.

3 Melt the remaining butter or margarine in the saucepan. Add the flour and cook for 5 minutes, stirring constantly. Stir in the stock, sherry and wine. Bring the sauce to a boil and continue boiling for 1 minute, stirring continuously.

4 Add the cream, peas, chicken, thyme and parsley to the sauce. Season to taste with salt and pepper. Simmer for 1 minute, stirring. Transfer to an 8¾-cup ovenproof dish.

5 On a lightly floured surface, roll out the pastry to ½-inch thickness. Lay the pastry on the dish and trim off the excess. Dampen the rim of the dish. Using a fork, press the pastry to the rim to seal.

6 Lightly whisk the egg with the milk. Brush the pastry all over with the egg glaze. Cut decorative shapes from the pastry trimmings and arrange on top of the pie. Brush again with the egg glaze. Make one or two holes in the crust so that steam can escape during baking.

7 Bake the pie for about 35 minutes, until the pastry is golden brown. Serve hot.

Old-fashioned Chicken Pie

The chicken can be roasted and the sauce prepared a day in advance.

Serves 4

4-pound chicken
1 onion, quartered
1 fresh tarragon or
 rosemary sprig
2 tablespoons butter
1½ cups button mushrooms
2 tablespoons all-purpose flour

1¼ cups Chicken Stock
¾ cup cooked ham, diced
2 tablespoons chopped
 fresh parsley
1 pound ready-made puff or
 flaky pastry
1 egg, beaten
salt and freshly ground
 black pepper

1 Preheat the oven to 400°F. Put the chicken into a casserole with the onion and herbs. Add 1¼ cups water and season. Cover with a lid and bake for about 1¼ hours or until tender.

2 Remove the chicken from the casserole and strain the cooking liquid into a measuring cup. Let cool and remove any fat. Add water to make 1¼ cups.

3 Remove bones and skin from the chicken and cut the meat into cubes. Melt the butter in a pan and cook the mushrooms for 2–3 minutes. Sprinkle in the flour and blend in the stock. Bring to a boil, season and add the ham, chicken and parsley. Turn into a pie dish and cool before covering with pastry.

4 Roll out the pastry to 2 inches larger than the pie dish. Cut a narrow strip to place around the edge. Dampen with a little water and stick to the rim. Brush with beaten egg. Lay the pastry loosely on the pie and press firmly onto the rim. Trim off the excess and crimp the edge. Cut a hole in the center to let steam escape. Decorate with pastry leaves cut from the trimmings.

5 Brush the top of the pie with beaten egg and bake for about 35 minutes or until the pastry is golden brown.

Chicken Pie with Mushrooms

The filling in this pie has an intense mushroom flavor, using chicken stock rather than the more typical milk and butter.

Serves 4–6

2 pounds cooked roast or boiled chicken
3 tablespoons olive oil, plus extra for greasing
10 ounces mixed dark mushrooms, e.g. flat, oyster and chestnut
5 teaspoons all-purpose flour
1¼ cups Chicken Stock
1 tablespoon soy sauce
1 egg white
salt and freshly ground black pepper

For the pastry

generous ½ cup margarine, chilled
2 cups all-purpose flour
1 egg yolk
¼ cup cold water

1 To make the pastry, cut the margarine into small pieces and rub it into the flour until the mixture resembles bread crumbs. Mix the egg yolk with the water and stir it into the mixture. Form the dough into a ball, cover and chill for 30 minutes.

2 Preheat the oven to 425°F. Cut the cooked chicken into pieces and put them in a greased pie pan of about 7½ cups capacity.

3 Heat half the oil in a frying pan. Slice the mushrooms thickly and sauté them over high heat for about 3 minutes. Add the rest of the oil and stir in the flour. Season with pepper and gradually add the stock, stirring to make a thick sauce.

4 Stir in the soy sauce and adjust the seasoning. Pour the mushroom sauce over the chicken. Roll out the pastry and cut one piece slightly larger than the size of the dish. Also cut some long strips about ¾ inches wide. Place the strips around the rim of the pie pan, then lift the pastry lid on top, pressing it down on top of the strips. Knock up the edges with a knife.

5 Lightly whisk the egg white and brush it on the pie. Bake for 30–35 minutes or until golden brown.

Chicken & Leek Pie

Crisp, light pastry made with fresh herbs tops a tarragon-flavored chicken and leek sauce to make this tempting savory pie.

Serves 4

1½ cups all-purpose flour, plus extra
pinch of salt
7 tablespoons margarine
1 tablespoon chopped fresh mixed herbs
3 leeks, sliced
3 tablespoons cornstarch
1⅔ cups milk
1–2 tablespoons chopped fresh tarragon
12 ounces cooked, skinless, boneless chicken breast, diced
7-ounce can corn kernels, drained
salt and freshly ground black pepper
fresh herb sprigs and coarse sea salt, to garnish

1 To make the pastry, place the flour and salt in a bowl and rub in 6 tablespoons of the margarine until the mixture resembles bread crumbs. Stir in the mixed herbs and add a little cold water to make smooth, firm dough. Put the pastry in a plastic bag and chill for 30 minutes.

2 Preheat the oven to 375°F. Steam the leeks for about 10 minutes, until just tender. Drain and keep warm.

3 Meanwhile, blend the cornstarch with 5 tablespoons of the milk. Heat the remaining milk in a saucepan to the boiling point, then pour it onto the cornstarch mixture, stirring constantly. Return the mixture to the pan and heat gently until the sauce comes to a boil and thickens, stirring constantly. Simmer gently for about 2 minutes, stirring. Add the remaining margarine to the pan with the chopped tarragon, leeks, chicken and corn. Season to taste with salt and pepper, and combine well.

4 Spoon the mixture into a 5-cup pie pan. Roll out the pastry on a lightly floured surface to a shape slightly larger than the pie pan. Trim, decorate the top with the pastry trimmings, if desired, and make a slit in the center to let steam escape. Bake for 35–40 minutes, until the pastry is golden brown. Serve immediately, sprinkled with herbs and sea salt.

Chicken Bouchée

A spectacular centerpiece, this light pastry shell contains a delicious chicken and mushroom filling.

Serves 4

1 pound ready-made puff pastry
1 egg, beaten

For the filling
1 tablespoon oil
1 pound ground chicken
¼ cup all-purpose flour
⅔ cup milk
⅔ cup Chicken Stock
4 scallions, chopped
¼ cup red currants
generous 1 cup button
  mushrooms, sliced
1 tablespoon chopped
  fresh tarragon
salt and freshly ground
  black pepper

1 Preheat the oven to 400°F. Roll out half the pastry on a lightly floured surface into a 10-inch oval. Roll out the remainder into an oval of the same size and draw a smaller 8-inch oval in the center.

2 Brush the edge of the first pastry shape with the beaten egg and place the smaller oval on top. Place on a dampened baking sheet and bake for 30 minutes.

3 To make the filling, heat the oil in a large pan. Cook the ground chicken for 5 minutes, stirring frequently to break up any lumps. Add the flour and cook for another minute. Stir in the milk and stock, and bring to a boil. Add the scallions, red currants and mushrooms. Cook for 20 minutes. Stir in the tarragon and season to taste.

4 Place the pastry bouchée on a serving plate, remove the oval center and spoon in the filling. Replace the pastry oval to form a lid. Serve immediately.

> **Variation**
> *You can also use shortcrust pastry for this dish and cook as a traditional chicken pie.*

Kotopitta

This is based on a Greek chicken pie. Serve hot or cold with a Greek salad made from tomatoes, cucumber and cubes of feta cheese.

Serves 4

10 ounces phyllo pastry, thawed
  if frozen
2 tablespoons olive oil
¾ cup chopped
  toasted almonds
2 tablespoons milk

Greek salad, to serve

For the filling
1 tablespoon olive oil
1 medium onion, finely chopped
1 garlic clove, crushed
1 pound boneless cooked chicken
2 ounces feta cheese, crumbled
2 eggs, beaten
1 tablespoon chopped fresh
  parsley
1 tablespoon chopped cilantro
1 tablespoon chopped fresh mint
salt and freshly ground black pepper

1 To make the filling, heat the oil in a large frying pan and cook the onion gently until soft. Add the garlic and cook for another 2 minutes. Transfer to a bowl.

2 Remove the skin from the chicken and grind or chop the meat finely. Add to the onion with the rest of the filling ingredients. Combine thoroughly and season to taste with salt and pepper.

3 Preheat the oven to 375°F. Have a damp dish towel ready to keep the phyllo pastry covered. Unravel the pastry and cut the whole batch into a 12-inch square. Taking half the sheets (cover the remainder), brush one sheet with a little olive oil, lay it on a well-greased 6¼-cup ovenproof dish and sprinkle with a few chopped, toasted almonds. Repeat with the other (uncovered) sheets of phyllo, overlapping them alternately in the dish. Spoon in the filling and cover the pie in the same way with the rest of the pastry.

4 Fold in the overlapping edges and mark a diamond pattern on the surface of the pie with a sharp knife. Brush with milk and sprinkle on any remaining almonds. Bake for 20–30 minutes or until golden brown on top. Serve with Greek salad.

Chicken Charter Pie

This dish comes from Cornwall in England, where cream is typically used in the filling.

Serves 4
4 tablespoons butter
4 chicken legs
1 onion, finely chopped
⅔ cup milk
⅔ cup sour cream
4 scallions, quartered
¾ ounces finely chopped
   fresh parsley
8 ounces ready-made puff pastry
2 eggs, beaten, plus extra
   for glazing
½ cup heavy cream
salt and freshly ground
   black pepper
lightly cooked carrots, to serve

1 Melt the butter in a heavy pan and brown the chicken legs. Transfer to a plate. Add the onion to the pan and cook until soft. Add the milk, sour cream, scallions, parsley and seasoning, bring to a boil, then simmer for 2 minutes.

2 Return the chicken to the pan with any juices, cover and cook very gently for 30 minutes. Transfer the chicken and sauce mixture to a 5-cup pie pan and let cool.

3 Meanwhile, roll out the pastry until about ¾ inch larger all around than the top of the pie pan. Let the pastry relax while the chicken is cooling.

4 Preheat the oven to 425°F. Cut off a narrow strip around the edge of the puff pastry and place it on the edge of the pie dish. Moisten the strip with cold water, then cover the dish with the pastry. Press the edges together. Make a hole in the center of the pastry and insert a small funnel of aluminum foil. Brush the pastry with a little beaten egg, then bake for 15–20 minutes.

5 Reduce the oven temperature to 350°F. Mix the cream and eggs and cream, and pour into the pie through the funnel. Shake gently, then return to the oven for 5–10 minutes. Remove from the oven and let sit for 5–10 minutes before serving hot with carrots.

Chicken & Ham Pie

This domed double-crust pie is suitable for a cold buffet and for picnics.

Serves 8
14 ounces ready-made
   shortcrust pastry
1¾ pounds chicken breast
   fillet, skinned
12 ounces ham
about ¼ cup heavy cream
6 scallions, finely chopped
1 tablespoon chopped
   fresh tarragon
2 teaspoons chopped fresh thyme
grated zest and juice of
   ½ large lemon
1 teaspoon ground mace
salt and freshly ground
   black pepper
beaten egg or milk, to glaze
salad, to serve

1 Preheat the oven to 375°F. Roll out one third of the pastry and use it to line an 8-inch pie pan 2 inches deep. Place on a baking sheet.

2 Grind 4 ounces of the chicken with the ham, then mix with the cream, scallions, herbs, lemon zest, 1 tablespoon of the lemon juice and the seasoning to make a soft mixture; add more cream if necessary. Cut the remaining chicken into ½-inch pieces and mix with the remaining lemon juice, the mace and seasoning.

3 Make a layer of one third of the ham mixture in the pastry shell, cover with half the chopped chicken, then add another layer of one third of the ham. Add all the remaining chicken followed by the remaining ham. Dampen the edges of the pastry shell. Roll out the remaining pastry to make a lid for the pie and place in position. Trim neatly and crimp the edges.

4 Use the pastry trimmings to make a lattice decoration on the pie lid. Make a small hole in the center of the lid, brush all over with beaten egg or milk, then bake for about 20 minutes. Reduce the oven temperature to 325°F and bake for another 1–1¼ hours; cover the top with aluminum foil if the pastry becomes too brown. Transfer the pie to a wire rack and let cool before serving, accompanied by salad.

Chicken Knish

These individual chicken and Stilton knishes are wrapped in crisp shortcrust pastry and shaped. They can be served hot or cold.

Makes 4

3 cups self-rising flour, plus extra
½ teaspoon salt
6 tablespoons lard, plus extra
  for greasing
6 tablespoons butter
4–5 tablespoons cold water

beaten egg, to glaze
salad, to serve

For the filling

1 pound boned and skinned
  chicken thighs
¼ cup chopped walnuts
1 ounces scallions, sliced
½ cup Stilton, crumbled
1 ounce celery, finely chopped
½ teaspoon dried thyme
salt and freshly ground
  black pepper

1 Preheat the oven to 400°F. Mix the flour and salt in a bowl. Rub in the lard and butter with your fingers until the mixture resembles fine bread crumbs. Using a knife to cut and stir, mix in the cold water to form a stiff, pliable dough.

2 Turn out onto a lightly floured surface and knead gently until smooth. Divide into 4 equal pieces and roll out each piece to a thickness of ¼ inch, keeping a good round shape. Cut each one into an 8-inch circle, using a plate as a guide.

3 Remove any fat from the chicken thighs and cut the meat into small cubes. Mix the chicken with the walnuts, scallions, Stilton, celery, thyme and seasoning, and divide among the four pastry circles.

4 Brush the edge of the pastry with beaten egg and fold over, pinching and crimping the edges together well. Place on a greased baking sheet and bake for about 45 minutes or until golden brown. Serve hot or cold, with salad.

Chicken Parcels with Herb Butter

These crisp, light, little phyllo pastry packets, dusted with Parmesan cheese, enclose chicken breast moistened with herb-flavored butter.

Serves 4

4 chicken breast fillets, skinned
10 tablespoons butter, softened,
  plus extra for greasing

6 tablespoons chopped fresh
  mixed herbs, e.g. thyme, parsley,
  oregano and rosemary
1 teaspoon lemon juice
5 large sheets phyllo pastry,
  thawed if frozen
1 egg, beaten
2 tablespoons grated
  Parmesan cheese
salt and freshly ground
  black pepper
salad greens, to serve

1 Season the chicken fillets and fry in 2 tablespoons of the butter to seal and brown lightly. Let cool.

2 Preheat the oven to 375°F. Put the remaining butter, the herbs, lemon juice and seasoning in a food processor and process until smooth. Melt half the herb butter.

3 Take one sheet of phyllo pastry and brush with a little melted herb butter. Fold the phyllo pastry sheet in half and brush again with butter. Place a chicken fillet about 1-inch from the top end.

4 Dot the chicken with a quarter of the remaining unmelted herb butter. Fold in the sides of the pastry, then roll up to enclose it completely. Place, seam-side down, on a lightly greased baking sheet. Repeat with the other chicken fillets.

5 Brush the phyllo parcels with beaten egg. Cut the last sheet of phyllo into strips, then scrunch and arrange on top. Brush the parcels once again with the egg glaze, then sprinkle with Parmesan. Bake for 35–40 minutes, until golden brown. Serve hot, accompanied by salad greens.

Chicken en Croûte

Chicken breasts layered with herbs and orange-flavored stuffing and wrapped in light puff pastry make an impressive dinner-party dish.

Serves 8
1 pound ready-made puff pastry
4 large chicken breast
  fillets, skinned
1 egg, beaten
lightly cooked vegetables,
  to serve

For the stuffing
4 ounces leeks, thinly sliced
⅓ cup chopped bacon
2 tablespoons butter
2 cups fresh white bread crumbs
2 tablespoons chopped fresh
  herbs, e.g. parsley, thyme,
  marjoram and chives
grated zest of 1 large orange
1 egg, beaten
salt and freshly ground
  black pepper

1 To make the stuffing, cook the leeks and bacon in the butter until soft. Put the bread crumbs, herbs and seasoning in a bowl. Add the leeks and butter with the orange zest and bind with beaten egg. If the mixture is too dry, add a little orange juice.

2 Preheat the oven to 400°F. Roll out the pastry to a large rectangle 12 x 16 inches. Trim the edges and reserve the trimmings for the decoration.

3 Place the chicken breasts between two pieces of plastic wrap and flatten to a thickness of ¼ inch with a rolling pin or meat mallet. Spread one-third of the stuffing over the center of the pastry. Lay two chicken breasts, side by side, over the stuffing. Cover with another third of the stuffing, then repeat with two more chicken breasts and the rest of the stuffing.

4 Cut diagonally from each corner of the pastry to the chicken. Brush with beaten egg. Bring up the sides and overlap them slightly. Trim any excess and fold the ends over like a parcel. Turn over onto a greased baking sheet. Using a sharp knife, lightly criss-cross the pastry into a diamond pattern. Brush with beaten egg and cut leaves from the trimmings to decorate the top. Bake for 50–60 minutes. Serve hot with vegetables.

Chicken & Apricot Phyllo Pie

The filling for this pie has a Middle Eastern flavor—ground chicken combined with apricots, bulghur wheat, nuts and spices.

Serves 6
½ cup bulghur wheat
6 tablespoons butter
1 onion, chopped
1 pound ground chicken
¼ cup dried apricots, finely
  chopped
¼ cup blanched almonds,
  chopped
1 teaspoon ground cinnamon
½ teaspoon ground allspice
¼ cup plain yogurt
1 tablespoon snipped fresh chives
2 tablespoons chopped
  fresh parsley
6 large sheets phyllo pastry,
  thawed if frozen
salt and freshly ground
  black pepper
fresh whole chives, to garnish

1 Preheat the oven to 400°F. Put the bulghur wheat in a bowl with ½ cup boiling water. Soak for 5–10 minutes, until the water is absorbed.

2 Heat 2 tablespoons of the butter in a pan and gently cook the onion and chicken until pale golden, stirring frequently. Add the apricots, almonds and bulghur wheat, and cook for another 2 minutes. Remove from heat and stir in the cinnamon, allspice, yogurt, chives and parsley. Season to taste.

3 Melt the remaining butter. Unroll the phyllo pastry and cut into 10-inch rounds. Keep the pastry rounds covered with a clean, damp dish towel to prevent them from drying out.

4 Line a 9-inch springform pan with three of the pastry rounds, brushing each one with melted butter as you layer them. Spoon in the chicken mixture and cover with three more pastry rounds, brushed with melted butter as before.

5 Crumple the remaining pastry rounds and place them on top of the pie, then brush on any remaining melted butter. Bake the pie for about 30 minutes, until the pastry is golden brown and crisp. Serve hot or cold, cut into wedges and garnished with whole chives.

Tandoori Chicken Kebabs

Before it is cooked, the chicken is marinated in a mixture of yogurt and lemon juice and flavored with tandoori paste, garlic and cilantro.

Serves 4

4 chicken breast fillets, about
  6 ounces each, skinned
1 tablespoon lemon juice
3 tablespoons tandoori paste
3 tablespoons plain yogurt
1 garlic clove, crushed
2 tablespoons chopped cilantro
1 small onion, cut into wedges
  and separated into layers
a little oil, for brushing
salt and freshly ground
  black pepper
cilantro sprigs, to garnish
rice pilaf and naan,
  to serve

1 Cut the chicken breasts into 1-inch cubes, place in a bowl and add the lemon juice, tandoori paste, yogurt, garlic, cilantro and seasoning. Cover and let marinate in the refrigerator for 2–3 hours.

2 Preheat the broiler to high. Thread alternate pieces of marinated chicken and onion onto four skewers.

3 Brush the onions with a little oil, lay on a broiler rack and cook under the preheated broiler for 10–12 minutes, turning once.

4 Garnish the kebabs with cilantro and serve immediately with rice pilaf and naan.

Cook's Tip
Use chopped, boned and skinned chicken thighs, or turkey breasts, for a cheaper alternative. Tandoori paste is available at specialty Indian food stores and many supermarkets.

Deviled Chicken

This spicy grilled chicken dish from southern Italy uses a marinade of dried red chiles, which are a colorful specialty of the Abruzzi region.

Serves 4
½ cup olive oil
finely grated zest and juice of
  1 large lemon
2 garlic cloves, finely chopped
2 teaspoons finely chopped or
  crumbled dried red chiles
12 skinless, boneless chicken
  thighs, each cut into
  3 or 4 pieces
salt and freshly ground
  black pepper
flat-leaf parsley, to garnish
lemon wedges and green salad,
  to serve

1 Make a marinade by mixing the oil, lemon zest and juice, garlic and chiles in a large, shallow nonmetallic dish. Add salt and pepper to taste, and whisk well.

2 Add the chicken pieces to the dish, turning to coat with the marinade. Cover and place in the refrigerator for at least 4 hours, or preferably overnight.

3 When ready to cook, prepare a grill or preheat the broiler and thread the chicken pieces onto eight oiled metal skewers. Cook on the grill or under a hot broiler for 6–8 minutes, turning frequently, until tender.

4 Serve hot, garnished with flat-leaf parsley and accompanied by lemon wedges for squeezing and a green salad.

Cook's Tip
Thread the chicken pieces zig-zag fashion onto the skewers so that they do not fall off during cooking.

Chicken Saté with Peanut Sauce

Marinated chicken kebabs
served with a peanut sauce.

Serves 4–6
4 chicken breast fillets
1 tablespoon coriander seeds
2 teaspoons fennel seeds
2 garlic cloves, crushed
2-inch piece lemongrass, shredded
1/2 teaspoon ground turmeric
2 teaspoons sugar
1/2 teaspoon salt
2 tablespoons soy sauce
1 tablespoon sesame oil
juice of 1/2 lime

mint leaves, lime wedges and
    cucumber batons, to garnish
lettuce, to serve

For the peanut sauce
1 1/4 cups raw peanuts
1 tablespoon vegetable oil,
    plus extra
2 shallots, finely chopped
1 garlic clove, crushed
1–2 small fresh chiles, seeded
    and finely chopped
1/2-inch cube shrimp paste
2 tablespoons tamarind sauce
1/2 cup coconut milk
1 tablespoon honey

1 Cut the chicken into thin strips and thread, zig-zag fashion,
onto 12 bamboo skewers. Arrange on a flat plate and set aside.

2 Dry-fry the coriander and fennel seeds in a wok. Grind with
a mortar and pestle or food processor, then return to the wok
and add the garlic, lemongrass, turmeric, sugar, salt, soy sauce,
sesame oil and lime juice. Let the mixture cool. Spread it onto
the chicken and set in a cool place for up to 8 hours.

3 For the sauce, stir-fry the peanuts with a little oil. Turn out
onto a cloth and rub with your hands to remove the skins.
Process in a food processor for 2 minutes. Heat the oil in a
wok and sauté the shallots, garlic and chiles until softened. Add
the shrimp paste, tamarind sauce, coconut milk and honey.
Simmer briefly, add to the peanuts and process into a thick
sauce. Pour into a serving bowl.

4 Brush the chicken with a little vegetable oil and cook under a
preheated broiler for 6–8 minutes. Serve on a bed of lettuce,
garnished with mint leaves, lime wedges and cucumber batons
and accompanied by the peanut sauce.

Chicken Tikka Masala

Tender chicken pieces
cooked in a creamy, spicy
sauce with a hint of tomato
and served on naan.

Serves 4
1 1/2 pounds chicken breast
    fillet, skinned
6 tablespoons tikka paste
1/4 cup plain yogurt
2 tablespoons oil
1 onion, chopped
1 garlic clove, crushed

1 fresh green chile, seeded
    and chopped
1-inch piece fresh ginger root,
    grated
1 tablespoon tomato paste
1 tablespoon ground almonds
1 cup water
3 tablespoons butter, melted
1/4 cup heavy cream
1 tablespoon lemon juice
cilantro sprigs, plain yogurt and
    toasted cumin seeds, to garnish
naan, to serve

1 Cut the chicken into 1-inch cubes. Put 3 tablespoons of the
tikka paste and all of the yogurt into a bowl. Add the chicken,
turn to coat well and let marinate for 20 minutes.

2 For the tikka sauce, heat the oil in a pan and sauté the onion,
garlic, chile and ginger for 5 minutes. Add the remaining tikka
paste and fry for 2 minutes. Add the tomato paste, ground
almonds and water, and simmer for 15 minutes.

3 Meanwhile, thread the chicken onto wooden kebab skewers.
Preheat the broiler.

4 Brush the chicken pieces with the melted butter and broil
under medium heat for 15 minutes, turning occasionally.

5 Put the tikka sauce into a food processor or blender and
process until smooth. Return to the pan and stir in the cream
and lemon juice.

6 Remove the chicken pieces from the skewers and add to the
tikka sauce, then simmer for 5 minutes. Serve on naan and
garnish with cilantro, yogurt and toasted cumin seeds.

Blackened Cajun Chicken & Corn

A classic Cajun method of cooking poultry in a spiced coating. Traditionally, the coating should begin to char and blacken slightly at the edges.

Serves 4

8 chicken joints, e.g. drumsticks, thighs or wings

2 whole ears corn

2 teaspoons garlic salt

2 teaspoons freshly ground black pepper

1 ½ teaspoons ground cumin

1 ½ teaspoons paprika

1 teaspoon cayenne pepper

3 tablespoons melted butter

chopped fresh parsley, to garnish

1 Cut any excess fat from the chicken, but leave the skin on. Slash the deepest parts with a knife to let the flavors penetrate the flesh.

2 Pull the husks and silks off the corn and discard. Cut the corn into thick slices.

3 In a small bowl, combine all the spices. Put the chicken and corn in a large bowl and brush with melted butter. Sprinkle the spices on them and toss well to coat evenly.

4 Cook the chicken pieces on a medium-hot grill or under a preheated broiler for about 25 minutes, turning occasionally. Add the corn after 15 minutes of the cooking time and cook, turning often, until golden brown. Serve hot, garnished with chopped parsley.

> **Cook's Tip**
> *The natural sugar that gives corn its characteristic flavor starts to turn to starch immediately after picking. When buying, look for plump kernels and always use on the day of purchase.*

Barbecued Jerk Chicken

Jerk refers to the blend of herb and spice seasoning rubbed into meat before it is roasted over charcoal, usually sprinkled with juniper berries, to make this tasty Caribbean dish.

Serves 4

8 chicken portions

oil, for brushing

salt and freshly ground black pepper

salad greens, to serve

For the marinade

1 teaspoon ground allspice

1 teaspoon ground cinnamon

1 teaspoon dried thyme

¼ teaspoon grated nutmeg

2 teaspoons sugar

2 garlic cloves, crushed

1 tablespoon finely chopped onion

1 tablespoon chopped scallion

1 tablespoon vinegar

2 tablespoons oil

1 tablespoon lime juice

1 fresh hot chile, chopped

1 To make the marinade, combine all the ingredients in a small bowl and mash them together well to form a thick paste.

2 Lay the chicken portions on a plate or board and make several lengthwise slits in the flesh. Rub the seasoning all over the chicken and into the slits.

3 Place the chicken portions in a dish, cover with plastic wrap and marinate for several hours, or preferably overnight, in the refrigerator.

4 Preheat the broiler or prepare the grill. Shake off any excess seasoning from the chicken. Brush with oil and place either on a baking sheet or on a grill. Cook under the broiler for 45 minutes, turning often, or over hot coals for 30 minutes, turning often. Serve hot with salad greens.

> **Cook's Tip**
> *The flavor is best if you marinate the chicken overnight. Sprinkle the charcoal with aromatic herbs, such as bay leaves, for even more flavor when grilling.*

Spicy Barbecued Chicken

A very easy dish that can be cooked either on the grill or in the oven. The sauce has all the hot, sharp and sweet flavors that you would expect.

Serves 4

3 tablespoons vegetable oil
1 large onion, chopped
³⁄₄ cup ketchup
³⁄₄ cup water
2¹⁄₂ tablespoons fresh lemon juice
1¹⁄₂ tablespoons grated
  horseradish
1 tablespoon light brown sugar
1 tablespoon French mustard
3 pounds chicken portions
cooked rice, to serve

1 Preheat the oven, if using, to 350°F. Heat 1 tablespoon of the oil in a saucepan. Add the onion and cook for about 5 minutes, until softened. Stir in the ketchup, water, lemon juice, horseradish, sugar and mustard, and bring to a boil. Reduce the heat and simmer the sauce for 10 minutes, stirring occasionally.

2 Meanwhile, heat the remaining oil in a heavy frying pan. Add the chicken portions and brown on all sides. Remove from the pan and drain on paper towels.

3 Place the chicken in an 11 x 9-inch ovenproof dish and pour the sauce on top.

4 Bake for about 1¼ hours, until the chicken is cooked and tender, basting occasionally. Alternatively, grill over medium heat for 40–50 minutes, turning once and brushing frequently with the sauce. Serve the chicken on a bed of cooked rice.

> **Cook's Tip**
> For a hotter flavor, use English mustard.

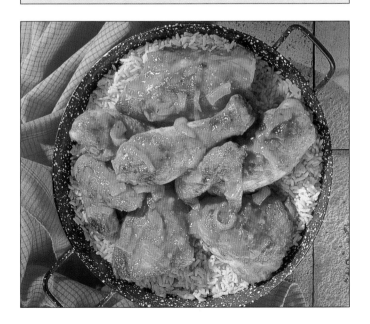

Thai-style Grilled Chicken

Grilled chicken is served almost everywhere in Thailand, from portable roadside stalls to sports stadiums and beaches.

Serves 4–6

3¹⁄₂-pound chicken, cut into
  8–10 pieces
lime wedges and finely sliced red
  chiles, to garnish
cooked rice, to serve

For the marinade

2 lemongrass stalks, chopped
1-inch piece fresh ginger root
6 garlic cloves
4 shallots
¹⁄₂ bunch cilantro roots
1 tablespoon sugar
¹⁄₂ cup coconut milk
2 tablespoons fish sauce
2 tablespoons soy sauce

1 To make the marinade, put all the ingredients into a food processor and process until smooth.

2 Put the chicken pieces in a wide, shallow dish and pour in the marinade. Let marinate in the refrigerator for at least 4 hours or overnight.

3 Prepare the grill or preheat the oven to 400°F. Cook the chicken over glowing coals, or place on a rack over a roasting pan and bake for 20–30 minutes or until the chicken is cooked and golden brown. Turn the pieces occasionally and brush frequently with the marinade.

4 Garnish with lime wedges and finely sliced red chiles, and serve with rice.

> **Cook's Tip**
> Made from salted anchovies, fish sauce—also known as nam pla—is widely used in Thai cooking in much the same way as soy sauce is used in Chinese cuisine. It is strongly flavored and very salty, so use with caution. It is available at Asian food stores and many supermarkets.

Thai Chicken

Thai chicken is especially delicious when cooked on the grill. It should be served with a dipping sauce.

Serves 4–6

2 pounds chicken drumsticks
   or thighs
1 teaspoon whole black
   peppercorns
½ teaspoon caraway or
   cumin seeds
4 teaspoons sugar
2 teaspoons paprika
¾-inch piece fresh ginger root,
   peeled
3 garlic cloves, crushed
½ ounce cilantro, white root or
   stem, finely chopped
3 tablespoons vegetable oil
salt
6–8 lettuce leaves, to serve

For the garnish

½ cucumber, cut into strips
4 scallions, trimmed
2 limes, quartered

1 Chop through the narrow end of each chicken drumstick with a heavy knife. Score the chicken pieces deeply to let the marinade penetrate. Set aside in a shallow bowl.

2 Grind the peppercorns, caraway or cumin seeds and sugar using a mortar and pestle or food processor. Add the paprika, ginger, garlic, cilantro and oil, and grind into a paste.

3 Spread the marinade on the chicken and place in the refrigerator for 6 hours.

4 Preheat the broiler or prepare the grill. Cook the chicken for 20 minutes, turning once. Season with salt to taste. Serve on a bed of lettuce leaves, garnished with cucumber, scallions and lime quarters.

> **Cook's Tip**
> Spices are more flavorful when freshly ground than bought ready ground. You can use a mortar and pestle or a small coffee mill kept especially for this purpose. Custom-made spice grinders are also available.

Broiled Spiced Chicken

The sharpness of fresh lime balances the heat and strength of the spices.

Serves 4

1 teaspoon coriander seeds
1 teaspoon cumin seeds
2 limes
2 garlic cloves, crushed
¼ cup chopped cilantro
1 small fresh green chile, seeded
   and finely chopped
2 tablespoons light soy sauce
¼ cup sunflower oil
4 chicken breast fillets, about
   6 ounces each, skinned
green vegetables, to serve

1 Crush the coriander and cumin seeds using a mortar and pestle or a spice or coffee grinder. Cut the zest from the limes into thin shreds using a zester. Squeeze the juice. Blend the spices, lime zest and juice, garlic, cilantro, chile, soy sauce and oil in a bowl. Add the chicken, turn to coat thoroughly, then cover and marinate in the refrigerator for 24 hours.

2 Remove the chicken from the marinade. Heat a broiler or ridged pan and cook the chicken for 4–6 minutes on each side or until cooked through. Serve with green vegetables.

Thai Dipping Sauce

This has a fiery strength, so use with caution.

Makes ½ cup

1 tablespoon vegetable oil
1 tablespoon fish sauce
2 garlic cloves, finely chopped
¾-inch piece ginger root,
   peeled and finely chopped
3 fresh red chiles, chopped
1 tablespoon finely chopped
   cilantro root
4 teaspoons sugar
3 tablespoons dark soy sauce
juice of ½ lime

1 Heat the oil, fish sauce, garlic, ginger and chiles for 1–2 minutes.
2 Remove from heat and add the remaining ingredients.

Indonesian Chicken

The flavor of this dish will be more intense if the chicken is marinated for several hours or overnight.

Serves 4
3½-pound chicken
4 garlic cloves, crushed
2 lemongrass stalks, lower
    2-inches sliced
½-inch fresh galangal, peeled
    and sliced
1 teaspoon ground turmeric
about 2 cups water
3–4 bay leaves
3 tablespoons each dark and
    light soy sauce
2 ounces butter or margarine
salt
cilantro, to garnish
boiled rice, to serve

1 Cut the chicken into four or eight portions. Slash the fleshy part of each portion twice and set aside.

2 Put the garlic, lemongrass, galangal, turmeric and salt into a food processor and process to a paste or grind using a mortar and pestle. Rub the paste into the chicken pieces and set aside for at least 30 minutes. Wear rubber gloves for this, as the turmeric will stain heavily; or wash your hands immediately after using.

3 Transfer the chicken pieces to a wok or heavy pan and pour in the water. Add the bay leaves and bring to a boil. Cover and cook gently for 30 minutes, adding a little more water if necessary. Stir occasionally.

4 Preheat the broiler or grill, or preheat the oven to 400°F. Just before transferring, add the two soy sauces to the pan together with the butter or margarine. Cook until the chicken is well coated and the sauce has almost been absorbed.

5 Transfer to the broiler, grill or oven and cook for another 10–15 minutes, turning the pieces often so that they become golden brown all over. Take care not to let them burn. Baste with the remaining sauce during cooking. Serve with boiled rice, garnished with cilantro leaves.

Broiled Cashew Chicken

This dish comes from the beautiful island of Bali where nuts are widely used as a base for sauces and marinades. Serve with a green salad and hot chili dipping sauce.

Serves 4–6
4 chicken legs
sliced radishes and sliced
    cucumber, to garnish
Chinese greens and chili dipping
    sauce, to serve

For the marinade
½ cup raw cashews or
    macadamia nuts
2 shallots or 1 small onion,
    finely chopped
2 garlic cloves, crushed
2 small fresh red chiles, chopped
2-inch piece lemongrass
1 tablespoon tamarind sauce
2 tablespoons dark soy sauce
1 tablespoon fish sauce (optional)
2 teaspoons sugar
½ teaspoon salt
1 tablespoon rice or white
    wine vinegar

1 Using a sharp knife, slash the chicken legs several times through to the bone and chop off the knuckle end. Place the chicken in a wide, shallow dish and set aside.

2 To make the marinade, grind the cashews or macadamia nuts in a food processor or using a mortar and pestle.

3 Add the shallots or onion, garlic, chiles and lemongrass, and blend. Add the remaining marinade ingredients.

4 Spread the marinade on the chicken and set aside in the refrigerator for up to 8 hours.

5 Preheat the broiler or prepare a grill. Cook the chicken under medium heat or cook on the grill for 15 minutes on each side. Transfer to a serving dish lined with Chinese greens, garnish with the sliced radishes and cucumber, and serve, accompanied by chili dipping sauce.

Chicken Breasts Cooked in Spices & Coconut

The chicken is marinated in a highly aromatic, spicy coconut mixture, which doubles as a sauce for the finished dish.

Serves 4

7 ounces coconut milk
1 1/4 cups boiling water
3 garlic cloves, chopped
2 scallions, chopped
1 fresh green chile, chopped
2-inch piece fresh ginger root, peeled and chopped
1 teaspoon fennel seeds
1/2 teaspoon black peppercorns
seeds from 4 cardamom pods
2 tablespoons ground coriander
1 teaspoon ground cumin
1 teaspoon ground star anise
1 teaspoon grated nutmeg
1/2 teaspoon ground cloves
1/2 teaspoon ground turmeric
4 large chicken breast
   fillets, skinned
onion rings and cilantro sprigs,
   to garnish
naan, to serve

1 Place the garlic, scallions, chile, ginger and all the spices in a blender or food processor. Add the coconut milk and process into a smooth paste.

2 Make several diagonal cuts across the chicken fillets. Arrange them in one layer in a shallow dish. Spoon on half the coconut mixture and toss well to coat the chicken evenly. Cover the dish and let marinate in the refrigerator for about 30 minutes, or overnight.

3 Cook the chicken under a preheated broiler or on a medium-hot grill for 12–15 minutes, turning once, until well browned and thoroughly cooked.

4 Heat the remaining coconut mixture gently until boiling. Serve with the chicken, garnished with onion rings and sprigs of cilantro, and accompanied by naan.

Drumsticks with Devilish Sauce

Chicken drumsticks marinated with spices, coated with a hot, tomato-based sauce and served on a bed of yellow rice.

Serves 4

8 large chicken drumsticks

For the dry marinade

2 teaspoons salt
2 teaspoons sugar
1 teaspoon freshly ground
   black pepper
1 teaspoon ground ginger
1 teaspoon dry English
   mustard powder
1 teaspoon paprika
2 tablespoons olive oil

For the sauce

2 tablespoons ketchup
1 tablespoon chili sauce
1 tablespoon soy sauce
1 tablespoon fruit sauce

For the yellow rice

2 tablespoons butter
1 medium onion, finely chopped
1 teaspoon ground turmeric
generous 1 cup cooked rice

1 To make the dry marinade, combine all the ingredients in a bowl. Place the chicken drumsticks in a wide, shallow dish. Rub the marinade into the drumsticks, cover with plastic wrap and let sit for at least 1 hour, or preferably overnight.

2 Preheat the broiler. Lay the drumsticks on a broiler rack and broil slowly under medium heat for 10 minutes, turning occasionally, until brown and crisp.

3 Meanwhile, to make the sauce, combine all the ingredients and spoon onto the chicken. Continue to cook the chicken for another 5–7 minutes, basting frequently.

4 To make the yellow rice, heat the butter in a large pan, add the onion and cook until tender. Add the turmeric and cook for another minute.

5 Add the cooked rice and stir to reheat and color. Spoon onto a serving plate and arrange the deviled drumsticks on top. Serve immediately.

Chicken with Pica de Gallo Salsa

This dish originates from Mexico. Its hot, fruity flavors form the essence of Tex-Mex cooking.

Serves 4
4 chicken breasts
pinch each of celery salt and
* cayenne pepper, combined*
2 tablespoons vegetable oil
cilantro sprigs, to garnish
tortilla chips, to serve

For the salsa
10 ounces watermelon
6 ounce cantaloupe
1 small red onion
1–2 fresh green chiles
2 tablespoons lime juice
¼ cup chopped cilantro
salt

1 Preheat a broiler to medium. Slash the chicken breasts deeply in several places to speed up cooking and to help them absorb the spice flavors.

2 Season the chicken with celery salt and cayenne, brush with oil and broil for about 15 minutes, turning occasionally.

3 To make the salsa, remove the rind and as many seeds as you can from the melons. Finely dice the flesh and put it into a bowl. Finely chop the onion. Split the chiles (discarding the seeds if you do not want a very hot salsa) and chop. Mix the onion and chiles with the melon. Add the lime juice and chopped cilantro, and season with a pinch of salt. Turn the salsa into a small bowl.

4 Arrange the chicken on a plate, and serve with the salsa and a handful of tortilla chips. Garnish with cilantro sprigs.

Cook's Tip
To capture the spirit of Tex-Mex food, cook the chicken on a grill and eat shaded from the hot summer sun.

Spiced Poussins

The coating of ground cumin and coriander on the poussins keeps them moist during cooking as well as giving them a delicious and unusual flavor.

Serves 4
2 garlic cloves, roughly chopped
1 teaspoon ground cumin
1 teaspoon ground coriander
pinch of cayenne pepper
½ small onion, chopped
¼ cup olive oil
½ teaspoon salt
2 poussins
lemon wedges, to garnish

1 Combine the garlic, cumin, coriander, cayenne pepper, onion, olive oil and salt in a blender or food processor. Process to make a paste that will spread smoothly.

2 Cut the poussins in half lengthwise. Place them skin-side up in a shallow dish and spread with the spice paste. Cover and let marinate in a cool place for 2 hours.

3 Grill or broil the poussins for 15–20 minutes, turning frequently, until cooked and lightly charred on the outside. Serve immediately, garnished with lemon wedges.

Cook's Tip
Quail can also be cooked in this way. Quail are quite small birds, weighing 4–5 ounces, but with a surprising amount of meat. One bird will usually make a substantial single portion. The meat has quite a delicate flavor and can dry out easily, so this is an especially good way of cooking quail. Wild quail is no longer available, but fresh or frozen Japanese quail is widely available at many supermarkets.

Spiced Honey Chicken Wings

Be prepared to get very sticky when you eat these wings, as the best way to enjoy them is by eating them with your fingers. Provide individual finger bowls for your guests.

1 teaspoon ground ginger
zest of 1 lime, finely grated
12 chicken wings
¼ cup sunflower oil
1 tablespoon chopped cilantro
2 tablespoons soy sauce
3½ tablespoons honey

Serves 4
1 fresh red chile, finely chopped
1 teaspoon chili powder

1 Combine the fresh chile, chili powder, ground ginger and lime zest in a small bowl. Place the chicken wings in a wide, shallow dish. Rub the spice mixture into the chicken skins and let sit for at least 2 hours so the flavors can penetrate.

2 Heat a wok or heavy frying pan and add half the oil. When the oil is hot, add half the wings and stir-fry for 10 minutes, turning regularly until crisp and golden. Drain on paper towels. Repeat with the remaining oil and wings.

3 Add the cilantro to the hot wok and stir-fry for 30 seconds, then return the wings to the wok and stir-fry for 1 minute.

4 Stir in the soy sauce and honey and stir-fry for 1 minute. Serve the chicken wings hot, with the sauce drizzled on them.

Cook's Tip
These wings are perfect party food, as they are inexpensive, take little time to cook and are easy to nibble. For a more filling meal, use the same flavorings for chicken drumsticks, but cook under the broiler for 12–15 minutes, turning frequently, until cooked through and golden.

Cajun-spiced Chicken

These chicken breast fillets are seared in a very hot frying pan which, for best results, should be of heavy cast iron and well seasoned.

2 teaspoons cayenne pepper
2 teaspoons paprika
1½ teaspoons salt
½ teaspoon freshly ground white pepper
1 teaspoon freshly ground black pepper
¼ teaspoon ground cumin
1 teaspoon dried thyme
salad greens and bell pepper strips, to garnish

Serves 6
6 medium chicken breast fillets, skinned
6 tablespoons butter or margarine
1 teaspoon garlic powder
2 teaspoons onion powder

1 Slice each chicken breast in half horizontally, making two pieces of about the same thickness. Flatten them slightly with the heel of your hand. Lay them on a large plate or place in a shallow dish.

2 Melt the butter or margarine in a small saucepan over low heat without letting it color.

3 Combine all the remaining ingredients, apart from the garnish, in a bowl and stir to blend well. Brush the chicken pieces on both sides with a little of the melted butter or margarine, then sprinkle evenly with the seasoning mixture.

4 Heat a large, heavy frying pan over high heat for 5–8 minutes, until a drop of water sprinkled on the surface sizzles.

5 Drizzle 1 teaspoon melted butter onto each chicken piece. Place them carefully in the frying pan in an even layer, two or three at a time, and cook for 2–3 minutes, until the underside begins to blacken. Turn and cook the other side for 2–3 more minutes. Serve hot, garnished with salad leaves and bell pepper strips.

Caribbean Fried Chicken

This crispy chicken is superb hot or cold. Served with a salad or vegetables, it makes a delicious lunch and is ideal for picnics and snacks too.

Serves 4–6
4 chicken drumsticks
4 chicken thighs
2 teaspoons curry powder
½ teaspoon garlic powder
½ teaspoon freshly ground black pepper
½ teaspoon paprika
about 1¼ cups milk
oil, for deep-frying
½ cup all-purpose flour
salt
mixed salad, to serve

1 Place the chicken pieces in a large bowl and sprinkle with the curry powder, garlic powder, black pepper, paprika and salt to taste. Rub the spices well into the chicken, then cover and let marinate in a cool place for at least 2 hours, or overnight in the refrigerator.

2 Preheat the oven to 350°F. Pour enough milk into the bowl to cover the chicken and let stand for another 15 minutes.

3 Heat the oil in a large, heavy saucepan or deep-fat fryer. Put the flour on a plate. Shake off excess milk from the chicken and dip each piece in the flour, turning it to coat well. Fry two or three pieces at a time until golden but not cooked. Continue until all the chicken pieces are fried.

4 Remove the chicken pieces from the oil using a slotted spoon and place on a baking sheet. Bake for about 30 minutes. Serve hot or cold with mixed salad.

Variation
This recipe would work just as well with turkey breasts, but would need only 15–20 minutes cooking time in the oven.

Spicy Fried Chicken

Chicken portions are soaked in buttermilk before they are coated with spiced flour and fried.

Serves 4
½ cup buttermilk
3 pounds chicken portions
vegetable oil, for frying
½ cup all-purpose flour
1 tablespoon paprika
¼ teaspoon pepper
1 tablespoon water

1 Pour the buttermilk into a large bowl and add the chicken pieces. Stir to coat, then set aside for 5 minutes.

2 Heat ¼-inch depth of oil in a large frying pan over medium-high heat. Do not let the oil overheat.

3 In a bowl or plastic bag, combine the flour, paprika and pepper. One by one, lift the chicken pieces out of the buttermilk and dip into the flour to coat well all over, shaking off any excess.

4 Add the chicken pieces to the hot oil and fry for about 10 minutes, until lightly browned, turning them over halfway through the cooking time.

5 Reduce the heat to low and add the water to the frying pan. Cover and cook for 30 minutes, turning the pieces over at 10-minute intervals. Uncover the pan and continue cooking for about 15 minutes, until the chicken is very tender and the coating is crisp, turning every 5 minutes. Serve hot.

Cook's Tip
Buttermilk, available at supermarkets, is a byproduct of the butter-making process. Nowadays, it is more often cultured skim milk produced under controlled conditions, which make it more stable.

Chicken Stir-fry with Five Spices

The chicken is marinated in an aromatic blend of spices and stir-fried with crisp vegetables. If you find it too spicy, serve with a spoonful of sour cream or yogurt.

Serves 4

¹/₂ teaspoon each ground
   turmeric and ground ginger
1 teaspoon each salt and freshly
   ground black pepper
2 teaspoons ground cumin
1 tablespoon ground coriander
1 tablespoon sugar
1 pound chicken breast
   fillet, skinned
1 bunch scallions
4 celery stalks
2 red bell peppers, seeded
1 yellow bell pepper, seeded
6 ounces zucchini
6 ounces snowpeas or
   sugar snap peas
about 3 tablespoons sunflower oil
1 tablespoon lime juice
1 tablespoon honey

1 Combine the turmeric, ginger, salt, pepper, cumin, coriander and sugar in a bowl until well combined. Cut the chicken into bite-size strips. Add to the spice mixture and stir to coat the chicken pieces thoroughly. Set aside.

2 Prepare the vegetables. Cut the scallions, celery and peppers into 2-inch long, thin strips. Cut the zucchini at a slight angle into thin rounds, and trim the snowpeas or sugar snap peas.

3 Heat 2 tablespoons oil in a large, heavy frying pan or wok. Stir-fry the chicken in batches until cooked through and golden brown, adding a little more oil if necessary. Remove the chicken from the pan and keep warm.

4 Add a little more oil to the pan and cook the onions, celery, peppers and zucchini over medium heat for 8–10 minutes until beginning to soften and turn golden. Add the snowpeas or sugar snap peas and cook for another 2 minutes.

5 Return the chicken to the pan, with the lime juice and honey. Cook for 2 minutes. Adjust the seasoning and serve.

Spiced Chicken Sauté

A rich tomato sauce coats this chicken, which is first oven-cooked or fried.

Serves 4

3¹/₂-pound chicken, cut into
   8 pieces
1 teaspoon each salt and freshly
   ground black pepper
2 garlic cloves, crushed
sunflower oil
sliced fresh red chile and
   deep-fried onions, to
   garnish (optional)
boiled rice, to serve

For the sauce

2 tablespoons butter
2 tablespoons sunflower oil
1 onion, sliced
4 garlic cloves, crushed
2 large ripe beefsteak tomatoes,
   chopped, or 14-ounce can
   chopped tomatoes with
   chile, drained
2¹/₂ cups water
¹/₄ cup dark soy sauce
salt and freshly ground
   black pepper

1 Preheat the oven to 375°F. Make two slashes in the fleshy part of each chicken piece. Rub well with the salt, pepper and garlic. Drizzle with a little oil and bake for 30 minutes, until brown. Alternatively, shallow-fry in hot oil for 12–15 minutes.

2 To make the sauce, heat the butter and oil in a wok or frying pan, and sauté the onion and garlic until soft. Add the tomatoes, water, soy sauce and seasoning. Boil briskly for 5 minutes to reduce the sauce and concentrate the flavor.

3 Add the chicken to the sauce in the wok. Turn the chicken pieces over in the sauce to coat them well. Continue cooking slowly for about 20 minutes, until the chicken pieces are tender. Stir the mixture occasionally.

4 Arrange the chicken on a warmed serving platter and garnish with the sliced chile and deep-fried onions, if using. Serve with boiled rice.

Deep-fried Onions

A traditional garnish and accompaniment to many Indonesian dishes. Asian stores sell them ready-prepared, but it is simple to make them at home.

Makes 1 pound

1 pound onions
oil, for deep-frying

1 Peel the onions and slice as evenly and thinly as possible. Spread out on paper towels, in an airy place, and set aside to dry for 30 minutes to 2 hours.

2 Heat the oil in a deep-fat fryer or wok to 375°F and fry the onions in batches until crisp and golden, turning constantly. Drain well on paper towels and let cool. Store in an airtight container for 2–3 days.

Adobo of Chicken & Pork

Four ingredients are essential in an adobo, one of the best-loved recipes in the Filipino repertoire: vinegar, garlic, peppercorns and bay leaves.

Serves 4
3-pound chicken or
*   4 chicken quarters*
12 ounces pork chops
2 teaspoons sugar
¼ cup sunflower oil
5 tablespoons wine vinegar or
*   cider vinegar*
4 plump garlic cloves, crushed
½ teaspoon black peppercorns,
*   lightly crushed*
1 tablespoon light soy sauce
4 bay leaves
½ teaspoon annatto seeds,
*   soaked in 2 tablespoons boiling*
*   water, or ½ teaspoon*
*   ground turmeric*
salt

For the plantain chips
vegetable oil, for deep-frying
1–2 large plantains and/or
*   1 sweet potato*

1 Wipe the chicken and cut into eight pieces, or halve the chicken quarters, if using. Cut the pork into neat pieces. Spread the meat out on a board, sprinkle lightly with sugar and set aside.

2 Heat the oil in a wok or large frying pan, and fry the chicken and pork pieces, in batches if necessary, until golden all over.

3 Add the vinegar, garlic, peppercorns, soy sauce and bay leaves and stir well. Strain the annatto seed liquid and stir it into the pan or stir in the turmeric. Add salt to taste. Bring to a boil, cover, lower the heat and simmer for 30–35 minutes. Remove the lid and simmer for 10 more minutes.

4 Meanwhile, to make the plantain chips, heat the oil in a deep-fat fryer to 383°F. Peel the plantains and/or sweet potato and slice into rounds or chips. Deep-fry them, in batches if necessary, until cooked but not brown. Drain on paper towels.

5 When ready to serve, reheat the oil and fry the plantains or sweet potato until crisp. Drain. Spoon the adobo into a serving dish and serve with the chips.

Chicken & Olives

A whole chicken is simmered gently with fresh ginger, paprika and saffron, and finished with lemon juice and green and black olives.

Serves 4
2 tablespoons olive oil
3½-pound chicken
1 large onion, sliced
1 tablespoon grated fresh
*   ginger root*
3 garlic cloves, crushed
1 teaspoon paprika
1 cup Chicken Stock
2–3 saffron threads, soaked in
*   1 tablespoon boiling water*
4–5 scallions, chopped
15–20 black and green
*   olives, pitted*
juice of ½ lemon
salt and freshly ground
*   black pepper*
boiled rice and mixed salad,
*   to serve*

1 Heat the oil in a large saucepan or flameproof casserole. Add the chicken and sauté until golden on all sides.

2 Add the onion, ginger, garlic and paprika, and season to taste with salt and pepper. Continue to cook over medium heat, coating the chicken with the mixture.

3 Add the chicken stock and saffron, and bring to a boil. Cover, lower the heat and simmer gently for 45 minutes.

4 Add the scallions and cook for another 15 minutes, until the chicken is well cooked and the sauce is reduced to about ½ cup. The chicken juices should run clear when the thickest part of the thigh is pierced with a skewer or the point of a sharp knife. Add the olives and lemon juice, and cook for another 5 minutes.

5 Transfer the chicken to a large, deep serving plate and pour on the sauce. Serve with rice and a mixed salad.

Peanut Chicken

In this Caribbean dish the rich, nutty sauce is best made from smooth peanut butter, though it can also be made with crushed peanuts.

Serves 4
2 pounds chicken breast fillet, skinned and cut into pieces
2 garlic cloves, crushed
$\frac{1}{2}$ teaspoon dried thyme
$\frac{1}{2}$ teaspoon freshly ground black pepper
1 tablespoon curry powder
1 tablespoon lemon juice
2 tablespoons butter or margarine
1 onion, chopped
3 tablespoons chopped tomatoes
1 fresh hot chile, chopped
2 tablespoons smooth peanut butter
about scant 2 cups warm water
salt
cilantro sprigs, to garnish
fried plantain, to serve

1 Place the chicken pieces in a large bowl and stir in the garlic, thyme, pepper, curry powder, lemon juice and a little salt. Cover loosely with plastic wrap and let marinate in a cool place for a few hours.

2 Melt the butter or margarine in a large saucepan, add the onion and sauté gently for 5 minutes. Add the seasoned chicken and cook over medium heat for 10 minutes, turning frequently. Stir in the tomatoes and chile.

3 Blend the peanut butter with a little of the warm water into a smooth paste and stir into the chicken mixture.

4 Slowly stir in the remaining water, then simmer gently for about 30 minutes, adding a little more water if necessary. Garnish with cilantro sprigs and serve with fried plantain.

> **Variation**
> You could substitute lime juice for the lemon juice and add 1 teaspoon ground allspice with the curry powder.

Chicken Sauce Piquante

Cajun Sauce Piquante is based on the brown Cajun *roux* and has chile peppers to give it heat: vary the heat by the number you use.

Serves 4
4 chicken legs or 2 legs and 2 breasts
5 tablespoons cooking oil
$\frac{1}{2}$ cup all-purpose flour
1 medium onion, chopped
2 celery stalks, sliced
1 green bell pepper, seeded and diced
2 garlic cloves, crushed
1 bay leaf
$\frac{1}{2}$ teaspoon dried thyme
$\frac{1}{2}$ teaspoon dried oregano
1–2 fresh red chile peppers, seeded and finely chopped
14-ounce can chopped tomatoes, with their juice
$1\frac{1}{4}$ cups Chicken Stock
salt and freshly ground black pepper
watercress, to garnish
boiled potatoes, to serve

1 Halve the chicken legs through the joint, or the breasts across the middle, to give 8 pieces. In a heavy frying pan, fry the chicken pieces in the oil until brown on all sides, lifting them out and setting them aside as they are done.

2 Strain the oil from the pan into a flameproof casserole. Heat it and stir in the flour. Stir constantly over low heat until the *roux* is the color of peanut butter. Immediately the *roux* reaches the right stage, add the onion, celery and green pepper, and stir over the heat for 2–3 minutes.

3 Add the garlic, bay leaf, thyme, oregano and chile pepper(s). Stir for 1 minute, then turn down the heat and stir in the tomatoes with their juice.

4 Return the casserole to the heat and gradually stir in the stock. Add the chicken pieces, cover and simmer for 45 minutes, until the chicken is tender.

5 If there is too much sauce or it is too runny, remove the lid for the last 10–15 minutes of the cooking time and raise the heat a little. Adjust the seasoning to taste and serve, garnished with watercress and accompanied by boiled potatoes.

Tagine of Chicken

Based on a traditional Moroccan recipe, this spicy chicken stew is served with vegetable couscous.

Serves 8
2 tablespoons olive oil
8 chicken legs, cut in half
1 medium onion, finely chopped
2 garlic cloves, crushed
1 teaspoon ground turmeric
1/2 teaspoon ground ginger
1/2 teaspoon ground cinnamon
scant 2 cups Chicken Stock
1 1/4 cups pitted green olives
1 lemon, sliced
salt and freshly ground black pepper
cilantro sprigs, to garnish

For the vegetable couscous
2 1/2 cups Chicken Stock
2 2/3 cups couscous
4 zucchini, thickly sliced
2 carrots, thickly sliced
2 small turnips, cubed
3 tablespoons olive oil
15-ounce can chickpeas, drained
1 tablespoon chopped cilantro

1 Preheat the oven to 350°F. Heat the oil in a flameproof casserole and brown the chicken all over. Remove from the casserole and keep warm. Add the onion and garlic to the casserole and cook until tender. Add the spices and cook for 1 minute. Pour in the stock and bring to a boil. Return the chicken to the casserole. Cover and bake for 45 minutes.

2 Transfer the chicken to a bowl, cover and keep warm. Skim any fat from the cooking liquid and boil to reduce by one third.

3 Meanwhile, blanch the olives and lemon slices in a pan of boiling water for 2 minutes. Drain and add to the cooking liquid in the casserole. Adjust the seasoning to taste.

4 To make the vegetable couscous, bring the stock to a boil in a large pan and sprinkle in the couscous slowly, stirring. Remove from heat, cover and set aside for 5 minutes. Cook the vegetables, drain and place in a bowl. Add the couscous, oil and seasoning. Stir the grains and add the remaining ingredients. Garnish, and serve the couscous with the chicken and sauce.

Chicken Bobotie

Perfect for a buffet party, this mild curry dish is set with savory custard, which makes serving easy.

Serves 8
2 thick slices white bread
scant 2 cups milk
2 tablespoons olive oil
2 medium onions, finely chopped
2 1/2 tablespoons medium curry powder
2 1/2 pounds ground chicken
1 tablespoon apricot jam, chutney or sugar
2 tablespoon wine vinegar or lemon juice
3 large eggs, beaten
1/3 cup raisins or golden raisins
butter, for greasing
12 almonds
salt and freshly ground black pepper
boiled rice, to serve

1 Preheat the oven to 350°F. Soak the bread in 2/3 cup of the milk.

2 Heat the oil in a frying pan and sauté the onions until tender. Add the curry powder and cook for another 2 minutes.

3 Add the ground chicken and brown all over, stirring to break up any lumps. Remove from heat, season and add the apricot jam, chutney or sugar and vinegar or lemon juice.

4 Mash the bread in the milk and add to the pan together with one of the beaten eggs and the raisins or golden raisins.

5 Grease a 6 1/4-cup shallow ovenproof dish with butter. Spoon in the chicken mixture and level the top. Cover with buttered foil and bake for 30 minutes.

6 Meanwhile, beat the remaining eggs with the rest of the milk. Remove the dish from the oven and lower the temperature to 300°F. Break up the meat using two forks and pour in the beaten egg mixture. Sprinkle the almonds on top and return to the oven, uncovered, for 30 minutes, until set and golden brown all over. Serve immediately with rice.

Chicken Thighs Wrapped in Bacon

These tasty chicken "parcels" are first marinated and then baked in a spicy garlic and citrus sauce.

Serves 4
16 strips bacon
8 chicken thighs, skinned
cooked rice, to serve

For the marinade
finely grated zest and juice of
*   1 orange*
finely grated zest and juice of
*   1 lime*
5 garlic cloves, finely chopped
1 tablespoon chili powder
1 tablespoon paprika
1 teaspoon ground cumin
½ teaspoon dried oregano
1 tablespoon olive oil

1 To make the marinade, combine the citrus zest and juice, garlic, chili powder, paprika, cumin, oregano and olive oil in a small bowl.

2 Wrap 2 strips of bacon around each chicken thigh in a cross shape. Secure with wooden toothpicks. Arrange the wrapped chicken thighs in an ovenproof dish.

3 Pour the marinade onto the chicken, cover and let stand for 1 hour at room temperature or for several hours in the refrigerator.

4 Preheat the oven to 375°F. Place the dish and bake until the chicken is cooked through and the bacon is crisp; this will take about 40 minutes for small thighs and 1 hour for large thighs. Skim excess fat from the sauce and serve with rice.

Cook's Tip
Chili powder varies widely in strength, although it is always hot, and some varieties have other spices or herbs added. It is best to buy pure ground chili powder and add your own flavorings if you want to.

Aromatic Chicken from Madura

An Indonesian dish which is best cooked ahead so that the flavors permeate the chicken flesh, making it even more delicious.

Serves 4
3½-pound chicken, cut into
    quarters, or 4 chicken quarters
1 teaspoon sugar
2 tablespoons coriander seeds
2 teaspoons cumin seeds

6 whole cloves
½ teaspoon grated nutmeg
½ teaspoon ground turmeric
1 small onion
1-inch piece fresh ginger root,
    sliced
1¼ cups Chicken Stock
    or water
salt and freshly ground
    black pepper
boiled rice and Deep-fried
    Onions, to serve

1 Cut each chicken quarter in half. Place in a flameproof casserole, sprinkle with sugar and salt, and toss together.

2 Dry-fry the coriander, cumin and whole cloves in a heavy frying pan until the spices give off a good aroma. Add the nutmeg and turmeric, and heat briefly. Grind in a food processor or using a mortar and pestle.

3 If using a processor, process the onion and ginger until finely chopped. Otherwise, finely chop the onion and ginger, and pound into a paste using a mortar and pestle. Add the spices and stock or water, and mix well. Season to taste.

4 Pour the mixture onto the chicken in the casserole. Cover and cook over low heat for 45–50 minutes, until the chicken pieces are really tender. Serve portions of the chicken, with the sauce, on a bed of boiled rice, sprinkled with crisp deep-fried onions.

Cook's Tip
Add a large piece of bruised ginger and a small onion to the chicken stock to ensure a good flavor.

Curried Apricot & Chicken Casserole

A mild curried and fruity chicken dish served with almond rice, this makes a good winter meal.

Serves 4
1 tablespoon oil
8 large boned and skinned
  chicken thighs
1 medium onion, finely chopped
1 teaspoon medium curry powder
2 tablespoons all-purpose flour
scant 2 cups Chicken Stock
juice of 1 large orange

8 dried apricots, halved
1 tablespoon golden raisins
salt and freshly ground
  black pepper

For the almond rice
1 cup cooked rice
1 tablespoon butter
½ cup toasted almonds

1 Preheat the oven to 375°F. Heat the oil in a large frying pan. Cut the chicken into cubes and brown quickly all over in the oil. Add the onion and cook gently until soft and lightly browned.

2 Transfer to a large, flameproof casserole, sprinkle in the curry powder and cook again for a few minutes. Add the flour, and blend in the stock and orange juice. Bring to a boil and season with salt and pepper.

3 Add the apricots and golden raisins, cover and cook for 1 hour or until tender. Adjust the seasoning to taste.

4 To make the almond rice, reheat the precooked rice with the butter and season to taste. Stir in the toasted almonds. Serve with the chicken.

> **Variation**
> This recipe would also work well with diced turkey breast or other boneless turkey meat.

Spiced Chicken & Apricot Pie

This pie is unusually sweet and sour. Use boneless turkey instead of chicken, if desired or even some leftovers from a roast turkey—the dark, moist leg meat is best.

Serves 6
2 tablespoons sunflower oil
1 large onion, chopped
1 pound boneless chicken,
  roughly chopped
1 tablespoon curry paste
  or powder

2 tablespoons apricot or
  peach chutney
½ cup dried apricots, halved
4 ounces cooked carrots, sliced
1 teaspoon dried mixed herbs
¼ cup crème fraîche
12 ounces ready-made
  shortcrust pastry
a little egg or milk, to glaze
salt and freshly ground
  black pepper
cooked vegetables, to serve

1 Heat the oil in a large, heavy frying pan and cook the onion and chicken until just coloring. Add the curry paste or powder and fry, stirring constantly, for 2 more minutes.

2 Add the chutney, apricots, carrots, herbs and crème fraîche to the pan, and season to taste with salt and pepper. Mix well, then transfer to a deep 3¾–5-cup pie pan.

3 Preheat the oven to 375°F. Roll out the pastry to 1 inch wider than the pie dish. Cut a strip of pastry from the edge. Dampen the rim of the dish, press on the strip, then brush this strip with water and place the sheet of pastry on top. Press to seal and trim to fit.

4 Use the pastry trimmings to decorate the top of the pie if desired. Brush all over with beaten egg or milk, to glaze, and bake for 40 minutes, until crisp and golden. Serve hot with vegetables.

Chicken with Turmeric

Colorful, aromatic and creamy, this is a perfect dish to serve to guests for an informal supper.

Serves 4

3½-pound chicken, cut into
    8 pieces, or 4 chicken quarters,
    each halved
1 tablespoon sugar
3 macadamia nuts or 6 almonds
2 garlic cloves, crushed
1 large onion, quartered
1-inch piece fresh galangal, peeled
    and sliced, or 1 teaspoon
    powdered galangal
1–2 lemongrass stalks, lower
    2 inches sliced, top bruised
½-inch cube terasi
    (fermented shrimp paste)
1½-inch piece fresh turmeric,
    peeled and sliced, or
    1 tablespoon ground turmeric
1 tablespoon tamarind pulp,
    soaked in ⅔ cup warm water
4–6 tablespoons oil
1⅔ cups coconut milk
salt and freshly ground
    black pepper
Deep-fried Onions, to garnish

1 Rub the chicken joints with a little sugar and set them aside.

2 Grind the nuts and garlic in a food processor with the onion, galangal, sliced lemongrass, *terasi* and turmeric. Alternatively, pound the ingredients to a paste using a mortar and pestle. Strain the tamarind pulp and reserve the juice. Discard the contents of the strainer.

3 Heat the oil in a wok or heavy frying pan and cook the paste, without browning, until it gives off a spicy aroma. Add the pieces of chicken and toss well in the spices. Add the strained tamarind juice.

4 Spoon the coconut cream off the top of the milk and set it to one side. Add the coconut milk to the pan. Cover and cook for 45 minutes or until the chicken is tender.

5 Just before serving, stir in the reserved coconut cream while bringing to a boil. Season to taste with salt and pepper, and serve immediately, garnished with deep-fried onions.

Mole Poblano de Guajolote

This is the greatest festive dish of Mexico, served at any special occasion. The traditional accompaniments are rice, beans, tortillas and guacamole.

Serves 6–8

6–8-pound turkey, cut into
    serving portions
1 onion, chopped
1 garlic clove, chopped
6 tablespoons lard or corn oil
salt
cilantro and 2 tablespoons
    toasted sesame seeds,
    to garnish

For the sauce

6 dried ancho chiles
4 dried pasilla chiles
4 dried mulato chiles
1 drained canned chipotle chile,
    seeded and chopped (optional)
2 onions, chopped
2 garlic cloves, chopped
1 pound tomatoes, peeled
    and chopped
1 stale tortilla, torn into pieces
⅓ cup seedless raisins
1 cup ground almonds
3 tablespoons sesame
    seeds, ground
1 teaspoon ground cinnamon
½ teaspoon ground anise
¼ teaspoon ground
    black peppercorns
¼ cup lard or corn oil
1½ ounces unsweetened
    chocolate, broken into squares
1 tablespoon sugar
salt and freshly ground
    black pepper

1 Put the turkey pieces into a large flameproof casserole in one layer. Add the onion, garlic and enough cold water to cover. Season with salt, bring to a gentle simmer, cover and cook for about 1 hour or until the turkey is tender.

2 Lift the turkey out of the casserole and pat dry with paper towels. Reserve the stock. Heat the lard or oil in a large frying pan and sauté the turkey until lightly browned all over. Transfer to a plate and set aside. Reserve the oil in the pan.

3 Meanwhile, to make the sauce, put the dried chiles in a dry frying pan over low heat and roast them for a few minutes, shaking the pan frequently. Remove the stems and shake out the seeds. Tear the pods into pieces and put these into a small bowl. Add sufficient warm water just to cover and soak, turning occasionally for 30 minutes, until soft.

4 Transfer the chiles with their soaking water into a food processor. Add the *chipotle* chile, if using, with the onions, garlic, tomatoes, tortilla, raisins, ground almonds, ground sesame seeds and spices. Process into a purée. Do this in batches if necessary.

5 Add the lard or oil to the fat remaining in the frying pan used for sautéing the turkey. Heat the mixture, then add the chile and spice paste. Cook, stirring, for 5 minutes.

6 Transfer the cooked spice mixture to the casserole in which the turkey was originally cooked. Stir in 2 cups of the reserved turkey stock (make it up with water if necessary). Add the chocolate, and season with salt and pepper. Cook over low heat until the chocolate has melted. Stir in the sugar. Add the turkey to the casserole and more stock if needed. Cover and simmer very gently for 30 minutes. Serve, garnished with cilantro and sprinkled with toasted sesame seeds.

Chicken Korma

A korma is a rich, creamy Moghulai dish that originates from northern India. This recipe uses a combination of yogurt and cream that gives the sauce a delicious, subtle flavor.

Serves 4

1½ pounds chicken breast
   fillet, skinned
¼ cup blanched almonds
2 garlic cloves, crushed
1-inch piece fresh ginger root,
   peeled and roughly chopped
2 tablespoons oil
3 green cardamom pods
1 onion, finely chopped
2 teaspoons ground cumin
¼ teaspoon salt
⅔ cup plain yogurt
¾ cup light cream
toasted sliced almonds and
   cilantro, to garnish
boiled rice, to serve

1 Cut the chicken breasts into 1-inch cubes. Put the almonds, garlic and ginger into a food processor or blender with 2 tablespoons water, and process to a smooth paste.

2 Heat the oil in a large frying pan and cook the chicken for 8–10 minutes or until browned. Remove using a slotted spoon and set aside.

3 Add the cardamom pods to the pan and cook for 2 minutes. Add the onion and cook for another 5 minutes.

4 Stir in the almond and garlic paste, cumin and salt, and cook, stirring, for another 5 minutes.

5 Add the yogurt, a tablespoonful at a time, and cook over low heat, until it has all been absorbed. Return the chicken to the pan. Cover and simmer over low heat for 5–6 minutes or until the chicken is tender.

6 Add the cream and simmer for another 5 minutes. Serve with boiled rice and garnish with toasted sliced almonds and cilantro.

Simple Chicken Curry

Curry powder can be bought in three different strengths—mild, medium and hot. Use the type you prefer to suit your taste.

Serves 4

8 chicken legs (thighs
   and drumsticks)
2 tablespoons olive oil
1 onion, thinly sliced
1 garlic clove, crushed
1 tablespoon medium
   curry powder
1 tablespoon all-purpose flour
scant 2 cups Chicken Stock
1 beefsteak tomato
1 tablespoon mango chutney
1 tablespoon lemon juice
salt and freshly ground
   black pepper
boiled rice, to serve

1 Cut the chicken legs in half. Heat the oil in a large, flameproof casserole and brown the chicken on all sides. Remove from the casserole and keep warm.

2 Add the onion and garlic to the casserole and cook over fairly low heat until tender. Add the curry powder and cook gently for 2 minutes, stirring.

3 Stir in the flour and gradually blend in the stock. Season to taste with salt and pepper. Bring to a boil, return the chicken pieces to the casserole, cover and simmer for 20–30 minutes or until tender.

4 Peel the tomato by blanching in boiling water for 15 seconds, then plunging into cold water to loosen the skin. Peel and cut into small cubes, discarding the seeds.

5 Add the tomato to the chicken, with the mango chutney and lemon juice. Heat through gently and adjust the seasoning to taste. Serve with plenty of boiled rice.

Moghul-style Chicken

This delicate curry can be served as an appetizer followed by stronger curries and rice. Saffron is a crucial ingredient, but as it is very expensive, save the dish for special occasions.

Serves 4–6

4 chicken breasts, rubbed with a little garam masala
2 eggs, beaten with salt and pepper
6 tablespoons ghee or melted butter
1 large onion, finely chopped
2-inch piece fresh ginger root, peeled and crushed
4 garlic cloves, crushed
4 cloves
4 green cardamoms
2-inch piece cinnamon stick
2 bay leaves
15–20 saffron threads
⅔ cup plain yogurt, beaten with 1 teaspoon cornstarch
salt
5 tablespoons heavy cream
½ cup ground almonds

1 Brush the chicken breasts with the beaten eggs. Heat the ghee or butter in a frying pan and fry the chicken. Remove from the pan and keep warm.

2 In the remaining fat, sauté the onion, ginger, garlic, cloves, cardamoms, cinnamon and bay leaves. When the onion turns golden, remove the pan from heat, let cool a little and stir in the saffron and yogurt.

3 Return the chicken to the pan with any juices and gently cook until the chicken is tender. Taste and adjust the seasoning as necessary.

4 Just before serving, fold in the cream and ground almonds. Serve hot.

> **Cook's Tip**
> If you don't have time to make your own ghee, clarified butter and vegetable ghee are available at Indian food stores and supermarkets.

Special Chicken Curry

Chicken curry is always popular when served at a family dinner. This version is cooked covered, giving a thin consistency. If you would prefer it thicker, cook uncovered for the last 15 minutes.

Serves 4–6

¼ cup vegetable oil
4 cloves
4–6 green cardamoms
2-inch piece cinnamon stick
3 whole star anise
6–8 curry leaves
1 large onion, finely chopped
2-inch piece fresh ginger root, crushed
4 garlic cloves, crushed
¼ cup mild curry paste
1 teaspoon ground turmeric
1 teaspoon five-spice powder
3-pound chicken, skinned and jointed
14-ounce can chopped tomatoes
4 ounces coconut milk
½ teaspoon sugar
1 cup cilantro, chopped
salt

1 Heat the oil in a frying pan and fry the cloves, cardamoms, cinnamon stick, star anise and curry leaves until the cloves swell and the curry leaves are slightly burned.

2 Add the onion, ginger and garlic, and sauté until the onion turns brown. Add the curry paste, turmeric and five-spice powder, and cook until the oil separates.

3 Add the chicken pieces and mix well. When all the pieces are evenly sealed, cover and cook until the meat is nearly done.

4 Add the chopped tomatoes and the coconut milk. Simmer gently until the coconut dissolves. Mix well, add the sugar and salt to taste. Fold in the cilantro leaves, reheat gently and serve hot.

> **Cook's Tip**
> Indian five-spice powder is different from Chinese. Make sure you buy Indian.

Tandoori Chicken

A popular party dish. The chicken is marinated the night before, so all you have to do on the day is to cook it in a very hot oven and serve with wedges of lemon and green salad.

Serves 4

3½-pound chicken, cut into
   8 pieces
juice of 1 large lemon
⅔ cup plain yogurt

3 garlic cloves, crushed
2 tablespoons olive oil
1 teaspoon ground turmeric
2 teaspoons paprika
1 teaspoon grated fresh ginger root
   or ½ teaspoon ground ginger
2 teaspoons garam masala
1 teaspoon salt
a few drops of red food
   coloring (optional)
green salad and lemon wedges,
   to serve

1 Skin the chicken pieces and cut two slits in each piece. Arrange in a single layer in a nonmetallic dish and pour in the lemon juice.

2 Combine the remaining ingredients and pour over the chicken pieces, turning them to coat thoroughly. Cover with plastic wrap and chill overnight.

3 Preheat the oven to 425°F. Remove the chicken from the marinade and arrange in a single layer in a shallow ovenproof dish. Bake for 15 minutes, then turn over and cook for another 15 minutes or until tender.

4 Serve hot with green salad, plus lemon wedges for squeezing.

Cook's Tip
The red color of tandoori chicken is traditional, but some people are allergic to food coloring. Fortunately, omitting it has no effect on the flavor of the dish.

Fragrant Chicken Curry

Tender pieces of chicken breast are lightly cooked with fresh vegetables and aromatic spices in the traditional style.

Serves 4

1½ pounds chicken breast
   fillet, skinned
2 tablespoons oil
½ teaspoon cumin seeds
½ teaspoon fennel seeds
1 onion, thickly sliced

2 garlic cloves, crushed
1-inch piece fresh ginger root,
   finely chopped
1 tablespoon curry paste
8 ounces broccoli, broken
   into florets
4 tomatoes, cut into thick wedges
1 teaspoon garam masala
2 tablespoons chopped cilantro
naan, to serve

1 Remove any fat from the chicken and cut the meat into 1-inch cubes.

2 Heat the oil in a wok or heavy frying pan, and fry the cumin and fennel seeds for 2 minutes, until the seeds begin to splutter. Add the onion, garlic and ginger, and cook for 5–7 minutes. Stir in the curry paste and cook for another 2–3 minutes.

3 Add the broccoli florets and stir-fry for about 5 minutes. Add the chicken cubes and cook for 5–8 minutes.

4 Add the tomatoes, garam masala and chopped cilantro. Cook for another 5–10 minutes or until the chicken is tender. Serve with naan.

Cook's Tip
This dish is traditionally cooked—and often served—in a karahi, a pan that is very similar to a wok. Karahis are available in a wide range of sizes.

Chicken with Mild Spices

This recipe has a beautifully delicate flavor and makes a very delicious dish.

Serves 4–6
3 tablespoons corn oil
3 medium onions, sliced
3 medium tomatoes, halved and sliced
1-inch piece cinnamon stick
2 large black cardamom pods
4 black peppercorns
½ teaspoon black cumin seeds
1 teaspoon grated fresh ginger root
1 teaspoon crushed garlic
1 teaspoon garam masala
1 teaspoon chili powder
1 teaspoon salt
3-pound chicken, skinned and cut into 8 pieces
2 tablespoons plain yogurt
¼ cup lemon juice
2 tablespoons chopped cilantro
2 fresh green chiles, chopped

1 Heat the oil in a wok or heavy frying pan. Add the onions and sauté until they are golden brown. Add the tomatoes and stir well. Add the cinnamon stick, cardamoms, peppercorns, black cumin seeds, ginger, garlic, garam masala, chili powder and salt. Lower the heat and stir-fry for 3–5 minutes.

2 Add the chicken pieces, two at a time, and stir-fry for at least 7 minutes or until the spice mixture has completely penetrated the chicken. Add the yogurt and mix well.

3 Lower the heat and cover the pan with a piece of aluminum foil, making sure that the foil does not touch the food. Cook very gently for about 15 minutes, checking once to make sure the sauce is not sticking to the bottom of the pan. Finally, add the lemon juice, cilantro and green chiles, and serve immediately.

Cook's Tip
Chicken cooked on the bone is both tender and flavorful. However, you can substitute the whole chicken with 1½ pounds boned and cubed chicken, if wished. The cooking time can be reduced at step 3 too.

Butter Chicken

Another favorite mild dish, especially in the West. Cooked in butter, with aromatic spices, cream and almonds, it will be enjoyed by everyone.

Serves 4–6
⅔ cup plain yogurt
½ cup ground almonds
1½ teaspoons chili powder
¼ teaspoon crushed bay leaves
¼ teaspoon ground cloves
¼ teaspoon ground cinnamon
1 teaspoon garam masala
4 green cardamom pods
1 teaspoon grated fresh ginger root
1 teaspoon crushed garlic
14-ounce can tomatoes
1 teaspoon salt
2¼-pound chicken, skinned, boned and cubed
6 tablespoons butter
1 tablespoon corn oil
2 medium onions, sliced
2 tablespoons chopped cilantro
¼ cup light cream
cilantro sprigs, to garnish

1 Put the yogurt, ground almonds, all the dry spices, the ginger, garlic, tomatoes and salt into a bowl, and blend together.

2 Place the chicken in a large bowl and pour over the yogurt mixture. Set aside.

3 Heat the butter and oil in a medium karahi or deep, round-bottomed frying pan. Add the onions and sauté for about 3 minutes.

4 Add the chicken mixture and stir-fry for 7–10 minutes. Stir in about half of the cilantro and mix well.

5 Pour in the cream and stir in well. Bring to a boil. Sprinkle with the remaining chopped cilantro, garnish with cilantro sprigs and serve.

Cook's Tip
Substitute the plain yogurt with Greek-style yogurt for an even richer and creamier flavor.

Chicken Saag

A mildly spiced dish using a popular combination of spinach and chicken. It is best made using fresh spinach, but if this is unavailable, you can substitute frozen. Do not use canned.

Serves 4

8 ounces spinach leaves, washed
    but not dried
1-inch piece fresh ginger root,
    grated
2 garlic cloves, crushed
1 fresh green chile,
    roughly chopped

scant 1 cup water
2 tablespoons oil
2 bay leaves
1/4 teaspoon black peppercorns
1 onion, finely chopped
4 tomatoes, peeled and
    finely chopped
2 teaspoons curry powder
1 teaspoon salt
1 teaspoon chili powder
3 tablespoons plain yogurt
8 chicken thighs, skinned
plain yogurt and chili powder,
    to garnish
masala naan, to serve

1 Cook the spinach, without water, in a tightly covered saucepan for 5 minutes. Put the spinach, ginger, garlic and chile with 1/4 cup of the water into a food processor or blender, and process into a thick purée.

2 Heat the oil in a large saucepan, add the bay leaves and peppercorns, and fry for 2 minutes. Add the onion and sauté for 6–8 minutes or until the onion has browned.

3 Add the tomatoes and simmer for about 5 minutes. Stir in the curry powder, salt and chili powder, and cook for 2 minutes.

4 Add the spinach purée and the remaining water, and simmer for 5 minutes. Add the yogurt, 1 tablespoon at a time, and simmer for 5 minutes.

5 Add the chicken. Cover and cook for 25–30 minutes or until the chicken is tender. Serve on masala naan, drizzle on some yogurt and dust with chili powder.

Chicken Dhansak

Dhansak curries originate from the Parsee community and are traditionally made with lentils and meat.

Serves 4

scant 1/2 cup green lentils
2 cups Chicken Stock
3 tablespoons oil
1 teaspoon cumin seeds
2 curry leaves
1 onion, finely chopped
1-inch piece fresh ginger root,
    chopped
1 fresh green chile, finely chopped

1 teaspoon ground cumin
1 teaspoon ground coriander
1/4 teaspoon salt
1/4 teaspoon chili powder
1 4-ounce can
    chopped tomatoes
8 chicken portions, skinned
1/4 cup chopped cilantro
1 teaspoon garam masala
cilantro sprigs, to garnish
cooked plain and yellow rice,
    to serve

1 Rinse the lentils under cold running water. Put them into a large, heavy saucepan with the stock. Bring to a boil, lower the heat, cover and simmer for 15–20 minutes. Set aside without draining.

2 Heat the oil in a large saucepan, and fry the cumin seeds and curry leaves for 2 minutes. Add the onion, ginger and chile, and cook for about 5 minutes. Stir in the cumin, coriander, salt and chili powder with 2 tablespoons water.

3 Add the tomatoes and chicken. Cover and cook over medium heat for 10–15 minutes.

4 Add the lentils and their stock, the cilantro and garam masala, and cook for 10 minutes or until the chicken is tender. Garnish with cilantro sprigs and serve immediately with plain and yellow rice.

Chicken in a Thick Creamy Coconut Sauce

If you like the flavor of coconut, you will really love this curry, which contains both dry coconut and coconut milk.

Serves 4

1 tablespoon ground almonds
1 tablespoon dry, shredded coconut
⅔ cup coconut milk
¾ cup fromage frais
1½ teaspoons ground coriander
1 teaspoon chili powder
1 teaspoon crushed garlic
1½ teaspoons grated fresh ginger root
1 teaspoon salt
1 tablespoon corn oil
8 ounces boneless chicken, skinned and cubed
3 green cardamom pods
1 bay leaf
1 dried red chile, crushed
2 tablespoons chopped cilantro

1 Using a heavy saucepan, dry-roast the ground almonds and dry, shredded coconut until they turn a shade darker. Transfer to a mixing bowl.

2 Add the coconut milk, fromage frais, ground coriander, chili powder, garlic, ginger and salt to the mixing bowl.

3 Heat the oil in a nonstick wok or frying pan and add the chicken cubes, cardamoms and bay leaf. Stir-fry for about 2 minutes to seal the chicken.

4 Pour in the coconut milk mixture and blend everything together. Lower the heat, add the crushed dried chile and cilantro, cover and cook for 10–12 minutes, stirring occasionally. Uncover, then stir and cook for another 2 minutes before serving.

> **Cook's Tip**
> Cut the chicken into small, equal-size cubes for speedy and even cooking.

Chicken in Hara Masala Sauce

A little fresh and dried fruit with mint, cilantro leaves and scallions flavor the creamy sauce of this chicken dish.

Serves 4

1 crisp green apple, peeled, cored and cut into small cubes
4 tablespoons cilantro leaves
2 tablespoons fresh mint leaves
½ cup plain yogurt
3 tablespoons fromage frais
2 medium fresh green chiles, seeded and chopped
1 bunch scallions, chopped
1 teaspoon salt
1 teaspoon sugar
1 teaspoon crushed garlic
1 teaspoon grated fresh ginger root
1 tablespoon corn oil
8 ounces chicken breast fillet, skinned and cubed
¼ cup golden raisins

1 Place the apple, 3 tablespoons of the cilantro, half the mint, yogurt, fromage frais, chiles, scallions, salt, sugar, garlic and ginger in a food processor, and process for about 1 minute, using the pulsing action.

2 Heat the oil in a nonstick wok or frying pan, pour in the yogurt mixture and cook over low heat for about 2 minutes.

3 Add the chicken pieces and blend everything together. Cook over medium-low heat for 12–15 minutes or until the chicken is fully cooked.

4 Finally, add the golden raisins and remaining cilantro leaves and mint leaves, and serve immediately.

> **Cook's Tip**
> This dish makes a good dinner-party centerpiece.

Jeera Chicken

An aromatic dish with a delicious, distinctive taste of cumin. Serve simply with a cooling cucumber raita.

Serves 4

3 tablespoons cumin seeds
3 tablespoons oil
½ teaspoon black peppercorns
4 green cardamom pods
2 fresh green chiles,
   finely chopped
2 garlic cloves, crushed
1-inch piece fresh ginger root,
   grated
1 teaspoon ground coriander
2 teaspoons ground cumin
½ teaspoon salt
8 chicken portions, e.g. thighs and
   drumsticks, skinned
1 teaspoon garam masala
cilantro and chili powder,
   to garnish
cucumber raita, to serve

1 Dry-roast 1 tablespoon of the cumin seeds for 5 minutes and set aside.

2 Heat the oil in a large saucepan and fry the remaining cumin seeds, peppercorns and cardamoms for 2–3 minutes. Add the chiles, garlic and ginger, and cook for 2 minutes. Add the ground coriander, cumin and salt, and cook for 2–3 minutes. Add the chicken. Cover and simmer for 20–25 minutes.

3 Add the garam masala and toasted cumin seeds, and cook for another 5 minutes. Serve with cucumber raita, garnished with chili powder and cilantro.

Cook's Tip

Raitas are very easy to make. For a cucumber raita, combine 1¼ cups lightly beaten plain yogurt, ½ diced cucumber and 1 seeded and chopped fresh green chile. Season with salt and a pinch of ground cumin. Cover and chill before serving. For a tomato raita, mix the yogurt with 2 peeled, seeded and finely chopped tomatoes, season with salt and stir in 1 tablespoon chopped cilantro.

Chicken in a Spicy Yogurt Marinade

Plan this dish well in advance; the extra-long marinating time is necessary to develop a really mellow, spicy flavor.

Serves 6

6 chicken portions
juice of 1 lemon
1 teaspoon salt

For the marinade

1 teaspoon coriander seeds
2 teaspoons cumin seeds
6 cloves
2 bay leaves
1 onion, quartered
2 garlic cloves
2-inch piece fresh ginger root,
   roughly chopped
½ teaspoon chili powder
1 teaspoon ground turmeric
⅔ cup plain yogurt
salad greens and lemon or lime
   slices, to serve

1 Skin the chicken portions and make deep slashes in the fleshiest parts with a sharp knife. Place in a dish, sprinkle on the lemon juice and salt, and rub in. Set aside.

2 Spread the coriander and cumin seeds, cloves and bay leaves in the bottom of a large frying pan and dry-fry over medium heat until the bay leaves are crispy.

3 Let the spices cool, then grind coarsely using a mortar and pestle.

4 Finely grind the onion, garlic and ginger in a food processor or blender. Add the ground spices, the chili powder, turmeric and yogurt, then strain in the lemon juice from the chicken.

5 Arrange the chicken in a single layer in a roasting pan. Pour on the spice mixture, then cover and let marinate for 24–36 hours in the refrigerator. Turn the chicken pieces occasionally in the marinade.

6 Preheat the oven to 400°F. Cook the chicken for 45 minutes. Serve hot or cold, with salad greens and slices of lemon or lime.

Chicken Jalfrezi

A Jalfrezi curry is a stir-fried dish cooked with onions, ginger and garlic in a rich pepper sauce.

Serves 4

1½ pounds chicken breast
   fillet, skinned
2 tablespoons oil
1 teaspoon cumin seeds
1 onion, finely chopped
1 green bell pepper, seeded and
   finely chopped
1 red bell pepper, seeded and
   finely chopped
1 garlic clove, crushed
¾-inch piece fresh ginger root,
   finely chopped
1 tablespoon curry paste
¼ teaspoon chili powder
1 teaspoon ground coriander
1 teaspoon ground cumin
½ teaspoon salt
1 4-ounce can
   chopped tomatoes
2 tablespoons chopped cilantro
cilantro sprig, to garnish
cooked rice, to serve

1 Remove any visible fat from the chicken and cut the meat into 1-inch cubes.

2 Heat the oil in a wok or frying pan and fry the cumin seeds for 2 minutes, until they splutter. Add the onion, peppers, garlic and ginger, and cook for 6–8 minutes.

3 Add the curry paste and cook for about 2 minutes. Stir in the chili powder, ground coriander, cumin and salt. Add 1 tablespoon water and cook for another 2 minutes.

4 Add the chicken and fry for about 5 minutes. Add the tomatoes and chopped cilantro. Cover and cook for about 15 minutes or until the chicken is tender. Garnish with cilantro and serve with rice.

Cook's Tip

Curry paste is a "wet" blend of spices cooked with oil and vinegar, which helps to preserve them. Many brands are available at supermarkets and Indian food stores.

Chicken Dopiazza

Dopiazza literally translates as "two onions;" in this chicken dish, two types of onions are used at different stages during cooking.

Serves 4

3 tablespoons oil
8 small onions, halved
2 bay leaves
8 green cardamom pods
4 cloves
3 dried red chiles
8 black peppercorns
2 onions, finely chopped
2 garlic cloves, crushed
1-inch piece fresh ginger root,
   finely chopped
1 teaspoon ground coriander
1 teaspoon ground cumin
½ teaspoon ground turmeric
½ teaspoon chili powder
½ teaspoon salt
4 tomatoes, peeled and
   finely chopped
½ cup water
8 chicken pieces, e.g. thighs and
   drumsticks, skinned
boiled rice, to serve

1 Heat 2 tablespoons of the oil in a large saucepan and sauté the small onions for 10 minutes or until golden brown. Remove from the pan and set aside.

2 Add the remaining oil to the pan and fry the bay leaves, cardamoms, cloves, chiles and peppercorns for 2 minutes. Add the chopped onions, garlic and ginger, and cook for 5 minutes. Stir in the ground spices and salt, and cook for 2 minutes.

3 Add the tomatoes and the water, and simmer for 5 minutes, until the sauce thickens. Add the chicken and cook for about 15 minutes.

4 Add the reserved small onions, then cover and cook for another 10 minutes or until the chicken is tender. Serve with boiled rice.

Khara Masala Chicken

Whole spices *(khara)* are used in this recipe, giving it a wonderfully rich flavor. This is a dry dish, so it is best served with a refreshing raita and paratha.

Serves 4

3 curry leaves
¼ teaspoon mustard seeds
¼ teaspoon fennel seeds
¼ teaspoon onion seeds
½ teaspoon crushed dried red chiles
½ teaspoon white cumin seeds
¼ teaspoon fenugreek seeds
½ teaspoon crushed pomegranate seeds
1 teaspoon salt
1 teaspoon grated fresh ginger root
3 garlic cloves, sliced
¼ cup corn oil
4 fresh green chiles, slit
1 large onion, sliced
1 medium tomato, sliced
1½ pounds chicken, skinned, boned and cubed
1 tablespoon chopped cilantro

1 Combine the curry leaves, mustard seeds, fennel seeds, onion seeds, crushed red chiles, cumin seeds, fenugreek seeds, crushed pomegranate seeds and salt in a large bowl. Add the ginger and garlic.

2 Heat the oil in a medium karahi or deep round frying pan. Add the spice mixture, then the green chiles. Add the onion and stir-fry over medium heat for 5–7 minutes.

3 Add the tomato and chicken pieces, and cook over medium heat for about 7 minutes. The chicken should be cooked through and the sauce reduced.

4 Stir over medium heat for another 3–5 minutes, then serve hot, garnished with chopped cilantro.

> **Cook's Tip**
> *Paratha is unleavened bread with a flaky texture, much like chapati. It is available at Indian food stores.*

Chicken & Tomatoes

If you like tomatoes, you will love this chicken recipe. It is good served with a lentil dish and plain boiled rice.

Serves 4

¼ cup corn oil
6 curry leaves
½ teaspoon mixed onion and mustard seeds
8 medium tomatoes, sliced
1 teaspoon ground coriander
1 teaspoon chili powder
1 teaspoon salt
1 teaspoon ground cumin
1 teaspoon crushed garlic
1½ pounds chicken, skinned, boned and cubed
⅔ cup water
1 tablespoon sesame seeds, roasted
1 tablespoon chopped cilantro

1 Heat the oil in a medium karahi or a deep, round-bottomed frying pan. Add the curry leaves and mixed onion and mustard seeds, and stir thoroughly. Lower the heat slightly and add the sliced tomatoes.

2 While the tomatoes are gently cooking, combine the ground coriander, chili powder, salt, ground cumin and garlic in a bowl. Sprinkle the spices onto the tomatoes.

3 Add the chicken pieces and combine well. Stir-fry for about 5 minutes.

4 Pour on the water and continue cooking, stirring occasionally, until the sauce thickens and the chicken is cooked through.

5 Sprinkle the sesame seeds and cilantro on top of the dish and serve.

> **Cook's Tip**
> *Although it takes very little time to roast sesame seeds, you may find it more convenient to buy them ready-roasted from an Indian food store.*

Chicken with Vegetables

In this recipe, the chicken and vegetables are cut into strips, which makes the dish particularly attractive.

Serves 4–6
¼ cup corn oil
2 medium onions, sliced
4 garlic cloves, thickly sliced
1 pound chicken breast, skinned, boned and cut into strips
1 teaspoon salt
2 tablespoons lime juice

3 fresh green chiles, chopped
2 medium carrots, cut into batons
2 medium potatoes, cut into ½-inch strips
1 medium zucchini, cut into batons

For the garnish
4 lime slices
1 tablespoon chopped cilantro
2 fresh green chiles, cut into strips (optional)

1 Heat the oil in a large karahi or deep, round frying pan. Lower the heat slightly and add the onions. Sauté until lightly browned.

2 Add half the garlic slices and cook for a few seconds before adding the chicken and salt. Cook, stirring, until all the moisture has evaporated and the chicken is lightly browned.

3 Add the lime juice, chopped chiles and all the vegetables to the pan. Increase the heat and add the rest of the garlic. Stir-fry for 7–10 minutes or until the chicken is cooked through and the vegetables are just tender.

4 Transfer to a serving dish and garnish with the lime slices, chopped cilantro and chile strips, if using.

Cook's Tip
A good rule of thumb—but there are exceptions—is that dark green chiles tend to be hotter than pale green ones, and pointed chiles tend to be hotter than those with rounded ends.

Sweet-&-Sour Chicken

This dish combines a sweet-and-sour flavor with a creamy texture. It is delicious served with rice or naan.

Serves 4
3 tablespoons tomato paste
2 tablespoons plain yogurt
1½ teaspoons garam masala
1 teaspoon chili powder
1 teaspoon crushed garlic

2 tablespoons mango chutney
1 teaspoon salt
½ teaspoon sugar (optional)
¼ cup corn oil
1½ pounds chicken, skinned, boned and cubed
⅔ cup water
2 fresh green chiles, chopped
2 tablespoons chopped cilantro
2 tablespoons light cream

1 Blend together the tomato paste, yogurt, garam masala, chili powder, garlic, mango chutney, salt and sugar, if using, in a medium mixing bowl.

2 Heat the corn oil in a large karahi or a deep, round frying pan. Lower the heat slightly and pour in the spice mixture. Bring to a boil and cook for about 2 minutes, stirring occasionally.

3 Add the chicken pieces and stir until they are well coated. Add the water to thin the sauce slightly. Continue cooking for 5–7 minutes or until the chicken is tender.

4 Finally, add the fresh chiles, cilantro and cream, and mix well. Cook for another 2 minutes, until the chicken is cooked through. Serve hot.

Cook's Tip
There is no set recipe for garam masala, but this spice mixture typically contains black cumin seeds, peppercorns, cloves, cinnamon and black cardamom pods.

Chicken with Lentils

This is rather an unusual combination of flavors, but well worth a try. The sour-tasting mango powder gives a delicious tangy flavor to this spicy dish.

Serves 4–6

scant ½ cup chana dhal (split yellow lentils)
¼ cup corn oil
2 medium leeks, chopped
6 large dried red chiles
4 curry leaves
1 teaspoon mustard seeds
2 teaspoons mango powder
2 medium tomatoes, chopped
½ teaspoon chili powder
1 teaspoon ground coriander
1 teaspoon salt
1 pound chicken, skinned, boned and cubed
1 tablespoon chopped cilantro
paratha, to serve

1 Wash the lentils carefully and remove any stones. Put the lentils into a saucepan with enough water to cover, and boil for about 10 minutes, until they are soft but not mushy. Drain and set to one side in a bowl.

2 Heat the oil in a medium karahi or deep, round frying pan. Lower the heat slightly and throw in the leeks, dried red chiles, curry leaves and mustard seeds. Stir-fry gently for a few minutes.

3 Add the mango powder, tomatoes, chili powder, ground coriander, salt and chicken, and stir-fry for 7–10 minutes.

4 Mix in the cooked lentils and cook for another 2 minutes or until the chicken is cooked right through. Garnish with cilantro and serve with paratha.

Cook's Tip
Chana dhal, a split yellow lentil, is available at Asian stores. However, split yellow peas are a good substitute.

Chicken in Spicy Onions

One of the few dishes of India in which onions appear prominently. Chunky onion slices infused with toasted cumin seeds and shredded ginger add a delicious contrast to the flavor of the chicken.

Serves 4–6

3-pound chicken, jointed and skinned
½ teaspoon turmeric
½ teaspoon chili powder
¼ cup oil
4 small onions, finely chopped
2½ cups cilantro leaves, coarsely chopped
2-inch piece fresh ginger root, finely shredded
2 fresh green chiles, finely chopped
2 teaspoons cumin seeds, dry roasted
5 tablespoons plain yogurt
5 tablespoons heavy cream
½ teaspoon cornstarch
salt

1 Rub the chicken joints with the turmeric, chili powder and salt to taste. Heat the oil in a frying pan and fry the chicken pieces without overlapping until both sides are sealed. Remove from the pan and keep warm.

2 Reheat the oil and sauté 3 of the chopped onions, 2¼ cups of the cilantro leaves, half the ginger, the green chiles and the cumin seeds until the onions are translucent.

3 Return the chicken to the pan with any juices and mix well. Cover and cook gently for 15 minutes.

4 Remove the pan from heat and let cool a little. Combine the yogurt, cream and cornstarch in a bowl, and gradually fold into the chicken, mixing well.

5 Return the pan to the heat and gently cook until the chicken is tender. Just before serving, stir in the reserved onion, cilantro and ginger. Serve hot.

Chicken in Saffron Sauce

A beautifully aromatic
chicken dish that is partly
cooked in the oven, this is
sure to impress your guests.

Serves 4–6
¼ cup butter
2 tablespoons corn oil
3-pound chicken, skinned and cut
   into 8 portions
1 medium onion, chopped
1 teaspoon crushed garlic
½ teaspoon crushed
   black peppercorns
½ teaspoon crushed
   cardamom pods
¼ teaspoon ground cinnamon
1½ teaspoons chili powder
⅔ cup plain yogurt
½ cup ground almonds
1 tablespoon lemon juice
1 teaspoon salt
1 teaspoon saffron threads
⅔ cup water
⅔ cup light cream
2 tablespoons chopped cilantro
boiled rice, to serve

1 Preheat the oven to 350°F. Heat the butter and oil in a
medium karahi or deep, round frying pan. Add the chicken
portions and fry for about 5 minutes, until lightly browned.
Remove from the pan using a slotted spoon, leaving behind as
much of the fat as possible, and set aside.

2 Add the onion to the pan, and sauté over medium heat.
Combine the garlic, peppercorns, cardamom, cinnamon, chili
powder, yogurt, ground almonds, lemon juice, salt and saffron
threads in a mixing bowl. When the onions are lightly browned,
pour the spice mixture into the pan and stir-fry for about
1 minute. Return the chicken to the pan and continue to
stir-fry for another 2 minutes. Add the water and bring to
a simmer.

3 Transfer the contents of the pan to an ovenproof casserole and
cover with a lid, or, if using a karahi, cover with aluminum foil.
Transfer to the oven and cook for 30–35 minutes.

4 When the chicken is cooked through, remove it from the
oven. Transfer to a frying pan and stir in the cream. Reheat
gently over low heat for about 2 minutes. Garnish with
chopped cilantro and serve with boiled rice.

Baby Chicken in Tamarind Sauce

The tamarind in this recipe
gives the dish a sweet-and-
sour flavor; this is also
quite hot.

Serves 4–6
¼ cup ketchup
1 tablespoon tamarind paste
¼ cup water
1½ teaspoons chili powder
1½ teaspoons salt
1 tablespoon sugar
1½ teaspoons grated fresh
   ginger root
1½ teaspoons crushed garlic
2 tablespoons dry,
shredded coconut
2 tablespoons sesame seeds
1 teaspoon poppy seeds
1 teaspoon ground cumin
1½ teaspoons ground coriander
2 1-pound poussins, skinned and
   each cut into 6–8 pieces
5 tablespoons corn oil
8 tablespoons curry leaves
½ teaspoon onion seeds
3 large dried red chiles
½ teaspoon fenugreek seeds
10–12 cherry tomatoes
3 tablespoons chopped cilantro
2 fresh green chiles, chopped

1 Put the ketchup, tamarind paste and water into a large mixing
bowl, and use a fork to blend together. Add the chili powder,
salt, sugar, ginger, garlic, coconut, sesame seeds, poppy seeds,
ground cumin and ground coriander to the mixture. Add the
poussins and stir until they are well coated with the spice
mixture. Set to one side.

2 Heat the oil in a large karahi or deep, round frying pan. Add
the curry leaves, onion seeds, dried red chiles and fenugreek
seeds, and fry for about 1 minute.

3 Lower the heat to medium and add the poussins, two or
three pieces at a time, along with their sauce, mixing as you go.
When all the pieces are in the pan, stir them around well using
a slotted spoon.

4 Simmer gently for 12–15 minutes or until the poussins are
thoroughly cooked. Finally, add the tomatoes, cilantro and green
chiles, and serve.

Chili Chicken

Hot and spicy would be the best way of describing this mouthwatering dish. The smell of the fresh chiles cooking is quite pungent but delicious.

Serves 4–6

5 tablespoons corn oil
8 large fresh green chiles, slit
½ teaspoon mixed onion and
   cumin seeds
4 curry leaves
1 teaspoon grated fresh ginger root

1 teaspoon chili powder
1 teaspoon ground coriander
1 teaspoon crushed garlic
1 teaspoon salt
2 medium onions, chopped
1½ pounds chicken, skinned,
   boned and cubed
1 tablespoon lemon juice
1 tablespoon roughly chopped
   fresh mint
1 tablespoon roughly chopped
   cilantro
8–10 cherry tomatoes

1 Heat the oil in a medium karahi or deep, round frying pan. Lower the heat slightly and add the slit green chiles. Fry until the skin starts to change color.

2 Add the onion and cumin seeds, curry leaves, ginger, chili powder, ground coriander, garlic, salt and onions, and sauté for a few seconds, stirring continuously.

3 Add the chicken cubes and stir-fry for 7–10 minutes or until the chicken is cooked through.

4 Sprinkle on the lemon juice, and add the mint and cilantro. Add the cherry tomatoes and serve immediately.

> **Cook's Tip**
> *A good raita to serve with this can be made by combining 1 peeled and diced cucumber, 2 finely diced tomatoes, 1 finely chopped onion, 1¼ cups plain yogurt, 1 teaspoon ground cumin, 1 teaspoon lightly fried black mustard seeds and a pinch of salt. Chill before serving.*

Chicken & Pasta

This is not a traditional dish, as pasta is not eaten widely in India or Pakistan. However, it is no less enjoyable for that. The pomegranate seeds give an unusual, tangy flavor.

Serves 4–6

¾ cup small pasta shells
   (the colored ones look
   most attractive)
5 tablespoons corn oil
4 curry leaves
4 dried red chiles
1 large onion, sliced

1 teaspoon crushed garlic
1 teaspoon chili powder
1 teaspoon grated fresh ginger root
1 teaspoon crushed
   pomegranate seeds
1 teaspoon salt
2 medium tomatoes, chopped
6 ounces chicken, skinned,
   boned and cubed
1 cup canned chickpeas, drained
⅔ cup corn kernels
2 ounces snowpeas,
   sliced diagonally
1 tablespoon chopped cilantro,
   to garnish (optional)

1 Cook the pasta in boiling salted water, according to the directions on the package, until *al dente*. Add 1 tablespoon of the oil to the water to prevent the pasta from sticking together. When it is cooked, drain and set to one side in a sieve.

2 Heat the remaining oil in a large karahi or deep, round frying pan. Add the curry leaves, dried chiles and onion, and sauté for about 5 minutes.

3 Add the garlic, chili powder, ginger, pomegranate seeds, salt and tomatoes. Stir-fry for about 3 minutes.

4 Next, add the chicken, chickpeas, corn and snowpeas to the onion mixture. Cook over medium heat for about 5 minutes, stirring constantly.

5 Add the pasta to the chicken mixture and stir well. Cook for another 7–10 minutes, until the chicken is cooked through. Serve, garnished with the cilantro, if using.

Chicken Pasanda

Pasanda dishes are favorites in Pakistan, but they are also becoming well known in the West.

Serves 4

¼ cup plain yogurt
½ teaspoon black cumin seeds
4 cardamom pods
6 black peppercorns
2 teaspoons garam masala
1-inch piece cinnamon stick
1 tablespoon ground almonds

1 teaspoon crushed garlic
1 teaspoon grated fresh ginger root
1 teaspoon chili powder
1 teaspoon salt
1½ pounds chicken, skinned, boned and cubed
5 tablespoons corn oil
2 medium onions, diced
3 fresh green chiles, chopped
2 tablespoons chopped cilantro, plus extra to garnish
½ cup light cream

1 Mix the yogurt, cumin seeds, cardamoms, peppercorns, garam masala, cinnamon stick, ground almonds, garlic, ginger, chili powder and salt in a medium mixing bowl. Add the chicken and let marinate for about 2 hours.

2 Heat the oil in a large karahi or deep, round frying pan. Add the onions and sauté for 2–3 minutes.

3 Pour in the chicken mixture and stir until it is well blended with the onions. Cook over medium heat for 12–15 minutes or until the sauce thickens and the chicken is cooked through.

4 Add the green chiles and cilantro, and pour in the cream. Bring to a boil and serve immediately, garnished with more cilantro.

Cook's Tip
Ground ginger is no substitute for fresh, as it burns very easily. Wrap fresh ginger root, unpeeled, in plastic wrap and store in the refrigerator for up to six weeks.

Chicken in Hot Red Sauce

In India, small chickens are used for this dish and served as an appetizer with chapatis. If you wish to serve it as an appetizer, use four poussins instead of chicken pieces. Skin them first and make small gashes with a sharp knife to let the spices seep in.

Serves 4–6

4 teaspoons kashmiri masala paste
¼ cup ketchup
1 teaspoon Worcestershire sauce
1 teaspoon Indian five-spice powder
1 teaspoon sugar
8 chicken portions, skinned but not boned
3 tablespoons vegetable oil
4 garlic cloves, crushed
2-inch piece fresh ginger root, finely shredded
juice of 1 lemon
a few cilantro leaves, finely chopped
salt

1 In a bowl, combine the kashmiri masala, ketchup, Worcestershire sauce, five-spice powder, sugar and salt. Let rest in a warm place until the sugar has dissolved.

2 Place the chicken portions in a wide, shallow dish and rub with the mixture. Set aside to marinate for 2 hours, or overnight if possible.

3 Heat the oil in a large frying pan and sauté the garlic and half the ginger until golden brown. Add the chicken pieces and the marinade, and fry without overlapping until both sides are sealed. Cover the pan and cook gently until the chicken is nearly tender and the gravy clings to it, with the oil separating.

4 Sprinkle the chicken with the lemon juice, the remaining ginger and cilantro leaves. Mix well, reheat and serve hot.

Spicy Chicken Dhal

The chicken is coated in a spiced lentil sauce and finished with a tarka, a seasoned oil, which is poured onto the dish just before serving.

Serves 4

2 tablespoons chana dhal
  (split yellow lentils)
¼ cup masoor dhal
1 tablespoon corn oil
2 medium onions, chopped
1 teaspoon crushed garlic
1 teaspoon grated fresh ginger root
½ teaspoon ground turmeric
1½ teaspoons chili powder
1 teaspoon garam masala
½ teaspoon ground coriander
1½ teaspoons salt
6 ounces chicken breast fillet,
  skinned and cubed
3 tablespoons cilantro leaves
1–2 fresh green chiles, seeded
  and chopped
2–3 tablespoons lemon juice
1¼ cups water
2 tomatoes, peeled and halved

For the tarka

1 teaspoon corn oil
½ teaspoon cumin seeds
2 garlic cloves
2 dried red chiles
4 curry leaves

1 Boil the chana dhal and masoor dhal together in a saucepan of water until soft and mushy. Set aside.

2 Heat the oil in a wok or frying pan and sauté the onions until soft and golden brown. Stir in the garlic, ginger, turmeric, chili powder, garam masala, ground coriander and salt. Add the chicken cubes and stir-fry for 5–7 minutes.

3 Add half the cilantro, the green chiles, lemon juice and water, and cook for another 3–5 minutes.

4 Pour in the chana dhal and masoor dhal, followed by the tomatoes. Add the remaining cilantro. Remove from heat and set aside.

5 To make the tarka, heat the oil and add the cumin seeds, whole garlic cloves, dried chiles and curry leaves. Heat for about 30 seconds and, while it is still hot, pour it on top of the chicken and lentils. Serve immediately.

Chicken Vindaloo

This is considered rather a hot curry and is probably one of the best-known Indian dishes, especially in the West.

Serves 4

1 large potato
⅔ cup malt vinegar
1½ teaspoons crushed
  coriander seeds
1 teaspoon crushed cumin seeds
1½ teaspoons chili powder
¼ teaspoon ground turmeric
1 teaspoon crushed garlic
1 teaspoon grated fresh ginger root
1 teaspoon salt
1½ teaspoons paprika
1 tablespoon tomato paste
large pinch of ground fenugreek
1¼ cups water
8 ounces chicken breast fillet,
  skinned and cubed
1 tablespoon corn oil
2 medium onions, sliced
4 curry leaves
2 fresh green chiles, chopped

1 Peel the potato, cut it into large, irregular shapes, place in a bowl of water and set aside.

2 In a bowl, mix the vinegar with the coriander and cumin seeds, chili powder, turmeric, garlic, ginger, salt, paprika, tomato paste, fenugreek and water. Pour this mixture onto the chicken and set aside.

3 Heat the oil in a wok or frying pan and sauté the onions with the curry leaves for 3–4 minutes.

4 Lower the heat and add the chicken mixture to the pan. Continue to stir for another 2 minutes. Drain the potato pieces and add to the pan. Cover and cook over medium to low heat for 5–7 minutes or until the sauce has thickened slightly, and the chicken and potatoes are cooked through. Stir the chopped green chiles into the dish and serve hot.

Cook's Tip
The best thing to drink with a hot curry is either ice water or a yogurt-based lassi.

Hot Chili Chicken

Not for the weak or faint-hearted, this fiery, hot curry is made with a spicy chili masala paste.

Serves 4

2 tablespoons tomato paste
2 garlic cloves, roughly chopped
2 fresh green chiles,
   roughly chopped
5 dried red chiles
½ teaspoon salt
¼ teaspoon sugar
1 teaspoon chili powder
½ teaspoon paprika
1 tablespoon curry paste

2 tablespoons oil
½ teaspoon cumin seeds
1 onion, finely chopped
2 bay leaves
1 teaspoon ground coriander
1 teaspoon ground cumin
¼ teaspoon ground turmeric
14-ounce can
   chopped tomatoes
⅔ cup water
8 chicken thighs, skinned
1 teaspoon garam masala
sliced fresh green chiles,
   to garnish
chapatis and plain yogurt,
   to serve

1 Put the tomato paste, garlic, fresh and dried chiles, salt, sugar, chili powder, paprika and curry paste into a food processor or blender, and process into a smooth paste.

2 Heat the oil in a large saucepan and fry the cumin seeds for 2 minutes. Add the onion and bay leaves, and cook over medium heat for about 5 minutes.

3 Add the spice paste and fry for 2–3 minutes. Add the remaining ground spices and cook for 2 minutes. Add the chopped tomatoes and water. Bring to a boil and simmer for 5 minutes, until the sauce thickens.

4 Add the chicken and garam masala. Cover and simmer for 25–30 minutes, until the chicken is tender. Serve with chapatis and plain yogurt, garnished with sliced green chiles.

Chicken with Ginger & Lemongrass

This Vietnamese dish can also be prepared using duck legs. Be sure to remove the jointed parts of the drumsticks and thigh bones to make the meat easier to eat with chopsticks.

Serves 4–6

3 chicken legs (thighs
   and drumsticks)
1 tablespoon vegetable oil
¾-inch piece fresh ginger root,
   finely chopped
1 garlic clove, crushed

1 small fresh red chile, seeded
   and finely chopped
2-inch piece lemongrass, shredded
⅔ cup Chicken Stock
1 tablespoon fish sauce (optional)
2 teaspoons sugar
½ teaspoon salt
juice of ½ lemon
½ cup raw peanuts
2 scallions, shredded
thinly pared zest of 1 mandarin
   orange or satsuma, shredded
2 tablespoons chopped fresh mint
cooked rice or rice noodles,
   to serve

1 Using the heel of a knife, chop through the narrow end of the chicken drumsticks. Remove the jointed parts of the drumsticks and thigh bones, then remove the skin.

2 Heat the vegetable oil in a large wok or frying pan. Add the chicken, ginger, garlic, chile and lemongrass, and cook over medium heat for 3–4 minutes. Add the chicken stock, fish sauce, if using, sugar, salt and lemon juice. Cover and simmer for 30–35 minutes.

3 Roast the peanuts under steady heat for 2–3 minutes, until evenly browned. Turn the nuts out onto a clean dish towel and, when cool enough to handle, rub briskly to loosen the skins. Discard the skins.

4 Serve the chicken, sprinkled with the roasted peanuts, shredded scallions, the shredded zest of the mandarin orange or satsuma and mint. Serve with rice or rice noodles.

Soy-braised Chicken

This chicken is cooked whole and divided after cooking. It can be served hot or cold as part of a buffet-style meal.

Serves 6–8

3–3½-pound chicken
1 tablespoon ground
  Szechuan peppercorns
2 tablespoons grated fresh
  ginger root

3 tablespoons light soy sauce
2 tablespoons dark soy sauce
3 tablespoons Chinese rice wine
  or dry sherry
1 tablespoon light brown sugar
vegetable oil, for deep-frying
about 2½ cups water
2 teaspoons salt
1 ounce rock sugar
lettuce leaves, to serve

1 Rub the chicken both inside and out with the ground pepper and fresh ginger root. In a bowl, combine the soy sauces, wine or sherry and sugar. Place the chicken in a bowl, pour in the soy mixture and let marinate for at least 3 hours, turning several times.

2 Heat the oil in a preheated wok. Remove the chicken from the marinade and deep-fry for 5–6 minutes or until brown all over. Remove and drain.

3 Pour off the excess oil from the wok. Add the marinade with the water, salt and rock sugar, and bring to a boil. Return the chicken to the wok and braise in the sauce for 35–40 minutes, covered, turning once or twice.

4 Remove the chicken from the wok and let it cool a little before cutting it into approximately 30 bite-size pieces. Arrange the pieces on a bed of lettuce leaves, then pour some of the sauce onto the chicken and serve. Any leftover sauce can be stored in the refrigerator for use in another dish.

Cook's Tip
Rock sugar is also known as crystal sugar.

Chicken & Ham with Green Vegetables

This dish originates from China, where its name means "Golden Flower and Jade Tree Chicken." It makes a great buffet-style dish for all occasions.

Serves 6–8

2¼–3-pound chicken
2 scallions
2–3 pieces fresh ginger root
1 tablespoon salt
8 ounces honey-roast ham
10 ounces broccoli
3 tablespoons vegetable oil
1 teaspoon light brown sugar
2 teaspoons cornstarch

1 Place the chicken in a large pan and add enough cold water to cover. Add the scallions, ginger and about 2 teaspoons of the salt. Bring to a boil, then cover with a tight-fitting lid, reduce the heat and simmer for 10–15 minutes. Remove from heat and set aside to let the chicken cook itself in the hot water for at least 4–5 hours—you must not lift the lid, as this will let out the heat.

2 Remove the chicken from the pan, reserving the liquid, and carefully cut the meat off the bones, keeping the skin on. Slice both the chicken and ham into pieces, each about the size of a matchbox, and arrange the meats in alternating layers on a serving plate.

3 Cut the broccoli into small florets. Heat the oil in a wok and stir-fry the broccoli with the remaining salt and the sugar for about 2–3 minutes. Arrange the broccoli between the rows of chicken and ham, and around the edge of the plate, making a border around the meat.

4 Heat a small amount of the reserved chicken stock and thicken with the cornstarch. Stir until smooth, then pour it evenly all over the chicken and ham so that it forms a thin coat of transparent jelly resembling "jade." Let cool before serving.

Szechuan-style "Kung Po" Chicken

Kung Po was the name of a court official in the Szechuan province of China; his cook created this dish.

Serves 4

12 ounces chicken thighs, boned and skinned
¼ teaspoon salt
½ egg white, lightly beaten
2 teaspoons cornstarch
1 medium green bell pepper
¼ cup vegetable oil

3–4 dried red chiles, soaked in water for 10 minutes
1 scallion, cut into short sections
a few small pieces of fresh ginger root
1 tablespoon sweet bean paste or hoisin sauce
1 teaspoon chili bean paste
1 tablespoon Chinese rice wine or dry sherry
1 cup roasted cashews
a few drops of sesame oil

1 Cut the chicken meat into small cubes, each about the size of a sugar lump. In a bowl, mix the chicken with the salt and egg white. Mix the cornstarch into a thin paste with a little water and stir into the chicken.

2 Cut the green pepper into cubes about the same size as the chicken, discarding the core and seeds.

3 Heat a wok and pour in the oil. When the oil is hot, add the chicken cubes and stir-fry for about 1 minute or until they change color. Remove from the wok using a slotted spoon and keep warm.

4 Add the green pepper, dried red chiles, scallion and ginger to the wok, and stir-fry for about 1 minute. Return the chicken and add the sweet bean paste or hoisin sauce, chili bean paste and wine or sherry. Blend well and cook for another minute. Finally, add the cashews and sesame oil. Serve hot.

Spicy Clay-pot Chicken

Clay-pot cooking stems from the Malaysian practice of burying a glazed pot in the embers of a fire. The low heat keeps the liquid inside at a slow simmer.

Serves 4–6

3½-pound chicken
3 tablespoons grated fresh coconut
2 tablespoons vegetable oil
2 shallots, finely chopped
2 garlic cloves, crushed
2-inch piece lemongrass

1-inch piece galangal or fresh ginger root, thinly sliced
2 small fresh green chiles, seeded and finely chopped
½-inch cube shrimp paste or 1 tablespoon fish sauce
14-fluid ounce can coconut milk
1¼ cups Chicken Stock
2 kaffir lime leaves (optional)
1 tablespoon sugar
1 tablespoon rice or white wine vinegar
2 ripe tomatoes
2 tablespoons chopped cilantro leaves, to garnish
boiled rice, to serve

1 Remove the chicken legs and wings with a chopping knife, skin the pieces and divide the drumsticks from the thighs. Using a pair of kitchen scissors, remove the lower part of the chicken, leaving the breast piece. Remove as many of the bones as you can. Cut the breast piece into fourths. Set the chicken aside.

2 Dry-fry the coconut in a large wok until evenly brown. Add the oil, shallots, garlic, lemongrass, galangal or ginger, chiles and shrimp paste or fish sauce. Fry briefly to release the flavors.

3 Preheat the oven to 350°F. Add the chicken joints to the wok and brown evenly with the spices for 2–3 minutes. Strain the coconut milk and add the thin part to the wok with the stock, lime leaves, if using, sugar and vinegar. Transfer to a glazed clay pot, cover and bake for 50–55 minutes. Stir in the thick part of the coconut milk and return to the oven for 5–10 minutes to simmer and thicken.

4 Scald the tomatoes in boiling water, then plunge into cold water. Peel, halve, seed and dice the tomatoes. Add them to the dish, sprinkle on the cilantro and serve with rice.

Bang Bang Chicken

What a descriptive name this special dish from Szechuan has! Use toasted sesame paste to give the sauce an authentic flavor, although crunchy peanut butter can be used instead.

Serves 4
3 chicken breast fillets, total
    weight about 1 pound, skinned
1 garlic clove, crushed
½ teaspoon black peppercorns
1 small onion, halved
1 large cucumber, peeled, seeded
    and cut into thin strips
salt

For the sauce
3 tablespoons toasted
    sesame paste
1 tablespoon light soy sauce
1 tablespoon wine vinegar
2 scallions, finely chopped
2 garlic cloves, crushed
2 ½-inch pieces fresh ginger root,
    cut into matchsticks
1 tablespoon Szechuan
    peppercorns, dry-fried
    and crushed
about 1 teaspoon light brown sugar

For the chili oil
¼ cup peanut oil
1 teaspoon chili powder

1 Place the chicken in a saucepan. Just cover with water, add the garlic, peppercorns and onion, and bring to a boil. Skim the surface, stir in salt to taste, then cover the pan. Cook for 25 minutes or until the chicken is just tender. Drain, reserving the stock.

2 To make the sauce, mix the toasted sesame paste with 3 tablespoons of the chicken stock, saving the rest for soup. Add the soy sauce, vinegar, scallions, garlic, ginger and crushed Szechuan peppercorns. Stir in sugar to taste.

3 To make the chili oil, gently heat the peanut oil and chili powder together in a pan until gently foaming. Simmer for 2 minutes, then strain off the red-colored oil and discard the sediment.

4 Spread out the cucumber batons on a serving platter. Cut the chicken into pieces of about the same size as the cucumber strips and arrange them on top. Pour on the sauce, drizzle on the chili oil and serve.

Cashew Chicken

In this Chinese-inspired dish, tender pieces of chicken are stir-fried with cashews, red chiles and a touch of garlic for a delicious combination.

Serves 4–6
1 pound chicken breast fillets
2 tablespoons vegetable oil
2 garlic cloves, sliced

4 dried red chiles, chopped
1 red bell pepper, seeded and cut
    into ¾-inch dice
2 tablespoons oyster sauce
1 tablespoon soy sauce
pinch of sugar
1 bunch scallions, cut into
    2-inch lengths
1½ cups cashews, roasted
cilantro leaves, to garnish

1 Remove and discard the skin from the chicken breasts. Using a sharp knife, cut the chicken into bite-size pieces. Set aside.

2 Heat the oil in a wok and swirl it around. Add the garlic and dried chiles, and sauté until golden.

3 Add the chicken and stir-fry until it changes color, then add the red pepper. If necessary, add a little water.

4 Stir in the oyster sauce, soy sauce and sugar. Add the scallions and cashews. Stir-fry for another 1–2 minutes. Serve, garnished with cilantro leaves.

Variations
For an extra-spicy dish, season with cayenne pepper to taste just before serving. For a slightly different flavor, substitute halved walnuts for the cashews. For a more substantial dish, add 2 cups sliced mushrooms and 5 ounces snowpeas with the red pepper in step 3.

Fragrant Chicken Curry with Thai Spices

To create this wonderful, aromatic dish you need Thai red curry paste—homemade is best, but for speed you could use ready-made.

Serves 4

3 tablespoons oil
1 onion, roughly chopped
2 garlic cloves, crushed
1 tablespoon Thai red curry paste
    (see Red Chicken Curry with
    Bamboo Shoots)
½ cup coconut milk
2 lemongrass stalks,
    roughly chopped
6 kaffir lime leaves, chopped
⅔ cup plain yogurt
2 tablespoons apricot jam
1 cooked chicken,
    about 3½ pounds
2 tablespoons chopped cilantro
salt and freshly ground
    black pepper
kaffir lime leaves, shredded
    coconut and cilantro,
    to garnish
boiled rice, to serve

1 Heat the oil in a saucepan. Add the onion and garlic, and sauté over low heat for 5–10 minutes, until soft. Stir in the curry paste and cook, stirring, for 2–3 minutes. Stir in the coconut milk, then add the lemongrass, lime leaves, yogurt and apricot jam. Stir well. Cover and simmer for 30 minutes.

2 Process the sauce in a blender or food processor, then strain it back into a clean pan, pressing as much of the puréed mixture as possible through the sieve.

3 Remove the skin from the chicken. Slice the meat off the bones and cut it into bite-size pieces. Add to the sauce. If the sauce seems too thin, add a little more coconut milk.

4 Bring the sauce back to the simmering point. Stir in the cilantro, and season to taste with salt and pepper. Serve with boiled rice, garnished with extra lime leaves, shredded coconut and cilantro.

Thai Chicken & Vegetable Curry

For this curry, chicken and vegetables are cooked in an aromatic Thai-spiced coconut sauce.

Serves 4

1 tablespoon sunflower oil
6 shallots, finely chopped
2 garlic cloves, crushed
1 pound chicken breast fillet,
    cut into ½-inch cubes
1 teaspoon ground coriander
1 teaspoon ground cumin
4 teaspoons Thai green curry
    paste (see Green Curry
    Coconut Chicken)
1 green bell pepper,
    seeded and diced
6 ounces baby corn, halved
4 ounces green beans, halved
⅔ cup Chicken Stock
⅔ cup coconut milk
2 tablespoons cornstarch
fresh herb sprigs and toasted
    cashews, to garnish
boiled rice, to serve

1 Heat the oil in a saucepan, add the shallots, garlic and chicken, and cook for 5 minutes, until the chicken is colored all over, stirring occasionally. Add the coriander, cumin and curry paste, and cook for 1 minute.

2 Add the green pepper, baby corn, beans, stock and coconut milk, and stir to mix. Bring to a boil, stirring constantly, then cover and simmer for 20–30 minutes, until the chicken is tender, stirring occasionally.

3 Blend the cornstarch with about 3 tablespoons water in a small bowl. Stir into the curry, then simmer gently for about 2 minutes, stirring constantly, until the sauce thickens slightly. Serve hot, garnished with fresh herb sprigs and toasted cashews, and accompanied by boiled rice.

Chicken Rendang

This Malaysian dish is great served with shrimp crackers or with deep-fried anchovies.

Serves 4
4 chicken breast fillets, skinned
1 teaspoon sugar
1 cup dry, shredded coconut
4 small red or white onions, roughly chopped
2 garlic cloves, chopped
1-inch piece fresh ginger root, sliced
1–2 lemongrass stalks, root trimmed
1-inch piece galangal, peeled and sliced
5 tablespoons peanut oil or vegetable oil
2–3 teaspoons chili powder, or to taste
14-fluid ounce can coconut milk
about 2 teaspoons salt
fresh chives and deep-fried anchovies, to garnish

1 Halve the chicken breast fillets, sprinkle on the sugar and let stand for about 1 hour.

2 Dry-fry the coconut in a wok over low heat, turning constantly until crisp and golden. Transfer to a food processor and process into an oily paste. Transfer to a bowl and reserve.

3 Add the onions, garlic and ginger to the processor. Cut off the lower 2 inches of the lemongrass, chop and add to the processor with the galangal. Process into a fine paste.

4 Heat the oil in a wok or large saucepan. Fry the onion mixture for a few minutes. Reduce the heat, stir in the chili powder and cook for 2–3 minutes, stirring. Spoon in ½ cup of the coconut milk, with salt to taste. As soon as the mixture bubbles, add the chicken, turning until well coated with the spices. Pour in the remaining coconut milk, stirring. Bruise the top of the lemongrass stalks and add to the wok or pan. Cover and cook over low heat for 40–45 minutes, until the chicken is tender.

5 Stir in the reserved coconut paste. Bring to just below the boiling point, then simmer for 5 minutes. Transfer to a serving bowl, and garnish with chives and deep-fried anchovies. Serve immediately.

Stir-fried Chicken with Basil & Chiles

Deep-frying the basil adds another dimension to this easy Thai dish. Thai basil, which is sometimes known as Holy basil, has a unique, pungent flavor that is both spicy and sharp. The dull leaves have serrated edges.

Serves 4–6
3 tablespoons vegetable oil
4 garlic cloves, sliced
2–4 fresh red chiles, seeded and chopped
1 pound boneless chicken
2–3 tablespoons fish sauce
2 teaspoons dark soy sauce
1 teaspoon sugar
10–12 Thai basil leaves

For the garnish
2 fresh red chiles, finely sliced
20 Thai basil leaves, deep-fried (optional)

1 Heat the oil in a wok or large frying pan and swirl it around. Add the garlic and chiles, and stir-fry until golden.

2 Cut the chicken into bite-size pieces, add to the wok or pan and stir-fry until it changes color.

3 Season with fish sauce, soy sauce and sugar. Continue to stir-fry for 3–4 minutes or until the chicken is cooked.

4 Stir in the fresh Thai basil leaves. Garnish with sliced chiles and the deep-fried basil, if using.

Cook's Tip
To deep-fry Thai basil leaves, make sure that the leaves are completely dry. Deep-fry in hot oil for 30–40 seconds, lift out and drain on paper towels.

Chicken Cooked in Coconut Milk

Traditionally the chicken for this dish would be part-cooked by frying, but here it is roasted in the oven. This is an unusual recipe in that the sauce is white, as it does not contain chiles or turmeric, unlike many other Indonesian dishes.

Serves 4

3½-pound chicken or
    4 chicken quarters
4 garlic cloves
1 onion, sliced
4 macadamia nuts or 8 almonds

1 tablespoon coriander seeds,
    dry-fried, or 1 teaspoon
    ground coriander
3 tablespoons oil
1-inch piece fresh galangal, peeled
    and bruised
2 lemongrass stalks, fleshy
    part bruised
3 kaffir lime leaves
2 bay leaves
1 teaspoon sugar
2½ cups coconut milk
salt
boiled rice and Deep-fried Onions,
    to serve

1 Preheat the oven to 375°F. If using a whole chicken, cut it into 4 or 8 pieces. Season with salt. Put into an oiled roasting pan and bake for 25–30 minutes.

2 Meanwhile, prepare the sauce. Grind the garlic, onion, nuts and coriander into a fine paste in a food processor or using a mortar and pestle. Heat the oil in a frying pan and fry the paste to bring out the flavor. Do not let it brown.

3 Add the part-cooked chicken pieces to a wok, together with the galangal, lemongrass, lime and bay leaves, sugar, coconut milk and salt to taste. Mix well to coat in the sauce.

4 Bring to a boil, then reduce the heat and simmer gently for 30–40 minutes, uncovered, until the chicken is tender and the coconut sauce is reduced and thickened. Stir the mixture occasionally during cooking.

5 Just before serving, remove and discard the galangal and lemongrass. Serve with boiled rice and sprinkle with crisp deep-fried onions.

Green Curry Coconut Chicken

The recipe given here for green curry paste is a slightly complex one, so allow time to make it properly—your efforts will be well rewarded.

Serves 4–6

2½-pound chicken
2½ cups canned coconut milk
scant 2 cups Chicken Stock
2 kaffir lime leaves
12 ounces sweet potatoes, peeled
    and roughly chopped
12 ounces winter squash, peeled,
    seeded and roughly chopped
4 ounces green beans, halved
1 small bunch cilantro, shredded,
    to garnish

For the green curry paste

2 teaspoons coriander seeds
½ teaspoon caraway or
    cumin seeds
3–4 medium fresh green chiles,
    finely chopped
4 teaspoons sugar
2 teaspoons salt
3-inch piece lemongrass
¾-inch piece galangal or fresh
    ginger root, finely chopped
3 garlic cloves, crushed
4 shallots or 1 medium onion,
    finely chopped
¾-inch shrimp paste cube
3 tablespoons finely chopped
    cilantro
3 tablespoons finely chopped
    fresh fresh mint or basil
½ teaspoon grated nutmeg
2 tablespoons vegetable oil

1 To prepare the chicken, remove the legs, then separate the thighs from the drumsticks. Separate the lower part of the chicken carcass by cutting through the rib section with kitchen scissors. Divide the breast part in half down the middle, then chop each half in two. Remove the skin from all the pieces. Set the chicken aside.

2 Strain the coconut milk into a bowl, reserving the thick part. Place the chicken in a stainless steel or enamel saucepan, cover with the thin part of the coconut milk and the stock. Add the lime leaves and simmer, uncovered, for 40 minutes. Lift the chicken out of the pan, cut the meat off the bones and set aside. Reserve the stock.

3 To make the green curry paste, dry-fry the coriander and caraway or cumin seeds. Grind the chiles with the sugar and salt in a food processor or using a mortar and pestle to make a smooth paste. Combine the dry-fried seeds with the chiles, add the lemongrass, galangal or ginger, garlic and shallots or onion, then grind smoothly. Add the shrimp paste, chopped herbs, nutmeg and oil.

4 Place 1 cup of the reserved chicken stock in a large wok. Add 4–5 tablespoons of the curry paste to the liquid according to taste. Boil rapidly until the liquid has reduced completely. Add the remaining chicken stock, the chicken meat, sweet potatoes, squash and beans. Simmer for 10–15 minutes, until all the vegetables are cooked.

5 Just before serving, stir in the thick part of the coconut milk and simmer gently to thicken. Serve, garnished with the shredded cilantro.

Red Chicken Curry with Bamboo Shoots

Bamboo shoots have a great texture. It is quite acceptable to use canned ones, as fresh bamboo is not readily available in the West. Buy canned whole bamboo shoots, which are crisper and of better quality than sliced shoots. Rinse well before using.

Serves 4–6

4 cups coconut milk
1 pound chicken breast fillet, skinned and cut into bite-size pieces
2 tablespoons fish sauce
1 tablespoon sugar
8 ounces drained canned bamboo shoots, rinsed and sliced
5 kaffir lime leaves, torn

salt and freshly ground black pepper
chopped fresh red chiles and kaffir lime leaves, to garnish

For the red curry paste
1 teaspoon coriander seeds
½ teaspoon cumin seeds
12–15 fresh red chiles, seeded and roughly chopped
4 shallots, thinly sliced
2 garlic cloves, chopped
1 tablespoon chopped galangal
2 lemongrass stalks, chopped
3 kaffir lime leaves, chopped
4 cilantro roots
10 black peppercorns
good pinch of ground cinnamon
1 teaspoon ground turmeric
½ teaspoon shrimp paste
1 teaspoon salt
2 tablespoons vegetable oil

1 To make the red curry paste, dry-fry the coriander and cumin seeds for 1–2 minutes, then put in a mortar or food processor with all the remaining ingredients except the oil. Pound or process into a paste.

2 Add the oil, a little at a time, mixing or processing well after each addition. Transfer to a jar and place in the refrigerator until ready to use.

3 Pour half of the coconut milk into a large saucepan. Bring to a boil, stirring constantly until the milk has separated.

4 Stir in 2 tablespoons of the red curry paste and cook the mixture for 2–3 minutes, stirring constantly. (The remaining red curry paste can be stored in the refrigerator for 3–4 weeks.)

5 Add the chicken pieces, fish sauce and sugar to the pan. Mix well, then cook for 5–6 minutes, until the chicken changes color and is cooked through, stirring constantly to prevent the mixture from sticking to the bottom of the pan.

6 Pour the remaining coconut milk into the pan, then add the bamboo shoots and kaffir lime leaves. Bring back to a boil over medium heat, stirring constantly to prevent the mixture from sticking, then taste and add salt and pepper if necessary.

7 To serve, spoon the curry into a warmed serving dish and garnish with chopped chiles and kaffir lime leaves.

Chicken with Spices & Soy Sauce

A very simple Indonesian recipe, which often appears on Padang restaurant menus. Any leftovers taste equally good when reheated the following day.

Serves 4
3½-pound chicken, jointed and cut into 16 pieces
3 onions, sliced
about 4 cups water
3 garlic cloves, crushed

3–4 fresh red chiles, seeded and sliced, or 1 tablespoon chili powder
3–4 tablespoons oil
½ teaspoon grated nutmeg
6 cloves
1 teaspoon tamarind pulp, soaked in 3 tablespoons warm water
2–3 tablespoons dark or light soy sauce
salt
fresh red chile shreds, to garnish
boiled rice, to serve

1 Place the chicken pieces in a large pan with one of the onions. Pour in enough water just to cover. Bring to a boil, then reduce the heat and simmer gently for 20 minutes.

2 Process the remaining onions, with the garlic and chiles, into a fine paste in a food processor or using a mortar and pestle. Heat a little of the oil in a wok or frying pan and cook the paste to bring out the flavor, but do not let it brown.

3 When the chicken has cooked for 20 minutes, lift it out of the stock in the pan using a slotted spoon and put it into the spicy mixture. Toss everything together over fairly high heat so that the spices permeate the chicken pieces. Reserve 1¼ cups of the chicken stock.

4 Stir the nutmeg and cloves into the chicken. Strain the tamarind, and add the tamarind juice and the soy sauce to the chicken. Cook for another 2–3 minutes, then add the reserved stock.

5 Taste and adjust the seasoning and cook, uncovered, for another 25–35 minutes, until the chicken pieces are tender. Transfer the chicken to a serving bowl, top with shredded chile and serve with boiled rice.

Chicken & Basil Coconut Rice

For this dish, the rice is partially boiled before being simmered with coconut so that it fully absorbs the flavors of the chiles, basil and spices. Serve in a halved coconut.

Serves 4
1⅔ cups Thai fragrant rice
2–3 tablespoons peanut oil
1 large onion, thinly sliced into rings
1 garlic clove, crushed
1 fresh red chile, seeded and thinly sliced
1 fresh green chile, seeded and thinly sliced
generous handful of basil leaves
12 ounces chicken breast fillet, skinned and thinly sliced
¼-inch piece lemongrass, pounded or finely chopped
2½ cups coconut milk
salt and freshly ground black pepper

1 Bring a saucepan of water to a boil. Add the rice to the pan and boil for about 6 minutes, until partially cooked. Drain and let cool.

2 Heat the oil in a frying pan and fry the onion rings for 5–10 minutes, until golden and crisp. Lift out using a slotted spoon, drain on paper towels and set aside but keep warm.

3 Fry the garlic and chiles in the oil remaining in the pan for 2–3 minutes, then add the basil leaves and fry briefly until they begin to wilt. Remove a few leaves and set them aside for the garnish, then add the chicken slices and lemongrass to the pan and cook for 2–3 minutes, until golden.

4 Add the rice. Stir-fry for a few minutes to coat the grains, then pour in the coconut milk. Cook for 4–5 minutes or until the rice is tender, adding a little more water if necessary.

5 Adjust the seasoning to taste. Pile the rice into halved coconut or warmed serving dish, sprinkle on the fried onion rings and reserved basil leaves, and serve immediately.

Thai Fried Rice

This recipe uses Thai fragrant rice, which is sometimes known as jasmine rice.

Serves 4
2 cups coconut milk
1⅔ cups Thai fragrant rice
2 tablespoons peanut oil
2 garlic cloves, chopped
1 small onion, finely chopped
⅔ cup baby corn, sliced
1-inch piece fresh ginger root, grated
8 ounces chicken breast fillet, skinned and cut into ½-inch dice
1 red bell pepper, seeded and diced
⅔ cup drained canned corn kernels
1 teaspoon chili oil
1 tablespoon hot curry powder
salt
2 eggs, beaten
scallion shreds, to garnish

1 In a saucepan, add the coconut milk and the rice. Bring to a boil and stir once. Lower the heat to a gentle simmer, cover and cook for 10 minutes or until the rice is tender and the liquid has been absorbed. Spread the rice on a baking sheet and let sit until completely cold.

2 Heat the oil in a wok, add the garlic, onion, baby corn and ginger, and stir-fry for 2 minutes. Push the vegetables to the sides of the wok, add the chicken to the center and stir-fry for 2 minutes. Add the rice and stir-fry over high heat for 3 more minutes.

3 Stir in the red pepper, corn kernels, chili oil and curry powder, and season with salt. Toss over the heat for 1 minute. Stir in the beaten egg and cook for 1 more minute. Garnish with scallion shreds and serve.

Cook's Tips
The rice must be completely cold before it is fried, and the oil should be very hot, or the rice will absorb too much oil. Add sliced baby corn along with the rice, if desired.

Indonesian Pineapple Rice

This way of presenting rice not only looks spectacular, it also tastes so delicious that it can easily be served solo.

Serves 4

¾ cup unsalted peanuts
1 large pineapple
3 tablespoons peanut or
    sunflower oil
1 onion, chopped
1 garlic clove, crushed
about 8 ounces chicken breast
    fillet, cut into strips
generous 1 cup Thai fragrant rice
2½ cups Chicken Stock
1 lemongrass stalk, bruised
2 thick slices ham, cut into
    julienne strips
1 fresh red chile, seeded and very
    thinly sliced
salt

1 Dry-fry the peanuts in a nonstick frying pan until golden. When cool, grind one sixth of them in a coffee or spice mill and chop the remainder.

2 Cut a lengthwise slice of pineapple, slicing through the leaves, then cut out the flesh to leave a neat shell. Chop 4 ounces of the pineapple into cubes, saving the remainder for another dish.

3 Heat the oil in a saucepan and sauté the onion and garlic for 3–4 minutes, until soft. Add the chicken strips and stir-fry over medium heat for a few minutes, until evenly brown.

4 Add the rice to the pan. Toss with the chicken mixture for a few minutes, then pour in the stock, with the lemongrass and a little salt. Bring to just below the boiling point, lower the heat, cover the pan and simmer gently for 10–12 minutes, until both the rice and the chicken pieces are tender.

5 Stir the chopped peanuts, the pineapple cubes and the ham into the rice, then spoon the mixture into the pineapple shell. Sprinkle the ground peanuts and the sliced chile on top, and serve immediately.

Chicken Biryani

A classic rice and chicken dish, prepared with whole and ground spices and finished in the oven.

Serves 4

1½ cups basmati rice
½ teaspoon salt
5 whole cardamom pods
2–3 whole cloves
1 cinnamon stick
3 tablespoons vegetable oil
3 onions, sliced
1½ pounds chicken breast fillet,
    skinned and cubed
¼ teaspoon ground cloves
5 cardamom pods, seeds removed
    and ground
¼ teaspoon hot chili powder
1 teaspoon ground cumin
1 teaspoon ground coriander
½ teaspoon freshly ground
    black pepper
3 garlic cloves, finely chopped
1 teaspoon finely chopped fresh
    ginger root
juice of 1 lemon
4 tomatoes, sliced
2 tablespoons chopped
    cilantro
⅔ cup plain yogurt
½ teaspoon saffron threads,
    soaked in 2 teaspoons hot milk
⅔ cup water
3 tablespoons toasted sliced
    almonds and cilantro sprigs,
    to garnish
plain yogurt, to serve

1 Preheat the oven to 375°F. Bring a pan of water to a boil and add the rice, salt, whole cardamom pods, whole cloves and cinnamon stick. Boil for 2 minutes and then drain, leaving the whole spices in the rice.

2 Heat the oil in a large frying pan and sauté the onions for 8 minutes, until browned. Add the chicken, then all the ground spices, the garlic, ginger and lemon juice. Stir-fry for 5 minutes.

3 Transfer the mixture to a casserole. Lay the tomatoes on top, sprinkle with the cilantro, spoon on the yogurt and top with the drained rice. Drizzle the saffron and milk onto the rice and pour in the water. Cover and bake for 1 hour.

4 Transfer the rice to a warmed serving platter and discard the whole spices. Garnish with toasted almonds and cilantro, and serve with yogurt.

Chicken & Mushroom Donburi

"Donburi" is a one-dish meal that is eaten from a bowl and takes its name from the eponymous Japanese porcelain food bowl. As in most Japanese dishes, the rice here is completely plain, but is nevertheless an integral part of the dish.

Serves 4

generous 1–1½ cups Japanese
   rice or Thai fragrant rice
2 teaspoons peanut oil
¼ cup butter
2 garlic cloves, crushed
1-inch piece fresh ginger root,
   grated
5 scallions, sliced diagonally
1 green fresh chile, seeded and
   thinly sliced
3 chicken breast fillets, skinned
   and cut into thin strips
5 ounces tofu, cut into
   small cubes
1¾ cups shiitake mushrooms,
   stems discarded and cups sliced
1 tablespoon Japanese rice wine
2 tablespoons light soy sauce
2 teaspoons sugar
1⅔ cups Chicken Stock

1 Cook the rice following the instructions on the package.

2 Meanwhile, heat the oil and butter in a large frying pan. Stir-fry the garlic, ginger, scallions and chile for 1–2 minutes, until slightly softened. Add the chicken and cook, in batches if necessary, until all the pieces are evenly browned.

3 Using a slotted spoon, transfer the chicken mixture to a plate and add the tofu to the pan. Stir-fry for a few minutes, then add the mushrooms. Stir-fry for 2–3 minutes over medium heat until the mushrooms are tender.

4 Stir in the rice wine, soy sauce and sugar, and cook briskly for 1–2 minutes, stirring. Return the chicken to the pan, toss over the heat for about 2 minutes, then pour in the stock. Stir well and cook over low heat for 5–6 minutes, until bubbling.

5 Spoon the rice into individual serving bowls, and pile the chicken mixture and sauce on top.

Caribbean Chicken with Pigeon Pea Rice

Golden, spicy caramelized chicken tops richly flavored vegetables and rice in this hearty and delicious dish.

Serves 4

1 teaspoon ground allspice
½ teaspoon ground cinnamon
1 teaspoon dried thyme
pinch of ground cloves
¼ teaspoon freshly grated nutmeg
4 chicken breast fillets, skinned
3 tablespoons peanut or
   sunflower oil
1 tablespoon butter
1 onion, chopped
2 garlic cloves, crushed
1 carrot, diced
1 celery stalk, chopped
3 scallions, chopped
1 fresh red chile, seeded and
   thinly sliced
14-ounce can pigeon peas
generous 1 cup long-grain rice
½ cup coconut milk
2½ cups Chicken Stock
2 tablespoons sugar
salt and cayenne pepper

1 In a small bowl, combine the ground allspice, cinnamon, dried thyme, cloves and nutmeg. Place the chicken fillets on a plate and rub the spice mixture onto them. Set aside for 30 minutes.

2 Heat 1 tablespoon of the oil with the butter in a saucepan. Sauté the onion and garlic until soft and beginning to brown. Add the carrot, celery, scallions and chile. Sauté for a few minutes. Stir in the pigeon peas, rice, coconut milk and stock. Season with salt and cayenne pepper. Bring to the simmering point, cover and cook over low heat for about 25 minutes.

3 About 10 minutes before the rice mixture is cooked, heat the remaining oil in a heavy frying pan, add the sugar and cook, without stirring, until it begins to caramelize. Add the chicken. Cook for 8–10 minutes, until it is browned, glazed and cooked through. Transfer the chicken to a board and slice thickly. Serve the pigeon pea rice in individual bowls, with the chicken on top.

Cajun Chicken Jambalaya

For this dish, the chicken is cooked whole, and the resulting tasty stock is used to cook the rice.

Serves 4
2½-pound chicken
2½ cups water
1½ onions
1 bay leaf
4 black peppercorns
1 fresh parsley sprig
2 tablespoons vegetable oil
2 garlic cloves, chopped
1 green bell pepper, seeded
  and chopped
1 celery stalk, chopped
generous 1 cup long-grain rice

1 cup chorizo sausage, sliced
⅔ cup chopped cooked ham
14-ounce can chopped tomatoes
  with herbs
½ teaspoon hot chili powder
½ teaspoon cumin seeds
½ teaspoon ground cumin
1 teaspoon dried thyme
1 cup cooked, peeled shrimp
dash of Tabasco sauce
salt and freshly ground
  black pepper
chopped fresh parsley, to garnish
cooked green beans, to serve

1 Place the chicken in a large, flameproof casserole and add the water, the half onion, the bay leaf, peppercorns and parsley, and bring to a boil. Cover and simmer gently for about 1½ hours.

2 Remove the chicken from the stock, discard the skin and bones and chop the meat. Strain the stock and let cool.

3 Chop the remaining onion and heat the oil in a large frying pan. Add the onion, garlic, green pepper and celery. Cook for 5 minutes, then stir in the rice. Add the sausage, ham and chicken, and cook for another 2–3 minutes, stirring frequently.

4 Pour in the tomatoes and 1¼ cups of the reserved stock. Add the chili powder, cumin and thyme. Bring to a boil, cover and simmer for 20 minutes. Stir in the shrimp and Tabasco, and cook for another 5 minutes. Adjust the seasoning. Serve hot, garnished with chopped parsley and accompanied by green beans.

Rice Layered with Chicken & Potatoes

In India, this dish is mainly prepared for important occasions. Every cook in the country has a subtle and secret variation.

Serves 4–6
3 pounds chicken breast fillet,
  skinned and cut into
  large pieces
¼ cup biryani masala paste
2 fresh green chiles, chopped
1 tablespoon grated fresh
  ginger root
1 tablespoon crushed garlic
1 cup chopped cilantro leaves
6–8 fresh mint leaves, chopped
⅔ cup plain yogurt, beaten
2 tablespoons tomato paste
4 onions, finely sliced, deep-fried
  and crushed
2¼ cups basmati rice
1 teaspoon black cumin seeds

2-inch piece cinnamon stick
4 green cardamom pods
2 black cardamom pods
vegetable oil, for shallow frying
4 large potatoes, quartered
¾ cup milk, mixed with
  5 tablespoons water
1 envelope saffron powder,
  mixed with 6 tablespoons milk
2 tablespoons ghee or
  unsalted butter

For the garnish
ghee or unsalted butter, for
  shallow frying
½ cup cashews
scant ½ cup golden raisins
2 hard-boiled eggs, quartered
Deep-fried Onions

1 In a bowl, mix the chicken with the masala paste, chiles, ginger, garlic, cilantro, mint, yogurt, tomato paste, onions and salt to taste. Marinate for about 2 hours. Transfer to a heavy pan and cook gently for about 10 minutes. Set aside.

2 Boil a large pan of water and soak the rice with the cumin seeds, cinnamon stick and green and black cardamoms for about 5 minutes. Drain well. Some of the whole spices may be removed at this stage.

3 Heat the oil for shallow frying and cook the potatoes until they are evenly browned on all sides. Drain and set aside.

4 Place half the rice on top of the chicken in the pan in an even layer. Then make an even layer with the potatoes. Put the remaining rice on top of the potatoes and spread to make an even layer.

5 Sprinkle the milk mixed with water all over the rice. Make random holes in the rice with the handle of a spoon and pour into each a little saffron milk. Place a few pats of ghee or butter on the surface, cover and cook over low heat for 35–45 minutes.

6 Meanwhile, to make the garnish, heat a little ghee or butter and fry the cashews and golden raisins until they swell. Drain and set aside.

7 When the chicken dish is cooked, gently toss the rice, chicken and potatoes together, garnish with the nut mixture, hard-boiled eggs and deep-fried onions, and serve hot.

Chicken Chow Mein

Chow Mein, in which noodles are stir-fried with meat, seafood or vegetables, is arguably China's best-known noodle dish.

Serves 4
12 ounces noodles
8 ounces chicken breast
   fillet, skinned
3 tablespoons soy sauce
1 tablespoon rice wine or
   dry sherry

1 tablespoon dark sesame oil
¼ cup vegetable oil
1 teaspoon Chinese five-spice
   powder
2 garlic cloves, finely chopped
2 ounces snowpeas
½ cup bean sprouts
⅓ cup ham, finely shredded
4 scallions, finely chopped
salt and freshly ground
   black pepper

1 Cook the noodles in a saucepan of boiling water according to the package instructions until tender. Drain, rinse under cold water and drain well again.

2 Slice the chicken into fine shreds about 2 inches in length. Place in a bowl and add 2 teaspoons of the soy sauce, the rice wine or sherry and sesame oil.

3 Heat half the vegetable oil in a wok or large frying pan over high heat. When it starts smoking, add the chicken mixture. Stir-fry for 2 minutes until it begins to color, then transfer the chicken to a plate and keep it hot.

4 Wipe the wok clean and heat the remaining oil. Stir in the five-spice powder, garlic, snowpeas, bean sprouts and ham, stir-fry for another minute or so, and add the noodles.

5 Continue to stir-fry until the noodles are heated through. Add the remaining soy sauce to taste, and season with salt and pepper. Return the chicken and any juices to the noodle mixture, add the chopped scallions and give the mixture a final stir. Serve immediately.

Special Chow Mein

This recipe calls for lap cheong, an air-dried Chinese sausage available at most Chinese supermarkets. If you cannot buy it, substitute ham, chorizo or salami.

Serves 4–6
3 tablespoons vegetable oil
2 garlic cloves, sliced
1 teaspoon chopped fresh
   ginger root
2 fresh red chiles, chopped
2 lap cheong, about 3 ounces,
   rinsed and sliced (optional)
1 chicken breast fillet, thinly sliced

16 jumbo shrimp, peeled but tails
   left intact and deveined
4 ounces green beans
1 cup bean sprouts
1 cup garlic chives
1 pound egg noodles, cooked in
   boiling water until tender
2 tablespoons soy sauce
1 tablespoon oyster sauce
1 tablespoon sesame oil
salt and freshly ground
   black pepper
2 scallions, shredded and
   1 tablespoon cilantro leaves,
   to garnish

1 Heat 1 tablespoon of the oil in a wok or large frying pan and sauté the garlic, ginger and chiles. Add the lap cheong, chicken, shrimp and beans. Stir-fry for about 2 minutes over high heat or until the chicken and shrimp are cooked. Transfer the mixture to a bowl and set aside.

2 Heat the rest of the oil in the wok. Add the bean sprouts and garlic chives. Stir-fry for 1–2 minutes.

3 Add the noodles, and toss and stir to mix. Season with soy sauce, oyster sauce, salt and pepper.

4 Return the shrimp mixture to the wok. Reheat and mix well with the noodles. Stir in the sesame oil. Serve, garnished with scallions and cilantro leaves.

> **Cook's Tip**
> Garlic chives are also known as Chinese or flowering chives. They have a mild garlic and chive flavor.

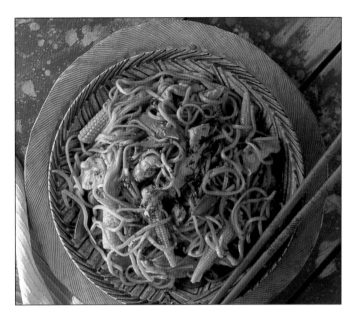

Chicken Curry with Rice Vermicelli

Lemongrass gives this Southeast Asian curry a wonderful, lemony flavor and fragrance.

Serves 4

3½-pound chicken
8 ounces sweet potatoes
4 tablespoons oil
1 onion, finely sliced
3 garlic cloves, crushed
2–3 tablespoons
   Thai curry powder
1 teaspoon sugar
2 teaspoons fish sauce

2½ cups coconut milk
1 lemongrass stalk, cut in half
12 ounces rice vermicelli,
   soaked in hot water until soft
salt

For the garnish

½ cup bean sprouts
2 scallions, thinly
   sliced diagonally
2 fresh red chiles, seeded and
   finely sliced
8–10 mint leaves

1 Skin the chicken and cut it into small pieces. Peel the sweet potatoes and cut them into large chunks.

2 Heat half the oil in a large, heavy saucepan. Add the onion and garlic, and sauté until the onion softens. Add the chicken pieces and stir-fry until they change color.

3 Stir in the curry powder. Season with salt and sugar, and mix thoroughly, then add the fish sauce, coconut milk and lemongrass. Cook over low heat for 15 minutes.

4 Meanwhile, heat the remaining oil in a large frying pan. Cook the sweet potatoes until lightly golden.

5 Using a slotted spoon, add the sweet potato pieces to the chicken. Cook for 10–15 more minutes or until both the chicken and sweet potatoes are tender.

6 Drain the rice vermicelli and cook in a saucepan of boiling water for 3–5 minutes. Drain well. Place in shallow serving bowls with the chicken curry. Garnish with bean sprouts, scallions, chiles and mint leaves, and serve.

Stir-fried Sweet-&-Sour Chicken

A quickly cooked, all-in-one stir-fry meal with a Southeast Asian influence.

Serves 4

10 ounces Chinese egg noodles
2 tablespoons vegetable oil
3 scallions, chopped
1 garlic clove, crushed
1-inch piece fresh ginger root,
   grated
1 teaspoon hot paprika
1 teaspoon ground coriander

3 chicken breast fillets, sliced
4 ounces sugar snap peas,
   trimmed
4 ounces baby corn, halved
1 cup bean sprouts
1 tablespoon cornstarch
3 tablespoons soy sauce
3 tablespoons lemon juice
1 tablespoon sugar
salt
3 tablespoons chopped cilantro or
   scallion tops, to garnish

1 Bring a large saucepan of salted water to a boil. Add the noodles and cook according to the package instructions. Drain, cover and keep warm.

2 Heat the oil in a wok or frying pan. Add the scallions and cook over low heat. Mix in the garlic, ginger, paprika and ground coriander, and stir for a minute or so. Add the chicken and stir-fry for 3–4 minutes.

3 Add the peas, corn and bean sprouts, cover the wok and steam briefly. Stir in the noodles.

4 Combine the cornstarch, soy sauce, lemon juice and sugar in a small bowl. Add to the wok and simmer briefly to thicken. Serve, garnished with chopped cilantro or scallion tops.

> **Cook's Tip**
> *Large wok lids are cumbersome and can be difficult to store in a small kitchen. Consider placing a circle of waxed paper on the surface of the food to keep cooking juices in.*

Spicy Szechuan Noodles

Cooked noodles, chicken and roasted cashews tossed in a spicy dressing and served cold.

Serves 4
12 ounces thick noodles
6 ounces cooked chicken, shredded
½ cup roasted cashews
salt

For the dressing
4 scallions, chopped
2 tablespoons chopped cilantro
2 garlic cloves, chopped
2 tablespoons smooth peanut butter
2 tablespoons sweet chili sauce
1 tablespoon soy sauce
1 tablespoon sherry vinegar
1 tablespoon sesame oil
2 tablespoons olive oil
2 tablespoons Chicken Stock or water
10 toasted Szechuan peppercorns, ground

1 Bring a large saucepan of salted water to a boil. Add the noodles and cook according to the package instructions. Drain, rinse under cold running water and drain well.

2 Meanwhile, to make the dressing, combine all the ingredients in a large bowl and whisk together well.

3 Add the noodles, shredded chicken and cashews to the dressing, toss gently to coat and adjust the seasoning to taste. Serve immediately.

Variation
You can substitute cooked turkey or duck for the chicken.

Mee Krob

The basis of this dish is fried rice vermicelli: be careful when frying, as it has a tendency to spit when added to hot oil.

Serves 4
½ cup vegetable oil
8 ounces rice vermicelli
5 ounces green beans, trimmed and halved lengthwise
1 onion, finely chopped
2 chicken breast fillets, about 6 ounces each, skinned and cut into strips
1 teaspoon chili powder
8 ounces cooked peeled shrimp
3 tablespoons dark soy sauce
3 tablespoons white wine vinegar
2 teaspoons sugar
cilantro sprigs, to garnish

1 Heat a wok, then add ¼ cup of the oil. Break up the rice vermicelli into 3-inch lengths. When the oil is hot, fry the vermicelli in batches. Remove from the wok and keep warm.

2 Heat the remaining oil in the wok, then add the beans, onion and chicken, and stir-fry for 3 minutes, until the chicken is cooked.

3 Sprinkle in the chili powder. Stir in the shrimp, soy sauce, vinegar and sugar, and stir-fry for 2 minutes.

4 Serve the chicken, shrimp and vegetables on the vermicelli, garnished with sprigs of cilantro.

Variation
Usually served at celebrations, this dish often includes other ingredients. You could add 4 ounces ground pork and 3–4 seeded and chopped dried chiles in step 2. Black bean sauce may be substituted for the soy sauce. For a more elaborate garnish, make an omelet from 2 eggs, roll it up and cut into thin slices. Shredded scallion and chopped fresh red chiles can also be sprinkled over the finished dish.

Chili Chicken

This simple supper dish can be prepared in next to no time using ingredients from the pantry.

Serves 4
12 chicken thighs
1 tablespoon olive oil
1 medium onion, thinly sliced
1 garlic clove, crushed
1 fresh green chile, chopped, or
  1 teaspoon chili powder

14-ounce can chopped tomatoes,
  with their juice
1 teaspoon sugar
15-ounce can red kidney beans,
  drained and rinsed
salt and freshly ground
  black pepper
fresh parsley sprig, to garnish
cooked rice, to serve

1 Cut the chicken into large cubes, removing all the skin and bones. Heat the oil in a large, flameproof casserole and brown the chicken pieces on all sides. Remove from the casserole and keep warm.

2 Add the onion and garlic to the casserole, and cook gently until tender. Stir in the fresh chile or chili powder and cook for 2 minutes. Add the tomatoes with their juice, sugar and seasoning. Bring to a boil.

3 Return the chicken pieces to the casserole, cover and simmer for about 30 minutes, until tender.

4 Add the kidney beans and cook over low heat for another 5 minutes to heat them through. Serve with rice, garnished with fresh parsley.

Variation
You could substitute canned chickpeas for the kidney beans and add 2 chopped or sliced medium carrots to the casserole with the onion and garlic in step 2. For an extra spicy touch, add a dash of Tabasco sauce with the seasoning.

Chicken Naan Pockets

This quick-and-easy dish is ideal for a snack and makes excellent picnic fare. For speed, use the ready-to-bake naan available at some supermarkets and Asian stores, or try warmed pita bread instead.

Serves 4
4 naan
1 pound chicken, skinned, boned
  and cubed
3 tablespoons plain yogurt
1½ teaspoons garam masala
1 teaspoon chili powder
1 teaspoon salt

3 tablespoons lemon juice
1 tablespoon chopped cilantro
1 fresh green chile, chopped
1 tablespoon vegetable oil
8 onion rings
2 tomatoes, quartered
½ white cabbage, shredded

For the garnish
lemon wedges
2 small tomatoes, halved
mixed salad leaves
cilantro

1 Cut into the middle of each naan to make a pocket, then set aside. Place the chicken cubes in a dish.

2 In a small bowl, combine the plain yogurt, garam masala, chili powder, salt, lemon juice, chopped cilantro and chopped fresh green chile. Pour the mixture onto the cubed chicken pieces and let marinate for about 1 hour.

3 Preheat the broiler to very hot, then lower the heat to medium. Place the chicken in a flameproof dish and cook under the broiler for 15–20 minutes, until tender and cooked through, turning the pieces at least twice. Baste frequently with the vegetable oil during cooking.

4 Fill each naan with the chicken and then with the onion rings, tomatoes and cabbage.

5 Serve hot, garnished with lemon wedges, tomato halves, mixed salad leaves and cilantro.

Mixed Tostadas

Like little edible plates, these fried Mexican tortillas can support any filling that is not too juicy.

Makes 14
oil, for shallow frying
14 freshly prepared unbaked
 corn tortillas
1 cup mashed cooked or canned
 red kidney or pinto beans
1 iceberg lettuce, shredded
vinaigrette dressing (optional)
2 cooked chicken breast fillets,
 skinned and thinly sliced
8 ounces ready-made guacamole
1 cup coarsely grated
 Cheddar cheese
pickled jalapeño chiles, seeded
 and sliced, to taste

1 Heat the oil in a frying pan and fry the tortillas until golden brown on both sides and crisp but not hard.

2 Spread each tortilla with a layer of mashed beans. Put a layer of shredded lettuce (which can be left plain or lightly tossed with a little dressing) over the beans.

3 Arrange pieces of chicken in a layer on top of the lettuce. Carefully spread over a layer of the guacamole and finally sprinkle with the grated cheese. Sprinkle sliced pickled chiles on top, to taste.

4 Arrange the mixed tostadas on a large serving platter. Serve on individual plates but eat using your hands.

Cook's Tip
To make a vinaigrette dressing, whisk together 3 tablespoons wine vinegar, 1 tablespoon Dijon mustard, and salt and pepper to taste. Gradually whisk in ⅔ cup olive oil. Alternatively, put all the ingredients in a screw-top jar and shake vigorously until thoroughly combined.

Mexican Chicken

Warm taco shells filled with chicken in a spicy sauce, served with lettuce, tomatoes, sour cream and grated cheese.

Serves 4
3-pound chicken
1 teaspoon salt
12 taco shells
1 small iceberg lettuce, shredded
6 ounces tomatoes, chopped
1 cup sour cream
1 cup grated
 Cheddar cheese

For the sauce
1 cup fresh tomatoes, peeled,
 cooked and sieved
1–2 garlic cloves, crushed
½ teaspoon cider vinegar
½ teaspoon dried oregano
½ teaspoon ground cumin
1–2 tablespoons mild
 chili powder

1 Put the chicken in a large pan, and add the salt and enough water to cover. Bring to a boil. Reduce the heat and simmer for about 45 minutes to 1 hour until the chicken is thoroughly cooked. Remove the chicken from the pan and let cool. Reserve ½ cup of the stock for the sauce.

2 Remove the chicken meat from the bones, discarding all the skin. Chop the meat coarsely.

3 To make the sauce, combine all the ingredients with the reserved chicken stock in a saucepan and bring to a boil. Stir in the chicken meat. Simmer for about 20 minutes until the sauce thickens considerably, stirring occasionally.

4 Preheat the oven to 350°F. Spread out the taco shells on two baking sheets and heat for 7 minutes.

5 Meanwhile, put the shredded lettuce, chopped tomatoes, sour cream and grated cheese in individual serving dishes. To serve, spoon a little of the hot chicken mixture into each taco shell. Garnish with the lettuce, tomatoes, sour cream and grated Cheddar cheese.

Tortilla Flutes

These crisply fried rolled tortillas, stuffed with chicken in fresh tomato sauce, look as good as they taste.

Makes about 12

24 freshly prepared unbaked
   flour tortillas
2 tomatoes, peeled, seeded
   and chopped
1 small onion, chopped
1 garlic clove, chopped
2–3 tablespoons corn oil
2 freshly cooked chicken breast
   fillets, skinned and shredded
salt

For the garnish
sliced radishes
stuffed green olives
cilantro

1 Place the unbaked flour tortillas in pairs on a work surface, with the right-hand tortilla overlapping the left-hand one by about 2 inches.

2 Put the tomatoes, onion and garlic into a food processor and process into a purée. Season with salt to taste.

3 Heat 1 tablespoon of the corn oil in a frying pan and cook the tomato paste for a few minutes, stirring constantly to blend the flavors. Remove from heat and stir in the shredded chicken, mixing well.

4 Spread about 2 tablespoons of the chicken mixture on each pair of tortillas, roll them up into flutes and secure with a toothpick.

5 Heat a little more of the oil in a frying pan large enough to hold the flutes comfortably. Cook more than one at a time if possible, but don't overcrowd the pan. Fry the flutes until light brown all over. Add more oil if needed.

6 Drain the cooked flutes on paper towels and keep hot. When ready to serve, transfer to a platter and garnish with radishes, olives and cilantro.

Chicken Fajitas

Fajitas are warmed soft tortillas, filled and folded like an envelope. They are traditional Mexican fast food, delicious and easy to prepare, and a favorite for family supper.

Serves 4

generous ½ cup long-grain rice
3 tablespoons wild rice
1 tablespoon olive oil
1 tablespoon sunflower oil
1 onion, cut into thin wedges
4 chicken breast fillets, skinned
   and cut into thin strips
1 red bell pepper, seeded and
   thinly sliced
1 teaspoon ground cumin
generous pinch of cayenne pepper
½ teaspoon ground turmeric
¾ cup passata
½–¾ cup Chicken Stock
12 small or 8 large wheat
   tortillas, warmed
sour cream, to serve

For the salsa
1 shallot, roughly chopped
1 small garlic clove
½–1 fresh green chile, seeded and
   roughly chopped
small bunch of fresh parsley
5 tomatoes, peeled, seeded
   and chopped
2 teaspoons olive oil
1 tablespoon lemon juice
2 tablespoons tomato juice
salt and freshly ground
   black pepper

For the guacamole
1 large ripe avocado
2 scallions, chopped
1–2 tablespoons fresh lime or
   lemon juice
generous pinch of cayenne pepper
1 tablespoon chopped
   cilantro

1 Cook the long-grain and wild rice separately, following the instructions on the packages. Drain and set aside.

2 To make the salsa, finely chop the shallot, garlic, chile and parsley in a blender or food processor. Spoon into a bowl. Stir in the tomatoes, olive oil, lemon juice and tomato juice. Season to taste with salt and pepper. Cover with plastic wrap and chill.

3 To make the guacamole, scoop the avocado flesh into a bowl. Mash it lightly with the scallions, citrus juice, cayenne, cilantro and seasoning, so that small pieces still remain. Cover the surface closely with plastic wrap and chill.

4 Heat the olive and sunflower oils in a frying pan and sauté the onion wedges for 4–5 minutes, until softened. Add the chicken strips and red pepper slices, and cook until evenly browned.

5 Stir in the cumin, cayenne and turmeric. Cook, stirring, for about 1 minute, then stir in the passata and chicken stock. Bring to a boil, then lower the heat and simmer gently for 5–6 minutes, until the chicken is cooked through. Season to taste.

6 Stir both types of rice into the chicken and cook for 1–2 minutes, until the rice is warmed through.

7 Spoon a little of the chicken mixture onto each warmed tortilla. Top with salsa, guacamole and sour cream, and roll up. Alternatively, let everyone assemble their own fajita at the table.

Enchiladas with Hot Chili Sauce

By Mexican standards, this is a low-heat version of the popular chicken enchiladas. If you like your food hot, you can add extra chiles to the sauce.

Serves 4
butter, for greasing
8 wheat tortillas
1½ cups grated Cheddar cheese
1 onion, finely chopped
12 ounces cooked chicken, cut
   into small chunks
1¼ cups sour cream

1 avocado, sliced and tossed in
   lemon juice, to garnish

For the salsa picante
1–2 fresh green chiles
1 tablespoon vegetable oil
1 onion, chopped
1 garlic clove, crushed
14-ounce can
   chopped tomatoes
2 tablespoons tomato paste
salt and freshly ground
   black pepper

1 To make the salsa picante, halve the chiles, and remove the cores and seeds. Slice the chiles very thinly. Heat the oil in a frying pan, and sauté the onion and garlic for 3–4 minutes, until softened. Add the tomatoes, tomato paste and chiles. Simmer gently, uncovered, for 12–15 minutes, stirring frequently.

2 Pour the sauce into a food processor or blender and process until smooth. Return to the heat and cook very gently, uncovered, for another 15 minutes. Season and set aside.

3 Preheat the oven to 350°F and butter a shallow, ovenproof dish. Sprinkle each tortilla with grated cheese and chopped onion, about 1½ ounces of the chicken and 1 tablespoon of the salsa. Pour on 1 tablespoon of the sour cream, roll up and place, seam-side down, in the dish.

4 Pour the remaining salsa picante on top of the enchiladas and sprinkle with the remaining cheese and onion. Bake for about 25–30 minutes, until the top is golden. Serve with the remaining sour cream either poured on or in a separate pitcher, and garnish with the sliced avocado.

Turkey-chorizo Tacos

Chopped spicy chorizo sausage and ground turkey make a warming filling for Mexican taco shells.

Serves 4
1 tablespoon vegetable oil
1 pound ground turkey
1 teaspoon salt
1 teaspoon ground cumin

12 taco shells
3 ounces chorizo, finely chopped
3 scallions, chopped
2 tomatoes, chopped
1 small head lettuce, shredded
2 cups grated Cheddar cheese
tomato salsa and guacamole,
   to serve

1 Preheat the oven to 350°F. Heat the oil in a nonstick frying pan and add the turkey, salt and cumin. Sauté over medium heat for 5–8 minutes, until the turkey is cooked through, stirring frequently to break up any lumps.

2 Meanwhile, arrange the taco shells in one layer on a large baking sheet and heat in the oven for about 10 minutes or according to the directions on the package.

3 Add the chopped chorizo and scallions to the turkey, and stir to mix. Cook until just warmed through, stirring the mixture occasionally.

4 To assemble each taco, place 1–2 spoonfuls of the turkey mixture in the bottom of a warmed taco shell. Top with a generous sprinkling of chopped tomato, shredded lettuce and grated cheese.

5 Serve immediately, with tomato salsa and guacamole.

Variation
You can use ground chicken for these tacos, if preferred.

Hot Turkey Chili

This nutritious and tasty dish, perfect for a family supper, is made economically with ground turkey.

Serves 8
2 tablespoons corn oil
1 medium onion, halved and
  thinly sliced
1 green bell pepper,
  seeded and diced
3 garlic cloves, crushed

2 pounds ground turkey
2–3 tablespoons chili powder
1½ teaspoons ground cumin
1 teaspoon dried oregano
14-ounce can
  chopped tomatoes
2 tablespoons tomato paste
1 cup Chicken Stock
15-ounce can red kidney beans,
  drained and rinsed
¼ teaspoon salt
boiled rice, to serve

1 Heat the oil in a large saucepan over medium heat. Add the onion, green pepper and garlic, and cook for about 5 minutes, until softened, stirring frequently.

2 Add the turkey and cook for about 5 minutes, until it is lightly browned, stirring to break up any lumps.

3 Stir in the chili powder, cumin and oregano. Add the tomatoes, tomato paste, chicken stock, kidney beans and salt, and stir well.

4 Bring the mixture to a boil, then reduce the heat and simmer for 30 minutes, stirring occasionally. Serve the chili with boiled rice.

Cook's Tip
Canned kidney beans are quick and convenient, but you could use dried beans, which are more economical. Soak them in cold water to cover for 3–4 hours, drain and place in a saucepan. Add fresh cold water to cover and bring to a boil. Boil vigorously for 15 minutes. This is essential, as it destroys a naturally occurring toxin in the skin of the beans. Lower the heat and simmer for 1½–2 hours, until tender, then drain.

Turkey Sosaties with a Curried Apricot Sauce

This is a South African way of cooking poultry in a delicious sweet-and-sour sauce that is spiced with curry powder.

Serves 4
1 tablespoon oil
1 onion, finely chopped
1 garlic clove, crushed

2 bay leaves
juice of 1 lemon
2 tablespoons curry powder
¼ cup apricot jam
¼ cup apple juice
salt
1½ pounds turkey fillet
¼ cup crème fraîche

1 Heat the oil in a saucepan. Add the onion, garlic and bay leaves, and cook over low heat for 10 minutes, until the onions are soft.

2 Add the lemon juice, curry powder, apricot jam and apple juice with salt to taste. Cook gently for 5 minutes. Remove from heat and let cool.

3 Cut the turkey into ¾-inch cubes and place in a dish. Add the cooled onion mixture and stir thoroughly. Cover and set in a cool place to marinate for at least 2 hours or overnight in the refrigerator.

4 Preheat the broiler or prepare a grill. Thread the turkey onto skewers, letting the marinade run back into the dish. Broil or grill the sosaties for 6–8 minutes, turning several times, until cooked.

5 Meanwhile, transfer the marinade to a pan and simmer for 2 minutes. Stir in the crème fraîche and serve with the sosaties.

Variation
This marinade is equally good with cubes of chicken.

Stuffed Turkey in Lemon Sauce

Sweet potatoes and shrimp flavored with herbs and chile make an unusual stuffing for turkey fillets. Use orange-fleshed potatoes.

Serves 4

6 ounces sweet potato
1 onion, finely chopped
1 teaspoon dried tarragon, crushed
½ teaspoon dried basil
1 fresh green chile, seeded and finely chopped
1 garlic clove, crushed
½ teaspoon dried thyme
4 ounces cooked peeled shrimp, chopped

4 turkey fillets, about 8 ounces each
butter, for greasing
salt and freshly ground black pepper
cooked root vegetables, bulghur wheat or rice, to serve

For the lemon sauce

1 tablespoon olive oil
½ onion, finely chopped
2 garlic cloves, crushed
1¼ cups Chicken Stock
¾ teaspoon dried thyme
½ teaspoon dried basil
2 tablespoons finely chopped fresh parsley
2 tablespoons lemon juice
mint leaves, to garnish

1 Preheat the oven to 350°F. Cook the sweet potato in boiling water until tender, drain, transfer to a bowl and mash. Add the onion, tarragon, basil, chile, garlic, thyme and shrimp to the sweet potato, season with pepper and mix well.

2 Lay the turkey fillets on a plate and season. Place a little of the sweet potato stuffing in the center of each, fold over the sides and roll up. Secure with a wooden cocktail stick and place in a buttered ovenproof dish, seam-side down.

3 To make the sauce, heat the oil in a frying pan and sauté the onion and garlic for 5–7 minutes, until soft. Stir in the stock and simmer briefly. Add the herbs and lemon juice, and simmer for 2 minutes. Season to taste.

4 Pour the sauce around the turkey, cover with foil and bake for 1½ hours, basting frequently with the sauce to keep the rolls moist. Garnish with mint leaves and serve with bulghur wheat or rice.

Duck with Sherry & Pumpkin

For this dish, duck is marinated in a mixture of spices and cooked in a smooth pumpkin and tomato sauce enriched with medium-dry sherry.

Serves 6

1 whole duck, about 3 pounds
1 lemon
1 teaspoon garlic powder or 2 garlic cloves, crushed
1 teaspoon curry powder
½ teaspoon paprika

¾ teaspoon Indian five-spice powder
2 tablespoons soy sauce, plus extra to serve
vegetable oil, for frying
salt and freshly ground black pepper

For the sauce

3 ounces pumpkin
1 onion, chopped
4 canned plum tomatoes
1¼ cups medium-dry sherry
about 1¼ cups water

1 Cut the duck into 10 pieces and place in a large bowl. Halve the lemon and squeeze the juice onto the duck. Set aside.

2 In a small bowl, combine the garlic, curry powder, paprika, five-spice powder and salt and pepper, and rub into the duck pieces. Sprinkle the duck with the soy sauce, cover loosely with plastic wrap and marinate overnight.

3 To make the sauce, cook the pumpkin in boiling water until tender. Blend into a purée with the onion and tomatoes in a food processor or blender.

4 Pat the duck pieces dry with paper towels. Heat a little oil in a wok or large frying pan and fry the duck for 15 minutes, until crisp and brown. Remove from the pan and set aside.

5 Wipe the excess oil from the wok or frying pan with paper towels and pour in the pumpkin purée. Add the sherry and a little of the water, then bring to a boil and add the fried duck. Simmer for about 1 hour, until the duck is cooked, adding more water if the sauce becomes too thick. Serve hot and pass soy sauce separately.

Hot Chili Duck with Crabmeat & Cashew Sauce

Perhaps a surprising partner for duck, crabmeat nonetheless makes a wonderful rich sauce with Thai spices and coconut.

Serves 4–6

6-pound duck
about 5 cups water
2 kaffir lime leaves
2–3 small fresh red chiles, seeded and finely chopped
5 teaspoons sugar
2 tablespoons coriander seeds
1 teaspoon caraway seeds
1 cup cashews, chopped
3-inch piece lemongrass, shredded
1-inch piece galangal or fresh ginger root, finely chopped
2 garlic cloves, crushed
4 shallots or 1 medium onion, finely chopped
¾-inch cube shrimp paste
½ cup cilantro white root or stem, finely chopped
6 ounces frozen white crabmeat, thawed
2 ounces coconut milk
salt
1 small bunch cilantro, chopped, to garnish
cooked Thai fragrant rice, to serve

1 To divide the duck into manageable pieces, first remove the legs. Separate the thighs from the drumsticks and chop each thigh and drumstick into two pieces. Trim away the lower half of the duck with kitchen scissors. Cut the breast piece in half down the middle, then chop each half into four pieces.

2 Put the duck flesh and bones into a large saucepan and add the water—it should just cover the meat. Add the lime leaves and 1 teaspoon salt, bring to a boil and simmer, uncovered, for 35–40 minutes, until the duck is tender. Discard the bones, skim off the fat from the stock and place in a clean pan.

3 Grind the chiles together with the sugar and ½ teaspoon salt using a food processor. Dry-fry the coriander and caraway seeds and the cashews in a wok for 1–2 minutes. Add to the food processor with the lemongrass, galangal or ginger, garlic and shallots or onion, and process into a smooth paste. Add the shrimp paste and cilantro root or stem.

4 Add 1 cup of the duck stock to the spicy mixture in the food processor and blend to make a thin paste.

5 Pour the spicy paste from the food processor in with the duck, bring to a boil and simmer, uncovered, for 20–25 minutes.

6 Add the crabmeat and coconut milk, and simmer briefly. Turn out onto a serving dish, garnish with chopped cilantro and serve, accompanied by Thai fragrant rice.

205

Hot Sweet-&-Sour Duck Casserole

This dish has a distinctively sweet, sour and hot flavor, and is best eaten with rice as an accompaniment.

Serves 4–6

3-pound duck, jointed and skinned
4 bay leaves
3 tablespoons salt
5 tablespoons vegetable oil
juice of 5 lemons
8 medium onions, finely chopped
2 ounces garlic, crushed
2 ounces chili powder
1¼ cups pickling vinegar
4 ounces fresh ginger root, thinly sliced or shredded
generous ½ cup sugar
2 ounces garam masala

1 Place the duck, bay leaves and salt in a large pan, and cover with cold water. Bring to a boil, then simmer until the duck is fully cooked: the juices should run clear when the thickest part of the thigh is pierced with a skewer or knife. Remove the duck from the pan and keep warm. Reserve the liquid to use as a base for stock or soups.

2 In a large pan, heat the oil and lemon juice until it reaches the smoking point. Add the onions, garlic and chili powder, and sauté until the onions are golden brown.

3 Add the vinegar, ginger and sugar, and simmer until the sugar dissolves and the oil has separated.

4 Add the duck to the pan with the garam masala. Mix well, then reheat until the masala clings to the pieces of duck and the gravy is thick. Taste and adjust the seasoning as necessary. If you prefer a thinner gravy, add a little of the reserved stock. Serve hot.

Cook's Tip
Shrimp paste is made from dried shrimp fermented in brine. It both smells and tastes strongly, so add it with caution. It is used widely throughout Southeast Asia, where it is known as blacan *or* blachan. *The Japanese variety is called* terasi.

Variation
This recipe also works well with most game birds. Try it with guinea fowl, pheasant or partridge—or, of course, wild duck, such as teal or widgeon.

Chicken Pitas with Red Coleslaw

Pitas are convenient for simple snacks and packed lunches and it's easy to cram in lots of fresh, healthy ingredients.

Serves 4

$^1/_4$ red cabbage
I small red onion
2 radishes
I red apple
I tablespoon lemon juice
3 tablespoons low-fat fromage frais
I cooked chicken breast without
   skin, about 6 ounces
4 large or 8 small pita breads
salt and freshly ground
   black pepper
chopped fresh parsley, to garnish

I Remove the tough central spine from the cabbage leaves, then finely shred the leaves using a large, sharp knife. Thinly slice the onion. Thinly slice the radishes. Peel, core and grate the apple. Place the cabbage, onion, radishes and apple in a bowl and stir in the lemon juice.

2 Stir the fromage frais into the shredded cabbage mixture, and season well with salt and pepper.

3 Thinly slice the cooked chicken breast and stir into the shredded cabbage mixture until well coated in fromage frais.

4 Preheat the broiler. Warm the pitas under the broiler, then split them along one edge using a round-bladed knife. Spoon the filling into the pitas, garnish with chopped fresh parsley and serve immediately.

Cook's Tip
If the filled pita breads need to be made more than an hour in advance, line them with crisp lettuce leaves before adding the filling.

Caribbean Chicken Kebabs

These kebabs have a rich, Caribbean flavor and the marinade keeps them moist without the need for oil. Serve with a colorful salad and rice.

Serves 4

I$^1/_4$ pounds chicken breast
   fillet, skinned
finely grated zest of I lime
2 tablespoons lime juice
I tablespoon rum or sherry
I tablespoon light brown sugar
I teaspoon ground cinnamon
2 mangoes, peeled and cubed
rice and salad, to serve

I Cut the chicken into bite-size chunks and place in a non-metallic bowl with the lime zest and juice, rum or sherry, sugar and ground cinnamon. Toss well to coat, cover and let stand for I hour.

2 Drain the chicken and reserve the marinade. Thread the chicken onto four wooden skewers, alternating with the mango cubes. Preheat the broiler or prepare the grill.

3 Cook the chicken skewers under the broiler or on the grill for 8–10 minutes, turning occasionally and basting frequently with the reserved marinade until the chicken is tender and golden brown. Serve immediately with rice and salad.

Cook's Tip
The rum or sherry adds a wonderfully rich flavor, but it can be omitted if you prefer or if you are preparing the kebabs for children, in which case, you might wish to add an extra I tablespoon lime juice.

Chicken Tortellini

These tasty little parcels, with a chicken and ham filling, are poached in stock.

Serves 4–6
4 ounces smoked lean ham, diced
4 ounces chicken breast
   fillet, skinned and diced
3¾ cups vegetable or
   Chicken Stock
cilantro stalks
2 tablespoons grated Parmesan
   cheese, plus extra to serve
1 egg, beaten, plus egg white
   for brushing
2 tablespoons chopped cilantro
1 batch Basic Pasta Dough
all-purpose flour, for dusting
salt and freshly ground
   black pepper
cilantro leaves, to garnish

1 Put the ham and chicken into a saucepan with ⅔ cup of the stock and some cilantro stalks. Bring to a boil, cover and simmer for 20 minutes. Set aside to cool slightly.

2 Drain the ham and chicken, reserving the stock, and grind finely. Put the meat into a bowl with the Parmesan, beaten egg and chopped cilantro. Season with salt and pepper.

3 Roll the pasta into thin sheets and cut into 1½-inch squares. Put ½ teaspoon of the meat mixture on each. Brush the edges with egg white and fold each square into a triangle; press out any air and seal firmly. Curl each triangle around the tip of a forefinger and press the two ends together firmly. Lay on a lightly floured dish towel to rest for 30 minutes before cooking.

4 Strain the reserved stock and add to the remainder. Put into a pan and bring to a boil. Lower the heat and add the tortellini. Cook for 5 minutes. Turn off the heat, cover and let stand for 20–30 minutes. Ladle into soup plates with some of the stock and garnish with cilantro leaves. Serve, with extra grated Parmesan passed separately.

Lasagne

You can still enjoy classic pasta dishes even if you are reducing the fat content of your diet, as this version of lasagne, made with ground chicken or turkey, shows.

Serves 6–8
1 large onion, chopped
2 garlic cloves, crushed
1¼ pounds ground chicken
   or turkey
1-pound carton passata
1 teaspoon dried mixed herbs
8 ounces frozen leaf
   spinach, thawed
7 ounces lasagne verdi
scant 1 cup low-fat cottage
   cheese
salt and freshly ground
   black pepper
mixed salad, to serve

For the sauce
2 tablespoons low-fat margarine
¼ cup all-purpose flour
1¼ cups skim milk
¼ teaspoon grated nutmeg
⅓ cup grated
   Parmesan cheese

1 Put the onion, garlic and ground chicken or turkey into a nonstick saucepan. Brown quickly for 5 minutes, stirring with a wooden spoon to break up any lumps.

2 Add the passata, herbs and seasoning. Bring to a boil, cover and simmer for 30 minutes.

3 To make the sauce, put all the ingredients, except the Parmesan cheese, into a saucepan. Heat to thicken, whisking constantly until bubbling and smooth. Season to taste, add the cheese to the sauce and stir.

4 Preheat the oven to 375°F. Lay the spinach leaves out on paper towels and pat dry.

5 Layer the chicken or turkey mixture, dried lasagne, cottage cheese and spinach in a 9-cup ovenproof dish, starting and ending with a layer of chicken or turkey.

6 Spoon the sauce on top to cover and bake for 45–50 minutes or until bubbling. Serve with a mixed salad.

Rolled Stuffed Cannelloni

These cannelloni are made by rolling cooked lasagne sheets around the herbed chicken filling.

Serves 4
12 sheets lasagne
2 tablespoons grated
   Parmesan cheese
fresh basil leaves, to garnish

For the filling
2–3 garlic cloves, crushed
1 small onion, finely chopped
²/₃ cup white wine
1 pound ground chicken
1 tablespoon dried basil
1 tablespoon dried thyme
³/₄ cup fresh white bread crumbs
salt and freshly ground
   black pepper

For the sauce
2 tablespoons low-fat margarine
2¹/₄ cups all-purpose flour
1¹/₄ cups skim milk
4 sun-dried tomatoes, chopped
1 tablespoon chopped mixed
   fresh herbs (basil, parsley,
   marjoram)

1 To make the filling, put the garlic, onion and half the wine into a pan. Cover and cook for 5 minutes. Add the chicken and break up with a spoon. Cook until all the liquid has evaporated and the chicken begins to brown, stirring constantly. Add the remaining wine, seasoning and herbs. Cover and simmer for 20 minutes. Remove from heat and stir in the bread crumbs.

2 Cook the lasagne sheets in a large pan of boiling salted water according to the package instructions until *al dente*. Drain and rinse in cold water. Pat dry on a clean dish towel.

3 Spread out the lasagne. Spoon the chicken mixture along one short edge and roll up into a tube. Cut the tubes in half.

4 Preheat the oven to 400°F. To make the sauce, put the margarine, flour and milk into a pan, heat and whisk until thickened. Add the tomatoes and herbs. Season to taste.

5 Spoon a layer of sauce into an ovenproof dish and place a layer of cannelloni on top. Repeat, then sprinkle with Parmesan. Bake for 10–15 minutes. Garnish and serve.

Minty Yogurt Chicken

Marinating skinned chicken in yogurt infused with fresh mint and lime or lemon juice is an excellent way to give it flavor with a minimum of fat.

Serves 4
8 chicken thighs, skinned
1 tablespoon honey
2 tablespoons lime or lemon juice
2 tablespoons plain yogurt
¹/₄ cup chopped fresh mint
salt and freshly ground
   black pepper
boiled new potatoes and tomato
   salad, to serve

1 Slash the flesh of the chicken thighs at intervals with a sharp knife. Place in a bowl.

2 In another small bowl, mix the honey, lime or lemon juice, yogurt, seasoning and half the mint.

3 Spoon the yogurt mixture over the chicken and let marinate for 30 minutes. Preheat the broiler and line a broiler pan with aluminum foil.

4 Cook the chicken under a medium-hot broiler until thoroughly cooked and golden brown, turning occasionally during cooking.

5 Sprinkle the chicken with the remaining mint and serve immediately with new potatoes and tomato salad.

> **Cook's Tip**
> *There are several different types of yogurt. Ordinary plain yogurt is made by adding a culture to full-fat milk. Its fat content varies, but can be as high as 7.5 percent. Low-fat yogurt is made from concentrated skim milk and has a fat content of 0.5–2 percent. Very low-fat yogurt, made from skim milk, contains less than 0.5 percent fat.*

Chicken with Mixed Vegetables

A riot of color, this delectable dish has plenty of contrasts in terms of texture and taste.

Serves 4

12 ounces chicken breast
  fillets, skinned
4 teaspoons vegetable oil
1 ¼ cups Chicken Stock
¾ cup drained, canned straw
  mushrooms
½ cup drained, canned bamboo
  shoots, sliced
⅓ cup drained, canned water
  chestnuts, sliced
1 small carrot, sliced
2 ounces snowpeas
1 tablespoon dry sherry
1 tablespoon oyster sauce
1 teaspoon sugar
1 teaspoon cornstarch
1 tablespoon cold water
salt and freshly ground
  white pepper

1 Put the chicken in a shallow bowl. Add 1 teaspoon of the oil, ¼ teaspoon salt and a pinch of pepper. Cover and set aside for 10 minutes in a cool place.

2 Bring the stock to a boil in a saucepan. Add the chicken and cook for 12 minutes or until tender. Drain, reserving 5 tablespoons of the stock. Slice the chicken.

3 Heat the remaining oil in a nonstick frying pan or wok, add all the vegetables and stir-fry for 2 minutes. Stir in the sherry, oyster sauce, sugar and reserved stock. Add the chicken to the pan and cook for 2 more minutes.

4 Mix the cornstarch to a smooth, thin paste with the water. Add the mixture to the pan and cook, stirring constantly, until the sauce thickens slightly. Season to taste with salt and pepper, and serve immediately.

Cook's Tip
Popular in Chinese and Southeast Asian cuisine, straw mushrooms are valued less for their flavor than for their slippery texture.

Chicken Baked with Lima Beans & Garlic

A one-pot meal that combines chicken with leeks, fennel and garlic-flavored lima beans.

Serves 6

2 leeks
1 small fennel bulb
4 garlic cloves
2 14-ounce cans lima beans,
  drained and rinsed
2 large handfuls fresh
  parsley, chopped
1 ¼ cups dry white wine
1 ¼ cups vegetable stock
3 ½-pound chicken
fresh parsley sprigs, to garnish
lightly cooked green vegetables,
  to serve

1 Preheat the oven to 350°F. Slit the leeks, wash out any grit, then slice them thickly. Cut the fennel into quarters, remove the core and chop the flesh roughly. Peel the garlic cloves, leaving them whole.

2 Mix the leeks, fennel, whole garlic cloves, lima beans and parsley in a bowl. Spread out the mixture on the bottom of a heavy flameproof casserole that is large enough to hold the chicken. Pour in the white wine and vegetable stock, and stir well.

3 Place the chicken on top of the vegetable mixture. Bring to a boil, cover the casserole and transfer it to the oven. Bake for 1–1½ hours, until the chicken is cooked and so tender that it falls off the bone. Garnish with parsley and serve with lightly cooked green vegetables.

Cook's Tip
Stock can be made with almost any vegetables, but not green leafy ones. Add a few fresh herbs, garlic and a strip of lemon zest, cover with water and simmer for about 30 minutes.

Two-way Chicken with Vegetables

This tender, slow-cooked chicken makes a tasty lunch or supper, with the stock and remaining vegetables providing a nourishing soup for a second meal.

Serves 6
3½-pound chicken
2 onions, quartered
3 carrots, thickly sliced
2 celery stalks, chopped
1 parsnip or turnip, thickly sliced
¾ cup button mushrooms, with
   stalks, roughly chopped
1–2 fresh thyme sprigs or
   1 teaspoon dried thyme
4 bay leaves
large bunch of fresh parsley
1 cup whole-wheat
   pasta shapes
salt and freshly ground
   black pepper
cooked new potatoes or pasta
   and snowpeas or green beans,
   to serve (optional)

1 Trim the chicken of any extra fat. Put it into a flameproof casserole and add the vegetables and herbs. Pour in sufficient water to cover. Bring to a boil over medium heat, skimming off any scum. When the water boils, lower the heat and simmer for 2–3 hours.

2 Lift the chicken out of the stock and carve the meat neatly, discarding the skin and bones, and returning any small pieces of meat to the pan. Serve the chicken with some of the vegetables from the pan, plus new potatoes or pasta and snowpeas or green beans, if desired.

3 Remove the bay leaves and any large pieces of parsley and thyme from the pan, and discard. Set the remaining mixture aside to cool, then chill it overnight in the refrigerator. Next day, lift off the fat that has solidified on the surface. Reheat the soup over low heat.

4 When the soup comes to a boil, add the pasta shapes, with salt if required, and cook for 10–12 minutes or until the pasta is *al dente*. Adjust the seasoning to taste, and serve.

Chicken Kiev with Ricotta

Cut through the crispy-coated chicken to reveal a creamy filling with just a hint of garlic—proof that a lower-fat chicken Kiev can be delicious.

Serves 4
4 large chicken breast
   fillets, skinned
1 tablespoon lemon juice
½ cup ricotta cheese
1 garlic clove, crushed
2 tablespoons chopped
   fresh parsley
¼ teaspoon grated nutmeg
2 tablespoons all-purpose flour
pinch of cayenne pepper
¼ teaspoon salt
2 egg whites, lightly beaten
2 cups fresh white bread crumbs
duchesse potatoes, green beans
   and broiled tomatoes, to serve

1 Place the chicken breasts between two sheets of plastic wrap and gently beat with a meat mallet or rolling pin until flattened. Sprinkle with the lemon juice.

2 Mix the ricotta cheese with the garlic, 1 tablespoon of the parsley and the nutmeg. Shape into four 2-inch long cylinders. Put one portion of the cheese and herb mixture in the center of each chicken breast and fold the meat over, tucking in the edges to enclose the filling completely. Secure the chicken with wooden toothpicks pushed through the center of each.

3 Combine the flour, cayenne pepper and salt on a plate. Place the egg whites in a bowl. Combine the bread crumbs and remaining parsley on another plate.

4 Dust the chicken with the seasoned flour, dip into the egg whites, then coat with the bread crumbs. Chill for 30 minutes in the refrigerator. Preheat the oven to 400°F. Dip the chicken into the egg white and bread crumbs for a second time.

5 Put the chicken on a nonstick baking sheet and spray with nonstick cooking spray. Bake for 25 minutes or until the coating is golden brown and the chicken completely cooked. Remove the toothpicks, and serve with duchesse potatoes, green beans and broiled tomatoes.

Chicken in Creamy Orange Sauce

This sauce is deceptively creamy—in fact it is made with low-fat fromage frais, which is virtually fat-free. The brandy adds a richer flavor, but is optional—omit it if you prefer and use orange juice alone.

Serves 4

8 chicken thighs or
   drumsticks, skinned
3 tablespoons brandy
1 ¼ cups orange juice
3 scallions, chopped
2 teaspoons cornstarch
6 tablespoons low-fat
   fromage frais
salt and freshly ground
   black pepper
boiled rice or pasta and
   green salad, to serve

1 Fry the chicken pieces without fat in a nonstick or heavy pan, turning until evenly browned.

2 Stir in the brandy, orange juice and scallions. Bring to a boil, then cover and simmer for 15 minutes or until the chicken is tender and the juices run clear, not pink, when the thickest part is pierced with a skewer or knife.

3 In a small bowl, blend the cornstarch with a little water, then mix into the fromage frais. Stir this into the sauce and stir over medium heat until boiling.

4 Adjust the seasoning to taste, and serve with boiled rice or pasta and green salad.

Cook's Tip
Adding a thin cornstarch paste to the fromage frais stabilizes it and helps prevent it from curdling. This is also a good technique with yogurt, which will also curdle if it is added to a dish that is going to be boiled.

Oat-crusted Chicken with Sage

A smooth sauce, lightly flavored with sage, makes a fine contrast to the crunchy oats coating these tender chicken pieces.

Serves 4

3 tablespoons skim milk
2 teaspoons English mustard
½ cup rolled oats
3 tablespoons chopped fresh sage
8 chicken thighs or
   drumsticks, skinned
½ cup low-fat
   fromage frais
1 teaspoon whole-grain mustard
salt and freshly ground
   black pepper
fresh sage leaves, to garnish

1 Preheat the oven to 400°F. Combine the milk and English mustard in a small bowl.

2 Mix the oats with 2 tablespoons of the chopped sage, and salt and freshly ground black pepper to taste on a plate. Brush the chicken with the milk and press into the oats to coat evenly.

3 Place the chicken on a baking sheet and bake for about 40 minutes or until the juices run clear, not pink, when the meat is pierced through the thickest part with a skewer or the point of a knife.

4 Meanwhile, in a bowl, combine the low-fat fromage frais, whole-grain mustard, the remaining sage and seasoning. Garnish the chicken with fresh sage and serve hot or cold, accompanied by the mustard sauce.

Cook's Tip
If fresh sage is not available, choose another fresh herb such as thyme or parsley, instead of using a dried alternative. Although sage can be dried successfully, unlike some herbs, it quickly loses its volatile aromatic oils and becomes very crumbly and dusty with little flavor.

Chicken & Bean Casserole

A delicious combination of chicken, fresh tarragon and mixed beans, topped with a layer of tender potatoes.

Serves 6
2 pounds potatoes
½ cup reduced-fat aged
    Cheddar cheese, finely grated
2½ cups plus 2–3 tablespoons
    skim milk
2 tablespoons snipped
    fresh chives
2 leeks, sliced
1 onion, sliced

2 tablespoons dry white wine
3 tablespoons low-fat spread
⅓ cup all-purpose flour
1¼ cups Chicken Stock
12 ounces cooked skinless chicken
    breast fillet, diced
3 cups brown-cap mushrooms,
    sliced
11-ounce can red kidney beans
14-ounce can small cannellini
    beans
14-ounce can black-eyed peas
2–3 tablespoons chopped
    fresh tarragon
salt and freshly ground
    black pepper

1 Preheat the oven to 400°F. Cut the potatoes into chunks and cook in boiling salted water for 15–20 minutes. Drain and mash. Add the cheese, 2–3 tablespoons milk and the chives, season and mix well. Set aside and keep warm.

2 Meanwhile, put the leeks and onion in a saucepan with the wine. Cover and cook gently for 10 minutes, until the vegetables are just tender, stirring occasionally.

3 Put the low-fat spread, flour, remaining milk and the stock in another pan. Heat gently, whisking, until the sauce boils and thickens. Simmer for 3 minutes, stirring. Remove the pan from heat and stir in the leek mixture, chicken and mushrooms.

4 Drain and rinse all the canned beans. Stir into the sauce with the tarragon and seasoning. Heat gently, stirring, until piping hot.

5 Transfer the mixture to an ovenproof dish and spoon or pipe the mashed potatoes on top. Bake for about 30 minutes until the potato topping is crisp and golden brown, and serve.

Chicken with an Herb Crust

The chicken breasts can be brushed with melted low-fat spread instead of Dijon mustard before being coated in the bread crumb mixture, if you prefer.

Serves 4
4 chicken breast fillets, skinned
a little oil, for greasing
1 tablespoon Dijon mustard
2 tablespoons chopped fresh parsley
1 cup fresh bread crumbs
1 tablespoon dried mixed herbs
2 tablespoons low-fat spread,
    melted
salt and freshly ground
    black pepper
boiled new potatoes and salad,
    to serve

1 Preheat the oven to 350°F. Lay the chicken breast fillets in a single layer in a greased ovenproof dish and spread with the mustard. Season with salt and pepper.

2 In a bowl, combine the parsley, bread crumbs and dried mixed herbs thoroughly.

3 Sprinkle the bread crumb mixture on the chicken to coat it and press in well. Spoon on the low-fat spread.

4 Bake uncovered, for 20 minutes or until the chicken is tender and the topping is crisp. Serve with new potatoes and salad.

Cook's Tip
Dijon mustard is made from black mustard seeds, spices and white wine. It has a clean, medium-hot flavor and a creamy texture. It is the type most widely used in cooking. However, if you prefer a hotter taste, you could use English mustard or for a sweet-sour flavor, use German mustard. American mustard is very mild and quite sweet.

Tuscan Chicken

This simple peasant casserole has all the flavors of traditional Tuscan ingredients. The wine can be replaced by chicken stock.

Serves 4
8 chicken thighs, skinned
1 teaspoon olive oil
1 medium onion, thinly sliced
2 red bell peppers, seeded and sliced
1 garlic clove, crushed
1¼ cups passata
⅔ cup dry white wine
1 large fresh oregano sprig or 1 teaspoon dried oregano
14-ounce can cannellini beans, drained and rinsed
3 tablespoons fresh bread crumbs
salt and freshly ground black pepper

1 Fry the chicken in the oil in a large nonstick or heavy frying pan until golden brown. Remove from the pan, set aside and keep hot.

2 Add the onion and peppers to the pan, and gently sauté until softened but not brown. Stir in the garlic.

3 Return the chicken to the pan, and add the passata, wine and oregano. Season well, bring to a boil, then cover the pan tightly. Lower the heat and simmer gently, stirring occasionally, for 30–35 minutes or until the chicken is tender and the juices run clear, not pink, when the thickest part is pierced with the point of a knife or skewer.

4 Stir in the cannellini beans and simmer for another 5 minutes, until heated through. Sprinkle with the bread crumbs and cook under a hot broiler until golden brown.

> **Cook's Tip**
> Passata is a pasteurized, sieved tomato sauce which, unlike tomato paste, has not been concentrated. It has a fine, full flavor, as it is usually made from sun-ripened tomatoes. It is available in bottles and cans at most supermarkets.

Chicken with Orange & Mustard Sauce

The beauty of this recipe is its simplicity; the chicken breasts continue to cook in their own juices while you prepare the sauce.

Serves 4
2 large oranges
4 chicken breast fillets, skinned
1 teaspoon sunflower oil
salt and freshly ground black pepper
new potatoes and sliced zucchini tossed in parsley, to serve

For the orange and mustard sauce
2 teaspoons cornstarch
⅔ cup plain low-fat yogurt
1 teaspoon Dijon mustard

1 Peel the oranges using a sharp knife, removing all the white pith. Remove the segments by cutting between the membranes, holding the fruit over a small bowl to catch any juice. Set aside with the juice until required.

2 Season the chicken with salt and pepper to taste. Heat the sunflower oil in a nonstick frying pan, add the chicken and cook for 5 minutes on each side. Remove the chicken from the frying pan and wrap it in aluminum foil; the meat will continue to cook for a while.

3 To make the orange and mustard sauce, blend the cornstarch with the juice from the orange into a smooth paste. Add the yogurt and mustard, and mix well. Pour the mixture into the frying pan and bring to a boil over low heat. Simmer for 1 minute.

4 Add the orange segments to the sauce and heat gently. Unwrap the chicken and add any excess juices to the sauce. Slice the chicken on the diagonal and serve with the sauce, new potatoes and sliced zucchini tossed in parsley.

Chicken Provençal

A richly flavored dish in which the chicken and vegetables are simmered slowly together until wonderfully tender.

Serves 4

1 medium eggplant, diced
2 teaspoons olive oil
8 chicken thighs, skinned
1 medium red onion, cut
   into wedges
1 green bell pepper, seeded and
   thickly sliced
2 garlic cloves, sliced
1 small fresh green chile, sliced
2 zucchini, thickly sliced
2 beefsteak tomatoes, cut
   into wedges
1 bouquet garni
salt and freshly ground
   black pepper

1 Sprinkle the eggplant with salt, then let drain for 30 minutes. Rinse and pat dry with paper towels.

2 Heat the oil in a large, nonstick pan and fry the chicken until golden. Add the eggplant, onion, green pepper and garlic, and cook gently until the vegetables are soft.

3 Add the chile, zucchini, tomatoes, bouquet garni and seasoning. Cover tightly and cook over low heat for 25–30 minutes, until the chicken and vegetables are tender. Remove the bouquet garni and serve immediately.

Cook's Tip
In the past, it was always necessary to sprinkle eggplant with salt to remove the bitter and unpalatable juices—a process known as degorging. Modern varieties, especially those grown under glass, have been selectively bred so that this is rarely essential. Nevertheless, it is worth doing if the eggplant is to be fried, as dégorging helps to reduce the amount of oil absorbed and improves the texture. Always rinse the eggplant thoroughly to get rid of all traces of salt and then pat dry before using. Baby eggplant never need salting.

Caribbean Ginger Chicken

Pineapple helps to keep the chicken moist during cooking, as well as providing flavor along with the other ingredients, without the addition of any fat. Pineapple also contains an enzyme that helps to tenderize meat.

Serves 4

4 chicken breasts, skinned
½ small fresh pineapple, peeled
   and sliced
2 scallions, chopped
2 tablespoons chopped fresh
   ginger root
1 garlic clove, crushed
1 tablespoon dark
   brown sugar
1 tablespoon lime juice
1 teaspoon hot pepper sauce
1 teaspoon tomato paste
salt and freshly ground
   black pepper
cooked plain and wild rice, and
   salad, to serve

1 Preheat the oven to 400°F. Slash the chicken at intervals with a sharp knife. Place in an ovenproof dish with the pineapple slices.

2 In a bowl, combine the scallions, ginger, garlic, sugar, lime juice, pepper sauce, tomato paste, salt and pepper. Spread the mixture on the chicken.

3 Cover and bake for 30 minutes or until the chicken juices run clear when the thickest part is pierced with a skewer or knife. Serve with plain and wild rice, and salad.

Cook's Tip
To prepare fresh pineapple, cut off the green spiky top and take a thin slice from the base, so that it will stand upright. Using a sharp, long-bladed knife, cut off the skin downward in wide strips. Carefully remove the hard brown "eyes" from the pineapple flesh with the point of the knife. Cut the flesh into slices, then remove the woody core from each slice with a knife.

Yakitori Chicken

These Japanese-style kebabs are easy to eat and ideal for grills or parties. Make extra yakitori sauce if you would like to serve it with the kebabs. For an authentic touch, serve the kebabs with *shichimi*—seven-spice flavor, usually made from ground chile, anise pepper, sesame seeds, rape seeds, poppy seeds, dried citrus peel and ground nori seaweed.

Serves 4
6 boneless chicken thighs, skinned
1 bunch scallions
shichimi (seven-flavor spice), to
    serve (optional)

For the yakitori sauce
²/₃ cup Japanese soy sauce
½ cup sugar
1½ tablespoons sake or
    dry white wine
1 tablespoon all-purpose flour

1 To make the sauce, stir the soy sauce, sugar and sake or wine into the flour in a small saucepan and bring to a boil, stirring. Lower the heat and simmer the mixture for 10 minutes, until the sauce is reduced by a third. Set aside.

2 Cut the chicken into bite-size pieces. Cut the scallions into 1¼-inch pieces. Preheat the broiler or prepare the grill.

3 Thread the chicken and scallions alternately onto 12 bamboo skewers. Broil under medium heat or cook on the grill for 5–10 minutes, until the chicken is cooked but still moist, brushing generously several times with the sauce.

4 Serve with a little extra yakitori sauce, offering shichimi with the kebabs if desired.

> **Cook's Tip**
> *There are several types of Japanese soy sauce—shoyu. Tamari is a thick, mellow-flavored sauce that is a popular choice for dips. Usukuchi is lighter, but quite salty. Do not substitute Chinese soy sauce, as it is much stronger than Japanese.*

Chicken Couscous

This simple-to-prepare dish has a low fat content and needs no accompaniment.

Serves 4
1⅓ cups couscous
4 cups boiling water
1 teaspoon olive oil
14 ounces skinless boneless
    chicken, diced
1 yellow bell pepper, seeded
    and sliced
2 large zucchinis, thickly sliced
1 small fresh green chile, thinly
    sliced, or 1 teaspoon chili sauce
1 large tomato, diced
15-ounce can chickpeas,
    drained and rinsed
salt and freshly ground
    black pepper
cilantro or parsley sprigs,
    to garnish

1 Place the couscous in a large bowl and pour in the boiling water. Cover and let stand for 30 minutes.

2 Heat the oil in a large, nonstick pan and stir-fry the chicken quickly to seal, then reduce the heat.

3 Stir in the yellow pepper, zucchini and fresh chile or chili sauce and cook for 10 minutes, until the vegetables are softened, stirring frequently.

4 Add the tomato and chickpeas, followed by the couscous. Adjust the seasoning to taste and stir over medium heat until heated through.

5 Transfer to a serving platter, garnish with sprigs of cilantro or parsley and serve hot.

> **Variation**
> *For a spicier dish, add ½ teaspoon each ground coriander, paprika, ground cumin, ground turmeric and ground cinnamon, together with ⅔ cup golden raisins, with the vegetables in step 3.*

Moroccan Spiced Roast Poussins

A flavorful stuffing of rice, apricots and fresh mint keeps these baby chickens moist inside, while a coating of spicy yogurt does the same outside.

Serves 4

scant ½ cup cooked long-grain rice
1 small onion, finely chopped
finely grated zest and juice of
   1 lemon
2 tablespoons chopped fresh mint

3 tablespoons chopped
   dried apricots
2 tablespoons plain yogurt
2 teaspoons ground turmeric
2 teaspoons ground cumin
2 1-pound poussins
salt and freshly ground
   black pepper
lemon slices and fresh mint
   sprigs, to garnish
cooked rice and wild rice, to serve

1 Preheat the oven to 400°F. Combine the rice, onion, lemon zest, mint and apricots. Stir in half each of the lemon juice, yogurt, turmeric and cumin. Season to taste with salt and pepper.

2 Stuff the poussins with the rice mixture at the neck end only. Any spare stuffing can be cooked with the chicken in aluminum foil parcels and served separately. Place the poussins on a rack in a roasting pan.

3 In a small bowl, combine the remaining lemon juice, yogurt, turmeric and cumin, then brush this mixture all over the poussins. Cover them loosely with foil and bake for 30 minutes.

4 Remove the foil and roast the poussins for another 15 minutes or until they are golden brown and the juices run clear when the thickest part of the thigh is pierced with a skewer or the point of a knife.

5 Cut the poussins in half with a knife or poultry shears. Transfer to serving plates, garnish with the lemon slices and mint, and serve with the reserved rice stuffing and mixed rice.

Curried Chicken Salad

The chicken is tossed in a curried yogurt dressing and served on a colorful bed of pasta and vegetables.

Serves 4

2 cooked chicken breast fillets
6 ounces green beans
3 cups multi-colored penne
⅔ cup plain low-fat yogurt
1 teaspoon mild curry powder
1 garlic clove, crushed

1 fresh green chile, seeded and
   finely chopped
2 tablespoons chopped cilantro
4 firm ripe tomatoes, peeled,
   seeded and cut into strips
salt and freshly ground
   black pepper
cilantro leaves, to garnish

1 Remove the skin from the chicken and cut the meat into strips. Cut the beans into 1-inch lengths and cook in boiling water for 5 minutes. Drain and rinse under cold water.

2 Cook the pasta in a large pan of boiling salted water according to the package instructions until al dente. Drain and rinse thoroughly.

3 Combine the yogurt, curry powder, garlic, chile and chopped cilantro in a bowl. Stir in the chicken pieces and let stand for 30 minutes.

4 Transfer the pasta to a large glass bowl and toss with the beans and tomatoes. Spoon on the chicken and sauce. Garnish with cilantro leaves and serve.

> **Variations**
> *For herbed chicken salad, substitute 2 tablespoons each finely chopped fresh parsley and watercress and 3 finely chopped scallions for the curry powder, chile and cilantro. For lemon chicken salad, substitute the juice of ½ lemon, 1 bunch snipped chives and 2 tablespoons finely chopped fresh mixed herbs for the same ingredients and omit the garlic.*

Gingered Chicken Noodles

A blend of ginger, spices and coconut milk flavors this delicious supper dish, which is made in minutes. For a real Asian touch, add a little fish sauce to taste, just before serving.

Serves 4

12 ounces chicken breast
 fillet, skinned
8 ounces zucchini
10 ounces eggplant
2 teaspoons oil
2-inch piece fresh ginger root,
 finely chopped

6 scallions, sliced
2 teaspoons Thai green
 curry paste
1²⁄₃ cups coconut milk
2 cups Chicken Stock
4 ounces medium egg noodles
3 tablespoons chopped cilantro,
 plus extra to garnish
1 tablespoon lemon juice
salt and freshly ground
 black pepper

1 Cut the chicken into bite-size pieces. Cut the zucchini in half lengthwise and roughly chop them. Cut the eggplant into similar-size pieces.

2 Heat half the oil in a large, nonstick saucepan. Add the chicken and fry over medium heat, stirring frequently, until golden all over. Remove from the pan using a slotted spoon and drain well on paper towels.

3 Add the remaining oil to the pan and cook the ginger and scallions, stirring frequently, for 3 minutes. Add the zucchini and cook for 2–3 minutes or until they are beginning to turn golden. Stir in the curry paste and cook over low heat for 1 minute.

4 Add the coconut milk, stock, eggplant and chicken, and simmer for 10 minutes. Add the noodles and cook for another 5 minutes or until the chicken is cooked and the noodles are tender. Stir in the cilantro and lemon juice, and adjust the seasoning to taste. Serve, garnished with more cilantro.

Chicken with Pineapple

This chicken has a delicate tang. The pineapple not only tenderizes the chicken, but also gives it a hint of sweetness.

Serves 6

1 cup canned pineapple, in
 natural juice
1 teaspoon ground cumin
1 teaspoon ground coriander
¹⁄₂ teaspoon crushed garlic
1 teaspoon chili powder
1 teaspoon salt

2 tablespoons plain low-fat yogurt
1 tablespoon chopped cilantro
a few drops of orange
 food coloring
10 ounces boneless
 chicken, skinned
¹⁄₂ red bell pepper
¹⁄₂ yellow or green bell pepper
1 large onion, chopped
6 cherry tomatoes
1 tablespoon vegetable oil
salad, to serve

1 Drain the pineapple juice into a bowl. Reserve eight chunks of pineapple and squeeze the juice from the remaining chunks into the bowl and set aside. You should have about ¹⁄₂ cup pineapple juice.

2 In a large mixing bowl, blend the cumin, ground coriander, garlic, chili powder, salt, yogurt, cilantro and food coloring. Pour in the reserved pineapple juice and mix well.

3 Cut the chicken into bite-size cubes, add to the yogurt and spice mixture, and let marinate for 1–1¹⁄₂ hours.

4 Cut the peppers into bite-size chunks, discarding the seeds.

5 Preheat the broiler to medium. Arrange the chicken pieces, peppers, onion, tomatoes and reserved pineapple chunks alternately on six wooden or metal skewers.

6 Brush the kebabs with the oil, then place the skewers on a flameproof dish or in a broiler pan. Grill, turning and basting the chicken with the marinade regularly, for about 15 minutes. Serve with salad.

Chicken Tikka

The red food coloring gives this dish its traditional bright color. Serve with lemon wedges.

Serves 4

3¹/₂-pound chicken
mixed salad greens, e.g. frisée and
    oakleaf lettuce or radicchio, and
    lemon wedges, to serve

For the marinade

²/₃ cup plain low-fat yogurt
1 teaspoon ground paprika
2 teaspoons grated fresh
    ginger root
1 garlic clove, crushed
2 teaspoons garam masala
¹/₂ teaspoon salt
red food coloring (optional)
juice of 1 lemon

1 Joint the chicken and cut it into eight pieces, using a sharp knife.

2 To make the marinade, mix all the ingredients in a large dish. Add the chicken pieces and turn to coat them thoroughly. Chill for 4 hours or overnight to let the flavors penetrate the flesh.

3 Preheat the oven to 400°F. Remove the chicken pieces from the marinade and arrange them in a single layer in a large, ovenproof dish. Bake for 30–40 minutes or until tender, basting with a little of the marinade while cooking.

4 Arrange the chicken on a bed of salad greens and serve hot or cold with lemon wedges for squeezing.

Cook's Tip

Poppadums can be a healthy accompaniment to a low-fat Indian meal. Instead of frying them, put them, one at a time, on the turntable of a microwave oven and cook on HIGH for 40–60 seconds. They will not be as crisp as fried poppadums, but will they still be crisp—and much healthier.

Tandoori Chicken

Although the authentic tandoori flavor is very difficult to achieve in conventional ovens, this low-fat version still makes a very tasty dish.

Serves 4

4 chicken quarters
³/₄ cup plain low-fat yogurt
1 teaspoon garam masala
1 teaspoon grated fresh
    ginger root

1 teaspoon crushed garlic
1¹/₂ teaspoons chili powder
¹/₄ teaspoon ground turmeric
1 teaspoon ground coriander
1 tablespoon lemon juice
1 teaspoon salt
a few drops of red food coloring
1 tablespoon corn oil

For the garnish

mixed salad greens
lime wedges

1 Skin and rinse the chicken quarters, then pat dry with paper towels. Make two slits into the flesh of each piece, place in a dish and set aside.

2 In a bowl, combine the yogurt, garam masala, ginger, garlic, chili powder, turmeric, coriander, lemon juice, salt, red food coloring and oil. Beat well so that all the ingredients are thoroughly combined.

3 Cover the chicken quarters with the yogurt and spice mixture, turning them to coat well and set aside to marinate for about 3 hours.

4 Preheat the oven to 475°F. Transfer the chicken pieces to an ovenproof dish. Bake for 20–25 minutes or until the chicken is cooked right through, browned on top, and the juices run clear when the thickest part is pierced with a skewer or the point of a knife.

5 Remove from the oven and transfer to a serving dish. Garnish with the salad leaves and lime, and serve.

Kashmiri Chicken Curry

This mild yet flavorful dish is given a special lift by the addition of apples.

Serves 4

2 teaspoons corn oil
2 medium onions, diced
1 bay leaf
2 cloves
1-inch piece cinnamon stick
4 black peppercorns
1 baby chicken, about 1½ pounds,
   skinned and cut into 8 pieces
1 teaspoon garam masala
1 teaspoon grated fresh ginger root

1 teaspoon crushed garlic
1 teaspoon salt
1 teaspoon chili powder
1 tablespoon ground almonds
⅔ cup plain low-fat yogurt
2 green apples, peeled, cored and
   roughly sliced
1 tablespoon chopped cilantro
½ ounce sliced almonds, lightly
   toasted, and cilantro leaves,
   to garnish

1 Heat the oil in a nonstick wok or frying pan, and sauté the onions with the bay leaf, cloves, cinnamon and peppercorns for 3–5 minutes. Add the chicken pieces and continue to stir-fry for at least 3 minutes.

2 Lower the heat and add the garam masala, ginger, garlic, salt, chili powder and ground almonds, and continue to stir for 2–3 minutes. Pour in the yogurt and stir over low heat for another 2–3 minutes. Add the apples and chopped cilantro, cover and cook for 10–15 minutes.

3 Check that the chicken is cooked through, and serve immediately, garnished with toasted sliced almonds and whole cilantro leaves.

> **Cook's Tip**
> *While less fat may be required, a wok with a nonstick lining cannot be heated to high temperatures. A well-seasoned cast-iron wok also works in a "nonstick" way.*

Karahi Chicken with Mint

For this tasty dish, the chicken is first boiled before being quickly stir-fried in a little oil, to ensure that it is cooked through despite the short cooking time.

Serves 4

10 ounces chicken breast fillet,
   skinned and cut into strips
1¼ cups water
1 tablespoon oil
2 small bunches scallions,
   roughly chopped

1 teaspoon grated fresh
   ginger root
1 teaspoon crushed dried
   red chiles
2 tablespoons lemon juice
1 tablespoon chopped cilantro
1 tablespoon chopped fresh mint
3 tomatoes, seeded and
   roughly chopped
1 teaspoon salt
fresh mint and cilantro sprigs,
   to garnish

1 Put the chicken and water into a saucepan, bring to a boil and lower the heat to medium. Cook for about 10 minutes or until the water has evaporated and the chicken is cooked. Remove from heat and set aside.

2 Heat the oil in a heavy nonstick frying pan or saucepan and add the scallions. Stir-fry over medium heat for about 2 minutes, until soft and translucent. Add a boiled chicken strips and stir-fry for another 3 minutes over medium heat.

3 Gradually add the ginger, dried chiles, lemon juice, cilantro, mint, tomatoes and salt, and gently stir for a few minutes to blend all the flavors together. Transfer to a serving dish, garnish with mint and cilantro sprigs, and serve immediately.

> **Cook's Tip**
> *If fresh mint is not available, use a jar of mint that has been shredded and preserved in salt and vinegar, rather than the dried herb. Once opened, the jar should be stored in the refrigerator.*

Ground Chicken with Green & Red Chiles

Ground chicken is seldom cooked in Indian or Pakistani homes. However, it works very well in this low-fat recipe.

Serves 4

10 ounces chicken breast fillet, skinned and cubed
2 thick fresh red chiles
3 thick fresh green chiles
2 tablespoons corn oil
6 curry leaves
3 medium onions, sliced
1½ teaspoons crushed garlic
1½ teaspoons ground coriander
1½ teaspoons grated fresh ginger root
1 teaspoon chili powder
1 teaspoon salt
1 tablespoon lemon juice
2 tablespoons chopped cilantro
chapatis and lemon wedges, to serve

1 Place the chicken cubes in a saucepan, cover with water and bring to a boil. Lower the heat and simmer for about 10 minutes, until tender and cooked through. Drain thoroughly. Place the chicken in a food processor and grind.

2 Cut the chiles in half lengthwise and, if desired, remove the seeds. Cut the flesh into strips.

3 Heat the oil in a nonstick wok or frying pan, and sauté the curry leaves and onions until the onions are a soft golden brown. Lower the heat and add the garlic, ground coriander, ginger, chili powder and salt.

4 Add the ground chicken and stir-fry for 3–5 minutes. Add the lemon juice, chile strips and most of the cilantro. Stir for another 3–5 minutes.

5 Transfer to a warmed serving dish and serve immediately, garnished with the remaining cilantro and accompanied by chapatis and lemon wedges.

Chicken Pieces with Cumin & Cilantro Potatoes

The spicy potatoes are cooked separately in the oven first.

Serves 4

⅔ cup plain low-fat yogurt
¼ cup ground almonds
1½ teaspoons ground coriander
½ teaspoon chili powder
1 teaspoon garam masala
1 tablespoon coconut milk
1 teaspoon crushed garlic
1 teaspoon grated fresh ginger root
2 tablespoons chopped cilantro
1 fresh red chile, seeded and chopped
8 ounces chicken breast fillet, skinned and cubed
1 tablespoon corn oil
2 medium onions, sliced
3 green cardamom pods
1-inch piece cinnamon stick
2 cloves

For the potatoes

1 tablespoon corn oil
8 baby potatoes, thickly sliced
¼ teaspoon cumin seeds
1 tablespoon finely chopped cilantro

1 In a bowl, combine the yogurt, ground almonds, ground coriander, chili powder, garam masala, coconut milk, garlic, ginger, half the cilantro and half the chile. Add the chicken cubes, mix well and let marinate for 2 hours.

2 Meanwhile, for the potatoes, preheat the oven to 350°F. Heat the oil in a nonstick wok or frying pan and stir-fry the potatoes, cumin seeds and coriander for 2–3 minutes. Transfer to an ovenproof dish, cover and cook in the oven for about 30 minutes or until the potatoes are cooked through.

3 Increase the oven temperature to 400°F. Wipe out the wok or frying pan and add the oil with the onions, cardamoms, cinnamon and cloves. Heat for about 1½ minutes. Pour the chicken mixture into the onions and stir-fry for 5–7 minutes. Lower the heat, cover and cook gently for another 5–7 minutes. Serve, topped with the cooked potatoes, and garnished with the remaining chopped cilantro and red chile.

Spicy Masala Chicken

These broiled chicken
pieces have a sweet-and-
sour taste. They can be
served either hot or cold.

Serves 6
12 chicken thighs, skinned
6 tablespoons lemon juice
1 teaspoon grated fresh
   ginger root
1 teaspoon crushed garlic

1 teaspoon crushed dried red chiles
1 teaspoon salt
1 teaspoon brown sugar
2 tablespoons honey
2 tablespoons chopped cilantro
1 fresh green chile, finely chopped
2 tablespoons vegetable oil
cilantro sprigs, to garnish
boiled rice and salad,
   to serve

1 Prick the chicken thighs with a fork. Rinse them in cold water,
pat dry with paper towels and set aside in a bowl.

2 In a large mixing bowl, thoroughly combine the lemon juice,
grated ginger, garlic, crushed dried red chiles, salt, brown sugar
and honey.

3 Transfer the chicken thighs to the spice mixture, turning to
coat all over. Set aside in a cool place to marinate for about
45 minutes.

4 Preheat the broiler to medium. Add the chopped cilantro and
fresh green chile to the chicken thighs, and place them in a
flameproof dish.

5 Pour any remaining marinade onto the chicken and baste
with the oil, using a pastry brush.

6 Broil the chicken thighs for 15–20 minutes, turning and
basting with the oil occasionally, until golden brown and the
juices run clear when the thickest part is pierced with a skewer
or the point of a knife.

7 Transfer to a serving dish, garnish with cilantro sprigs and
serve with rice and salad.

Hot Chicken Curry

This curry has a delicious,
thick sauce and is made
using red and green bell
peppers for extra color. It
can be served with either
chapatis or plain rice.

Serves 4
2 tablespoons corn oil
1/4 teaspoon fenugreek seeds
1/4 teaspoon onion seeds
2 medium onions, chopped
1/2 teaspoon crushed garlic
1/2 teaspoon grated fresh
   ginger root

1 teaspoon ground coriander
1 teaspoon chili powder
1 teaspoon salt
1 4-ounce can tomatoes
2 tablespoons lemon juice
12 ounces skinless boneless
   chicken, cubed
2 tablespoons chopped cilantro
3 fresh green chiles, chopped
1/2 red bell pepper, seeded and
   cut into chunks
1/2 green bell pepper, seeded and
   cut into chunks
cilantro sprigs, to garnish

1 Heat the oil in a heavy saucepan, and fry the fenugreek and
onion seeds until they turn a shade darker. Add the onions,
garlic and ginger, and cook for about 5 minutes, until the onions
turn golden brown.

2 Meanwhile, in a separate bowl, combine the ground coriander,
chili powder, salt, tomatoes and lemon juice. Pour the tomato
mixture into the saucepan and stir-fry over medium heat for
about 3 minutes.

3 Add the chicken cubes and stir-fry for 5–7 minutes. Add the
chopped cilantro, green chiles and chopped peppers. Lower the
heat, cover and simmer for about 10 minutes until the chicken
is cooked. Serve hot, garnished with cilantro sprigs.

Cook's Tip
Known as methi *in Indian, fenugreek seeds look like small, light
brown pebbles and have a pungent smell. It is these seeds that
give curry powder its characteristic aroma.*

Spaghetti with Turkey Ragout

Ground turkey is low in fat and makes a very tasty and economical sauce to serve with spaghetti.

Serves 4

1 pound ground turkey
1 medium onion, diced
1 medium carrot, diced
1 celery stalk, diced
14-ounce can tomatoes
1 tablespoon tomato paste
1 teaspoon dried oregano
2 bay leaves
8 ounces spaghetti
salt and freshly ground
    black pepper

1 In a nonstick pan, dry-fry the turkey and onion until lightly colored. Stir in the carrot and celery and cook, stirring constantly, for 5–8 minutes.

2 Add the tomatoes, tomato paste, oregano, bay leaves and seasoning, and bring to a boil. Cover and simmer gently for 40 minutes, until the turkey is tender and the sauce is reduced.

3 Meanwhile, cook the spaghetti in boiling salted water according to the package instructions until *al dente*. Drain well.

4 Place the spaghetti in a large bowl or on individual plates and spoon the turkey ragout on top. Serve immediately.

Cook's Tip
Always use a large saucepan of lightly salted boiling water for cooking pasta. Allow about 8 cups of water for every 8 ounces of pasta. Start timing it from the moment the water in the pan comes back to a boil after the pasta has been added. Cook dried pasta for 8–12 minutes and fresh pasta for 2–3 minutes, but remember that these are only guidelines. Start testing the pasta to see if it is done by biting a small piece between your front teeth. When it is tender but still firm to the bite, it is ready—al dente. Drain the pasta immediately and do not delay before serving or it will dry out and become sticky and inedible.

Turkey & Pasta Casserole

A sauce of ground and smoked turkey is combined with cooked rigatoni and finished in the oven under a Parmesan cheese topping.

Serves 4

10 ounces ground turkey
5 ounces smoked turkey
    bacon, chopped
1–2 garlic cloves, crushed
1 onion, finely chopped
2 carrots, diced
2 tablespoons concentrated
    tomato paste
1 1/4 cups Chicken Stock
2 cups rigatoni
2 tablespoons grated
    Parmesan cheese
salt and freshly ground
    black pepper

1 Dry-fry the ground turkey in a nonstick saucepan, breaking up any large pieces with a wooden spoon, until it is crumbly and well browned all over.

2 Add the chopped turkey, garlic, onion, carrots, tomato paste, stock and seasoning. Bring to a boil, cover and simmer for 1 hour, until tender.

3 Preheat the oven to 350°F. Cook the pasta in a large pan of boiling salted water according to the package instructions until *al dente*. Drain thoroughly and mix with the turkey sauce.

4 Transfer to a shallow, ovenproof dish and sprinkle with the grated Parmesan cheese. Bake for 20–30 minutes, until lightly browned. Serve hot.

Cook's Tip
Parmesan cheese can be expensive, but as it is strongly flavored, a little goes long way. This is especially true if you use freshly grated aged Parmesan. Reduced-fat versions of traditional cheeses are constantly improving in quality, but, as a rule, do not brown under the broiler, although they melt. If you want a browned topping, mix the cheese with bread crumbs.

Turkey Pastitsio

A traditional Greek pastitsio is a rich, high-fat dish made with ground beef, but this lighter version is just as tasty.

Serves 4–6
1 pound ground turkey
1 large onion, finely chopped
1/4 cup tomato paste
1 cup red wine or Chicken Stock
1 teaspoon ground cinnamon
3 cups macaroni
oil, for greasing

1 1/4 cups skim milk
2 tablespoons low-fat
   sunflower margarine
1/4 cup all-purpose flour
1 teaspoon grated nutmeg
2 tomatoes, sliced
1/4 cup whole-wheat
   bread crumbs
salt and freshly ground
   black pepper
green salad, to serve

1 Preheat the oven to 425°F. Dry-fry the turkey and onion in a nonstick pan over medium heat, stirring constantly, until lightly browned.

2 Stir in the tomato paste, red wine or stock and cinnamon. Season to taste with salt and pepper, then cover and simmer for 5 minutes.

3 Cook the macaroni in boiling salted water according to the package instructions until *al dente*, then drain. Make layers of the macaroni and the meat mixture in a lightly greased, wide, ovenproof dish, ending with a layer of macaroni.

4 Place the milk, margarine and flour in a saucepan, and whisk over medium heat until thickened and smooth. Stir in the nutmeg, and season with salt and pepper to taste.

5 Pour the sauce evenly on the pasta and meat to cover the surface completely. Arrange the tomato slices on top and sprinkle lines of bread crumbs over the surface.

6 Bake for 30–35 minutes or until golden brown and bubbling. Serve hot with a green salad.

Mediterranean Turkey Rolls

Turkey breast steaks have less than 2 percent fat, and they are very quick to cook.

Serves 4
4 thin turkey breast steaks
2 tablespoons Pesto Sauce

1/2 cup large basil leaves
1/2 cup Chicken Stock
1 cup passata
garlic salt and freshly ground
   black pepper
cooked noodles or rice, to serve

1 Place the turkey steaks between two sheets of plastic wrap and beat with a meat mallet or rolling pin until thin. Spread with the pesto sauce. Lay the basil leaves on each steak, then roll them up. Secure with wooden toothpicks.

2 Bring the stock and passata to a boil in a large saucepan. Add the turkey rolls, cover and simmer for 15–20 minutes or until the turkey is cooked through.

3 Adjust the seasoning and remove the toothpicks. Serve the turkey rolls hot with noodles or rice.

Pesto Sauce

A low-fat version of this Italian sauce is quick and easy.

Makes about 8 ounces
1 cup fresh basil leaves
1/2 cup fresh parsley sprigs
1 garlic clove, crushed
1/4 cup pine nuts
1/2 cup cottage cheese
2 tablespoons freshly grated
   Parmesan cheese
salt and freshly ground
   black pepper

1 Process half the herbs, the garlic, pine nuts and cottage cheese in a food processor until smooth.
2 Add the remaining herbs and the Parmesan, season to taste with salt and pepper, and process until all the herbs are finely chopped.

Turkey Tonnato

This low-fat version of the popular Italian dish *vitello tonnato* is garnished with fine strips of sweet red bell pepper instead of the traditional anchovy fillets.

Serves 4

1 pound turkey fillets
1 small onion, sliced
1 bay leaf
4 black peppercorns
1½ cups Chicken Stock
7-ounce can tuna in water, drained

5 tablespoons reduced-fat mayonnaise
2 tablespoons lemon juice
2 red bell peppers, seeded and thinly sliced
about 25 capers, drained
salt
mixed salad and lemon wedges, to serve

1 Put the turkey fillets in a single layer in a large, heavy saucepan. Add the onion, bay leaf, peppercorns and stock. Bring to a boil and reduce the heat. Cover and simmer for about 12 minutes or until the turkey is tender.

2 Turn off the heat and let the turkey cool in the stock, then lift it out with a slotted spoon. Slice thickly and arrange on a serving plate.

3 Boil the stock until reduced to about 5 tablespoons. Strain and set aside to cool.

4 Put the tuna, mayonnaise, lemon juice, 3 tablespoons of the reduced stock and a pinch of salt into a blender or food processor, and process until smooth. Stir in enough of the remaining stock to reduce the sauce to the thickness of heavy cream. Spoon over the turkey.

5 Arrange the strips of red pepper in a lattice pattern on the turkey. Put a caper in the center of each diamond shape. Chill in the refrigerator for 1 hour, then serve with a mixed salad and lemon wedges.

Turkey Picadillo

Using ground turkey rather than beef for this Mexican-style dish makes it much lower in fat. Serve as a filling for soft wheat tortillas or baked potatoes and then top with some plain low-fat yogurt for a tasty meal.

Serves 4

1 tablespoon sunflower oil
1 onion, chopped
1 pound ground turkey
1–2 garlic cloves, crushed
1 fresh green chile, seeded and finely chopped
6 tomatoes, peeled and chopped

1 tablespoon tomato paste
½ teaspoon ground cumin
1 yellow or orange bell pepper, seeded and chopped
⅓ cup raisins
½ cup sliced almonds, toasted
3 tablespoons chopped cilantro
⅔ cup plain low-fat yogurt
2–3 scallions, finely chopped
4 soft tortillas
salt and freshly ground black pepper
shredded lettuce, to serve
lime wedges, to garnish

1 Heat the oil in a large frying pan and add the chopped onion. Cook gently for 5 minutes until soft. Stir in the ground turkey and garlic, and cook gently for another 5 minutes.

2 Add the chile, tomatoes, tomato paste, cumin, yellow or orange pepper and raisins. Cover and cook over low heat for 15 minutes, stirring occasionally and adding a little water if necessary.

3 Stir in the toasted almonds, with about two thirds of the chopped cilantro. Season to taste.

4 Transfer the yogurt to a bowl. Stir in the remaining chopped cilantro and the scallions.

5 Heat the tortillas in a dry frying pan, without oil, for 15–20 seconds. Place some shredded lettuce and turkey mixture on each tortilla, roll up like a pancake and transfer to a plate. Top with a generous spoonful of the yogurt and cilantro mixture, and serve immediately, garnished with lime wedges.

Mandarin Sesame Duck

Duck is a high-fat meat, but it is possible to get rid of a good amount of the fat by cooking it in this way. (If you remove the skin completely, the meat can be dry.) For a special occasion duck breasts are a good choice, though they are more expensive.

Serves 4

4 duck leg or boneless
   breast portions
2 tablespoons light soy sauce
3 tablespoons honey
1 tablespoon sesame seeds
4 mandarin oranges
1 teaspoon cornstarch
salt and freshly ground
   black pepper
lightly cooked snowpeas, carrots
   and bean sprouts, to serve

1 Preheat the oven to 350°F. Prick the duck skin all over. Slash the breast skin (if using) diagonally at intervals.

2 Place the duck on a rack in a roasting pan and roast for 1 hour. Mix 1 tablespoon of the soy sauce with 2 tablespoons of the honey and brush onto the duck. Sprinkle with sesame seeds. Roast for 15–20 minutes, until golden brown.

3 Meanwhile, grate the zest from 1 mandarin and squeeze the juice from 2 of them. Place in a small saucepan. Mix in the cornstarch, then stir in the remaining soy sauce and honey. Heat, stirring, until thickened and clear. Season to taste.

4 Peel and slice the remaining mandarins. Place the duck on individual plates, and top with the mandarin slices and the sauce. Serve with snowpeas, carrots and bean sprouts.

> **Variations**
> If desired, you could substitute black or white poppy seeds for the sesame seeds, satsumas for the mandarin oranges and tamari for the soy sauce.

Udon Pot

A quick and easy Japanese dish, this combines chicken with jumbo shrimp, vegetables and noodles in a flavorful stock.

Serves 4

12 ounces dried udon noodles
1 large carrot, cut into bite-
   size chunks
8 ounces chicken breast fillet or
   boneless thighs, skinned and
   cut into bite-size pieces
8 jumbo shrimp, peeled
   and deveined
4–6 Chinese cabbage leaves, cut
   into short strips

8 shiitake mushrooms,
   stems removed
2 ounces snowpeas
6¼ cups Chicken Stock or
   instant bonito stock
2 tablespoons mirin
soy sauce, to taste

To serve

1 bunch scallions, finely chopped
2 tablespoons grated fresh
   ginger root
lemon wedges
cilantro sprigs
soy sauce

1 Cook the noodles until just tender, following the directions on the package. Drain, rinse under cold water and drain thoroughly again.

2 Blanch the carrot in boiling water for 1 minute, then drain.

3 Spoon the noodles and carrot chunks into a large saucepan or flameproof casserole and arrange the chicken breasts or thighs, shrimp, Chinese cabbage leaves, mushrooms and snowpeas on top.

4 Bring the stock to a boil in another saucepan. Add the mirin and soy sauce to taste. Pour the stock onto the noodles. Cover the pan or casserole, bring to a boil over medium heat, then simmer gently for 5–6 minutes, until all the ingredients are cooked.

5 Transfer to a serving dish and serve with chopped scallions, grated ginger, lemon wedges, cilantro sprigs and a little soy sauce.

Poached Chicken

An organic free-range bird is the best choice for this simply cooked dish.

Serves 4
1 leek, roughly chopped
1 large carrot, roughly chopped
1 celery stalk, roughly chopped
1 medium onion, roughly chopped

3¹/₂-pound chicken
1 tablespoon roughly chopped fresh parsley
2 teaspoons roughly chopped fresh thyme
6 fresh green peppercorns
Mustard Mayonnaise, green salad and lightly cooked baby carrots, to serve

1 Put the leek, carrot, celery and onion in a large saucepan. Place the chicken on top, cover with water and bring to a boil. Remove any scum that comes to the surface.

2 Add the herbs and peppercorns. Simmer gently for 1 hour. Remove from heat and let the chicken cool in the stock.

3 Transfer the chicken to a board or plate and carve, discarding the skin. (Save the stock for another dish.) Arrange the slices on a serving platter. Serve with mustard mayonnaise, green salad and lightly cooked baby carrots.

Mustard Mayonnaise

Homemade mayonnaise is a really special treat.

Makes 1½ cups
2 egg yolks
1–2 tablespoons lemon juice
1–2 tablespoons Dijon mustard
1½ cups olive oil
salt and freshly ground black pepper

1 Process the egg yolks, lemon juice and mustard in a food processor.
2 With the motor running, add the oil, a few drops at a time at first, then in a thin stream. Season to taste with salt and pepper.

Chicken with Lemon Sauce

Succulent chicken with a light, refreshing, lemony sauce and just a hint of lime is a sure winner.

Serves 4
4 chicken breast fillets, skinned
1 teaspoon sesame oil
1 tablespoon dry sherry
1 egg white, lightly beaten
2 tablespoons cornstarch
1 tablespoon vegetable oil

salt and freshly ground white pepper
chopped cilantro leaves, chopped scallions and lemon wedges, to garnish

For the sauce
3 tablespoons lemon juice
2 tablespoons lime cordial
3 tablespoons sugar
2 teaspoons cornstarch
6 tablespoons cold water

1 Arrange the chicken fillets in a single layer in a shallow bowl. Mix the sesame oil with the sherry, and season with salt and pepper. Pour onto the chicken, cover and let marinate for 15 minutes. Combine the egg white and cornstarch. Add the mixture to the chicken and turn to coat thoroughly.

2 Heat the vegetable oil in a heavy frying pan or wok and fry the chicken fillets for about 15 minutes, until they are golden brown on both sides.

3 Meanwhile, to make the sauce, combine all the ingredients in a small pan. Add a pinch of salt. Bring to a boil over low heat, stirring constantly, until the sauce is smooth and has thickened slightly.

4 Cut the chicken into pieces and arrange on a warmed serving plate. Pour on the sauce, garnish with the cilantro leaves, scallions and lemon wedges, and serve.

Variation
You can replace the dry sherry with white port or dry Madeira, if desired.

Chicken with Asparagus

Canned asparagus may be used, but will not need any cooking—simply add at the very end to warm through.

Serves 4

4 large chicken breast
  fillets, skinned
1 tablespoon ground coriander
2 tablespoons olive oil

20 slender asparagus spears, cut
  into 3–4-inch lengths
1¼ cups Chicken Stock
1 tablespoon cornstarch
1 tablespoon lemon juice
salt and freshly ground
  black pepper
1 tablespoon chopped fresh
  parsley, to garnish

1 Divide each chicken breast fillet into two natural pieces. Place each between two sheets of plastic wrap and flatten to a thickness of ¼ inch with a rolling pin. Cut into 1-inch strips diagonally across the fillets. Sprinkle on the ground coriander and toss to coat each piece.

2 Heat the oil in a large frying pan and fry the chicken very quickly in small batches for 3–4 minutes, until lightly colored. Season each batch with a little salt and pepper. Remove from the pan and keep warm while frying the rest of the chicken.

3 Add the asparagus and chicken stock to the pan, and bring to a boil. Cook for another 4–5 minutes or until the asparagus is tender.

4 Mix the cornstarch into a thin paste with a little cold water and stir into the sauce to thicken. Return the chicken to the pan together with the lemon juice. Reheat and then serve immediately, garnished with the chopped parsley.

Cook's Tip
You can use green or white asparagus for this dish, but whichever you choose, the buds should be plump and the stems evenly colored.

Chicken with White Wine, Olives & Garlic

The chicken portions are browned without fat before being simmered in a rich white wine sauce.

Serves 4

3½-pound chicken, cut into
  serving portions
1 onion, sliced
1 tablespoon olive oil

3–5 garlic cloves, to taste, crushed
1 teaspoon dried thyme
2 cups dry white wine
16–18 green olives, pitted
1 bay leaf
1 tablespoon lemon juice
1–2 tablespoons butter
salt and freshly ground
  black pepper

1 Heat a deep, heavy, nonstick frying pan, add the chicken portions, skin-side down, and cook over medium heat for about 10 minutes until browned. Turn the chicken portions and cook for another 5–8 minutes to brown the other side. (Work in batches if necessary.) Transfer the chicken to a plate and set aside.

2 Heat the oil in the same pan. Add the onion and a pinch of salt, and cook for 5 minutes, stirring occasionally until just soft. Add the garlic and thyme, and cook for 1 minute.

3 Add the wine and stir, scraping up any sediment that clings to the bottom of the pan. Bring to a boil and boil for 1 minute. Stir in the green olives.

4 Return the chicken to the pan. Add the bay leaf and season lightly with pepper. Lower the heat, cover and simmer for 20–30 minutes, until the chicken is cooked through.

5 Transfer the chicken portions to a warmed platter. Stir the lemon juice into the sauce. Whisk in the butter, a little at a time, to thicken the sauce slightly. Spoon the sauce onto the chicken and serve immediately.

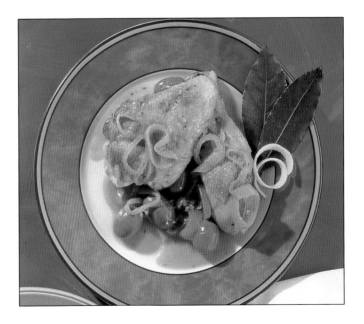

Lemon Chicken with Guacamole Sauce

Guacamole, which is very easy to prepare and looks stunning on the plate, is a great partner for chicken.

Serves 4
juice of 2 lemons
3 tablespoons olive oil
2 garlic cloves, finely chopped
4 chicken breasts,
   about 7 ounces each
2 tomatoes, cored and cut in half

salt and freshly ground
   black pepper
chopped cilantro and frisée
   lettuce, to garnish

For the guacamole sauce
1 ripe avocado
1/4 cup sour cream
3 tablespoons fresh lemon juice
1/2 teaspoon salt
about 1/4 cup water

1 Combine the lemon juice, oil, garlic, 1/2 teaspoon salt and a little pepper in a bowl. Arrange the chicken breasts, in one layer, in a shallow nonmetallic dish. Pour in the lemon mixture and turn to coat evenly. Cover and let marinate for at least 1 hour at room temperature, or chill overnight.

2 To make the sauce, halve the avocado, remove the pit and scrape the flesh into a food processor. Add the sour cream, lemon juice and salt, and process until smooth. Add the water and process to blend. If necessary, add a little more water to thin the sauce. Transfer to a bowl and set aside.

3 Preheat the broiler and heat a ridged frying pan. Remove the chicken breasts from the marinade and pat dry. When the frying pan is hot, add the chicken breasts and cook for about 10 minutes, turning frequently, until they are cooked through.

4 Meanwhile, arrange the tomato halves, cut sides up, on a baking sheet and season lightly. Broil for about 5 minutes, until hot and bubbling.

5 To serve, place a chicken breast, tomato half and a spoonful of sauce on each plate. Garnish with cilantro and lettuce.

Chicken Breasts with Prunes & Almonds

An excellent dish for a winter dinner party. Chicken is cooked in a lightly spiced, fruity sauce that is thickened with ground almonds.

Serves 4
2 tablespoons butter
   or margarine
1 tablespoon vegetable oil
about 2 1/2-pound chicken
   breast halves
3 cups Chicken Stock
3/4 cup raisins
1 tablespoon fresh thyme or
   1 teaspoon dried thyme
3 fresh sage leaves, chopped

3 tablespoons chopped
   fresh parsley
1 tablespoon chopped fresh
   marjoram or 1 teaspoon
   dried marjoram
1 cup fresh bread crumbs
1/2 cup ground almonds
12 prunes, pitted
4–6 cloves
1/2 teaspoon ground mace
pinch of saffron threads, crumbled
salt and freshly ground
   black pepper
1/3 cup sliced almonds, toasted,
   to garnish
lightly cooked zucchini and baby
   carrots, to serve

1 Heat the butter or margarine with the oil in a frying pan. Add the chicken and fry for 10 minutes, until browned on all sides. Transfer the chicken pieces to a large, flameproof casserole.

2 Pour the stock into the casserole and bring to a boil. Add all the remaining ingredients, up to the toasted almonds, and stir well to mix. Simmer over low heat for 45 minutes, until the chicken is tender.

3 Lift the chicken out of the casserole and set aside until cool enough to handle. Bring the cooking liquid back to a boil and boil for about 10 minutes, until well reduced, stirring frequently.

4 Remove the bones from the chicken and return the meat to the sauce. Heat through. Serve, sprinkled with the toasted almonds and accompanied by lightly cooked zucchini and baby carrots.

Chicken with Red Wine Vinegar

This is an easy version of the modern classic invented by a French master chef.

Serves 4
4 chicken breast fillets, about
   7 ounces each, skinned
¼ cup unsalted butter
8–12 shallots, halved

¼ cup red wine vinegar
2 garlic cloves, finely chopped
¼ cup dry white wine
½ cup Chicken Stock
1 tablespoon chopped
   fresh parsley
freshly ground black pepper
green salad, to serve

1 Cut each chicken breast in half crosswise to make 8 pieces. Melt half the butter in a large, heavy frying pan over a medium heat. Add the chicken and cook for 3–5 minutes, until golden brown, turning once, then season with pepper.

2 Add the shallot halves to the pan, cover and cook over low heat for 5–7 minutes, shaking the pan and stirring occasionally.

3 Transfer the chicken pieces to a plate. Add the vinegar to the pan and cook, stirring frequently, for about 1 minute, until the liquid is almost evaporated. Add the garlic, wine and stock, and stir to blend.

4 Return the chicken to the pan with any juices. Cover and simmer for 2–3 minutes, until the chicken is tender.

5 Transfer the chicken and shallots to a serving dish and keep warm. Increase the heat and boil the cooking liquid until it has reduced by half. Remove the pan from heat. Gradually add the remaining butter, whisking until the sauce is slightly thickened and glossy. Stir in the parsley, and pour the sauce over the chicken pieces and shallots. Serve with a green salad.

> **Variation**
> *You could use different flavored vinegars. Try tarragon vinegar and substitute fresh tarragon for the parsley.*

Chicken Cordon Bleu

Perennially popular, this dish consists of breasts of chicken stuffed with smoked ham and Gruyère cheese, then coated in egg and bread crumbs, and fried.

Serves 4
4 chicken breast fillets, about
   3½ ounces each, skinned
4 very thin slices smoked ham,
   halved

about 3½ ounces Gruyère cheese,
   thinly sliced
all-purpose flour, for coating
2 eggs, beaten
generous 1 cup dried
   bread crumbs
1 teaspoon dried thyme
3 tablespoons butter
2 tablespoons olive oil
salt and freshly ground
   black pepper
salad, to serve

1 Slit the chicken breasts about three quarters of the way through, then open them up and lay them flat. Place a slice of ham on each cut side of the chicken, trimming to fit if necessary.

2 Top with the Gruyère slices, making sure that they are well within the ham slices. Fold over the chicken and reshape, pressing well to seal and ensuring that no cheese is visible.

3 Put the flour into a shallow bowl. Pour the beaten eggs into another bowl, and mix the bread crumbs with the thyme and seasoning in a third bowl. Toss each stuffed breast in the flour, then coat in egg and bread crumbs, shaking off any excess. Lay the crumbed breasts flat on a plate, cover and chill for 1 hour.

4 To cook, heat the butter and oil in a frying pan. Slide in the coated breasts, two at a time. Fry over medium-low heat for about 5 minutes on each side, turning carefully with a spatula. Drain on paper towels and keep hot while you cook the remaining breasts. Serve with a side salad.

> **Variation**
> *Instead of Gruyère, try one of the herb-flavored hard cheeses, such as Gloucester with chives.*

Chicken Breasts with Grapes

Reducing the sauce is important for really concentrating the flavor, so take the time to do this fully before adding the cream.

Serves 4

4 chicken breast fillets, about 7 ounces each, well trimmed
2 tablespoons butter
I large or 2 small shallots, chopped
½ cup dry white wine
I cup Chicken Stock
½ cup whipping cream
5 ounces seedless green grapes
salt and freshly ground black pepper
fresh parsley sprigs, to garnish

I Season the chicken breast fillets. Melt half the butter in a frying pan over medium-high heat and cook the chicken for 4–5 minutes on each side, until golden.

2 Transfer the chicken to a plate and cover to keep warm. Add the remaining butter to the pan and sauté the shallots until just softened, stirring frequently.

3 Add the wine, bring to a boil and boil to reduce by half, then add the stock and continue boiling to reduce by half again.

4 Add the cream to the sauce, bring back to a boil and pour in any juices from the chicken. Add the grapes and cook gently for 5 minutes. Slice the chicken and serve with the sauce, garnished with parsley.

> **Variation**
> This recipe also works well with poussins. Cook 4 poussins and the shallots as in steps I and 2 in a flameproof casserole. After adding the wine and stock in step 3, return the poussins to the casserole and simmer for 20–25 minutes. Transfer to a serving platter and finish the sauce as above.

Tarragon Chicken Breasts

The original version of this dish, created in France, uses a whole chicken, but boneless breasts are quick to cook and elegant. The combination of dried and fresh tarragon makes a wonderfully aromatic sauce.

about 1¼ cups Chicken Stock
I tablespoon dried tarragon
I garlic clove, finely chopped
¾ cup whipping cream
I tablespoon chopped fresh tarragon
salt and freshly ground black pepper
fresh tarragon sprigs, to garnish

Serves 4

4 chicken breast fillets, about 5–6 ounces each, skinned
½ cup dry white wine

I Season the chicken breast fillets lightly with salt and pepper, and put them in a saucepan just large enough to hold them in one layer. Pour in the wine and stock, adding more stock to cover, if necessary, then add the dried tarragon and garlic.

2 Bring the stock just to a simmer over medium heat and cook gently for 8–10 minutes, until the chicken juices run clear when the thickest part is pierced with a knife or skewer.

3 Using a slotted spoon, transfer the chicken to a plate and cover to keep warm. Strain the cooking liquid into a small saucepan, skim off any fat and boil to reduce by two thirds.

4 Add the cream and boil to reduce by half. Stir in the fresh tarragon and adjust the seasoning to taste. Slice the chicken, spoon on a little sauce, garnish with fresh tarragon sprigs and serve immediately.

> **Cook's Tip**
> Tarragon is traditionally paired with chicken, but you could, of course, use chopped fresh basil or parsley instead. Do not use dried versions of these two herbs.

Stuffed Chicken Breasts with Cream Sauce

The chicken meat encloses a delicately flavored leek filling with a hint of lime.

Serves 4
4 large chicken breast fillets, skinned, or chicken suprêmes
4 tablespoons butter
3 large leeks, white and pale green parts only, thinly sliced
1 teaspoon grated lime zest
1 cup Chicken Stock or half stock and half dry white wine
½ cup heavy cream
1 tablespoon lime juice
salt and freshly ground black pepper
lime twists and fresh parsley sprigs, to garnish

1 Cut horizontally into the thickest part of each chicken fillet or suprême to make a deep, wide pocket. Take care not to cut all the way through. Set the chicken aside.

2 Melt half the butter in a large, heavy frying pan over low heat. Cook the leeks and lime zest, stirring occasionally, for 15–20 minutes or until the leeks are soft but not colored. Turn them into a bowl, season and let cool.

3 Divide the leeks among the chicken pockets, packing them full. Secure the openings with wooden toothpicks.

4 Melt the remaining butter in a clean frying pan over medium heat. Add the chicken pockets and brown lightly on both sides. Pour in the stock, and wine if using, and bring to a boil. Cover and simmer for about 10 minutes or until the chicken is cooked through.

5 Using a slotted spoon, remove the chicken from the pan and keep warm. Boil the cooking liquid until it is reduced by half. Stir the cream into the cooking liquid and boil until reduced by about half again. Stir in the lime juice and season to taste.

6 Remove the toothpicks. Cut each pocket into ½-inch slices. Pour on the sauce and garnish with lime and parsley.

Lavender Chicken

Here, lavender flowers are used to perfume and flavor chicken cooked with red wine, oranges and thyme. The heady aroma of this dish will be a hit with your guests.

Serves 4
1 tablespoon butter
1 tablespoon olive oil
8 chicken portions
8 shallots
2 tablespoons all-purpose flour
1 cup red wine
1 cup Chicken Stock
4 fresh thyme sprigs
2 teaspoons fresh thyme flowers, removed from stalk
2 teaspoons lavender flowers
grated zest and juice of 1 orange
salt and freshly ground black pepper

To garnish
1 orange, divided into segments
12 fresh lavender sprigs
4 teaspoons fresh lavender flowers

1 Heat the butter and oil in a heavy pan and add the chicken portions. Fry until brown all over, then transfer to a large casserole. Add the shallots to the frying pan and cook for 2 minutes. Transfer to the casserole.

2 Add the flour to the frying pan and cook, stirring constantly, for 2 minutes. Pour in enough wine and stock to make a thin sauce, bring to a boil, stirring constantly, and season to taste.

3 Stir in the thyme sprigs, thyme and lavender flowers, orange zest and juice. Pour the sauce onto the chicken. Cover and simmer for 30–40 minutes, until the chicken is tender.

4 Remove the thyme sprigs. Serve, garnished with orange segments and lavender sprigs and flowers.

Cook's Tip
Do not use lavender flowers that may have been sprayed with a toxic substance, or that grow near a busy road and so may have been polluted by traffic fumes.

Roly Poly Chicken & Chanterelle Dumpling

A warming treat for misty autumn days, this dish is broiled in the old-fashioned way, wrapped in muslin.

Serves 4

1 medium onion, chopped
1 celery stalk, sliced
2 teaspoons chopped fresh thyme
2 tablespoons vegetable oil
2 chicken breast fillets, skinned
1 1/2 cups chanterelles, trimmed
   and sliced
1/3 cup all-purpose flour

1 1/4 cups boiling Chicken Stock
1 teaspoon Dijon mustard
2 teaspoons wine vinegar
salt and freshly ground
   black pepper

For the roly poly dough
3 cups self-rising flour, plus extra
1/2 teaspoon salt
10 tablespoons chilled unsalted
   butter, diced
5 tablespoons cold water

1 Sauté the onion, celery and thyme gently in the oil without coloring. Cut the chicken into bite-size pieces, add to the pan with the mushrooms and cook briefly. Stir in the flour, then remove from heat. Gradually stir in the chicken stock. Return to the heat, simmer to thicken, then add the mustard, vinegar and seasoning. Set aside to cool.

2 To make the dough, sift the flour and salt into a bowl. Add the butter and rub in until it resembles coarse bread crumbs. Add the water all at once and combine without over-mixing.

3 Roll out the dough on a floured surface into a 10 x 12-inch rectangle. Rinse a piece of muslin, about twice as big as the dough, in a little water and lay it on a clean, flat surface. Spread the chicken filling onto the dough and roll up from the short end, using the muslin to help, to make a fat sausage. Enclose in the muslin and tie each end with cooking string.

4 Lower the dumpling into a pan of boiling water, cover and simmer for 1 1/2 hours. Lift out, untie and discard the muslin. Slice and serve hot.

Stuffed Chicken Rolls

These are simple to make, but sophisticated enough to serve at a dinner party.

Serves 4
2 tablespoons butter
1 garlic clove, chopped
1 1/4 cups cooked white
   long-grain rice
3 tablespoons ricotta cheese
2 teaspoons chopped fresh
   flat-leaf parsley

1 teaspoon chopped fresh
   tarragon
4 chicken breast fillets, skinned
3–4 slices prosciutto
1 tablespoon olive oil
1/2 cup white wine
salt and freshly ground
   black pepper
fresh flat-leaf parsley sprigs,
   to garnish
cooked tagliatelle and sautéed
   mushrooms, to serve (optional)

1 Preheat the oven to 350°F. Melt about 1 1/2 teaspoons of the butter in a small pan and sauté the garlic for a few seconds without browning. Spoon into a bowl. Add the rice, ricotta, parsley and tarragon to the garlic, and season with salt and pepper. Stir to mix.

2 Place each chicken breast fillet in turn between two sheets of plastic wrap and flatten by beating lightly, but firmly, with a rolling pin or meat mallet.

3 Lay a slice of prosciutto on each chicken breast, trimming to fit if necessary. Place a spoonful of the rice stuffing at the wider end of each breast. Roll up carefully and tie in place with cooking string or secure with a wooden toothpick.

4 Heat the oil and the remaining butter in a frying pan and lightly fry the chicken rolls until browned on all sides. Place side by side in a shallow, ovenproof dish and pour in the wine.

5 Cover the dish with waxed paper and cook in the oven for 30–35 minutes, until the chicken is tender.

6 Cut the rolls into slices and serve on a bed of tagliatelle with sautéed mushrooms, if desired. Garnish with fresh, flat-leaf parsley.

Chicken with Wild Mushrooms & Vermouth

Tender chicken slices are folded into a rich sour-cream sauce, spiked with dry white vermouth.

Serves 4

2 tablespoons oil
1 leek, finely chopped
4 chicken breast fillets, skinned and sliced
3 cups wild mushrooms, sliced if large
1 tablespoon brandy
pinch of grated nutmeg
¼ teaspoon chopped fresh thyme
⅔ cup dry white vermouth
⅔ cup Chicken Stock
6 green olives, pitted and quartered
⅔ cup sour cream
salt and freshly ground black pepper
fresh thyme sprigs and croutons, to garnish

1 Heat the oil and sauté the leek until softened but not browned. Add the chicken slices and mushrooms. Cook, stirring occasionally, until just beginning to brown.

2 Pour in the brandy and ignite. When the flames have died down, stir in the nutmeg, chopped thyme, vermouth and stock, with salt and pepper to taste.

3 Bring to a boil, lower the heat and simmer for 5 minutes. Stir in the olives and most of the sour cream. Reheat gently, but do not let the mixture boil.

4 Garnish with the remaining sour cream, the thyme sprigs and croutons. Serve immediately.

Cook's Tip
Chinese dried mushrooms work well in this dish. Soak them for 1 hour in cold water before use.

Whiskey Chicken with Onion Marmalade

Whiskey-flavored roasted chicken portions are served with meltingly tender onions and green bell pepper.

Serves 4

¼ cup sesame seeds, crushed
2 garlic cloves, crushed
pinch of paprika
2 tablespoons oil
2 tablespoons whiskey
2 tablespoons honey
4 chicken portions
salt and freshly ground black pepper

For the onion marmalade
2 tablespoons oil
2 large onions, finely sliced
1 green bell pepper, seeded and sliced
⅔ cup vegetable stock

1 Preheat the oven to 375°F. In a bowl, make a paste with the sesame seeds, garlic, paprika, oil, whiskey and honey. Season and add a little water if the paste is too thick.

2 Make several cuts in the chicken portions and place them in an ovenproof dish. Spread on the paste. Roast for 40 minutes or until cooked through.

3 Meanwhile, to make the marmalade, heat the oil in a frying pan and sauté the onions over medium heat for 15 minutes. Add the green pepper and cook for 5 more minutes. Stir in the stock, season with salt and pepper, and cook gently, stirring occasionally, for about 20 minutes.

4 Transfer the chicken to warmed plates and serve with the warm onion marmalade.

Variation
Instead of making cuts in the chicken portions, ease the skin away from the flesh and push the paste underneath.

Chicken with Sloe Gin & Juniper

Juniper is used in the manufacture of gin, and the reinforcement of the flavor by using both sloe gin and juniper berries is delicious. Sloe gin is easy to make, but can also be bought.

Serves 8
2 tablespoons butter
2 tablespoons sunflower oil
8 chicken breast fillets

12 ounces carrots, cooked
1 garlic clove, crushed
1 tablespoon finely chopped
   fresh parsley
1/4 cup Chicken Stock
1/4 cup red wine
1/4 cup sloe gin
1 teaspoon crushed juniper
   berries
salt and freshly ground
   black pepper
chopped fresh basil, to garnish

1 Heat the butter with the oil in a pan and sauté the chicken until browned on all sides.

2 In a food processor, combine all the remaining ingredients except the basil and process into a smooth purée. If the mixture seems too thick, add a little more red wine or water until a thinner consistency is reached.

3 Put the chicken breasts in a heavy pan, pour the sauce on top and cook for about 15 minutes, until the chicken is cooked through.

4 Adjust the seasoning to taste and serve, garnished with chopped fresh basil.

Variation
Instead of sloe gin, you could make this dish with an herb-flavored liqueur, such as Benedictine or Galliano, a plum brandy, such as slivovitz or kirsch, or an herb- or plum-flavored vodka, but still using the juniper berries.

Herbed Chicken with Apricot & Pecan Potato Baskets

The potato baskets make a pretty addition to the chicken and could easily have different fillings when you need a change.

Serves 8
8 chicken breast fillets, skinned
2 tablespoons butter
6 mushrooms, chopped
1 tablespoon chopped pecans
1/3 cup chopped cooked ham
1 cup whole-wheat bread crumbs
1 tablespoon chopped fresh
   parsley, plus a few whole leaves
   to garnish
salt and freshly ground
   black pepper

For the sauce
2 teaspoons cornstarch
1/2 cup white wine
1/4 cup butter
2 ounces apricot chutney

For the potato baskets
4 large baking potatoes
6 ounces pork sausagemeat
8-ounce can apricots in natural
   juice, drained and quartered
1/4 teaspoon ground cinnamon
1/2 teaspoon grated orange zest
2 tablespoons maple syrup
2 tablespoons butter
1/4 cup chopped pecans, plus
   some pecan halves to garnish

1 Preheat the oven to 325°F. Place the potatoes in the oven. Place the chicken breast fillets between two sheets of plastic wrap and beat lightly with a rolling pin or meat mallet to flatten.

2 Melt the butter in a pan and sauté the mushrooms, pecans and ham. Stir in the bread crumbs and parsley, and season.

3 Divide the mushroom mixture among the chicken fillets. Roll up and secure each one with a wooden toothpick. Chill while making the sauce.

4 To make the sauce, mix the cornstarch with a little of the wine to make a smooth paste. Put the remaining wine in a pan and add the paste. Simmer until smooth, then add the butter and chutney, and cook for about 5 minutes, stirring constantly.

5 Place the chicken breasts in a shallow, ovenproof dish and pour on the sauce. Bake (do not adjust the temperature) for 20 minutes, basting several times.

6 To make the potato baskets, cut the baked potatoes in half and scoop out the inside, leaving a reasonable layer within the shell. Mash the potato and place in a mixing bowl.

7 Fry the sausagemeat, discarding some of the fat that comes off. Add the remaining ingredients and cook for 1 minute. Add the mixture to the mashed potato, blend and use to fill the potato shells. Sprinkle the pecan halves on top, place in the oven with the chicken and bake for another 30 minutes.

8 Remove the chicken from the oven and drain the sauce into a pitcher. Slice the chicken, arrange on plates and pour on the sauce. Garnish with parsley and serve with the potato baskets.

Persian Chicken with Walnut Sauce

This distinctive dish is traditionally served on festive occasions in Iran.

Serves 4
2 tablespoons oil
4 chicken portions (leg or breast)
I large onion, grated
I cup water
I cup finely chopped walnuts
¼ cup pomegranate purée
I tablespoon tomato paste
2 tablespoons lemon juice
I tablespoon sugar
3–4 saffron threads dissolved in
    I tablespoon boiling water
salt and freshly ground
    black pepper
rice and salad greens, to serve

I Heat I tablespoon of the oil in a large saucepan or flameproof casserole and stir-fry the chicken portions until golden brown. Add half of the grated onion and sauté until slightly softened.

2 Add the water and seasoning, and bring to a boil. Cover the pan, reduce the heat and simmer for 15 minutes.

3 Heat the remaining oil in a small saucepan or frying pan and sauté the rest of the onion for 2–3 minutes, until soft. Add the walnuts and cook for another 2–3 minutes over low heat, stirring frequently and taking care that the walnuts do not burn.

4 Stir in the pomegranate purée and tomato paste, lemon juice, sugar and the dissolved saffron. Season to taste and then simmer over low heat for 5 minutes.

5 Pour the walnut sauce onto the chicken, ensuring that it is well covered. Cover and simmer for 30–35 minutes, until the meat is cooked and the oil of the walnuts has risen to the top. Serve immediately with rice and salad greens.

Cook's Tip
Pomegranate purée is available at Middle Eastern food stores.

Chicken with Prosciutto & Cheese

An Italian way of making a special meal of chicken, using Fontina cheese and cured ham.

Serves 4
2 thin slices prosciutto
2 thin slices Fontina cheese
4 part-boned chicken breasts
4 fresh basil sprigs
2 tablespoons olive oil
I tablespoon butter
½ cup dry white wine
salt and freshly ground
    black pepper
tender young salad greens,
    to serve

I Preheat the oven to 400°F. Lightly oil an ovenproof dish. Cut the prosciutto and cheese slices in half crosswise.

2 Skin the chicken breasts and open out the slit in the center of each one. Fill each cavity with half a prosciutto slice and a fresh basil sprig.

3 Heat the oil and butter in a wide, heavy frying pan until foaming. Cook the chicken breasts over medium heat for 1–2 minutes on each side, until they change color.

4 Transfer the chicken to the ovenproof dish. Add the wine to the pan juices, stir until sizzling, then pour onto the chicken and season to taste.

5 Top each chicken breast with a slice of Fontina. Bake for 20 minutes or until the chicken is tender. Serve hot, with tender young salad leaves.

Cook's Tip
There is nothing quite like the buttery texture and nutty flavor of Fontina cheese, and it also has superb melting qualities, but you could use a Swiss or French mountain cheese, such as Gruyère or Emmental. Ask for the cheese to be sliced thinly on the machine slicer, as you will find it difficult to slice it thinly enough yourself.

Chicken Kiev

This popular recipe is a modern Russian invention. These chicken breasts filled with garlic butter should be prepared in advance to allow time for chilling.

Serves 4

½ cup butter, softened
2 garlic cloves, crushed
finely grated zest of 1 lemon
2 tablespoons chopped
   fresh tarragon
pinch of grated nutmeg
4 chicken breast fillets with wing
   bones attached, skinned
1 egg, lightly beaten
2 cups fresh bread crumbs
oil, for deep frying
salt and freshly ground
   black pepper
lemon wedges, to garnish
potato wedges, to serve

1 Mix the butter in a bowl with the garlic, lemon zest, tarragon and nutmeg. Season to taste with salt and pepper. Shape the butter into a rectangular block about 2 inches long, wrap in aluminum foil and chill for 1 hour.

2 Place the chicken on a piece of oiled plastic wrap. Cover with a second piece of plastic wrap and gently beat the pieces with a meat mallet or rolling pin until fairly thin.

3 Cut the butter lengthwise into four pieces and put one in the center of each chicken fillet. Fold the edges over the butter and secure with wooden toothpicks.

4 Put the beaten egg and the bread crumbs into separate dishes. Dip the chicken pieces first in the beaten egg and then in the bread crumbs to coat evenly. Dip them a second time in egg and crumbs, then put them on a plate and chill for at least 1 hour.

5 Heat the oil in a large pan or deep-fat fryer to 350°F. Deep-fry the chicken for 6–8 minutes or until the chicken is cooked and the coating golden brown and crisp. Drain on paper towels and remove the toothpicks. Garnish with wedges of lemon and serve with potato wedges.

Chicken with Tomatoes & Shrimp

This dish was created especially for Napoleon after the battle of Marengo.

Serves 4

½ cup olive oil
8 chicken thighs on the
   bone, skinned
1 onion, finely chopped
1 celery stalk, finely chopped
1 garlic clove, crushed
12 ounces ripe Italian plum
   tomatoes, peeled and
   roughly chopped
1 cup dry white wine
½ teaspoon finely chopped
   fresh rosemary
1 tablespoon butter
8 small triangles thinly sliced
   white bread, without crusts
6 ounces large shrimp, peeled
salt and freshly ground
   black pepper
finely chopped flat-leaf parsley,
   to garnish

1 Heat 2 tablespoons of the oil in a frying pan and sauté the chicken over medium heat for 5 minutes, until it has changed colour on all sides. Transfer to a flameproof casserole.

2 Add the onion and celery to the pan and cook gently, stirring frequently, for 3 minutes, until softened. Add the garlic, tomatoes, wine, rosemary and seasoning. Bring to a boil, stirring.

3 Pour the tomato sauce onto the chicken. Cover and cook gently for 40 minutes or until the chicken juices run clear when the thickest part is pierced with a knife or skewer.

4 About 10 minutes before serving, heat the remaining oil and the butter in the frying pan. Add the triangles of bread and fry until crisp and golden on each side. Drain on paper towels.

5 Add the shrimp to the casserole and heat until they are cooked. Taste the sauce and adjust the seasoning as necessary.

6 Dip one of the tips of each fried bread triangle in the chopped parsley. Serve the chicken dish hot, garnished with the bread triangles.

Bisteeya

This intriguing dish is a simplified version of a Moroccan specialty.

Serves 4

2 tablespoons sunflower oil, plus
    extra for brushing
2 tablespoons butter
3 chicken quarters,
    preferably breasts
1½ Spanish onions, grated or
    very finely chopped
good pinch of ground ginger
good pinch of saffron powder

2 teaspoons ground cinnamon,
    plus extra for dusting
¼ cup sliced almonds
1 large bunch cilantro,
    finely chopped
1 large bunch fresh parsley,
    finely chopped
3 eggs, beaten
about 6 ounces phyllo pastry
1–2 teaspoons confectioners'
    sugar (optional), plus extra
    for dusting
salt and freshly ground
    black pepper

1 Heat the oil and butter in a large, flameproof casserole or saucepan and brown the chicken pieces for about 4 minutes. Add the onions, ginger, saffron, ¼ teaspoon of the cinnamon and enough water (about 1¼ cups) so that the chicken braises, rather than boils. Season well.

2 Bring to a boil, then cover and simmer very gently for 45–55 minutes or until the chicken is tender. Meanwhile, dry-fry the almonds until golden and set aside.

3 Transfer the chicken to a plate. When cool enough to handle, remove the skin and bones and cut the flesh into pieces.

4 Stir the cilantro and parsley into the pan, and simmer the sauce until well reduced and thick. Add the beaten eggs and cook over very low heat until they are lightly scrambled.

5 Preheat the oven to 350°F. Oil a shallow, round ovenproof dish, about 10 inches in diameter. Place one or two sheets of phyllo pastry in a single layer on the bottom of the dish (it will depend on the size of your phyllo pastry), so that it is completely covered and the edges of the pastry sheets hang over the sides. Brush lightly with oil and make two more layers of phyllo, brushing with oil between the layers.

6 Place the chicken on the pastry and then spoon the egg and herb mixture on top.

7 Place a single layer of phyllo pastry on top of the filling (you may need to use more than one sheet of phyllo pastry) and sprinkle on the almonds. Sprinkle with the remaining cinnamon and the confectioners' sugar, if using.

8 Fold the edges of the phyllo over the almonds and then make four more layers of phyllo (using one or two sheets per layer, depending on size), brushing each layer with a little oil. Tuck the phyllo edges under the pie (as if you were making a bed) and brush the top layer with oil.

9 Bake for 40–45 minutes, until golden. Dust the top with confectioners' sugar and use the extra cinnamon to make criss-cross or diagonal lines. Serve immediately.

Chicken in Badacsonyi Wine

A Hungarian recipe, originally made with a Balatan wine called *Badacsonyi Kékryalii* ("Blue Handled"), which has a full body and distinctive bouquet.

Serves 4

¼ cup butter
4 scallions, chopped
4 ounces bacon, diced
2 bay leaves
1 fresh tarragon sprig

3½-pound corn-fed chicken
¼ cup sweet sherry or mead
1½ cups button mushrooms,
    sliced
1¼ cups Badacsonyi or
    dry white wine
salt
fresh tarragon and bay leaves,
    to garnish
steamed rice, to serve

1 Heat the butter in a large, heavy pan or flameproof casserole and sweat the scallions for 1–1½ minutes. Add the bacon, bay leaves and tarragon, stripping the leaves from the stem. Cook for another 1 minute.

2 Add the whole chicken to the pan and pour in the sherry or mead. Cook, covered, over very low heat for 15 minutes.

3 Sprinkle the mushrooms into the pan and pour in the wine. Cook, covered, for 1 hour. Remove the lid, baste the chicken with the wine mixture and cook, uncovered, for another 30 minutes, until almost all the liquid has evaporated.

4 Skim the fat from the cooking liquid remaining in the pan. Taste and adjust the seasoning as necessary. Transfer the chicken, vegetables and bacon to a serving dish. Garnish with tarragon and bay leaves, and serve with rice.

Cook's Tip
Traditionally, this recipe also used a sweet drink with a honeyed caramel flavor called marc. If you can obtain this, use it instead of the sweet sherry or mead.

Chicken with Morels

Morels are among the tastiest dried mushrooms and, although they are expensive, a small amount goes a long way and is certainly worth investing in for this wonderful dinner party dish.

Serves 4

1½ ounces dried morel
   mushrooms
1 cup Chicken Stock
4 tablespoons butter

5 or 6 shallots, thinly sliced
1½ cups button mushrooms,
   thinly sliced
¼ teaspoon dried thyme
2–3 tablespoons brandy
¾ cup heavy or whipping cream
4 chicken breast fillets, about
   7 ounces each, skinned
1 tablespoon vegetable oil
¾ cup Champagne or
   dry sparkling wine
salt and freshly ground
   black pepper

1 Put the morels in a sieve and rinse well under cold running water, shaking to remove as much grit as possible. Put them in a saucepan with the stock and bring to a boil over medium heat. Remove the pan from heat and set aside for 1 hour.

2 Remove the morels from the cooking liquid. Strain the liquid through a very fine, muslin-lined sieve and set aside. Reserve a few whole morels and slice the rest.

3 Melt half the butter in a frying pan over medium heat. Add the shallots and cook for 2 minutes, until softened, then add the morels and button mushrooms and cook, stirring frequently, for 2–3 minutes.

4 Season and add the thyme, brandy and ⅓ cup of the cream. Reduce the heat and simmer gently for 10–12 minutes, until any liquid has evaporated, stirring occasionally. Remove the mixture from the pan and set aside.

5 Pull off the small fillet (the finger-shaped piece on the underside) from each chicken breast and reserve for another use. Make a pocket in each breast by cutting a slit along the thicker edge, taking care not to cut all the way through.

6 Using a small spoon, fill each pocket with one quarter of the mushroom mixture, then, if necessary, close with a wooden toothpick.

7 Melt the remaining butter with the oil in a heavy frying pan over medium-high heat and cook the chicken breasts on one side for 6–8 minutes, until golden. Transfer to a plate. Add the Champagne or sparkling wine to the pan and boil to reduce by half. Add the reserved strained morel cooking liquid and boil to reduce by half again.

8 Add the remaining cream and cook over medium heat for 2–3 minutes, until the sauce thickens slightly and coats the back of a spoon. Adjust the seasoning. Return the chicken to the pan with any accumulated juices and the reserved whole morels, and simmer for 3–5 minutes over medium-low heat, until the chicken is hot and the juices run clear when the thickest part is pierced with a knife or skewer. Serve immediately.

Pan-fried Marinated Poussin

These small birds are full of flavor when marinated for several hours before they are cooked.

Serves 3–4

2 poussins, about 1 pound each
5–6 fresh mint leaves,
   torn into pieces

1 leek, sliced into thin rings
1 garlic clove, finely chopped
¼ cup olive oil
2 tablespoons lemon juice
¼ cup dry white wine
salt and freshly ground
   black pepper
fresh mint leaves, to garnish

1 Cut the poussins in half down the backbone, dividing the breast. Flatten the four halves with a meat mallet. Place them in a bowl with the mint, leek and garlic. Season with pepper, and sprinkle with oil and half the lemon juice. Cover and let stand in a cool place for 6 hours.

2 Heat a large, heavy frying pan. Place the poussins and their marinade in the pan, cover and cook over medium heat for about 45 minutes, turning them occasionally. Season with salt during the cooking. Transfer the poussins to a warmed serving platter.

3 Tilt the pan and spoon off any fat on the surface of the liquid. Pour in the white wine and the remaining lemon juice, and cook until the sauce reduces by about half.

4 Strain the sauce, pressing the vegetables to extract all the juices. Place the poussins on individual plates and spoon on the sauce. Garnish with mint and serve.

Cook's Tip
While bottled lemon juice is very convenient, it does not have the same flavor as freshly squeezed juice. Let citrus fruits come to room temperature before squeezing for the maximum amount of juice.

Steamboat

This Malaysian dish is named after the utensil in which it is cooked—a type of fondue with a funnel and a moat. The moat is filled with stock, which traditionally is kept hot with charcoal. An electric steamboat or any traditional fondue pot can be used instead.

Serves 8

8 Chinese dried mushrooms, soaked for 30 minutes in warm water to cover
6¼ cups Chicken Stock
2 teaspoons rice wine or medium-dry sherry
2 teaspoons sesame oil
8 ounces lean pork, thinly sliced
8 ounces rump steak, thinly sliced
1 chicken breast fillet, skinned and thickly sliced
2 chicken livers, trimmed and sliced
8 ounces shrimp, peeled
1 pound white fish fillets, skinned and cubed
7 ounces fish balls
4 ounces fried tofu, each piece halved
leafy green vegetables, such as lettuce, Chinese cabbage, spinach leaves and watercress, cut into 6-inch lengths
8 ounces Chinese rice vermicelli
8 eggs
selection of sauces, including soy with sesame seeds; soy with crushed ginger; chili; plum and hot mustard
½ bunch scallions, chopped
salt and freshly ground white pepper

1 Drain the mushrooms, reserving the soaking liquid. Cut off and discard the stems; slice the caps thinly.

2 Pour the stock into a large saucepan and add the rice wine or sherry, sesame oil and reserved mushroom liquid. Bring the mixture to a boil, then season with salt and pepper. Reduce the heat and simmer gently.

3 Put the meat, fish, tofu, green vegetables and mushrooms in bowls on the table. Soak the vermicelli in hot water for about 5 minutes, drain and place in 8 soup bowls on a small side table. Crack an egg in a small bowl for each diner; place on the side table. Put the sauces in bowls beside each other.

4 Add the scallions to the pan of stock, bring it to a full boil and fuel the steamboat. Pour the stock into the moat and seat your guests immediately. Each guest lowers a few chosen morsels into a boiling stock, using chopsticks or fondue forks, leaves them for a minute or two, then removes them with a small wire mesh ladle, a fondue fork or pair of chopsticks.

5 When all the meat, fish, tofu and vegetables have been cooked, the stock will be concentrated and wonderfully enriched. Add a little boiling water if necessary. Bring the soup bowls containing the soaked noodles to the table, pour in the hot soup and slide a whole egg into each, stirring until it cooks and forms threads.

Cook's Tip
Fresh or frozen fish balls are available at Asian food stores and Chinese supermarkets.

Drunken Chicken

In China, "drunken" foods are usually served cold as part of an appetizer to a Chinese meal or as canapés.

Serves 4–6

1 chicken, about 3 pounds
½-inch piece fresh ginger root, thinly sliced
2 scallions, trimmed
7½ cups water or to cover
1 tablespoon salt
1¼ cups dry sherry
1–2 tablespoons brandy
shredded scallions and fresh herbs, to garnish

1 Rinse and dry the chicken inside and out. Place the ginger and scallions in the body cavity. Put the chicken in a large saucepan or flameproof casserole and just cover with water. Bring to a boil, skim and cook for 15 minutes.

2 Turn off the heat, cover the pan or casserole tightly and leave the chicken in the cooking liquid for 3–4 hours, by which time it will be cooked. Drain well. Pour 1¼ cups of the stock into a pitcher. Freeze the remaining stock for another dish.

3 Leaving the skin on the chicken, joint it neatly. Divide each leg into a drumstick and thigh. Make two more portions from the wings and some from the breast. Finally, cut off the remainder of the breast pieces (still on the bone) and divide each breast into two even-size portions.

4 Arrange the chicken portions in a shallow dish. Rub salt into the skin and cover with plastic wrap. Set aside in a cool place for several hours or overnight in the refrigerator.

5 Next day, lift off and discard any fat from the stock. Mix the sherry and brandy in a pitcher, add the stock and pour onto the chicken. Cover again and put in the refrigerator to marinate for 2–3 days, turning occasionally.

6 When ready to serve, remove the chicken skin. Cut the chicken through the bone into chunky pieces and arrange on a serving platter, garnished with scallion shreds and herbs.

Poussins Véronique

A double poussin is six to ten weeks old and weighs about 2 pounds, so one bird is large enough to serve two people.

Serves 4
2 fresh tarragon or thyme sprigs
2 double poussins
2 tablespoons butter
¼ cup white wine
grated zest and juice of ½ lemon

1 tablespoon olive oil
1 tablespoon all-purpose flour
⅔ cup Chicken Stock
4 ounces seedless green grapes,
  cut in half if large
salt and freshly ground
  black pepper
chopped fresh parsley, to garnish
lightly cooked green beans,
  to serve

1 Preheat the oven to 350°F. Put a sprig of tarragon or thyme inside the cavity of each poussin and tie the birds into a neat shape.

2 Heat the butter in a flameproof casserole, add the poussins and brown them lightly all over. Pour in the white wine, season with salt and pepper to taste, cover and transfer the casserole to the oven. Cook for 20–30 minutes or until tender and the juices run clear when the thickest part is pierced with a skewer or the point of knife.

3 Remove the poussins from the casserole and cut in half with a pair of kitchen scissors, removing the backbones and small rib-cage bones. Arrange in a shallow, ovenproof dish (that will slide under the broiler). Sprinkle with lemon juice and brush with oil. Broil until lightly browned. Keep warm.

4 Mix the flour into the butter and wine in the casserole, and blend in the stock. Bring to a boil, adjust the seasoning to taste and add the lemon zest and grapes, then simmer for 2–3 minutes.

5 Spoon the sauce onto the poussins, garnish with chopped fresh parsley and serve immediately with lightly cooked green beans.

Baby Chickens with Lime & Chili

Kept succulent with a sun-dried tomato-flavored butter, these poussins make a splendid meal for friends, and cook well under the broiler or on a grill.

Serves 4
4 poussins, about 1 pound each
3 tablespoons butter

2 tablespoons sun-dried
  tomato paste
finely grated zest of 1 lime
2 teaspoons chili sauce
juice of ½ lime
fresh flat-leaf parsley sprigs,
  to garnish
lime wedges, to serve

1 Prepare the grill or preheat the broiler. Spatchcock the poussins and turn the flattened birds breast-side up. Lift the breast skin carefully and gently ease your fingertips underneath, to loosen it from the flesh.

2 In a bowl, combine the butter, tomato paste, lime zest and chili sauce. Spread about three quarters of the mixture under the skin of each poussin, smoothing it evenly.

3 To hold the poussins flat during cooking, thread two skewers through each bird, crossing at the center. Each skewer should pass through a wing and then out through a drumstick.

4 Combine the remaining butter mixture with the lime juice and brush it onto the skin of the poussins. Cook on a medium-hot grill or under the broiler, turning occasionally, for 25–30 minutes or until the juices run clear when the thickest part of the thigh is pierced with a skewer or knife. Garnish with flat-leaf parsley and serve with lime wedges.

Cook's Tip
If you wish to serve half a poussin per portion, you may find it easier simply to cut the birds in half lengthwise. Use poultry shears or a large, sharp knife to cut through the breastbone and backbone.

Poussins with Zucchini & Apricot Stuffing

If possible, buy very small poussins for this recipe. If these are not available, buy slightly larger poussins and serve half per person.

Serves 4

4 small poussins
about 3 tablespoons butter
1–2 teaspoons ground coriander
1 large red bell pepper, seeded and cut into strips
1 fresh red chile, seeded and thinly sliced
1–2 tablespoons olive oil
$^{1}/_{2}$ cup Chicken Stock
2 tablespoons cornstarch
salt and freshly ground black pepper
fresh flat-leaf parsley, to garnish

For the stuffing
$2^{1}/_{2}$ cups vegetable or Chicken Stock
$1^{2}/_{3}$ cups couscous
2 small zucchini
8 dried apricots
1 tablespoon chopped fresh flat-leaf parsley
1 tablespoon chopped cilantro
juice of $^{1}/_{2}$ lemon

1 To make the stuffing, bring the stock to a boil and pour it onto the couscous in a large bowl. Stir once and then set aside for 10 minutes.

2 Meanwhile, trim the zucchini and then grate coarsely. Roughly chop the apricots and add to the zucchini. Preheat the oven to 400°F.

3 When the couscous has swollen, fluff up with a fork and then spoon 6 tablespoons into a separate bowl and add the zucchini and chopped apricots. Add the herbs, seasoning and lemon juice, and stir to make a fairly loose stuffing. Set aside the remaining couscous for serving.

4 Spoon the apricot stuffing loosely into the body cavities of the poussins and secure with cooking string or wooden toothpicks. Place the birds in a roasting pan so that they fit comfortably but not too closely. Rub the butter into the skins, and sprinkle with ground coriander and a little salt and pepper. Place the red pepper and chile in the roasting pan around the poussins and spoon on the olive oil.

5 Roast for 20 minutes, then reduce the temperature to 350°F. Pour the stock around the poussins and baste them with the stock and red pepper/chile mixture. Return the pan to the oven and cook for another 30–35 minutes, until the poussins are cooked through. Baste occasionally with the stock.

6 Transfer the poussins to a warmed serving plate. Steam the reserved couscous to reheat. Blend the cornstarch with 3 tablespoons cold water, stir into the stock and peppers in the roasting pan and heat gently on top of the stove, stirring, until the sauce is slightly thickened. Taste and adjust the seasoning.

7 Pour the sauce into a pitcher or over the poussins. Garnish the birds with parsley and serve with the reserved couscous.

Chicken Liver Risotto

The combination of chicken livers, bacon, parsley and thyme gives this risotto a wonderfully rich flavor. Serve it as an appetizer for four or a lunch for two or three.

Serves 2–4

6 ounces chicken livers
about 1 tablespoon olive oil
about 2 tablespoons butter
3 strips bacon, finely chopped
2 shallots, finely chopped
1 garlic clove, crushed
1 celery stalk, finely sliced
$1^{1}/_{2}$ cups risotto rice
$^{3}/_{4}$ cup dry white wine
$3^{3}/_{4}$–4 cups simmering Chicken Stock
1 teaspoon chopped fresh thyme
1 tablespoon chopped fresh parsley
salt and freshly ground black pepper
fresh parsley and thyme sprigs, to garnish

1 Clean the chicken livers, removing any fat or membrane. Rinse, pat dry with paper towels and cut into small pieces.

2 Heat the oil and butter in a frying pan and fry the bacon for 2–3 minutes. Add the shallots, garlic and sliced celery, and fry for 3–4 minutes over low heat, until the vegetables are softened.

3 Increase the heat and add the livers. Stir-fry for a few minutes, until they are brown all over but still slightly pink in the center.

4 Add the rice. Cook, stirring, for a few minutes, then pour in the wine. Bring to a boil, stirring frequently, taking care not to break up the livers. When all the wine has been absorbed, add the hot stock, a ladleful at a time, stirring constantly. About halfway through the cooking, add the thyme and season with salt and pepper. Continue to add the stock, making sure that it has been absorbed before adding more.

5 When the risotto is creamy and the rice is tender, stir in the parsley. Adust the seasoning. Remove the pan from heat, cover and let rest for a few minutes before serving, garnished with parsley and thyme sprigs.

Mushroom Picker's Chicken Paella

A good paella is based on a few well-chosen ingredients. Here, chicken combines with mixed wild mushrooms and vegetables.

Serves 4
3 tablespoons olive oil
1 medium onion, chopped
1 small fennel bulb, sliced
generous 3 cups assorted
   wild and cultivated mushrooms,
   trimmed and sliced
1 garlic clove, crushed
3 chicken legs, chopped through
   the bone
1 2/3 cups short-grain Spanish
   or Italian rice
3 3/4 cups Chicken Stock, boiling
pinch of saffron threads or
   1 envelope saffron powder
1 fresh thyme sprig
14-ounce can lima beans, drained
   and rinsed
3/4 cup frozen peas

1 Heat the oil in a 14-inch paella pan or a large frying pan. Add the onion and fennel, and sauté over low heat for 3–4 minutes.

2 Add the mushrooms and garlic, and cook until the juices begin to run, then increase the heat to evaporate them. Push the vegetables to one side. Add the chicken and fry briefly.

3 Stir in the rice, add the stock, saffron, thyme, lima beans and peas. Bring to the simmering point and cook gently for 15 minutes without stirring.

4 Remove the pan from heat and cover the surface of the paella with a circle of greased waxed paper. Cover the paper with a clean dish towel and let the paella finish cooking in its own heat for about 5 minutes. Bring to the table, uncover and serve.

> **Cook's Tip**
> It is best to use an assortment of wild mushrooms for this dish—the more the better. Feel free to use as many kinds as you want.

Seven-vegetable Couscous

In this glorious, magically numbered Moroccan dish, chicken is partnered with lamb, carrots, parsnips, turnips, onions, zucchini, tomatoes and green beans. You can substitute different vegetables if desired.

Serves 6
2 tablespoons sunflower or
   olive oil
1 pound lean lamb, cut into
   bite-size pieces
2 chicken breast quarters, halved
2 onions, chopped
12 ounces carrots, cut into chunks
8 ounces parsnips, cut into chunks
4 ounces turnips, cut into cubes
6 tomatoes, peeled and chopped
3 3/4 cups Chicken Stock
good pinch of ground ginger
1 cinnamon stick
14-ounce can chickpeas, drained
2 1/3 cups couscous
2 small zucchini, cut into
   julienne strips
4 ounces green beans, halved
   if necessary
1/3 cup raisins
a little harissa or Tabasco sauce
salt and freshly ground
   black pepper

1 Heat half the oil in a large, heavy saucepan or flameproof casserole and add the lamb, in batches if necessary, and fry until evenly browned, stirring frequently. Transfer to a plate using a slotted spoon. Add the chicken pieces to the pan and cook, turning occasionally, until evenly browned. Transfer to the plate with the lamb.

2 Heat the remaining oil and add the onions. Sauté over low heat for 2–3 minutes, stirring occasionally, until softened, but not colored. Add the carrots, parsnips and turnips. Stir well, cover with a lid and sweat over low heat for 5–6 minutes, stirring once or twice.

3 Add the tomatoes, and return the lamb and chicken to the pan. Pour in the chicken stock. Season with salt and pepper to taste, and add the ground ginger and cinnamon stick. Bring to a boil and simmer gently for 35–45 minutes, until the meat is nearly tender.

4 Skin the chickpeas by placing them in a bowl of cold water and rubbing them between your fingers. The skins will rise to the surface. Discard the skins and drain. Prepare the couscous according to the instructions on the package.

5 Add the skinned chickpeas, zucchini, beans and raisins to the meat mixture, stir gently and continue cooking for 10–15 minutes, until the vegetables and meat are tender. Pile the couscous onto a large warmed serving platter, making a slight well in the center.

6 Transfer the chicken to a plate, and remove the skin and bones, if desired. Spoon 3–4 large spoonfuls of stock into a separate saucepan. Stir the chicken back into the stew, add harissa or Tabasco sauce to taste to the separate pan of stock and heat both gently. Remove and discard the cinnamon stick, spoon the stew onto the couscous and serve. Pass the harissa sauce in a separate bowl.

Turkey Cutlets with Capers

These thin slices of turkey, coated in bread crumbs, cook very quickly. Here they are enhanced with the fresh, sharp flavors of lemon, capers and sage.

Serves 2

4 thin turkey breast cutlets, about 3 ounces each
1 large unwaxed lemon
½ teaspoon chopped fresh sage
4–5 tablespoons extra virgin olive oil
¾ cup fine dry bread crumbs
1 tablespoon capers, rinsed and drained
salt and freshly ground black pepper
fresh sage leaves and lemon wedges, to garnish

1 Place the turkey cutlets between two sheets of plastic wrap and pound with the flat-side of a meat mallet or rolling pin to flatten to a thickness of about ¼ inch.

2 With a vegetable peeler, remove four thin pieces of zest from the lemon. Cut them into fine julienne strips, cover with plastic wrap and set aside. Grate the remainder of the lemon zest and squeeze the lemon.

3 Put the grated zest in a large, nonmetallic shallow dish and add the chopped sage, salt and pepper. Stir in 1 tablespoon of the lemon juice, reserving the rest, and about 1 tablespoon of the oil, then add the turkey, turn to coat and let marinate for 30 minutes.

4 Place the bread crumbs in another shallow dish. Dip the turkey cutlets in the crumbs, coating them on both sides.

5 In a heavy frying pan, heat 2 tablespoons of the oil over high heat, add the cutlets and cook for 2–3 minutes, turning once, until golden. Transfer to warmed plates and keep warm.

6 Wipe out the pan, add the remaining oil, the lemon julienne strips and the capers, and heat through, stirring. Spoon a little sauce onto the turkey, garnish with sage leaves and lemon wedges, and serve.

Turkey Breasts with Wine & Grapes

Good stock and wine provide the flavor in this velvety sauce.

Serves 3

1 pound turkey breast, thinly sliced
3 tablespoons flour
3–4 tablespoons oil
½ cup white wine or sherry
½ cup Chicken Stock
5 ounces white grapes
salt and freshly ground black pepper
fresh flat-leaf parsley, to garnish
boiled new potatoes or rice, to serve

1 Put the turkey slices between two sheets of plastic wrap and flatten them with a rolling pin or meat mallet. Spread out the flour on a plate, and season with salt and pepper. Toss each turkey slice in it so that both sides are thoroughly coated and shake off any excess.

2 Heat the oil in a large frying pan and sauté the turkey slices for about 3 minutes on each side. Pour in the wine or sherry and boil rapidly to reduce it slightly.

3 Stir in the chicken stock, lower the heat and cook for another few minutes, until the turkey is cooked through.

4 Halve and seed the grapes, and stir them into the sauce. Adjust the seasoning to taste. Transfer to a warmed serving platter and serve, garnished with flat-leaf parsley, accompanied by new potatoes or rice.

Cook's Tip
For a dark sauce, you could use red wine and black grapes, and also add a scant 2 cups sliced chestnut mushrooms. Sauté them in the oil before you cook the turkey in Step 2.

Turkey with Fig, Orange & Mint Marmalade

This unusual fruity sauce gives a tremendous lift to the rather bland flavor of turkey breast fillets.

Serves 4

1 pound dried figs
1/2 bottle sweet, fruity white wine
1 tablespoon butter

4 turkey breast fillets, about
   6–8 ounces each
2 tablespoons dark
   orange marmalade
10 fresh mint leaves, finely
   chopped, plus extra to garnish
juice of 1/2 lemon
salt and freshly ground
   black pepper

1 Place the dried figs in a saucepan with the white wine and bring to a boil, then simmer very gently for about 1 hour. Let the figs cool in the cooking liquid and chill overnight.

2 Melt the butter in a frying pan and fry the turkey fillets, turning them once, until they are cooked through. Transfer to a warmed serving dish and keep warm.

3 Drain any fat from the pan and pour in the cooking liquid from the figs. Bring to a boil and reduce until about 2/3 cup remains.

4 Add the marmalade, chopped mint and lemon juice, and simmer for a few minutes. Season to taste with salt and pepper. Add the figs and heat through.

5 When the sauce is thick and shiny, pour it onto the meat and serve, garnished with plenty of mint leaves.

> **Cook's Tip**
> Some of the more unusual varieties of mint would be ideal for this dish. Try apple or pineapple, for example. A variety with variegated leaves would make an attractive garnish.

Turkey with Marsala Cream Sauce

Marsala makes a very rich and tasty sauce. The addition of lemon juice gives it a sharp edge, which helps to balance the richness.

Serves 6

6 turkey breast steaks
3 tablespoons all-purpose flour
2 tablespoons olive oil
2 tablespoons butter

3/4 cup dry Marsala
1/4 cup lemon juice
3/4 cup heavy cream
salt and freshly ground
   black pepper
lemon wedges and chopped fresh
   parsley, to garnish
steamed snowpeas and
   green beans, to serve

1 Put each turkey steak between two sheets of plastic wrap and pound with a meat mallet or rolling pin to flatten and stretch. Cut each steak in half or into quarters, discarding any sinew.

2 Spread out the flour in a shallow dish and season well. Dip the turkey steaks in the flour, turning them to coat thoroughly.

3 Heat the oil and butter in a wide saucepan or frying pan. Add as many pieces of turkey as the pan will hold in a single layer and sauté over medium heat for 3 minutes on each side, until colored on the outside and cooked. Transfer to a warmed serving dish and keep hot. Repeat with the remaining turkey.

4 Lower the heat. Mix the Marsala and lemon juice in a pitcher, add to the pan and raise the heat. Bring to a boil, stirring in the sediment, then add the cream. Simmer, stirring constantly, until the sauce is reduced and glossy. Taste and adjust the seasoning. Spoon onto the turkey, garnish with lemon wedges and parsley, and serve immediately with snowpeas and green beans.

> **Variations**
> Chicken breast fillets can be used instead of the turkey, and 1/4 cup mascarpone cheese can be substituted for the heavy cream.

Turkey Zador with Mlinces

In this Croatian recipe for special occasions, the unusual *mlinces* are used to soak up the juices from a roast turkey.

Serves 10–12
6¹/₂-pound turkey
2 garlic cloves, halved
4 ounces bacon, finely chopped
2 tablespoons chopped
   fresh rosemary

¹/₂ cup olive oil
1 cup dry white wine
fresh rosemary sprigs, to garnish
bacon, to serve

For the mlinces
3 cups all-purpose flour, sifted
¹/₂–²/₃ cup warm water
2 tablespoons oil
salt

1 Preheat the oven to 400°F. Dry the turkey well inside and out. Rub all over with the garlic cloves.

2 Toss the bacon and rosemary together, and use to stuff the turkey neck flap. Secure the skin with a wooden toothpick. Brush the bird with the oil. Place in a roasting pan and cover loosely with aluminum foil. Roast for 45–50 minutes. Remove the foil and reduce the oven temperature to 325°F. Baste the turkey with the juices and pour on the wine. Cook for 1 hour, basting occasionally. Reduce the temperature to 300°F and cook for another 45 minutes, basting occasionally.

3 Meanwhile, to make the *mlinces*, sift the flour with a little salt into a bowl. Add the water and oil, and mix into a soft but pliable dough. Knead briefly and divide equally into four pieces. Roll out thinly on a lightly floured surface into 16-inch circles. Sprinkle with salt. Bake on baking sheets alongside the turkey for 25 minutes, until crisp. Crush into pieces about 2¹/₂–4 inches.

4 About 6–8 minutes before the end of the cooking time for the turkey, add the *mlinces* to the meat juices in the roasting pan alongside the bird. Let the turkey rest for 10–15 minutes before carving, then serve, garnished with rosemary and accompanied by the *mlinces* and bacon.

Turkey with Sage, Prunes & Brandy

This stir-fry has a very rich sauce based on a good-quality brandy—use the best you can afford.

Serves 4
¹/₂ cup prunes
1¹/₂ pounds turkey breast fillet
1¹/₄ cups brandy

1 tablespoon chopped fresh sage
5 ounces bacon, in
   one piece
¹/₄ cup butter
24 baby onions, peeled
   and quartered
salt and freshly ground
   black pepper
fresh sage sprigs, to garnish

1 Pit the prunes and cut them into slivers. Remove the skin from the turkey and cut the breast into thin pieces.

2 Combine the prunes, turkey, brandy and chopped sage in a nonmetallic dish. Cover and set aside to marinate overnight in the refrigerator.

3 Next day, strain the turkey and prunes, reserving the marinade, and pat dry with paper towels. Dice the bacon.

4 Heat a wok or heavy frying pan and add half the butter. When the butter is hot, add the onions and stir-fry for 4 minutes, until crisp and golden. Set aside.

5 Add the bacon to the wok and stir-fry for 1 minute, until it begins to release some fat. Add the remaining butter, and stir-fry the turkey and prunes for 3–4 minutes, until the turkey and bacon are crisp and golden.

6 Push the turkey mixture to one side of the wok, add the reserved marinade and simmer until thickened. Stir the turkey into the sauce, season well with salt and pepper, and serve, garnished with sage.

Cook's Tip
"VSOP" on the label is a guarantee of the quality of the brandy.

Breast of Turkey with Mango & Wine

Fresh mango gives this Caribbean-inspired dish a truly tropical taste.

Serves 4

4 turkey breast steaks, about
  6 ounces each
2 garlic cloves, crushed
1/4 teaspoon ground cinnamon
1 tablespoon finely chopped fresh
  parsley, plus extra to garnish
1 tablespoon crushed crackers
2 tablespoons diced ripe mango,
  plus extra to garnish
3 tablespoons butter
  or margarine
6 shallots, sliced
2/3 cup white wine
salt and freshly ground
  black pepper

1 Cut a slit horizontally into each turkey steak to make a "pocket."

2 Put half the garlic, the cinnamon, parsley, cracker crumbs, mango, 1 tablespoon of the butter or margarine and salt and pepper in a bowl, and mash together.

3 Spoon a little of the mango mixture into each of the "pockets." If necessary, secure with a wooden toothpick. Season the turkey with a little extra pepper.

4 Melt the remaining butter or margarine in a large frying pan, and sauté the remaining garlic and the shallots for 5 minutes. Add the turkey and cook for 15 minutes, turning once.

5 Add the wine, cover, and simmer gently, until the turkey is fully cooked. Add the extra diced mango, heat through for a minute or two, then serve, garnished with chopped parsley.

> **Cook's Tip**
> If a mango "gives" when gently squeezed in the palm of the hand, it is ripe, regardless of the color of its skin.

Grape-leaf Wrapped Turkey with Noilly Prat

Pretty grape-leaf parcels conceal turkey cutlets filled with a delicious wild rice and pine nut stuffing flavored with Noilly Prat.

Serves 4

4 ounces drained grape leaves
  in brine
4 turkey cutlets, about
  4–6 ounces each
1 1/4 cups Chicken Stock

For the stuffing

2 tablespoons sunflower oil
3 shallots, chopped
3/4 cup cooked wild rice
4 tomatoes, peeled and chopped
3 tablespoons Noilly Prat
1/4 cup pine nuts, chopped
salt and freshly ground
  black pepper

1 Preheat the oven to 375°F. Rinse the grape leaves a few times in cold water and drain.

2 To make the stuffing, heat the oil in a frying pan. Add the shallots and sauté gently until soft. Remove the pan from heat and stir in the cooked rice, tomatoes, Noilly Prat and pine nuts. Season with salt and pepper to taste.

3 Put the turkey cutlets between sheets of plastic wrap and flatten with a rolling pin or meat mallet. Top each cutlet with a quarter of the stuffing and roll the meat over the filling.

4 Overlap a quarter of the grape leaves to make a rectangle. Center a turkey roll on top, roll up and tie with raffia or string. Repeat with the remaining leaves and turkey rolls.

5 Pack the rolls snugly in an ovenproof dish, pour in the stock and bake for 40 minutes. Skim any surface fat from the stock and pour the stock into a pitcher. Serve immediately with the turkey parcels.

Stuffed Turkey Breast with Lemon

This elegant dish of rolled turkey breast makes an impressive but economical main course.

Serves 4–5

1½-pound boneless turkey breast, in one piece
1 carrot, cut into matchsticks
1 medium zucchini, cut into matchsticks
3 ounces ham, cut into matchsticks
2 thick slices white bread, crusts removed, softened in a little milk
10 green olives, pitted and finely chopped
1 large garlic clove, finely chopped
¼ cup chopped fresh parsley
¼ cup finely chopped fresh basil
1 egg
¼ teaspoon grated lemon zest
2 tablespoons grated Parmesan cheese
¼ cup olive oil
1 cup hot Chicken Stock
½ lemon, cut into thin wedges
2 tablespoons butter
salt and freshly ground black pepper

1 Remove any skin or fat from the turkey. Using a sharp knife, cut part of the way through the turkey breast and open the two halves out like a book. Pound the meat with a mallet or rolling pin to obtain one large piece of meat of as even a thickness as possible.

2 Preheat the oven to 400°F. Blanch the carrot and zucchini pieces in a small saucepan of boiling water for 2 minutes, then drain. Combine with the ham.

3 Squeeze the bread and place in a mixing bowl, breaking it up with a fork. Stir in the olives, garlic, herbs and egg. Add the lemon zest and Parmesan. Season to taste with salt and pepper.

4 Spread the bread mixture onto the meat, leaving a small border all around. Cover with the ham and vegetable mixture. Roll up the turkey and tie in several places with cooking string.

5 Heat the oil in a flameproof casserole slightly larger than the turkey roll. Brown the meat on all sides. Remove the casserole from heat, add the stock and arrange the lemon wedges around the meat. Cover and place in the oven.

6 After 15 minutes, remove the lid, discard the lemon and baste the meat. Continue cooking, uncovered, for 25–30 minutes, basting occasionally. Transfer the turkey to a warmed serving plate and let rest for at least 10 minutes before slicing.

7 Strain the sauce. Stir in the butter and adjust the seasoning. Serve the sliced turkey roll warm with the sauce. If you wish to serve it cold, slice it just before serving and omit the sauce.

> **Variation**
> Substitute a generous 1 cup sliced mushrooms, sautéed lightly in 3 tablespoons butter, for the ham in Step 2. Omit the lemon wedges during cooking.

Turkey Rolls with Cranberries

Cranberry sauce is traditionally served with roast turkey, but here the berries are incorporated into a great stuffing.

Serves 4

4 turkey cutlets
2 tablespoons vegetable oil
½ cup cranberry juice or fruity red wine
½ teaspoon each arrowroot and water, mixed
salt and freshly ground black pepper
salad, to serve

For the stuffing

¾ cup cranberries
6 ounces seedless red grapes
1 large red apple, quartered and cored
1 tablespoon honey
2 teaspoons finely chopped fresh ginger root
½ teaspoon ground allspice

1 To make the stuffing, process the cranberries, grapes and apple in a food processor until finely chopped. Drain, pressing to extract the juice. Reserve the juice. Mix the fruit with the honey, ginger and allspice.

2 Place each turkey cutlet between two sheets of plastic wrap and beat with a meat mallet or rolling pin until ¼ inch thick. Season, then divide the stuffing among them, spreading almost to the edges. Roll up, tucking in the sides. Tie in two or three places with cooking string or secure with toothpicks.

3 Heat the oil in a large frying pan and brown the rolls on all sides over medium-high heat for 5–7 minutes. Add the reserved fruit juice and the cranberry juice or wine, and bring to a boil. Cover and simmer for 20 minutes, until tender and cooked through. Turn the rolls halfway through the cooking.

4 Remove the turkey rolls from the pan and keep warm. Boil the cooking liquid until it has reduced to about ¾ cup. Stir in the arrowroot mixture and boil for 2 minutes.

5 Remove the string or toothpicks from the turkey rolls and cut into slices. Serve the sliced rolls with the cooking liquid as a sauce and accompanied by salad.

Stir-fried Duck with Blueberries

Serve this conveniently quick dinner-party dish with sprigs of fresh mint, which will give a wonderful fresh aroma as you bring the meal to the table.

Serves 4

2 duck breast fillets, about
   6 ounces each
2 tablespoons sunflower oil
1 tablespoon red wine vinegar
1 teaspoon sugar
1 teaspoon red wine
1 teaspoon crème de cassis
1 cup fresh blueberries
1 tablespoon chopped fresh mint
salt and freshly ground
   black pepper
fresh mint sprigs, to garnish

1 Cut the duck breast fillets into neat slices. Season well with salt and pepper.

2 Heat a wok, then add the oil. When the oil is hot, add the duck and stir-fry for 3 minutes.

3 Add the red wine vinegar, sugar, red wine and crème de cassis. Bubble for 3 minutes to reduce to a thick syrup.

4 Stir in the blueberries, sprinkle on the chopped mint and serve, garnished with sprigs of mint.

Variations
You could substitute black currants, red currants or cranberries for the blueberries. If using cranberries—and if you can obtain a bottle—substitute Karpi, a Finnish liqueur made from cranberries, for the crème de cassis. Otherwise, use crème de cassis, which is a classic French liqueur made from black currants.

Duck with Peppercorns

Thick, meaty duck breast, like steak, should be served medium-rare. Green peppercorns make a zingy sauce, but choose pink peppercorns if you prefer a milder flavor.

¼ cup duck or Chicken Stock
6 tablespoons whipping cream
1 teaspoon Dijon mustard
1 tablespoon green or pink
   peppercorns in vinegar, drained
salt
fresh parsley, to garnish

Serves 2
1 teaspoon vegetable oil
2 duck breast fillets, about
   8 ounces each, skinned

1 Heat the oil in a heavy frying pan. Add the duck breast fillets and cook over medium-high heat for about 3 minutes on each side.

2 Transfer the duck to a plate and cover to keep warm. Pour off any fat from the pan and stir in the stock, cream, mustard and peppercorns. Boil for 2–3 minutes, until the sauce thickens slightly, then season with salt.

3 Pour any accumulated juices from the duck into the sauce, then slice the fillets diagonally.

4 Arrange the sliced duck on two warmed individual serving plates, pour on a little of the sauce, garnish with parsley and serve immediately.

Cook's Tip
Green peppercorns are the unripe berries of the same plant from which both black and white peppercorns come, Piper nigrum, although they have a milder flavor. They have a special affinity with poultry, especially duck. Pink peppercorns, however, are not really peppercorns at all, but the processed berries of a South American plant that is related to poison ivy.

Duck Risotto

This makes an excellent appetizer for six or could be served for half that number as a lunch or supper dish.

Serves 3–6
2 duck breast fillets
2 tablespoons brandy
2 tablespoons orange juice
1 tablespoon olive oil (optional)
1 onion, finely chopped
1 garlic clove, crushed
1 ½ cups risotto rice
4–5 cups simmering Chicken Stock
1 teaspoon chopped fresh thyme
1 teaspoon chopped fresh mint
2 teaspoons grated orange zest
½ cup grated Parmesan cheese
salt and freshly ground
    black pepper
strips of thinly pared orange zest,
    to garnish

1 Score the fatty sides of the duck and rub with salt. Dry-fry, fat-side down, in a heavy frying pan over medium heat for 6–8 minutes to render the fat. Transfer to a plate, and pull off and discard the fat. Cut the flesh into ¾-inch wide slices.

2 Pour all but 1 tablespoon of the rendered duck fat from the pan into a pitcher, then reheat the fat in the pan. Fry the duck slices for 2–3 minutes over medium-high heat, until evenly browned.

3 Add the brandy, heat to the simmering point and then ignite. When the flames have died down, add the orange juice and season. Remove from heat and set aside.

4 In a saucepan, heat either 1 tablespoon of the remaining duck fat or the olive oil. Sauté the onion and garlic over low heat until, the onion is soft but not browned. Add the rice and cook, stirring constantly, until the grains are coated in oil.

5 Add the stock, a ladle at a time, waiting for each addition to be absorbed completely before adding the next. Just before adding the final ladleful, stir in the duck with the thyme and mint. Continue cooking until the risotto is creamy and the rice is tender. Add the grated orange zest and Parmesan. Adjust the seasoning, then remove from heat, cover and let stand for a few minutes. Serve, garnished with the pared orange zest.

Peruvian Duck with Rice

This is a very rich dish, brightly colored with tomatoes, squash and fresh herbs.

Serves 4–6
4 duck breast fillets
1 Spanish onion, chopped
2 garlic cloves, crushed
2 teaspoons grated fresh
    ginger root
4 tomatoes (peeled, if
    desired), chopped
8 ounces kabocha or acorn squash,
    cut into ½-inch cubes
1 ½ cups long-grain rice
3 cups Chicken Stock
1 tablespoon finely chopped
    cilantro
1 tablespoon finely chopped
    fresh mint
salt and freshly ground
    black pepper

1 Heat a heavy frying pan or flameproof casserole. Using a sharp knife, score the fatty side of the duck breast fillets in a criss-cross pattern, rub the fat with a little salt, then dry-fry, skin-side down, for 6–8 minutes to render some of the fat.

2 Pour all but 1 tablespoon of the fat into a jar or cup, then fry the duck fillets, meat-side down, in the fat remaining in the pan for 3–4 minutes, until brown all over. Transfer to a board, slice thickly and set aside in a shallow dish. Deglaze the pan with a little water and pour this liquid onto the duck.

3 Sauté the onion and garlic in the same pan for 4–5 minutes, until the onion is fairly soft, adding a little extra duck fat if necessary. Stir in the ginger, cook for 1–2 more minutes, then add the tomatoes and cook, stirring, for another 2 minutes. Add the squash, stir-fry for a few minutes, then cover and let steam for about 4 minutes.

4 Stir in the rice and cook, stirring, until it is well coated. Pour in the stock, return the slices of duck to the pan and season.

5 Bring to a boil, then lower the heat, cover and simmer for 30–35 minutes, until the rice is tender. Stir in the cilantro and mint, and serve.

Roast Duckling on a Bed of Honeyed Potatoes

The rich flavor of duck combined with sweetened potatoes glazed with honey makes an excellent treat for a dinner party.

Serves 4
1 duckling
¼ cup light soy sauce

⅔ cup orange juice
3 large floury potatoes, cut
   into chunks
2 tablespoons honey
1 tablespoon sesame seeds
salt and freshly ground
   black pepper

1 Preheat the oven to 400°F. Place the duckling, breast-side up, in a roasting pan. Prick the skin well.

2 Combine the soy sauce and orange juice and pour onto the bird. Bake for 20 minutes.

3 Place the potato chunks in a bowl, stir in the honey and toss to mix well. Remove the duckling from the oven and spoon the potatoes all around and under the bird.

4 Roast for 35 minutes, then remove from the oven. Toss the potatoes in the duckling juices and turn the duckling over so that the underside will be cooked. Return to the oven and cook for another 30 minutes.

5 Remove the duckling from the oven and carefully scoop off the excess fat, leaving the juices behind.

6 Sprinkle the sesame seeds over the potatoes, season and turn the duckling back over, breast-side up, and cook for another 10 minutes. Remove the duckling and potatoes from the oven and keep warm, letting the bird rest for 10–15 minutes.

7 Pour off the excess fat from the roasting pan and simmer the juices on top of the stove for a few minutes. Serve the juices with the carved duckling and potatoes.

Duck with Orange Sauce

This is the classic French recipe.

Serves 2–3
4½-pound duck
2 oranges
½ cup sugar

6 tablespoons white wine vinegar
½ cup Grand Marnier or
   orange liqueur
salt and freshly ground
   black pepper
watercress and orange slices,
   to garnish

1 Preheat the oven to 300°F. Trim off the excess fat and skin from the duck, and prick the skin all over with a fork. Season the duck inside and out and tie the legs with cooking string. Place the duck on a rack in a large roasting pan. Cover tightly with aluminum foil and bake for 1½ hours.

2 With a vegetable peeler, remove the orange zest in wide strips, then slice into thin strips. Squeeze the juice from the oranges.

3 Place the sugar and vinegar in a small, heavy saucepan and stir to dissolve the sugar. Boil over high heat, without stirring, until the mixture is a rich caramel color. Remove from heat and carefully add the orange juice, pouring it down the side of the pan. Swirl the pan to blend, bring back to a boil, and add the orange zest and liqueur. Simmer for 2–3 minutes.

4 Remove the duck from the oven and pour off all the fat from the pan. Raise the oven temperature to 400°F. Return the duck to the oven and continue to roast, uncovered, for 25–30 minutes, basting a few times with some of the sauce, until the duck is brown and the juices run clear when the thickest part of the thigh is pierced with a knife or skewer.

5 Pour the juices from the duck cavity into the pan and transfer the bird to a carving board. Cover with foil and let rest for 10 minutes.

6 Pour the roasting juices into the saucepan with the remaining caramel mixture, skim off the fat and simmer gently. Serve the duck, garnished with watercress and orange slices, and accompanied by the sauce.

Spiced Duck with Pears

A delicious casserole based on a Catalan dish that uses goose or duck. The sautéed pears are added toward the end of cooking, along with picarda sauce, a pounded pine nut and garlic paste that both flavors and thickens.

Serves 6
1 tablespoon olive oil
6 duck portions
1 large onion, thinly sliced
1 cinnamon stick, halved
2 fresh thyme sprigs
2 cups Chicken Stock

To finish
3 firm ripe pears
2 tablespoons olive oil
2 garlic cloves, sliced
1/4 cup pine nuts
1/2 teaspoon saffron threads
2 tablespoons raisins
salt and freshly ground
    black pepper
fresh thyme or parsley sprigs,
    to garnish
mashed potatoes, to
    serve (optional)

1 Preheat the oven to 350°F. Heat the oil in a flameproof casserole and fry the duck portions for about 5 minutes, until the skin is golden. Transfer the duck to a plate and drain off all but 1 tablespoon of the fat left in the pan.

2 Add the onion to the casserole and sauté for 5 minutes. Add the cinnamon stick, thyme and stock. Return the duck to the casserole and bring the stock to a boil. Transfer to the oven and bake for 1 1/4 hours.

3 Meanwhile, peel, core and halve the pears. Heat the olive oil in a large frying pan and cook the pears until just golden on the cut sides.

4 Pound the garlic, pine nuts and saffron in a mortar with a pestle to make a thick, smooth paste. Add the paste to the casserole together with the raisins and pears. Bake for another 15 minutes, until the pears are tender.

5 Season to taste and garnish with thyme or parsley. Serve with mashed potatoes, if desired.

Duck Breasts with a Walnut & Pomegranate Sauce

This is an extremely exotic sweet-and-sour dish that originally came from Persia.

Serves 4
4 tablespoons olive oil
2 onions, very thinly sliced
1/2 teaspoon ground turmeric
3 1/2 cups walnuts, roughly
    chopped
4 cups duck or Chicken Stock
6 pomegranates
2 tablespoons sugar
1/4 cup lemon juice
4 duck breast fillets, about
    8 ounces each
salt and freshly ground
    black pepper

1 Heat half the oil in a frying pan. Add the onions and turmeric, and cook gently until soft. Transfer to a pan, add the walnuts and stock, then season with salt and pepper. Stir, bring to a boil and simmer, uncovered, for 20 minutes.

2 Cut the pomegranates in half and scoop out the seeds into a bowl. Reserve the seeds of one pomegranate. Transfer the remaining seeds to a blender or food processor and process to break them up. Strain through a sieve, to extract the juice, and stir in the sugar and lemon juice.

3 Score the skin of the duck breast fillets in a lattice fashion. Heat the remaining oil in a frying pan and place the duck in it, skin-side down. Cook gently for 10 minutes, pouring off the fat occasionally, until the skin is dark golden and crisp. Turn over the fillets and cook for another 3–4 minutes. Transfer to a plate and let rest.

4 Deglaze the frying pan with the pomegranate juice mixture, stirring with a wooden spoon, then add the walnut and stock mixture and simmer for 15 minutes, until slightly thickened.

5 Slice the duck breast fillets, drizzle with a little sauce and serve, garnished with the reserved pomegranate seeds. Serve the remaining sauce separately.

Apple-stuffed Duck

Stuffing the duck breast fillets with whole apples keeps the meat moist and gives them an attractive appearance when they are sliced and served cold, perhaps as part of a celebration buffet.

Serves 4

¼ cup raisins or golden raisins
2 tablespoons brandy

3 large onions
2 tablespoons oil
3 cups fresh bread crumbs
2 small apples
2 large duck breast fillets
salt and freshly ground
   black pepper
mixed salad, to serve

1 Place the dried fruit in a bowl, pour in the brandy and let soak. Preheat the oven to 425°F.

2 Chop one of the onions finely and sauté it in the oil until golden. Season with salt and pepper, and add ¼–½ cup water. Bring to a boil and then add bread crumbs until the stuffing is moist but not sloppy.

3 Core and peel the apples. Drain the raisins and press them into the center of the apples. Flatten the duck breast fillets and spread them out, skin-side down.

4 Divide the stuffing among the duck fillets and spread it on the meat. Place an apple at one end of each fillet and carefully roll up to enclose the apple and stuffing. Secure with fine cooking string. Quarter the remaining onions. Prick the duck skin in several places to release the fat.

5 Arrange the duck on a rack in a roasting pan with the onions underneath. Roast for about 35 minutes. Pour off the fat, then reduce the oven temperature to 325°F and roast for another 30–45 minutes.

6 Serve hot or cold. If serving cold, let cool, then chill and cut each breast into five or six thin slices. Arrange on a platter and bring to room temperature before serving with a salad.

Duck with Chestnut Sauce

This autumnal dish makes use of delicious sweet chestnuts that can be gathered in the woods.

Serves 4–5

1 fresh rosemary sprig, plus extra
   to garnish
1 garlic clove, thinly sliced
2 tablespoons olive oil
4 duck breast fillets, skin and
   fat removed

For the sauce

1 pound chestnuts
1 teaspoon oil
1½ cups milk
1 small onion, finely chopped
1 carrot, finely chopped
1 small bay leaf
salt and freshly ground
   black pepper
2 tablespoons cream, warmed

1 Pull the leaves from the sprig of rosemary. Combine them with the garlic and oil in a shallow bowl. Pat the duck fillets dry with paper towels and lay them in a shallow dish. Brush with the flavored oil and let marinate for at least 2 hours.

2 Preheat the oven to 350°F. To make the sauce, cut a cross in the flat-side of each chestnut with a sharp knife. Place the chestnuts in a roasting pan with the oil and shake the pan until the nuts are well coated. Bake for about 20 minutes, then peel.

3 Place the chestnuts in a heavy saucepan with the milk, onion, carrot and bay leaf. Cook for 10–15 minutes until the chestnuts are very tender. Season with salt and pepper. Discard the bay leaf. Press the mixture through a sieve.

4 Return the chestnut sauce to the pan and heat gently while the duck is cooking. Preheat the broiler or prepare a grill.

5 Broil the duck for 6–8 minutes, until medium rare. The meat should be pink when sliced. Slice into rounds and arrange on warmed plates.

6 Stir the cream into the sauce just before serving. Garnish the sliced duck with rosemary and serve with the sauce.

Pheasant Breast with Apples

This luxurious dish bears the signature of Normandy: Calvados, the regional apple brandy, and rich cream.

Serves 2
2 pheasant breast fillets
2 tablespoons butter
I onion, thinly sliced
I apple, peeled and quartered

2 teaspoons sugar
¼ cup Calvados
¼ cup Chicken Stock
¼ teaspoon dried thyme
½ cup whipping cream
salt and freshly ground
 white pepper
sautéed potatoes, to serve

1 Score the thick end of each pheasant breast fillet.

2 In a heavy frying pan, melt half of the butter over medium heat. Add the onion and cook for 8–10 minutes, until golden, stirring occasionally. Transfer to a plate.

3 Cut each apple quarter crosswise into thin slices. Melt half the remaining butter in the pan and add the apple. Sprinkle with the sugar and cook for 5–7 minutes, until caramelized, turning occasionally. Transfer to the plate with the onion.

4 Wipe out the pan, add the remaining butter and increase the heat to medium-high. Add the pheasant breast fillets, skin-side down, and cook for 3–4 minutes, until golden. Turn and cook for another 1–2 minutes, until the juices run slightly pink when the thickest part of the meat is pierced with a knife or skewer. Transfer to a board and cover to keep warm.

5 Add the Calvados to the pan and boil until reduced by half. Add the stock and thyme, season and reduce by half again. Stir in the cream, bring to a boil and cook for 1 minute. Return the onion and apple slices to the pan, and cook for 1 minute.

6 Slice the pheasant breasts diagonally and arrange on warmed plates. Spoon on a little sauce with the onion and apples.

Anita Wong's Duck

A Chinese recipe, which would be served at celebrations, such as weddings where it denotes marital harmony.

Serves 4–6
¼ cup vegetable oil
2 garlic cloves, chopped
5–5¼-pound duck, with giblets
 (if making your own stock)
I-inch piece fresh ginger root,
 thinly sliced

3 tablespoons bean paste
2 tablespoons light soy sauce
I tablespoon dark soy sauce
I tablespoon sugar
½ teaspoon Chinese five-spice
 powder
3 pieces star anise
scant 2 cups duck stock
 (see Cook's Tip)
salt
shredded scallions, to garnish

1 Heat the oil in a large pan. Sauté the garlic without browning, then add the duck. Turn frequently until the outside is slightly brown all over. Transfer to a plate.

2 Add the ginger to the pan, then stir in the bean paste. Cook for 1 minute, then add both soy sauces, the sugar and the five-spice powder. Return the duck to the pan and fry, turning, until the outside is coated. Add the star anise and stock, and season to taste. Cover tightly and simmer gently for 2–2½ hours or until the duck is tender. Skim off the excess fat. Leave the bird in the sauce to cool.

3 Cut the duck into serving portions and pour on the sauce. Garnish with shredded scallions and serve cold.

> **Cook's Tip**
> To make stock, put the duck giblets in a pan with a small onion and a piece of bruised fresh ginger root. Cover with 2½ cups water, bring to a boil and then simmer, covered, for 20 minutes. Strain and blot with paper towels to remove excess fat.

Index